Educational Television

edited by
Robert F. Arnove

Educational Television
A Policy Critique and Guide for Developing Countries

PRAEGER SPECIAL STUDIES IN INTERNATIONAL POLITICS AND GOVERNMENT

Praeger Publishers   New York   Washington   London

Library of Congress Cataloging in Publication Data
Main entry under title:

Educational television.

(Praeger special studies in international politics and
government)
  1. Television in education—Addresses, essays, lectures.
2. Underdeveloped areas—Education—Addresses, essays,
lectures. I. Arnove, Robert F.
LB1044.7.E369   384.55'44   75-19761
ISBN 0-275-55510-0

PRAEGER PUBLISHERS
111 Fourth Avenue, New York, N.Y. 10003, U.S.A.

Published in the United States of America in 1976
by Praeger Publishers, Inc.

Printed in the United States of America

ACKNOWLEDGMENTS

Initial funding for this study came from a Ford Foundation grant to the Stanford University School of Education in 1972 to prepare a report on educational television in developing countries. Four of the chapters in this book formed part of the report submitted to the Ford Foundation in 1973. Of these, three were published as journal articles. I wish to thank the following journals for granting permission to reprint these articles: Journal of Communication, "Sociopolitical Implications of Educational Television," by Robert F. Arnove, Vol. 25 (Spring 1975); Economic Development and Cultural Change, "The Economic Costs and Returns to Educational Television," by Martin Carnoy, Vol. 23 (January 1975); Educational Broadcasting, "The Samoan ETV Project: Some Cross-Cultural Implications of Educational Television," Parts I and II, by Lynne and Grant Masland (March/April and May/June 1975).

CONTENTS

LIST OF TABLES AND FIGURES

x

This book is intended as a critical guide for educational planners and administrators who are responsible for deciding (1) whether or not to establish large-scale systems of educational television, and (2) the set of conditions under which television can be used both effectively and efficiently as an instructional technology. We will analyze, from a variety of disciplinary viewpoints, the central issues and problems which are likely to arise in planning, implementing, and assessing the consequences of a national or regional educational television (ETV) system. The sociopolitical, economic, and cultural contexts of education systems and television are examined as well as the intraeducational issues of administration, curriculum, and pedagogy. The book contains case studies of three countries (El Salvador, Ivory Coast, and American Samoa) and one internationally disseminated television program ("Sesame Street"). These case studies provide more detailed analysis of issues which are likely to emerge with the introduction of ETV and comprehensive educational reform in developing countries; the latter two studies further point up the problems which result from cross-cultural contact.

BACKGROUND

This assessment of the promise and reality of television comes at an important point in the history of ETV in the Third World. Approximately ten years ago, the first large-scale projects were initiated in countries like American Samoa and Colombia. The groundwork was laid for innovative use of the medium in small-scale projects like Niger. Numerous experimental and pilot projects in both instructional television (ITV) for school-age children and ETV projects for adult basic education and social development proliferated throughout Africa, Asia, and Latin America.

By 1975, a decade later, many of the original proponents of massive utilization of television have doubts about the wisdom of their advice. The claims that ETV would serve as a catalytic agent for overall educational reform—upgrading the quality of instruction, reforming curriculum, reaching larger numbers of students, equalizing educational opportunity, and reducing unit costs of instruction—with few exceptions, have not materialized. School systems and educational opportunities in underdeveloped countries remain essentially the same. There has been some expansion and incremental reform, but few fundamental changes in the philosophy, structure, content, and outcomes of schooling. Nor, in most cases, could radical change in education systems be expected without transformations first taking place in the total society. In those exceptional cases, such as American Samoa, where substantial change occurred in the school system with the introduction of ETV, the price was disruption of existing cultural patterns and forced acculturation into Western social systems.

While early advocates of educational television are beginning to urge restraint in the headlong pursuit of educational modernization through sophisticated technologies, a number of countries (including the Ivory Coast, India, Brazil, Indonesia, and Korea) are moving ahead with ambitious educational programs based on utilization of television and advanced delivery systems, such as satellites. At the same time, exciting projects have emerged in the past few years in which television constitutes but one component of a total teaching-learning system. For example, the Open University in England and the high-school correspondence courses in Japan combine televised instruction with radio lectures, programmed correspondence materials, tutorial sessions, and intensive in-residence instruction.

Recent technological breakthroughs—portable and inexpensive videotaping, recording and playback equipment, cable television, and low-cost ways of establishing local TV transmitters—contain the potential for overcoming many of the confining and dangerous aspects of centrally controlled national ETV systems. These aspects include one-way communication and insignificant local control over the production, reception, and utilization of programs. Moreover, the educational potential of radio has been rediscovered, and advances are being made in radiovision and other ways of combining radio with pictorial and print material.

PARAMETERS

This study differs principally from other related publications on the subject of instructional technology in these respects: (1) its independent and multidisciplinary approach and (2) its almost exclusive focus on ETV at the systemic level in underdeveloped countries. The authors are nonpartisans; they have no stake in promoting or defending educational television. They are outsiders looking at television through the lenses of their respective disciplines: sociology of educational and political sociology, economics, anthropology, educational research and evaluation, educational finance and administration.

The exclusive focus on educational television is merited on the grounds that, of all the instructional technologies being transplanted to developing countries, television is the technology most promoted and most eagerly sought. It is the most glamorous, prestigious, and costly. When foreign aid donors and educational decision makers in developing countries discuss instructional technology, they basically mean television. According to the 1972 AID-commissioned study, Educational Technology and the Developing Countries:

> Simply going by what's happened so far, however, we must reach the tentative, pragmatic conclusion that the most impressive current uses of educational technology in the developing world, whether as part of integral school reform or to extend the reach of schooling or simply for enrichment, are those that use television [p. 90].

Our focus also is on those cases where television is utilized to extend or transform comprehensive education systems: (1) programs where television carries core curriculum or supplementary courses to substantial numbers of students in a school system; (2) pilot projects, as in Niger, which demonstrate alternative ways of reaching children and youths with useful educational content, and (3) nonschool programs for social development (for example, literacy and community action) and adult education. Because we are interested in employment of television for school-related instruction (ITV) as well as a broad range of educational activities outside the formal school curriculum, we use throughout our discussion the more inclusive term "educational television" (ETV).

With the exception of Goldsen's chapter, this book does not analyze aspects of commercial television and the interaction between commercial and educational broadcasting. However, in many countries the educational potential and impact of the private networks often exceeds that of ETV. Where private television sets are widespread, the commercial networks may reach larger numbers of people on a more systematic and repetitive basis, conveying information and skills, and shaping self-concepts and world views. The electronic media—and particularly television, with the high credibility people attach to it—permeate the entire cultural milieu of a country, presenting an agenda of what merits society's attention, portraying a select range of lifestyles and values, and offering explanations of social causality and change.

CONTENT

The content of each chapter is summarized below so that planners, administrators, researchers, and teachers can determine which sections are directly relevant to their interest. The guide is designed to be used both in its entirety and in parts, according to the information sought by the reader.

"Sociopolitical Implications of Educational Television"

This chapter, by Robert F. Arnove, analyzes the sociopolitical implications of educational television in particular and school systems in general—since television essentially represents a technological means to extend education to greater numbers of people and to upgrade the quality of instruction. Among the fundamental questions examined in the chapter are these: (1) who has access to educational programs and what groups systematically benefit from them? (2) whose values are transmitted and in which language? (3) what skills are developed in which groups and what opportunities are provided for the majority to employ their skills and participate meaningfully in important decision making?

The conclusion of the author is that ETV generally has not been aimed at reaching the most disadvantaged populations, the rural poor and the urban unemployed, and their children. In those cases where programs are underway to reach disadvantaged populations, the program content is often inappropriate and represents models of behavior and values characteristic of the dominant groups in society. The dominance of urban groups and external donor countries is also seen in the decision as to which language shall be used as the medium of instruction. With regard to ETV utilization for social development, these programs tend to be used for purposes of domesticating and channeling change in directions desired by existing elites, rather than in developing the critical conscience of program participants and equipping them with the means to actively determine their own individual and collective destinies.

The chapter also examines some of the unintended consequences and political repercussions of using technologies like television to expand and modify education systems. These include (1) increased rural-urban migration, (2) excessive strain on existing school resources, (3) the unemployed school-leaver problem, (4) raised aspirations of adults that cannot be fulfilled, and (5) increased dependence on foreign technical assistance and external models of development, circumscribing the autonomy of a country to decide its own future.

"The Economic Costs and Returns of Educational Television"

This chapter, by Martin Carnoy, points out that substantial investments of time, energy, and scarce resources are being made by low-income countries without adequate information on the economic returns to increasing the number of children schooled through educational television or even on the effectiveness of ETV compared to other educational improvements. In response to this problem, the author undertakes a comprehensive summary of available information from existing and planned projects on the economic value of education to a society and its costs. In his review of available data, he utilizes two basic approaches—cost-effectiveness analysis and cost-benefit analysis.

Carnoy's conclusions are that the main objective of ETV projects principally has been to produce more schooling and better schooling, primarily for children. Yet, from most of the results analyzed, the cost of ETV schooling is much higher per pupil than is classroom-teacher schooling and the performance of pupils is not significantly or consistently better when ETV is used than when teachers are simply retrained to use more effective curricula. Further, teacher retraining costs are usually a small fraction of the cost of operating an ETV system.

The most persuasive economic argument for ETV occurs in situations where there is a long-run shortage of qualified teachers needed to reach a significant fraction of the school-age population. On the grounds that it is important to put all children in school as rapidly as possible, it is argued that educational media are the only way to achieve this at acceptable costs. The importation of foreign teachers in large numbers is regarded as prohibitive. So in cases where the objective is rapid educational expansion, and it is not possible to train enough local qualified teachers in the short run, educational media are an important alternative to consider. Even so, it usually takes ten years or more to make the ETV system operational at intended capacity.

Carnoy suggests that radio may be substantially less expensive than television and just as effective in relation to student performance. There may also be inexpensive ways to expand education effectively without technology, using labor-intensive techniques. Given the future employment picture of even skilled labor in most low-income countries, these may be much more appropriate than methods which rely on labor-saving devices.

"Organizational and Administrative Considerations"

This chapter, by William Perron and Michael Kirst, is designed to provide ETV administrators with a broad administrative orientation to the implementation of educational television systems. Three general areas are identified for consideration: planning, management control, and operational control. Within each of these areas, Perron and Kirst illuminate the key issues involved by referring to appropriate examples from different country projects.

Related to planning considerations, the authors treat the preliminary decision-making process as comprised of three interrelated sets of activities: the "needs assessment" stage, the "solution selection" stage, and the "strategic planning" stage. Several of their principal concerns are the following: Are needs first assessed and then the role of ETV in meeting these problems determined, or does the existence of ETV define the educational needs? Is the full range of alternative solutions to educational problems explored, or are alternatives to ETV merely an afterthought? Are the major groups whose cooperation is critical to the success of the ETV project included in planning the new system from the outset? Do you start with a pilot project and expand gradually, or do you immediately start on a broad scale?

With respect to management control, Perron and Kirst first explore organizational and managerial considerations associated with the introduction of ETV into an existing educational situation. For example, where do you institutionally locate the ETV program? The authors suggest ways in which administrators of ETV projects can adapt to existing institutional arrangements without creating unnecessary problems. They then proceed to examine specific cost implications of ETV and how these costs relate to the overall financing of the reform endeavor. Finally, they analyze the administrative requirements for attending to the facility and equipment needs of the new technology.

With respect to operational control, the authors first assess the central issues relevant to the delivery and reception of the televised lesson. They continue by discussing media team staffing requirements (including the role of foreign technical advisors in building up local competencies) and examining the most common type of personnel stress precipitated by the introduction of ETV, that of teacher resistance. The section concludes with a discussion of the administrative coordination requirements of a research and evaluation unit, and emphasizes the unit's function as a basic tool of the decision-making process.

Case Studies

"Reconsidering the Use of Television for Educational Reform: The Case of El Salvador." Perhaps the best documented and studied effort to date on the use of educational television in a developing country is the Educational Reform program of El Salvador. In this chapter, Henry Ingle examines the reform program and the changes, both expected and unexpected, which the use of instructional television appears to have effected.

Television in El Salvador was integrated in a systematic manner within the larger effort for educational change; the project endeavored to put into operation the best theory and practice on the use of communication technology in education. However, the major changes in the educational system were not fully integrated within the broader framework of the country's socioeconomic development. To date, graduates from the reform program have not found employment in the middle-level technical job sectors that planners of the reform had envisioned; and those graduates desiring to continue their education have encountered limited enrollment possibilities at the secondary- and vocational/technical- school levels. Thus, rather than bringing about social and economic improvement, the reform appears, instead, to be reinforcing the status quo.

The Salvadoran experience supports the position that the relation- ship of an educational system to the society it serves should be rationalized in terms other than improved pedagogical quality or quanti- tative expansion. Attention needs to be given to the socioeconomic situation within a country and the extent to which aspirations of in- dividuals with increased schooling can be fulfilled. Simply providing individuals with more years of schooling, skills, and knowledge, as the Salvadoran Educational Reform seeks to do, will not automatically increase their wage- earning capacity nor reduce social inequalities. From a policy perspective, the case of El Salvador suggests that basic changes within the educational sector must be accompanied by sup- portive changes in nonschool sectors of the society—for example, by policies aimed at agrarian reform and generation of jobs.

The questions for El Salvador, therefore, are "education for what purpose," "education for whom," and to "what extent should invest- ment in education be complemented with investment in other sectors of the society" if the goal of more rapid socioeconomic development is to be accomplished.

"The Ivory Coast Educational Television Project." The Ivory Coast ETV Project is currently the most ambitious operation of its kind in the developing world in terms of its current and projected coverage. It is estimated that by 1986 about 1.5 million pupils will be studying in primary- school ETV classes, and at the moment there are nearly a quarter of a million children in ETV schools. Television programs for community education, with local teachers acting as animateurs, are now being received weekly in an estimated one thousand schools. And plans are under review for introducing a television-based component into secondary education.

The project also represents an interesting example of multilateral international cooperation: France, UNESCO, Canada, the World Bank, the United States, Belgium, the Federal Republic of Germany, and several other countries and agencies are involved to varying degrees.

The case study, by Anthony Kaye, attempts to relate the nature of the options taken in the ETV reform to the economic and social condi- tions of the Ivory Coast—in terms of average per capita GNP one of the most prosperous of the independent African states—and analyzes progress achieved since the start of the reform in September 1971.

The author, who was for two years director of the External Evalua- tion Unit of the project, points out, however, that it is too soon at this stage to make definitive judgments concerning the educational effectiveness of the system in terms of language and other skills ac- quired by the pupils. The first graduates of the system will not have completed their final grade studies until 1977, and accurate long-term testing and cost-effectiveness data will not be available until several years from now, when recently initiated research begins to bear fruit.

"Some Cross-Cultural Implications of Educational Television: The Samoan ETV Project." American Samoa represents the first project in the Third World where ETV was utilized to restructure totally a school system. The U.S. government was able to enforce in the territory of American Samoa rapid educational change by administrative fiat. In this respect, the Samoan case is unique. However, the issues that Samoa raises of cross-cultural contact and the impact of industrial technologies and value system on a non-Western indigenous society are applicable to many underdeveloped countries.

What is memorable in this case is the apparent failure of the proponents of ETV for Samoa to question the basic goals of the project. The objectives—"to equal, through . . . [an] 'explosive upgrading,' the educational standards of schools in the continental United States and to improve rapidly the Samoans' ability to speak English"—seemed to be accepted as given by members of the ETV project. The basic questions, then, became how best—and through what combination of technological means—to achieve the teaching of English and remodeling of academic programs along U.S. lines.

Lynne Masland and Grant Masland, who spent several years in Samoa with the project, carefully document the cultural differences between Americans and Samoans, and the insensitivity of the foreign education advisors and staff to these differences. Not only did the educational reform have a deleterious effect on the traditional Samoan way of life, but (ironically) the evidence is inconclusive on whether the project has been successful in achieving its overriding goal to raise significantly the level of English proficiency of Samoan children.

By 1974, an emerging Samoan drive for greater cultural autonomy and self-determination led to important changes in the ETV Project. Among these changes were the devolution of high-level decision-making positions to native-born Samoans and deemphasis on English as the primary language of instruction. Moreover, massive electrical power shortages in 1974 led to a dramatic reduction in the number of programs broadcast by television. The economic costs and technical difficulties associated with maintaining a highly sophisticated system of televised instruction were patently obvious to both Samoans and Americans. The future of the education system in American Samoa will be influenced by these technological and economic considerations as well as by the alternative models presented by neighboring island countries, which have recently gained their political independence and are pursuing different approaches to educational development.

"Literacy Without Books: The Case of 'Sesame Street.'" The hidden curriculum of television, the medium and the messages carried by it, is examined in both the Maslands' chapter on American Samoa and Rose K. Goldsen's study of "Sesame Street." Since its inauguration in 1969, "Sesame Street" has become the most widely disseminated and acclaimed educational television program in the United States. It is regularly viewed by some 15 million children. Overseas versions of "Sesame Street" have been produced in four different languages (Spanish, Portuguese, French, German) and are viewed by millions of children in over 60 countries.

What do children learn from "Sesame Street"? According to Goldsen, children essentially are being taught to read television rather than develop reading skills and an appreciation of books which would enable them to understand and explore their environment. They learn to "read" television's star system, show-business categories, action-adventure and crime-show formulas, and commercial messages. Indeed, as Goldsen points out, the programs are themselves full-length commercials, promoting the kind of world view that is compatible with a postindustrial, privatized, consumer society. The "show-and-tell" format of the programs sells the U. S. version of the "good life," paving the way for foreign subsidiaries, affiliates, clients, and imitators of American consumer-goods industries to capitalize on a growing market stimulated by the electronic media. The author then documents the support system of income-producing franchises which help finance and promote the program for distribution in the United States and abroad.

The chapter further analyzes how the program's format subtly but powerfully affects children's concepts of time and space, their language and play patterns, and their views of what is real and unreal. In the author's words: "It is the first time in the history of civilization that so many of the world's children will have been exposed simultaneously to the identical cultural materials—images, music, sounds, laughter, body movements, facial expressions—all feeding into a child's developing sense of self, all showing him particular ways of interacting in social relations." What is generally considered to be the best of educational television may have undesirable, unanticipated consequences for the countries importing the program.

CONSIDERATIONS

Although the authors represent a diversity of disciplines and varying experiences with ETV, a striking consensus of opinions emerges throughout the report. Among the common themes systematically emphasized by the different authors are the following:

● the need to examine critically the assumptions behind the claims made for ETV as an instructional technology that will substantially reform a country's education system—for example, the assumption that expanding school systems will necessarily improve the quality of instruction, or the assumption that improved schooling will lead to increased social mobility and increased economic productivity;

• the need to diagnose educational problems of a country, how these problems relate to overall development issues, and exactly how television in combination with other learning resources can help meet specific educational needs;

• the need to determine that television—as against alternative technologies and means—is cost effective and will not strain the economic resources of a country;

• the need for careful planning and pilot testing of a television project before large-scale implementation begins;

• the need to build upon and utilize the unique learning properties of television as a visual medium—but also the need to be aware of the powerful and subtle impact this medium has on individuals;

• the need to take into account how the classroom-teacher role is threatened or changed by the introduction of ETV and under what conditions teacher and technology interact effectively;

• the need for systematic research and evaluation which will assist production staff with the development of relevant learning materials and assist administrators with decisions pertaining to effective utilization of the medium;

• the need, in any assessment of the educational potential of ETV, to take into account its long-term consequences—the effects of importing this technology, for example, on the cultural autonomy of a country, and problems which are likely to arise from expanding schooling and raising expectations without tackling basic problems in the economy and polity;

• finally, the need to consider alternative uses of television for alternative populations—for example, decentralized systems aimed at disadvantaged and nonschool populations.

In reviewing the past experiences of many countries with ETV, the authors tend to be skeptical about the probability of long-lasting educational improvement occurring through the use of this medium—unless many of the provisos they raise in the subsequent chapters are taken into consideration by planners and decision makers. The limitations of television first must be recognized if its educational potential is to be realized.

Educational Television

SOCIOPOLITICAL IMPLICATIONS
OF EDUCATIONAL TELEVISION
Robert F. Arnove

Television represents a technological means to extend schooling to greater numbers of people and to upgrade the quality of instruction. Analysis of the sociopolitical implications of educational television (ETV) requires an examination of how schooling itself contributes to the overall maintenance, integration, and transformation of national societies. This framework further applies to endeavors to use mass media in combination with formal instruction for a variety of adult education programs related to social development.

In the post-World War II period, schooling has been heralded as the "key that unlocks the door to modernization."[1] The newly emergent states of Africa and Asia and the older states of the Third World struggling to overcome the conditions of underdevelopment have looked to schools as a manipulable institution that would enable them to (1) train and select the elite cadres of bureaucrats, technicians, professionals, and leaders required to manage more complex and specialized economic and political institutions; (2) transmit common values and develop a national identity and consensus among diverse, often conflicting, ethnic groups coexisting within the same territorial boundaries; (3) develop skills and outlooks in the population at large so that they could participate in the nation-building process.

Although these goals of schooling are laudable, a series of fundamental questions must be asked: Who has access to schooling and what groups systematically benefit from schooling? Whose values are transmitted and in which language? Moreover, who decides the content of the curriculum? What skills are developed in which groups? How extensive is participation? And how meaningful is this participation in relation to important decision making?

WHO BENEFITS?

Any technology that enables a country to expand and improve its schooling represents an instrument for change that can be utilized to overcome unequal opportunity, integrate previously excluded populations, contribute to the development of individuals and their social groupings, and help achieve widespread consensus and solidarity in a heterogeneous society. At the same time, the instrument can be utilized to favor already advantaged groups, establish barriers to massive incorporation of marginal populations, and rob people of their individual and collective identities.

Unless a country deliberately and systematically pursues a well-defined policy to achieve equality of both educational opportunity and educational outcomes (in terms of status, power, and wealth), the probability is strong that past inequities and injustices will continue. James S. Coleman describes the tendency of past inequalities to be self-perpetuating as the "law of unequal development advantage (or disadvantage)":

> Children of persons in the upper social stratum everywhere have greater access to higher education; areas more richly endowed by nature or possessing more development potential everywhere tend to attract investment, both public and private, more readily; and demographic groups whose members already have more skills, talents, and education everywhere have a differential advantage in further development. The process of uneven development tends to continue according to its own logic and dynamic unless countervailing influences, such as egalitarian political policies, provide for equal access to education, or deliberately allocate resources not only to ensure regional equality, but also to "level up" the less developed areas. [2]

In reviewing the worldwide use of television in underdeveloped countries, I find that television has not been aimed at reaching the most disadvantaged populations, the rural poor and the urban unemployed. In those cases where programs are directed to disadvantaged populations, the program content is often inappropriate and represents models of behavior and values characteristic of the dominant groups in society.

If we examine the showcase countries for educational television—El Salvador, Colombia, Niger, and American Samoa—we discover the following.

In El Salvador, television was initiated at the junior-high-school level (Plan Básico or Third Cycle, grades seven through nine). Before this level in the educational pyramid, approximately 75 percent of the children who have entered the first year of primary school have dropped out.

In Colombia, there is no apparent relationship between the widespread coverage of educational television (over one-half million primary school children out of three million) and the opening of educational opportunity to rural areas which systematically have been neglected. Due to lack of schooling facilities and public-sector investment in rural improvement, less than 10 percent of the children who start primary school in the countryside complete this level. For two-thirds of the rural population, schools are not available for the upper cycle of fourth and fifth grades. The overall efficiency of the school system itself has not been improved substantially by ETV, since even in the large cities only 50 percent complete five years of primary education.

In Niger, perhaps the most exciting and imaginative utilization of television in an underdeveloped country, the project (through 1972) had only an experimental status. The project consisted of some 800 students in 20 classes in small towns surrounding the capital of Niamey, with an additional two classes receiving instruction in the production studio. Plans to expand the television project, with French government assistance, were constrained by the overall poverty of Niger and the plans of the government to limit education to less than 50 percent of the relevant school-age population.

In American Samoa, the utilization of ETV to achieve near-universal primary and secondary schooling involved massive disruption of traditional cultural patterns (see Chapter 6). The negative consequences of this external intrusion into Samoan affairs and the attempts at acculturation into United States value systems and life-styles are likely to be felt for a long time.

WHOSE VALUES?

The extension of schooling through television to disadvantaged children and illiterate and unskilled adults raises the issue of what types of programs and curricular content are to be transmitted.

Rural Education

In the case of rural education, television theoretically presents an ideal opportunity to offer a curriculum that not only carries a common core of skills and messages and shared experiences to all children, but also the opportunity to transmit the particular skills, knowledge, and outlooks that enable rural populations to cope successfully with their own milieu and to attain a decent standard of living. Few countries, however, have systematically studied the type of curriculum that would be suited to the learning environment and development tasks of the rural area. Instead, ready-made urban programs are adopted in toto and broadcast to these areas. English or French will usually be included in the curriculum, but not the indigenous language spoken in the home. Universal history and geography will be included, but not the pressing social issues of everyday survival. The life-styles and values of the urban elite will be systematically portrayed, but not the daily routine and folkways of the peasant or farmer.

Adult Education

Similar distortions in content and images are to be found in adult basic-education programs broadcast over television. In some cases the decision is deliberate, but in others educators and communicators simply are unconscious of their biases in portraying elite mores and behaviors as models to be emulated by illiterate and unschooled adults.

In broadcasts and supplementary materials, intelligent adults are presented with a fantasy world—a world of plenitude and no crushing problems; with a world of people devoid of basic emotions of rage, fear, jealousy, and ecstasy. As in one Latin America program, they are presented with characters like Julio and Rosa, who love one another, never quarrel, are legally married, have but one child, hold down jobs, and possess all the latest electrical appliances and tools. In fact, this pattern of representing cardboard people over ETV is paralleled by the fare of commercial broadcasting, which usually presents a never-never land of fantasy for viewers.

As rural education programs are often repeats of urban curriculum, adult education programs also are often revisions of standard programs for children. As Paulo Freire has pointed out, many adult education and literacy programs view the unschooled adult as an empty receptacle to be "filled up" with requisite knowledge or as less than a complete human being who must be nurtured and restored to full life. [3] The considerable experiential base of adults, their talents and insights are not taken into account and do not form part of the pedagogy.

We must ask if the variety of adult education programs for social development represents the needs and desires of the target populations or the conceptions of national planners and technocrats as to what these populations want, or should want—and is therefore in their interest.

At another level of analysis, we can ask what explanations are offered to adults about the causes of poverty or backwardness; what institutionalized means are recommended for overcoming poverty and changing the pattern of being have-nots. Is poverty attributed to lack of education and personality traits (for example, laziness, irresponsibility, lack of punctuality) or to defects in the social system and economy (for example, land tenure patterns, employment opportunities, types of goods produced and marketed)?

WHOSE VALUES IN A HETEROGENEOUS SOCIETY?

The issues of whose values are reflected in the curriculum are more complex and volatile in the newly independent nations. Their territorial boundaries, drawn by colonial powers, embrace a potpourri of ethnic, tribal, and linguistic groups that share little in common and hold no strong allegiance to what is for them a remote national community. This phenomenon—the remoteness of national government— exists even in fairly homogeneous societies with over 100 years of political independence. In one Latin American country, approximately 45 percent of the adults who completed a nine-month basic education program, broadcast into community viewing centers and including civics and community education as a principal component of instruction, were unable to name the country they lived in.

The attempt to use school and the media to countersocialize individuals into a national culture by downplaying local or parochial identities—or completely excluding any reference to them—may have an opposite effect. Any threat to the social or cultural identity of individuals tends to represent a threat to their own self-identity and well-being. [4] Discriminatory policies of the national government, as manifested in schooling practices, can inflame local sentiments and loyalties, and arouse antagonism toward national authorities and members of different groups.

A more prudent policy, aimed at developing national loyalties and social solidarity, would accord (in the national curriculum) status and dignity to the values, outlooks, and ways of life of the different subcultures forming the society. By contributing to the self and social identity of individuals, a political regime is more likely to gain the allegiance of its citizens. By admitting these differences and not suppressing them, a country conceivably may advance toward social cohesiveness.*

----

*According to political scientists, society may be portrayed and analyzed in "consensual" or "conflictual" ways. According to the consensual model, the stability and progress of a political system depends on most people sharing the same basic values and allegiances. Conflict is to be kept at a minimum. According to the conflictual model, the health of a body politic, and particularly a democracy, depends upon the open expression of conflicting points of view. The emphasis in this model is on political change as new groups with new interests

In multiethnic, multilingual societies using ETV, I have not found a case where members of minority or nondominant social and cultural groups have actively participated in curriculum planning and development. For the most part, members of the urban elite have joined forces with the excolonial or trust power, to plan and develop curricula. In countries like Niger and Samoa, curriculum planning has been almost exclusively in the hands of the French and the Americans. In El Salvador and the Ivory Coast, outside curriculum specialists have played a key role in working with local educators to design a curriculum that reflects cosmopolitan values more than indigenous values. It should not be surprising to find that the "new" curricula of these countries are often mere transplants, with some trimming and pruning, of the standard curricula of the metropolitan country.

WHOSE LANGUAGE?

The dominance of urban groups and external donor countries is also seen in the decision as to which language will be used as the medium of instruction. In several multilingual societies, television is used to teach a common language within the country and with the outside world—usually the language of the excolonial or trust power. In Niger and the Ivory Coast, French is the language of instruction; in American Samoa, English.

The contradictions implicit in the use of the language of the metropolitan country become apparent in statements such as the following, made by a consulting team sent to the Trust Territory of the Pacific Islands in 1967:

---

emerge and make their claims on the society. Rose K. Goldsen, taking a slightly different point of view, calls for an "adversary" approach to the use of the mass media in development: " this means that airing different points of view, encouraging open discussion of clashing ideas and revealing clashing interests is absolutely essential." See Rose K. Goldsen, "Structure and Function of the Mass Media Viewed as a Sociological Institution," mimeographed (Ithaca, New York: Sociology Department, Cornell University, 1971), p. 4. Also see Hans Weiler, "Political Socialization and the Political System; Consensual and Conflictual Linkage Concepts," in Michael W. Kirst, ed., State, School, and Politics (Lexington, Massachusetts: Lexington Books, D. C. Heath and Company, 1972), pp. 57-72; and Harmon Zeigler and Wayne Peak, "The Political Functions of the Educational System", Sociology of Education 43 (Spring 1970): 115-42.

All twentieth century living is not alike, nor is it likely
that the people of the outlying and underdeveloped areas
of the world will have the same living and working conditions, and the same cultural and educational needs
during the last third of the twentieth century. All the
people everywhere have some common needs and common
goals, such as the ability to communicate freely and well,
but a good educational system ought to be designed to
separate the particular and unique needs of the society as
well as the general needs which that society shares with
others in the world. . . . When we say that we will provide a "sound education system of high quality based on
standards required elsewhere," we must define those
standards and carefully relate them to the particular and
unique needs of our relatively isolated people. Everyone
seems agreed that the social and economic development
of the Micronesian people depends upon the educational
development that they are able to achieve, and everyone
seems agreed that the success of their educational development will depend upon the speed and extent to which
they are able to use the English language. In other words,
the learning of English is the most basic and significant
item of educational development in the Trust Territory. . . .
The learner must not only be able to express his own
feelings, ideas, and concepts in English, but he must also
be able to understand fully such communication from others
in English . . . even though it [English] starts as a second
language, it must in effect become the first language of the
learner. [5]

The contradiction resides in the desire not to follow foreign models and
to respect the indigenous culture(s) in pursuing the elusive goals of
development, while establishing an education system and using a
language of instruction that inextricably tie the less developed to the
more powerful metropolitan country in thought patterns, life-styles,
organizational forms.

Undeniably, a strong case might be made for using an international
language as the language of instruction. Countries like Niger or the
Ivory Coast may opt for French as a lesser evil, because of the multiplicity of languages. In a multiethnic society, where no language group
predominates, to select arbitrarily one indigenous language over the
others would undoubtedly precipitate tremendous hostility among the
different groups within the society. At the same time, we must point
out some deleterious consequences that flow from the decision to use
the metropolitan language. Among these are (1) perpetuation of an
elite-mass gap, between the Western-educated and the majority of
people who have not been and will not be educated through the formal

school systems; (2) widening of a generational gap between children
who are brought up in the new cosmopolitan, foreign-oriented education
system and their parents who follow traditional patterns; (3) disruption
and destruction of indigenous value systems; and (4) the continuing
dependence of a country on the metropolitan center for technical assistance and cultural guidance.

The issue of which language to use obviously must be decided
within the context of each country and according to its own development goals. Some of the basic considerations are the following:

1. the relative priority that an overall development ideology or
strategy places on the achievement of a single language of instruction;

2. the extent to which interregional and interethnic communications depend on a single national language;

3. which language facilitates communication with neighboring
countries and the outside world;

4. the impact of a new official language on local bases of identity
and esteem;

5. the appropriateness of a language for the content being offered
and the level of complexity of the subject matter—for example, the
adequacy of language for teaching scientific or technical courses at
the secondary-school and university levels;

6. the language that is likely to facilitate literacy attainment for
both children and adults and serve as the base for later learning of
other languages and subjects;

7. the existence of printed materials in the language, so that
adequate textbooks would be available for children, or reading materials
for adults;

8. the availability of competent instructional personnel who speak
the language. [6]

Although many other important considerations could be included,
the central issue is the need to determine national language policy
first, and then decide the role television will play in language instruction. Under the appropriate conditions, television is an excellent
medium for language instruction. A country can bypass the need to
train a whole generation of teachers in the new language; native
speakers in natural contexts can be viewed and listened to by students
and teachers who learn together.

Unfortunately, the reverse happens. The existence of the technology and the preferences of foreign donors determine the policy; or
the technology becomes an instrument in the hands of the dominant
groups in a society to impose their view of development on the less
powerful, who may constitute the majority.

POLITICALLY RELEVANT TRAITS

Following our analysis of whose values and language comprise the curriculum, we ask which politically relevant dispositions are developed by the school system in general and by televised instruction in particular. Schooling can and does shape habits of passivity, conformity, and deference to existing hierarchical arrangements; but it also can stimulate students to become active, inquiring, and challenging citizens. Schooling can open minds or, conversely, circumscribe people's perceptions to "conventional truths" and routine modes of viewing the world.

Among the factors influencing the acquisition of politically relevant traits are the formal curriculum, classroom learning environments, the social relations of learning, and organizational properties of schools. The specific characteristics of televised instruction—and the dangers of "thought control"—will then be viewed against the general background of the different ways in which schooling can influence the prospective social and political roles of students.

School Factors

The Curriculum and Learning Environments

An examination of the impact of instructional programs on the social awareness and political self of individuals would embrace not only what is said (and not said), but how it is said, and under what conditions. For example, are critical social issues, such as poverty and racism or interethnic hostility, treated in the curriculum in an open and honest manner? Are these issues presented with some feeling for the full depth of their intensity and complexity, or are they presented in a bland, unrealistic way? To distort issues and problems beyond recognition, or to deny the full gravity of social issues, can only diminish the credibility of the curriculum for many students. They know that problems exist that are not being honestly treated.

Equally important is the classroom environment. Do the classroom teachers permit open discussion and controversial treatment of social issues, or do the teachers attempt to direct the students toward the correct answers, as perceived by them or by school authorities? In a study conducted by Lee H. Ehman on civics instruction in the United States, the researcher found that only an "open" classroom environment—where students felt free to raise questions, to critically appraise the ideas of the teacher and of one another, and to study and discuss controversial topics—was related to development of a high sense of political efficacy, low political cynicism, and a high sense of citizen duty among both blacks and whites. [7]

Social Relations of the Learning Process

Learning takes place in a total school environment that influences what is said and how it is said. The overall learning context shapes the transactions between student and student, student and teacher, and between student and environment that affect the development of politically relevant attitudes and values. According to Samuel Bowles:

> The "hidden" content of schooling—the values, expectations, and patterns of behavior which schools encourage—is primarily conveyed not by the formal curriculum, but by the social relations of the schooling process itself. Whether established relations among students are competitive or cooperative, whether relations between students and teachers are democratic or authoritarian, and whether relations between students and their work are creative or alienated, are better indicators of what is taught in schools than texts or curricula. [8]

In examining the learning environments of classrooms and schools, we may find a contradiction between the public goals of schooling and what is taught. For example, teachers preach democracy while acting in authoritarian ways; they exhort students to be creative, while establishing rigid criteria for what is acceptable.

Organizational Properties of Schools

Schools, in addition, have certain organizational properties that inculcate in students habits of punctuality, orderliness in work, deference to hierarchical authority, being treated as categories, and accepting public evaluations of one's work and one's own person. [9] The mass-production system of an industrial, bureaucratically managed society is mirrored in the way schools are organized to mass-produce school leavers with appropriate skills, habits, and outlooks. What is learned in school, then, may be predominantly obedience, deference, passivity, and orderliness.

Properties of ETV

When we examine the properties of television as a medium of instruction, we note that many of its inherent characteristics are those which tend to reinforce hierarchically arranged learning patterns and student passivity—one-way communication, authoritative teachers as role models, and self-contained instructional units with follow-up activities designed to reinforce a message. The assumption in the whole model is that learning results from the transmission of knowledge and information in a direct line from television set to pupil, who forms part of an inert mass quietly imbibing the information. Students and classroom teachers follow in lock-step fashion an inflexible schedule of broadcasts carrying the main load of instruction and the same messages for everyone. A number of countries are utilizing ETV for precisely the advantage to be derived from being able to transmit a uniform curriculum to all children at the same time, minimize discrepancies in messages that emanate from imperfectly trained or unreliable teachers, and force all schools to follow the same nationally determined pace.

One Latin American country, in making a case for using ETV in rural secondary schools, lists among the desired outcomes greater punctuality and orderliness on the part of students—as well as monitors who will now have "to show up on time" and follow nationally set standards. Trained teachers will not be necessary; television programs will teach the basic subjects. Monitors, primary school graduates with an intensive course preparing them for their role, will take classroom attendance, make sure that students are dutifully watching the television programs, distribute and guard supplementary materials, administer examinations, and keep records.

The properties and uses of television support the tendency for these patterns to occur unless a government makes a determined effort to provide means for two-way communication (feedback) and active learning. Niger is one example of a system where the television unit is meant to serve as a stimulus for children to go out and explore their environment, write a story, act out a play. Interestingly enough, Niger is also the exceptional case where research on the learning patterns and life-styles of the schoolchildren preceded the formulation of the curriculum. Again, it should be noted that Niger, between 1964 and 1971, was only an experimental project and its existence depended on substantial outside financing and management.

CENTRALIZATION OF CONTROL AND
UNIFORMITY OF MESSAGES

"Thought control" is a principal danger of a centrally managed and directed system of education using television to carry the main load of instruction. A uniform message can be beamed to all children and adults throughout a nation.

Military-run and one-party states generally will censor program content to eliminate conflicting and contrary points of view that do not serve development goals. But even in the so-called democracies, a process of implicit propagandizing is occurring, with the elimination or "blacking-out" of controversial issues and the presentation of only those points of view that support the ideal image of a country.

In developing countries, the mass media may be an effective instrument for social control. Wilbur Schramm has noted the high credibility assigned to electronic media, especially by people low in societal integration.

> It engineers change, and it keeps strain at a tolerable
> level. Therefore, wherever there is pending change or
> trouble in society, there is a great deal of communica-
> tion. When a group discovers it has a deviant member,
> it directs most of that communication to him until he
> returns to the fold or the cause is found to be hopeless.
> When a country decides it must industrialize, then it
> steps up its communication because the people must be
> informed and motivated. [10]

We must ask if the recent trend in a number of underdeveloped countries to use ETV for adult-education courses or nonformal education courses, hypothetically modeled after Freire and Ivan Illich, is not motivated by similar considerations of social control. Such programs are designed to meet pressures for some forms of participation by marginal groups, without fundamentally changing the structure of society by redistributing power and wealth. We believe that such programs are for the most part instituted and controlled by the government, without providing the opportunity for adults to articulate in a collective way demands for a basic reordering of priorities in a society.

TEACHER RESISTANCE

In countries attempting to inculcate a new system of values or bring about overall change, teachers often are unreliable agents of socialization. More often than not, they subscribe to a traditional system of values. And they will resist changes that threaten their status and prerogatives.

At the same time we must recognize that national authorities frequently contemplate using instructional television as a means of replacing or bypassing teachers or reshaping them to behave the way they must, if the new educational programs are to be successful. Television is rarely viewed as a means of improving teachers, so that, at a future date, television plays a minor role in classroom transactions and is only a learning aid. Therefore, when teachers resist introduction of ETV as a threat to their position in the classroom, their reasons are very well founded.

The teaching profession in a country, moreover, seldom plays an important role in the decision-making process that determines whether ETV should be used or not; it seldom participates to a significant extent in curriculum development and evaluation. Most activities that involve teachers in visiting the production studios for short periods, or have teachers review pilot programs, are essentially public-relations tactics. Decision makers make a show of consulting teachers—not because they believe classroom teachers can make an important professional contribution to curriculum development and program production—but because they want to avoid antagonizing teachers and win their support where necessary. (We also should note that the same ritualistic pattern may hold true when educational authorities consult local community leaders on use of educational television in their locales.)

UNANTICIPATED CONSEQUENCES

The preceding discussion has alluded to several negative consequences that are likely to occur when educational television is utilized on a large scale without prior planning. Inappropriate use of ETV can inflame local or ethnic sentiments against the government and outsiders, develop in students undesirable traits such as passivity, and antagonize teachers.

The expansion and modification of education systems through use of technologies like television furthermore may work to:
1. increase the flow of people from the countryside to the city;
2. expand schooling to the breaking point of financial resources and personnel, precipitating a variety of crises;
3. exacerbate the unemployed school-leaver problem;
4. raise the expectations of adults for social improvement when opportunities are not available.
All of these unanticipated consequences have sociopolitical implications, straining the capacities of a national government and creating social tensions not easily resolved.

Increased Rural-Urban Migration

The decision to use television as a means of providing advanced levels of education to rural areas is predicated upon the assumption that welfare and social-service programs, which make life more attractive for rural populations, will help stem the flood of migrants to the large urban centers. * Notwithstanding the various structural conditions

---

*Another purpose or objective of such programs would be the political support obtained at the grass-roots level by a government that offered greater schooling facilities.

that compel people to leave the countryside in search of greater opportunity in the cities, the very nature of the educational programs themselves may induce students to seek higher levels of education in urban
areas.

Mexico illustrates the contradictions inherent in ETV programs for
rural areas. Its program of televised instruction (telesecundaria) for
first-cycle secondary students living in small towns and rural concen-
trations, is basically a repeat of the urban, university-preparatory
curriculum. Since the curriculum is nonterminal and does not specifically prepare students for a vocation, it is certainly plausible to expect that many students will desire to continue their studies in the
cities where schools are available.

In general, urban curriculum does not prepare rural people to cope
with and improve their daily existence. The values implicit in this type
of curriculum convey the notion that the most desirable way of life is
that of the urban elites—notwithstanding an occasional message glori-
fying life in the rural areas and the importance of the agricultural sector
to national development.

Overexpansion of Schooling and Breakdowns

The use of television to expand one level of the school system
almost invariably places pressure on other rungs of the education ladder.
As a case in point, expansion of first-cycle secondary education will,
within several years, begin to place pressure on the upper level of
secondary education and subsequently on the higher education level.
Pressure for admission to higher and higher levels of the school system
will occur, unless there are adequate employment opportunities, close
linkages between academic training programs and the market, and appropriate curriculum and auxiliary counseling services—all dubious proba-
bilities.

The case of El Salvador is illustrative. Reform of the Plan Básico
(grades seven through nine) created a dynamic of change in the entire
preuniversity system, involving revised curriculum, administrative
reform, wide-scale teacher training, improved supervision, and "guided
promotion."* With the elimination of tuition fees at the middle-school
level in 1971, enrollment expanded by 35 percent over the previous

------

*"Guided promotion" is a variation of automatic promotion, in
the sense that most students will be promoted to the next higher grade
level. Students with academic problems at the beginning of each academic year will enter a special remedial course to bring them up to the
level of course work they will be required to do.

year. Schools had to go on double shifts, and teachers were required to take on additional work with no increase in pay. [11] The result—a teacher strike that shut down a majority of the schools for several months and disrupted the academic program tied to a fixed schedule of television broadcasts.

Future crises are likely at the secondary and university levels. According to the team evaluating the El Salvador educational reform, 95 percent of the students plan to go further than Plan Básico, and as many as 40 percent aspire to university studies. The researchers write that the two existing universities in the country could never handle this tidal wave of students. [12]

Unemployed School Leavers

In many countries, expansion of formal schooling is occurring at a rate exceeding the generation of employment opportunities in the market. This phenomenon is particularly true in countries that are copying capital intensive production processes from the advanced industrial center.

Planners, traditionally, have given insufficient consideration to the consequences of large numbers of school graduates not finding jobs or meaningful employment related to development. The deleterious consequences range from wasted human potential and inefficient allocation of scarce resources to the formation of a large group of dissatisfied individuals who may become a force for revolutionary change.

But change may not occur for a variety of reasons. Professionals may migrate—as they do in the case of El Salvador. School graduates may accept jobs previously occupied by individuals with less formal education. They may place blame on themselves or chance, not on the government. Individual frustration, therefore, does not necessarily become organized into collective dissent.

In the absence of planning and governmental policies aimed at generating employment, school expansion is likely to continue to have negative economic and social consequences. As John W. Hanson and Cole S. Brembeck have emphasized:

> education becomes a relevant factor in economic growth
> only when it is properly integrated with all the other
> factors in development. Moreover, it must be education
> of the right kind, in the proper balance, and suited to
> the stage of development. [13]

The case of El Salvador exemplifies the future pressures a government is likely to encounter as a consequence of expanded schooling. According to the initial research reports on student aspiration levels,

40 percent of all students in the Plan Básico (grades seven through nine) are aspiring toward professional occupations, and about 55 percent toward semiskilled jobs. In contrast to this, 70 percent of their fathers are working in unskilled jobs; only 10 percent are in semiskilled jobs; and less than 10 percent are in the professions. [14]

The Salvadoran economy, already characterized by a high brain drain of professionals unable to find work, is unlikely to provide adequate employment opportunities for school leavers. In addition, public expenditures on education represented 28 percent of the national budget in 1971, diverting funds from other ministries and programs concerned with employment generation and capital investment.

Frustrated Adults

The foregoing proviso of Hanson and Brembeck applies to social-development programs using television to carry new information and perspectives to disadvantaged farmers, mothers, urban unemployed, and illiterate adults. Exhortation by the public or private sectors for dispossessed individuals to join forces at the community level to bring about change, to learn to read and write in order to advance in life, to adopt new crops and farming methods, to seek an alternative role (for women) outside the household may be nothing more than one grand deception when:

● any militant pressure for change is met with repression;
● jobs are not available for people with mere literacy, and exaggerated credentials are required for employment;
● land, credit, fertilizer, and pesticides, irrigation and markets are not accessible to the poor peasant;
● women are discriminated against in the market and jobs are not available for them.

A recent study in Latin America reinforces these arguments. Research was conducted on the impact of an adult-education radio series on the innovative behaviors and modern attitudes of campesinos (country people) in rural Colombia. A comparison of the experimental groups that listened to the programs with control groups that did not, reveals that nonlisteners who live in relatively prosperous farming areas were more likely to exhibit innovative and modern attitudes than were listeners and program participants who live in impoverished areas. [15]

If televised educational programs are intended to make a substantial contribution to development processes, they must be accompanied by the requisite resources and means to transform promises into reality. Otherwise these education programs are likely to be more instrumental in enforcing social control than in facilitating social change. Many adults who join these programs in the hope of improvement soon become aware of the discrepancy between message and reality. It should not come as a surprise that attrition rates are high in these programs, and that the plight of the majority remains more or less unchanged.

ETV DEVELOPMENT STRATEGIES

The preceding discussion has analyzed some of the negative consequences that may flow from unplanned expansion of a school system through ETV. In this section, I will discuss how, in the absence of systematic planning, wholesale importation of technologies may compromise the autonomy of a country and determine the direction and pace of its development.

Ideally, utilization of technologies such as ETV should form part of an education plan reflecting overall national development goals. This set of ideal conditions presupposes that:

1. a national development strategy or ideology—for example, what kind of person in what type of society—exists, stipulating development goals and steps required to reach targets;

2. the role of different types of education programs in development processes has been defined; and

3. the part ETV can play in enhancing the overall performance and contribution of the education system to development has been carefully conceptualized.

Systematic planning of this type generally does not exist prior to the decision to adopt ETV on a massive scale. Instead, the decision to utilize television often is made on the grounds of expediency. An external technical assistance agency offers equipment, financing, and specialized personnel; a country has television sets sitting in a warehouse that must be used. More important, there is a certain symbolic value to establishing a national ETV system. It makes a country look modern; it leads people to believe that their government is doing something for them by offering new formal and nonformal education programs. At the same time foreign donors, who are pushing their technical assistance, have a showcase country to demonstrate the effectiveness of their technologies.

Aid recipients often assume that these technologies are "culturally neutral," and that a country's cultural integrity will not be compromised. These technologies, however, are not value free. Herbert I. Schiller and others have pointed out that, along with the hardware, a country is importing the values, behaviors, attitudes, and organizational patterns that sustain a technological society and keep the hardware running. [16]

Over and above the cultural penetration that occurs with uncritical adoption of foreign technologies—and accompanying education packages—the danger exists that a country will be financially indebted to the donor country. In a number of the showcase countries, the initial expenditures on capital equipment and construction of a communication infrastructure could not be met without substantial foreign investment. When the technical assistance terminates, will the country be able to sustain the project on its own? If it can, what other priorities are sacrificed?

A second danger is that a country's educational investment patterns will be determined by the piecemeal programs and projects supported from abroad. For example, if foreign loans are earmarked for expansion of secondary education, the matching national funds will have to be channeled to this level in preference to other levels. If money is given for televised instruction, then public resources will be directed toward this area as against others—which may be more necessary and less costly. Thus, instead of priorities first being determined by a national government—which seeks foreign aid as one source of financing nationally initiated change—the reverse may occur; foreign aid programs determine priorities for the recipient country.

Substantial foreign involvement in the internal affairs of a country is a price most countries have to pay to establish a national ETV system. Governments should question if the price is worth the advantage to be derived from using this technology.

The decision will be based in good part on how a country defines development. Kalman Silvert offers a provocative definition of the concept. According to Silvert, "development is the relationship between the range of choice open to a polity and the range it actually explores."[17] Among the essential sociopolitical questions we must ask of technologies like television are the following: Does it open options, or does it foreclose a number of opportunities? Does it facilitate greater learning and participation by larger numbers of people, or does it instead lead to greater formal control by those in power? Does it assist people in achieving a sense of who they are and what they can do to better their condition in life, or does it rob people of their individuality? Does it contribute to cultural autonomy and self-expression or to cultural emasculation and homogenization? (The question of the economic cost of achieving competing objectives is a separate issue analyzed in Chapter 2.) Do these technologies contribute to the decision-making capacities of a country or to continued dependency on outside powers?

These questions have to be answered within the social and cultural context of each country. What we must point out is the fallacy of technological determinism—that by adopting the technologies, organizational patterns, institutions, and behaviors of more industrialized and economically advanced countries, development will occur. Development is a matter of policy and strategy and ideology unique to each country; it is not an inevitable and unilinear unfolding toward Western models of industrialized society. The nature and direction of development is ultimately determined by the political process itself, which means the struggle for power to decide "who gets what, and when."

ALTERNATIVES

Depending on the development strategy of a country, television
may not be the most appropriate medium to use for instructional purposes—or it may be appropriate only under certain conditions and in
combination with other programs. For example, a country that assigns
high priority to rural transformation may find radio a less expensive
and more practical medium, able to reach isolated populations without
electricity. Aside from the electronic media, a country interested in
contributing to the enlightenment of rural populations might utilize a
broad range of means, such as mobile teams of educators and exten-
sionists, traveling popular cultural troupes, inexpensive print material—manuals, flyers, wall posters—and resident community organizers
and learning facilitators.

Attempts by the government to assist the urban poor might lead to
the establishment of community learning centers. These centers, as
envisioned by Arnove, would be one or more meeting places in a community where individuals of any age would go to take short courses,
receive counseling, share interests, teach skills, obtain learning
materials, participate in community activities, receive health and
nutritional care, and gain access to information on national welfare
services.[18] Radio and television would be one source of information,
along with the others.

The basic thrust in alternatives to present national systems of
educational television would be away from centralization of control,
uniformity of messages, and one-way vertical communication. The
movement would be in the direction of decentralized control over the
media and local participation in program development, reflecting the
needs and interests of the diverse populations comprising a society.
According to Hans Magnus Enzenberger, an "emancipatory use" of the
media would further involve a shift from one transmitter and many receivers to each receiver being a potential transmitter, a shift from
production by specialists to collective production, from control by
property owners or bureaucracy to social control by self-organization,
and from immobilization of isolated individuals to mobilization of the
masses.[19]

In essence, the movement would be away from the manipulative
aspects of the mass media toward its use as an instrument for enhancing
the self-awareness and self-expression of both individuals and their
communities. As Herbert Gintis has pointed up, "individuals must exercise direct control over technology in structuring their various social
environments, thereby developing and coming to understand their needs
through their exercise of power."[20]

A set of conditions favoring the emergence of community control
over educational processes would include a political regime dedicated
to a more participatory society as well as a substantial group of

individuals aware of contradictions in school systems and organized to establish an alternative system. A first step toward this more ideal state is the recognition and rejection of repressive aspects of present educational systems and technologies. This chapter has set out to illustrate the negative sociopolitical aspects of educational television as well as its emancipatory potential.

NOTES

1. James S. Coleman, ed., Education and Political Development (Princeton: Princeton University Press, 1965), p. 3.

2. Ibid., p. 31.

3. Paulo Freire, "The Adult Literacy Process as Cultural Action for Freedom," Harvard Educational Review 40 (May 1970): 202-25.

4. See, for example, the following: Robert Levine, "Political Socialization and Culture Change," in Clifford Geertz, ed., Old Societies and New States: The Quest for Modernity in Asia and Africa (New York: The Free Press of Glencoe, 1963), pp. 280-303; Clifford Geertz, "The Integrative Revolution: Primordial Sentiments and Civic Politics in the New States," in ibid., pp. 105-57; and Richard E. Dawson and Kenneth Prewitt, Political Socialization (Boston: Little, Brown and Company, 1969). These researchers have pointed up how individuals develop social identities and political loyalties at an early age, within the context of family and local authority groups. These identities and loyalties are emotionally charged, integrally related to the self-concepts of individuals, and resistant to outside forces for change.

5. NAEB, Educational Development in the Trust Territory of the Pacific Islands (Washington, D.C.: National Association of Educational Broadcasters, Office of Research and Development, 1967), p. 11.

6. For a general discussion of the language issue in national development, see Joshua A. Fishman, Charles A. Ferguson, and Jyotirinda Das Gapta, eds., Language Problems of Developing Nations (New York: John Wiley and Sons, 1968).

7. Lee H. Ehman, "An Analysis of the Relationships of Selected Educational Variables with the Political Socialization of High School Students," American Educational Research Journal 7 (1968): 580.

8. Samuel Bowles, "Cuban Education and the Revolutionary Ideology," Harvard Educational Review 41 (November 1971): 477-78.

9. See Robert Dreeben, On What is Learned in School (Reading, Massachusetts: Addison-Wesley Publishing Company, 1968); for an opposing point of view, see Carl Bereiter, "Schools without Education," Harvard Educational Review 42 (August 1972): 390-413.

10. Wilbur Schramm, "Communication Research in the United States," in Wilbur Schramm, ed., The Science of Human Communication:

New Directions and Findings in Communication Research (New York:
Basic Books, 1963), pp. 13-14.
11. Robert Hornik, Henry Ingle, John K. Mayo, Judith Mayo,
Emile G. McAnany, and Wilbur Schramm, Television and Educational
Reform in El Salvador, Report on the Third Year of Research (Stanford,
California: Institute for Communication Research, Stanford University,
Research Report No. 10, 1972), p. 1.
12. Wilbur Schramm, John K. Mayo, Emile G. McAnany, Robert C.
Hornik, Television and Educational Reform in El Salvador, Complete
Report of the Second Year of Research (Stanford, California: Institute
for Communication Research, Stanford University, Research Report
No. 7, 1971).
13. John W. Hanson, and Cole S. Brembeck, eds., Education and
the Development of Nations (New York: Holt, Rinehart and Winston,
1966), p. 148.
14. See Schramm et al., Television and Educational Reform in
El Salvador, 1972, p. 47.
15. Stefan A. Musto, Los Medios de Comunicación Social al
Servicio del Desarrollo Rural (Bogotá, Colombia: Editorial Andes,
1971).
16. Herbert I. Schiller, Mass Communications and American
Empire (New York: A. M. Kelley, 1969).
17. Kalman Silvert, Man's Power (New York: Viking Press, 1970).
18. Robert F. Arnove, "Community Learning Centers," UNICEF,
Assignment Children (April 1973): 94-105. Similarly, ETV, when used
in rural areas, might form part of the activities of rural development
centers that are being established in countries like Tanzania and Peru.
These centers would bring together in one place a variety of formal and
nonformal educational programs, along with credit, extension, and
health services.
19. Hans Magnus Enzenberger, "Constituents of a Theory of the
Mass Media," in Denis McQuail, ed., Sociology of Mass Communications (London: Penguin Books, Inc., 1972).
20. Herbert Gintis, "Toward a Political Economy of Education: A
Radical Critique of Ivan Illich's Deschooling Society," Harvard Educational Review 42 (February 1972): 84.

2

THE ECONOMIC COSTS
AND RETURNS TO
EDUCATIONAL TELEVISION
Martin Carnoy

Educational television (ETV) requires large investments of time, energy, and scarce resources by low-income countries. These investments are being made with minimal information concerning (1) the effectiveness of educational television compared to other educational improvements and (2) the economic returns to increasing the number of children schooled through educational television.

We first identify the nature of the problem and define two ways of dealing with it: cost-effectiveness analysis and cost-benefit analysis. Then we calculate costs of educational television projects and attempt some approximations of their effectiveness and economic benefits.

In this chapter we also examine from an economic perspective arguments proposed in favor of introducing educational reforms such as ETV. These arguments are based on assumptions that (1) innovations will improve average exam scores of students and (2) lead to an increased number of school graduates without a decrease in the "quality" of their education, and that (3) there is a substantial economic payoff both to improving individuals' cognitive skills, as measured by school tests, and graduating more students from higher levels of the education system. We argue, instead, there is no evidence that increasing the number of graduates has a higher economic return than investments in other forms of capital, nor that raising the average level of schooling in a country improves the distribution of income. Since ETV has often been introduced to expand schooling in nonindustrialized countries, this lack of evidence would have to be overcome in order to rationalize ETV on economic grounds.

Many countries, however, have already made a commitment to expand education even if the economic return is low. In that case, is ETV the least expensive way to achieve rapid expansion? We do not examine this question directly, but other studies indicate that radio is substantially cheaper than television and just as effective in relation to student performance.[1] There also may be inexpensive ways to expand education effectively without technology, using labor-intensive techniques. Given the future employment picture of even skilled labor in most low-income countries, these approaches may be much more appropriate than methods that rely on laborsaving devices. *

EVALUATING ETV

Does educational television save money? Usually the evaluation of alternatives in schooling is dealt with in terms of pure educational outcomes. The success of a teaching technique is measured by students' test scores or school retention rates or the acceptability of the method by teachers and students. But in situations where resources are scarce, the costs of achieving better educational outcomes through alternative means are a crucial variable. The issue of the cost-effectiveness of educational television and other media in comparison with traditional teaching techniques and alternatives that do not use the media has generally been avoided. The comparisons that were made in the United States, for example, did not evaluate ETV against alternatives that cost approximately the same amount; rather, they compared programs that used ETV with programs having no increase in cost per pupil. One of the most comprehensive reviews of educational media deals with the issue this way:

> The evidence on savings over potential expenses is rela-
> tively scarce and all we can say with confidence is that in
> the case of an expanding educational system (be it in quality
> or quantity), the new media may well save money. Introduc-
> ing a new media project into an existing system may possibly
> also lead to a redeployment of the resources employed in the
> system and end up producing a new structure. It is an open
> question at this stage whether this will produce any savings
> or not. At any rate, in this question we are forced on to slip-
> pery ground. We have to evaluate learning outputs against
> cost for we must deal with estimates of possible future costs
> that are far from firm. [2]

The principal difficulty with this and other treatments of educational television is that it evaluates ETV in absolute terms: does it or does it not do better than traditional schooling on some simple objective like an increase in test scores over a year of schooling? But the treatment does not compare the increase in test scores resulting from ETV and traditional schooling with the cost of the two methods. Obviously, we

---

*Studies show that there is sizable educated unemployment in India, the Philippines, and Kenya. See Table 2.8 for citations of these studies.

not only want to know if one method is more effective than another in attaining some objective, we also want to know what that increased effectiveness costs. We should therefore compare ETV with teacher re-training and other non-ETV educational improvements in terms of their effect on school performance and their costs. This is called cost-effectiveness analysis. In cost-effectiveness analysis, we measure how much change occurs in a particular objective (such as test score or behavior patterns) as a result of different treatments and compare this change with the cost of each treatment.

Furthermore, we can estimate the social value of unit increase in school output and compare the increase in social benefits resulting from the different treatments to their cost. This is called cost-benefit anal-ysis. The social value of an increased number of graduates that results from introducing ETV, for example, could be measured by the increased income earned by those additional graduates. In cost-benefit analysis, this increased income is compared to the extra resource cost required by ETV over and above providing traditional schooling. Relating the dollar increase in benefits with a dollar increase in costs yields a unit-less ratio that can be compared to the benefit-cost ratios of other in-vestments. [3] Cost-effectiveness analysis is limited to comparing projects that have the same objective (increased school performance in a particular subject, for example). Cost-benefit analysis can com-pare the effectiveness of projects with different objectives, as long as all those objectives can be translated into the common denominator of monetary benefits.

Another difficulty with previous assessments of educational media is the variety of uses to which the media have been put. Each use has different objectives. In some cases, like Hagerstown, television is used to supplement existing formal schooling. The primary objectives seem to be the increase in quality of existing courses, and the adding of new courses (like music and art) in all the schools of the district. In American Samoa and El Salvador the principal purpose of television is to provide the core curriculum. It is the means by which formal schooling is extended to more school-age children. The primary ob-jective is to overcome the shortage of primary- and secondary-school teachers through technology and to expand the formal school system.

The evaluation of supplementary objectives for educational tele-vision must be made in terms of the increase in quality of education it produces. Quality is itself a difficult concept to define. Is it the amount of cognitive learning the child accumulates? the nature of the teacher-student interaction? the breadth of the school experience? an index of "modernization?" Each of these definitions requires a dif-ferent measure.

The evaluation of extension objectives for television must be made in terms of the increase in the quantity of education it produces. Al-though this may seem simpler than the quality measure, there are prob-lems with defining quantity as well. Is it the number of students en-rolled? the number of students adjusted by an index of quality? the

number of graduates of each level of school? Again, each definition requires a different measure.

In both evaluations, we have only dealt with outputs as educational
outputs. This is adequate if we are comparing the unit cost of one method of producing such an output (by ETV, for example) with the unit cost
of producing the same output by another method (increasing the preparation or the number of conventional teachers, for example). In addition,
we may want to know whether the investment in increased quality or
quantity of education makes sense compared to other investments. We
would therefore have to measure the social benefits of investment in
ETV by assessing the social value of the educational results produced.
What is the value, for example, of increasing the number of graduates
at various levels of school? What is the value of increased math
scores?

These questions are difficult to answer, but if we are to answer
them at all, we must define the objectives of a particular project a
priori and gather the data necessary to perform the evaluation. Unfortunately, few ETV projects bother to do either of these things. The best
we can do at this point is an analytical beginning. First, we develop
some simple models of cost effectiveness and cost benefit as they could
be applied to educational television projects with various objectives.
We present some cost estimates for ETV and summarize the cost and
effect data available from existing projects. Finally, we enter into
some general issues concerning the impact of improved and increased
formal schooling on economic output and the distribution of income.

Cost-effectiveness Analysis

Educational outcomes like increasing test scores can themselves
be regarded as educational objectives without regard for their value in
the labor force or in the social structure. This is not to say that such
educational outcomes are free of cost or that they should not be evaluated in terms of their cost.

> The oft-encountered assertion that the results of the educa-
> tional process are so diverse and diffuse that they cannot be
> measured is either a semantic misunderstanding or pure ob-
> scurantism. Indeed, if it were true, educational decisions
> involving financial outlays would be impossible. [4]

We can measure many educational objectives with well-defined cardinal
indexes. * Cognitive learning, noncognitive behavior, and attitudes

---

*A cardinal index is one in which various outcomes are related to
each other with absolute and comparable values rather than simply
ranked (ordinal index).

toward school are all measurable, and various teaching techniques can be evaluated with regard to each of these objectives and with regard to the cost of each technique.

Let us assume that a school system is interested in improving the quality of its education. It has a choice of installing an educational television system that will deliver high-"quality" basic courses plus supplemental courses that do not exist in the present curriculum, or providing "better" teachers to teach the basic courses and additional teachers to teach the supplemental courses.* A cost-effectiveness analysis comparing the two alternatives requires information on (1) the change in the desired school output associated with each method of improved teaching and (2) the additional cost of each method. We want to know whether the ratio of change in school output associated with method I (ETV) is larger or smaller per unit cost than the change in the same school output associated with method II (improved conventional teaching).

$$\frac{\Delta \text{ school output (I)}}{\Delta \text{ cost (I)}} \underset{>}{<} \frac{\Delta \text{ school output (II)}}{\Delta \text{ cost (II)}} \qquad (2.1)$$

For example, the addition of ETV to the classroom may produce an average change in reading score of ten points per pupil in the third grade for an average annual cost increase per pupil of $50. Improved conventional teaching may produce an increase in average reading score of 15 points for an annual per-pupil-cost increase of $60. ETV in this example has a cost-effectiveness ratio of 0.20 points per dollar, while improved conventional teaching has a ratio of 0.25 points per dollar. In terms of an improved-reading-score objective, therefore, conventional teaching is more cost effective than ETV. But the objectives of the system may include much more than improving reading scores. Math scores may not improve as much with better conventional teaching as with the introduction of ETV. Certain behavior as measured by indexes may be "improved" more with better teaching as well. For each measure, we can estimate a cost-effectiveness ratio comparison for the two alternatives. Unless all the comparisons favor one method over the other, a choice will have to be made between the two based on the decision makers' "preference function," indicating their order of priority among objectives. Even in some ideal form of educational decision making, the best we can do is to present the decision makers with as many cost-effectiveness ratios as we can calculate, leaving it to them to attach weights to each one.

----

*There are many variables that can be used to measure teacher quality: academic preparation, years of experience, teacher modernity, or verbal ability, to name just a few. See, for example, Alexander Mood, ed., Do Teachers Make a Difference? (Washington, D.C.: U.S. Office of Education, 1970).

Cost-effectiveness analysis can also be applied to the <u>expansion</u> of schooling through ETV. Typically, a political decision has already been made to increase the number of children in school over a certain period of time. So the question is not <u>whether</u> to expand schooling, but <u>how</u> to do it for the lowest cost. Obviously, if the time period in which expansion will take place is short enough, the choice for most countries is either a massive infusion of educational technology or importing teachers. Often, the latter alternative is not politically acceptable, so the decision is made to import technology without any cost-effectiveness study. On the other hand, if the major expansion is allowed to take place over a 10-to-15-year period, a number of important alternatives are possible. * Thus, training or upgrading conventional teachers to provide schooling is an alternative to educational television, and the two can be compared by cost-effectiveness analysis. † In this case, the main objective of the educational expenditure is to maximize the enrollment of school-age children in school, or perhaps to maximize the number of primary-school graduates, or even the employment of people (teachers) in the education sector. Thus, we want to compare the cost per additional pupil enrolled or graduated between the two (or more) methods, or the number of teachers employed per dollar spent on additional schooling. Again, one method may result in lower costs per additional enrollee and higher cost per additional graduate, depending on the dropout rate associated with each method. One method may be higher on both enrollees and graduates but may employ far fewer teachers.

Cost-benefit Analysis

In the case of education, cost-benefit analysis permits us to compare the relative value of spending public funds on increasing the

---

*Should educational expansion take place over a short or longer period? This depends on the capacity of the economy to absorb schooled labor. If the economy is at full employment, additional schooling will at least be employed in the labor force even with rapid school expansion. But in economies characterized by significant unemployment, a rapid increase in schooling will result in increasing the average level of schooling among the unemployed. These are questions which can be treated better by cost-benefit rather than cost-effectiveness analysis, since they deal with the <u>social value</u> of school expansion over the short run or over the longer run.

†The problem of training teachers to serve in rural areas, or even getting them to serve there, has not been solved in societies where the most prestigious social and economic positions are in the largest cities. We deal with this issue in the last section of the chapter.

quantity or quality of schooling with other public investments (like
roads, sewer systems, agricultural extension services, or factories)
or with private ones. Although there may be a number of social benefits
and social costs of more and better schooling, cost-benefit analysis
is usually limited to estimating both costs and benefits in terms of
money. To estimate the value of an investment in ETV relative to its
costs in terms that are comparable to other investments requires measures of the monetary returns to and the monetary costs of the project.*
There may be other important social benefits from investing in an ETV
system, like a more equitable income distribution, greater political
participation, more political stability, or greater social integration;
the monetary product of these, however, would be indirect and would
not enter into the cost-benefit calculation. It is possible to do cost-
effectiveness analysis of different kinds of investments (roads versus
schools, for example) in terms of these nonpecuniary outputs. Thus,
a road may produce more social integration per dollar expended than
additional schools.

---

*Monetary returns are usually defined as the increased product or
earnings of labor as a result of taking additional or better schooling.
Usually, we compare incomes over lifetime of those taking a particular
level of schooling with the incomes of those taking the next highest
level. The difference in average incomes between those with these
different amounts of education can be called the monetary benefits of
schooling:

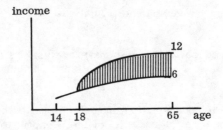

Thus, the shaded area represents the monetary value of six years of
additional schooling. Of course, the increased average income is not
only the result of additional schooling, but also the fact that those
with more schooling come from higher social-class backgrounds and
have higher IQs. They would probably earn more income than those
with six years of schooling even if they had six instead of 12 years of
education. Furthermore, more schooling generally leads to more on-
the-job training, so the income differences include a return to on-the-
job training as well as schooling. For more discussion of these points,
see Mark Blaug, An Introduction to the Economics of Education (London:
The Penguin Press, 1970).

Cost-benefit analysis yields a first estimate of the monetary payoff to à particular investment. If the payoff to that investment is high relative to other investments, then critics of the project would have to argue that particular nonpecuniary costs offset monetary benefits. For example, school may be such a dreary place that there is a high psychological cost of going to school.

If the payoff to a project is low, however, supporters of the project would have to show that nonpecuniary benefits make the project worthwhile. People with more schooling may not get higher salaries but may get more "prestigious" jobs. Prestige makes people feel better off.

In its simplest form, the information required for cost-benefit analysis could take the following form:

$$\frac{\Delta \text{ social output (project I)}}{\Delta \text{ cost (project I)}} \lessgtr \frac{\Delta \text{ social output (project II)}}{\Delta \text{ cost (project II)}} \quad (2.2)$$

The change in social output is taken here as the increased earnings of those who get the additional schooling or the better schooling. The cost of the projects is also taken in dollars. Since costs and additional social output are usually spread out over a considerable period of time (the schooling and working lives of those who get the additional schooling and even the lifetimes of succeeding generations), we have to have some way to adjust for different time patterns of costs and payoffs in different projects.

If the interest rate on capital were zero, there would be no problem; benefits received two or three years from now would have the same value as benefits received today. But the interest rate on capital is rarely less than 5 percent and is often much higher. Therefore, we must "discount" future earnings by the interest deferred income could earn if received today and invested. Taking account of people's time preference, equation (2.2) can be expressed:

$$P_I = \sum_{i=1}^{i=s} \frac{-C_i}{(1+r)^i} + \sum_{i=s+1}^{i=n} \frac{Y_i}{(1+r)^i} \lessgtr P_{II} \quad (2.3)$$

where P = present value

C_i = cost of schooling incurred in time period i

Y_i = benefits of schooling received in time period i

r = social discount rate

s = years of school

n = retirement age minus age at starting school

The present value of the project is the discounted stream of benefits and costs. Alternatively, we can set each project's present value equal to zero and solve for the internal discount rate, r. If $r_I > r_{II}$, the rate of return to the investment in project I is greater than to the alternative investment in II, and on economic grounds, project I is preferable. *

These are all different ways of determining the same thing: the pecuniary value of an ETV investment project compared to other public investments. When we consider the expansion of an educational system through ETV, we can measure the monetary benefits of the project by the average increase in earnings of those who get the additional schooling. † There are a number of problems associated with estimating such benefits—we deal with them in the last section of this chapter— but approximations have been made for a number of countries. [5] These approximations estimate the marginal rates of return to investing in more schooling at various levels. Of course, the estimations are based on the current costs and benefits of providing schooling. If ETV is more expensive than the present system, and if a large expansion of schooling inundates the labor market with schooled people, the estimated rates of return to such an investment could be considerably lower than those already estimated.

Thus, we can estimate the payoff providing more schooling for the population by estimating the costs of that additional schooling and the resultant increased income accruing to those who take the schooling. It is also possible to estimate the monetary payoff to increasing student performance in school. ‡ The benefits to better performance can be divided into the direct benefits—the increase in an individual's earnings due to improved performance in school—and the indirect benefits—the increased earnings due to the effect that improved performance has on the probability of staying longer in school. [6] Expressed in mathematical terms, the model has three components: (1) the direct benefits of an increase in school performance (taken as the measure of the increase

---

*See Martin Bailey, "Criteria for Investment Decision," Journal of Political Economy, October 1959, pp. 476-78.

†If the project consists of increasing the number of people who attend school by a small amount relative to the number currently in that level of schooling, we can measure the benefits by the increase of income at the "margin", that is, the average income difference that exists among those with different levels of schooling now in the labor force. We can assume that the small increase in graduates will affect the wage structure little. However, most ETV projects contemplate large increases in children attending school. We must therefore estimate the returns to additional schooling correcting for the probability that they will be employed in the future with much larger numbers of graduates in the labor market. This is defined here as the "average" return to those who get the additional schooling.

‡If we consider that pupil school performance is a function of school quality, pupil socioeconomic background, and pupil early IQ, a change in pupil performance as a result of additional school inputs could be regarded as a change in the quality of schooling.

in quality of schooling) for a given quantity of schooling;* (2) the increase in the quantity of schooling taken as a result of the increase in school performance (alternatively, the decrease in dropout resulting from improved performance); and (3) the benefits to taking more schooling. The last two components are multiplied to produce the indirect effect of better performance:

$$\frac{dB}{dQ}_i \quad \text{equals} \quad \frac{\partial B}{\partial Q}_i \quad \text{plus} \quad \frac{\partial S}{\partial Q} \quad \text{times} \quad \frac{\partial B}{\partial S}_i \qquad (2.4)$$

where $\dfrac{dB}{dQ}_i$ equals the total increase in benefits at age i from an increase in performance in schools;

$\dfrac{\partial B}{\partial Q}_i$ equals the <u>direct</u> increase in benefits at age i from an increase in performance alone;

$\dfrac{\partial S}{\partial Q}$ equals the increased years of schooling taken due to increased school performance;

and $\dfrac{\partial B}{\partial S}_i$ equals the benefits at age i of taking additional years of schooling.

The total benefits in time period i of an investment in improved schooling can therefore be estimated if we know these three components of benefits: How much more do people with a certain amount of schooling earn if, for example, their test scores are better? How much further in school do people go as a result of an improvement in their test scores? How much payoff is there to taking additional schooling?

Equation (2.4) shows the trade-off between improving pupil performance in school and increasing the quantity of schooling. If pupils perform better because of improved teaching, either through ETV or other means, the retention rate may rise (unless promotion is based on relative scores), and children will stay in school longer. The number of graduates should rise, provided that there are places for children in the higher grades. On the other hand, if the payoff to expenditures on schooling is higher for expanding the number of people coming out of a given level even with a fall in average performance—that is, the first term of equation (2.4) is very small—increasing the quality of schooling may be a poor investment.

Socioeconomic Background of Students

In most school systems, the distributional impact of educational expenditures is as important as their effectiveness. One way to assess

---

*An increase in the quality of schooling is usually measured by an increase in school inputs, but here it is measured by an increase in school output for a certain level or grade of school, with pupil background characteristics unchanged.

this impact is to estimate cost effectiveness and cost benefit by socioeconomic groups of students. If we define three socioeconomic class
groups, for example, we can estimate the increase in test scores with
ETV and compare it to the increase in test score from improved conventional teaching for each socioeconomic group. Similarly we can estimate the benefits to different groups resulting from an investment in
ETV, whether in improving the quality of schooling or extending the
school system.

One common error must be avoided: the school dropout rate among
lower-socioeconomic-class children is much higher than among higher-
class children. When we compare the increase in score for lower-class
students in the fourth year of primary school, for example, with the
increase in score for higher-class children, we may be comparing the
effectiveness of ETV for a very special selected group of lower-class
children (those left after many dropped out in earlier grades) with an
average group of higher-class children. We can begin to adjust for
these differences by taking account of ability of children in addition
to their social class. We would expect that by the fourth grade in many
underdeveloped countries the relationship between social class and
ability would be very low, since only the higher-ability children from
among the lower classes reach the fourth grade, while average-ability
children from the higher social classes have no difficulty staying in
school. [7]

It is therefore much better in the later grades to compare the effectiveness of ETV and conventional teaching on students defined by
a variable that combines social class and ability: low class/low ability;
low class/high ability; high class/low ability; and so on. The low-
class/low-ability group may be more representative of the average
lower-class child who is not in school by the fourth grade. The only
way to find that out is to sample all children, whether in school or not,
and test them for verbal and nonverbal ability.

The Use of Media in Different Educational Projects

ETV can be used to provide education in different ways. We have
discussed the trade-off between raising pupil performance in formal
schooling and extending formal schooling to additional school-age
population (increasing the quantity of schooling). But there are other
means of educating the population, and media may be more effective
in some means than others. In addition to examples of extending the
school to children who live in sparsely populated areas (Australia and
New Zealand), and of providing schooling to parts of the country that
are deficient in teachers (Italy and Mexico), ETV is also used to teach
technical subjects to factory workers (Poland) and in literacy programs
for adults (Italy, Peru, Niger). Since most countries have limited resources for education, it is important to know whether an investment

in literacy programs and/or on-the-job training have a higher payoff
than investment in formal schooling. Similarly, the effectiveness of
ETV in raising the quality and/or quantity of schooling may be better
served by concentrating it in rural areas rather than urban, or vice
versa. Perhaps the best use for ETV is in training teachers rather than
students, aiming for a rapid expansion of better-trained conventional
teachers.

Therefore, we do not have to limit cost-effectiveness or cost-benefit analysis to comparisons of ETV with conventional teaching or with
other investment projects, but can compare the benefits and/or effectiveness of different uses for ETV.

ESTIMATING THE COST OF EDUCATIONAL MEDIA
AND CONVENTIONAL SCHOOLING

No ETV project has yet been able to replace teachers completely.
It is supplemental to teachers, although it substitutes for certain kinds
of training and certification. In Niger, the ETV system used monitors
with low academic preparation (they did receive training in working
with the system) and little or no experience as teachers. In Hagerstown, the ETV was used in addition to the regular trained teachers to
provide special courses such as music and art and to supplement the
basic courses. In American Samoa, local teachers with low-level training continue in the classrooms as monitors, while ETV provides most
of the core curriculum. In Niger and Samoa, ETV has substituted in
considerable part for upgrading teachers through training.

A special consideration in the case of Hagerstown is that the city
has the option of drawing on the well-developed communications system of the area. Washington County, Maryland, is located between
two of the largest cities in the United States, Washington, D. C., and
Baltimore, about 70 miles apart. The countryside school district rented
coaxial cable space over which it runs its closed-circuit TV signals.
That option is open to few underdeveloped countries. They usually require the installation of TV transmission facilities in addition to the
other main components of ETV costs: production, reception, and classroom teacher training.

Each of these components (except, perhaps, teacher training) has
a fixed capital cost and a current, or operating, cost. Fixed capital
cost can be defined as the annual current resource cost of a fixed investment. One of the current costs of a fixed investment is depreciation
of capital such as equipment and buildings. Depreciation is charged on
current account on the assumption that if capital is used up it will have
to be replaced. We also usually count the implicit interest on the fixed
investment as another current cost of capital. Thus, the original investment could have yielded an interest return if it had not been used to

purchase machinery, equipment, and buildings. For example, an investment in a television transmitter could be used to buy machinery to produce fertilizer. The alternative yield on the fixed cost of a television
transmitter is called the implicit interest on that investment.

Fixed capital cost may be treated in many ways:

1. If the project has a finite life and the equipment is amortized
over the life of the project—that is, if it is considered to have no further use at the end of the project—total fixed capital investment is
divided by the expected number of years and the total number of students served by the project in order to get the annual depreciation cost
per student. Implicit interest cost based on the declining value of the
depreciated capital is added to this to get total capital cost.[8] In the
case of the Niger experiment, for example, capital costs contributed
by the French were $1.5 million. The experimental project had a life
of five years. Eight hundred students per year participated in this period. If the capital investment by the French is considered used up in
that time, the capital cost per student year was $562 (20 percent de-
preciation plus 10 percent interest per year).

2. The capital cost may not be considered at all in the estimate
of ETV costs. In estimates of Ivory Coast costs by IIEP,[9] for example,
capital costs were omitted, apparently because they were grant funded
or loan assisted, primarily by World Bank. If the country considers
that these foreign grants and loans will (a) be provided to replace capital equipment as long as it is needed; and (b) bear no interest and would
not have been available for any other use, then there are no capital
costs for the country.

Foreign aid, of course, raises a serious question about the kind of
leverage that foreign countries might have over the education policy of
an underdeveloped nation. A foreign agency could "induce" education
ministries to install ETV by giving them the necessary start-up capital
and making clear that capital is available only for ETV and ETV-related
activities, not for other kinds of educational reforms. Since capital
costs are an important component of total ETV costs, such a subsidy—
specified as a single available alternative—would be tempting to countries under pressure to expand the school system.

3. Ordinarily, capital cost is treated as the rate of depreciation
plus explicit or implicit interest (alternative yield of capital) on the
total investment (net of depreciation) in plant and equipment. The depreciation cost is like a savings fund to be used for capital replacement
once it is fully depreciated. The interest cost tells us the economic
cost to the society of the resources used to buy plant and equipment.
In some cases—if the capital is borrowed—this is a real cost and appears as interest charges (debt service) in the current account. But if
the investment is internally funded, the cost is implicit: what is the
return that capital could have yielded if invested somewhere else?

Typical amortization (depreciation) rates used in ETV projects are
the following: buildings—4 percent (25-year life); transmitter—10 per-

cent (10-year life); production equipment—10 percent (10-year life); television receivers and class equipment—20 percent (5-year life). [10] These depreciation rates depend on the climate and the level of main- tenance. For our purposes, we will use an average annual depreciation rate of 10 percent. Of course, alternative depreciation rates can be used to reflect particular country conditions.

Interest rates on capital also vary from country to country, and ob- viously with the risk of the investment and the length of debt amortiza- tion. In almost all cases, ETV is a public project, and so guaranteed by the government. We could take the rate of interest as that which the government pays in borrowing funds. But the funds would be used to finance private investments in factories, or public investments in roads or fertilizer plants or imports. For this reason it makes more sense to take as the implicit interest rate an average rate of return to long-term national investments. We shall use 10 percent for this annual rate. The total annual cost of capital (besides maintenance) is therefore approximately 20 percent of the total fixed capital investment in the ETV project.

Strictly speaking, the capital cost is lower than 20 percent of the initial fixed cost annually because of depreciation; as capital depreci- ates, the value of the initial investment declines by the annual amount of depreciation. Thus, after five years at a 10 percent depreciation rate, the initial investment has declined by 50 percent. According to the formula cited in note 8 above, the annual cost of capital using a ten-year capital life and a 10 percent implicit interest rate is $A = [0.10(1+.10)^{10}/(1+.10)^{10}-1)]P = 0.163P$, or 16.3 percent of the total capital investment.

Operating, or variable, cost is also divided into costs of produc- tion, distribution, reception, teacher training, and supporting materials. These are the cost of operation. They are proportional to the number of pupils or classrooms served. While fixed capital cost is fixed—it de- pends on the capacity of production versus actual production—variable costs depend on how much is actually produced annually. Where there is a large fixed-cost component, it is crucial to operate near capacity to keep costs low.

Costs of Some Operating ETV Projects

There have been a number of ETV cost studies. The most compre- hensive review of these studies is still The New Media: Memo to Edu- cational Planners, [11] but that includes data only to 1965. Table 2.1 summarizes the cost data from the IIEP study plus costs of three projects not reported there: El Salvador, Niger, and Ivory Coast. Most reports by foreign technical assistance agencies underestimate costs. Ivory Coast is a good example of such underestimates.

TABLE 2. 1

Estimated Total Current Annual Cost
(including depreciation and imputed interest)
of In-School ETV, by Project, Various Years
(thousands of dollars)

Project	Year	Production Cost	Distribution Cost	Reception Cost	Teacher Training
Hagerstown[a]	1965	349	161	53	—
MPATI[b]	1965	192	2,094	800	—
American Samoa[a]	1965	908	436	79	—
Colombia[a]	1965	287	312	208	141
Northern Nigeria[b]	1966	131	21	7	—
Ibaden[b]	1965	101	68	14	15
Lagos[b]	1965	62	26	6	5
Niger[c]	1969	—	—	—	—
El Salvador[d]	1972	242	411	208	188
Ivory Coast[e]	1972	1,719	173	935	—
	1976	1,962	282	2,745	—

[a]Schramm et al., The New Media: Memo to Educational Planners
(Paris: UNESCO, 1967). They use some depreciation costs as we do
(see text), but only 3 percent imputed interest rather than 10. For
Colombia data, we added $3,000 imputed cost per Peace Corps person
assisting on the project. In 1965 there were 18 on production, 47 on
teacher training, and six on reception. See Margaret Carpenter et al.,
"Analyzing the Use of Technology to Upgrade Education in a Developing
Country," Santa Monica: The Rand Corporation, March 1970, memo
RM-6179-RC, Table 10.
[b]IIEP, New Educational Media in Action: Case Studies for Planners,
Vol. 3 (Paris: UNESCO, 1967).

Total Cost	Approximate Number of Students Served	Student Hours Per Year	Cost Per Student	Cost Per Student Hour
613	20, 000	3, 300, 000	31	0. 20
3, 086	450, 000	35, 200, 000	7	0. 09
1, 423	16, 000	2, 409, 000	89	0. 59
948	250, 000	13, 820, 000	4	0. 07
159	—	54, 000	—	2. 95
198	3, 400	288, 900	58	0. 68
99	17, 200	448, 200	6	0. 21
925	800	—	1, 156	—
1, 050	40, 000	1, 040, 000	26	0. 10
2, 827	28, 000	—	101	—
4, 989	336, 000	—	13	—

cAID, Figures here do not include cost of classroom monitors.

dRichard Speagle, Educational Reform and Instructional Television in El Salvador, AID, October 1971. See our calculations in Table 2. 4 below. Method I costs used.

eIIEP (see Table 2. 6 for figures in CFA francs).

El Salvador

The El Salvador project is AID's showcase ETV project. It not only
incorporates educational media into the educational system (at the
junior-high-school level), but is the basis for a far-reaching reform of
Salvadoran education. Nevertheless, its costs have been somewhat
obscured by reports about the project.[12] Tables 2. 2 and 2. 3 taken from
the Speagle report (his Tables 2. 5 and 2. 14), summarize the reported
ETV costs of the educational reform. In Table 2. 4, we estimate the
costs of the project for 1972, assuming the kinds of capital cost estimates reviewed above. We find that the ETV investment cost up to 1971
includes 8. 3 million colones for buildings, remodeling of classrooms,
air conditioning, and transmission and reception equipment and 2. 9
million colones for planning and technical assistance. In addition, we
find that the investment in teacher retraining is 4. 7 million colones.

Speagle (and the government of El Salvador) count teacher-retrain-
ing cost and supervision training as current cost. However, it makes
much more sense to regard them as investment, since they continue to
yield additional product for a number of years after the retraining takes
place. We have not calculated the depreciation on the investment in
teachers, which could be anywhere from 3 to 10 percent, depending on
average teacher working life after retraining. The same is true for supervisors.

Capital cost is based on two different estimates. In Method I, imputed interest is calculated on the Government of El Salvador (GOES)
component of investment only. In this method, it is argued that foreign
lenders would lend for this project and no other. Therefore, the argument goes, the actual interest cost (debt service) is the interest cost
on foreign loans to El Salvador of the project plus the imputed interest
(10 percent) which GOES incurs on its own investment. Grants are cost-
less. The interest plus depreciation cost using Method I is 0. 96 million
colones. In Method II, all investment has an imputed interest of 10
percent. The interest plus depreciation cost from Method II is 1. 54
million colones.* Imputed interest on teacher investment is 0. 47 million colones. Total capital cost of ETV and retraining using Method I
is 1. 43 million colones; in Method II, it is 2. 01 million colones annually. This does not include maintenance of buildings and equipment or
the capital cost of technical assistance for non-ETV reform.

According to the Speagle report, annual operating costs of ETV in
1972 were approximately 1. 2 million colones. The total of capital costs
and operating costs is thus about 2. 63-3. 21 million colones, or

---

*Including depreciation on grant-financed equipment in both Meth-
od I and Method II assumes that the government of El Salvador will
have to replace that equipment themselves. AID could keep granting
equipment replacement.

TABLE 2. 2

El Salvador: Total Cost of ITV, 1966-73
(millions of colones)

Item	Totals	1966-67	1968	1969	1970	1971	1972-73
Major categories	(All Sources of Funds)						
Operating costs							
ITV Department	5.2	—	—	0.7	0.9	1.1	2.5
Investment costs							
Transmission equip.	4.7	—	0.1	0.6	0.1	3.9	—
Reception equip.	1.0	—	*	0.1	—	0.3	0.6
Bldg. and air cond.	1.1	—	—	—	0.6	0.3	0.2
Remodeling of classrooms	2.3	—	2.3	—	—	—	—
Subtotal	9.1	—	2.4	0.7	0.7	4.5	0.8
Nonrecurrent startup costs							
Preproduction planning, ITV Dept.	0.7	0.2	0.5	—	—	—	—
Technical assist.	3.2	—	0.3	0.8	0.6	0.5	1.0
Subtotal	3.9	0.2	0.8	0.8	0.6	0.5	1.0
Total cost	8.2	0.2	3.2	2.2	2.2	6.1	4.3
	(Foreign Sources of Funds)						
Grants and donations							
Investment costs	1.0	—	0.1	0.7	0.1	0.1	—
Technical assist.	2.7	—	0.3	0.8	0.6	0.4	0.6
Subtotal	3.7	—	0.4	1.5	0.7	0.5	0.6
Foreign loans							
Investment costs	4.8	—	—	—	—	4.2	0.6
Technical assist.	0.5	—	—	—	—	0.1	0.4
Subtotal	5.3	—	—	—	—	4.3	1.0
	(Domestic Sources of Funds)						
Use of Salvadoran funds							
D-(E+F)	9.2	0.2	2.8	0.7	1.5	1.3	2.7

*Small shipment of receivers included under transmission equipment.

Sources: Ministry of Education, ITV Department, AID/ES, Controller's Office, and Education Division (government of El Salvador).

TABLE 2. 3

El Salvador: Total Cost of Educational Reforms,
Exclusive of ITV, 1966-73
(millions of colones)

Item	Totals	1966-67	1968	1969	1970	1971	1972-73 [a]
Major Categories							
Operating costs							
Teacher retraining	6.7	—	—	1.6	2.1	1.0	2.0
Supervision	1.5	—	—	0.1	0.1	0.4	0.9
Reprinting of recap texts	0.6	—	—	—	—	0.1	0.5
Subtotal	8.8	—	—	1.7	2.2	1.5	3.4
Investment costs							
Constr. diversified high schools	19.6	—	—	—	1.2	10.3	8.1
School constr., AID loan 014 [b]	19.3	—	—	—	—	—	19.3
Central American Tech. Inst.	0.8	—	0.4	0.1	—	0.3	—
Sports and rec. fac.	1.2	—	0.1	—	0.2	0.9	—
Project plan. and supervision (COPLACE)	2.9	—	0.1	—	0.3	1.0	1.5
Subtotal	43.8	—	0.6	0.1	1.7	12.5	28.9
Nonrecurrent startup costs							
Non-ITV, tech. assist. for reform	0.9	—	—	—	—	0.4	0.5
Total GOES costs	53.5	—	0.6	1.8	3.9	14.4	32.8
Foreign grants							
Non-ITV, tech. assist. for reform	2.9	0.6	0.3	0.3	0.3	0.5	0.9
Total costs, reform without ITV	56.4 [c]	0.6	0.9	2.1	4.2	14.9	33.7

[a] Estimated.

[b] Technical assistance component included in (C) below.

[c] Excludes imputed cost of community-built schools of 10.6 million colones.

Sources: Ministry of Education, AID/ES, Controller's Office, UNESCO mission, El Salvador.

U. S. $1. 05-1. 29 million, annually. Forty thousand junior-high-school
students* were served by the ETV system in 1972 (Speagle, Table 2. 9),
which yields a cost per student year of U. S. $ 26-32. † The number of
hours per year per student of ITV time is about 260 (derived from figures
in Speagle), so that the minimum estimated cost per student per hour
is about U. S. $0. 10.

With expanded use of the system—extending it to more pupils—
costs could fall. But Speagle points out that reception costs would rise
rapidly if the system were extended to primary schools. Furthermore,
the system is also being used to train primary-school teachers, so not
all of the cost of the system should be allocated to junior-high-school
students. On the other side of the ledger, however, none of the costs
of administration of the school system are allocated to ETV costs, and
there is some doubt that maintenance costs of ETV plant and equipment
are included in ETV operating costs.

Even with the "low" estimated cost of $ 26 per pupil year, the total
annual cost per classroom of 30 pupils is $780, almost 60 percent of
full salary for a junior-high-school teacher in El Salvador (full salary
was about U. S. $1, 400 per year in 1970). It can only be concluded that
the system is much more expensive than its promoters would have us
believe. It does have a distinct advantage over the Samoan system, in
that it can be expanded to a much wider audience, but we only have
approximations of what the cost per student year and hour would be
under such an expansion.

Niger

The costs of the Niger ETV experiment are extremely high because
of the small number of students (800) who took part in the experiment.
The French contributed about $1. 5 million capital outlay to the project.
Recurring costs for the French were $600, 000 per year and for Niger,
about $175, 000. This includes $11, 000 for paying classroom monitor
salaries. If we assume 10 percent depreciation and 10 percent implicit
interest on the French capital, we get a total capital cost of $ 244, 500
annually and a total annual cost of $1, 019, 500 or $1, 274 per student
year. If we assume only depreciation charges on French capital, the
total annual cost is $ 925, 000, or $1, 156 per student year. In either
case, the costs are astronomical.

---

*It does not appear, however, that 40, 000 students were using
ETV in 1972. So the costs shown here are an underestimate.
 † Rate of exchange: U. S. $1. 00 = 2. 5 colones. Speagle shows a
cost per student of $17. 20, which was figured on 25, 000 students in
1971. This apparently does not include the debt service on loans for
the project. (See Academy for Educational Development, Summary of
Richard E. Speagle's Report, October 1972, p. 11.)

TABLE 2.4

El Salvador: Costs of ETV and Relevant Educational Reform, 1972
(millions of colones)

Item	Cost	Source
Operating costs of ETV, 1972	1.2	GOES
Nonrecurring startup costs, 1968-71	2.9	GOES = 0.7; foreign = 2.2
Depreciation plus interest costs		
Method I (foreign loans computed at actual interest cost; grants free):		
Transmission plus reception, 1968-71 (4.3 million loan of 5.1 million investment @ 10% depreciation and 3% implied interest cost = 0.122 × 4.3)	0.52*	Foreign loans and grants
Buildings and classroom remodeling, 1968-71 (3.2 million @ 4% depreciation and 10% implicit interest cost = 0.116 × 3.2)	0.37	GOES
Interest on GOES portion of startup costs (0.7 × 10%)	0.07	GOES
Total interest plus depreciation	0.96	
Method II (all investment @ 10% implied interest cost):		
Transmission, 1968-71 (4.7 million investment @ 10% depreciation plus 10% interest = 0.166 × 4.7)	0.78	Foreign loans and grants
Reception, 1968-71 (0.4 million @ 20% depreciation plus 10% implicit interest = 0.266 × 0.4)	0.10	Foreign loans and grants
Buildings and classroom remodeling, 1968-71 (3.2 million @ 4% depreciation and 10% implied interest = 0.116 × 3.2)	0.37	GOES
Interest on startup costs	0.29	GOES = 0.7; foreign = 2.2
Total interest plus depreciation	1.54	

Item	Cost	Source
Total current cost (operating cost + depreciation + imputed interest) of ETV		
Method I	2.16	
Method II	2.74	
Imputed interest cost of educational reform, not including construction of new schools		
Method I		
Teacher retraining, 1968-71		
(4.7 million × 0.10)	0.47	GOES
Supervision, 1968-71		
(0.6 million × 0.10)	0.06	GOES
Texts (0.1 million × 0.10)	0.01	GOES
Nonrecurrent startup, 1966-71		
(0.4 million, GOES; 2.0 million, foreign grants)	0.04	
Total interest plus depreciation	0.58	
Method II		
Imputed interest	0.78	
Total current cost, ETV and teacher retraining		
Method I (2.16 + 0.47)	2.63	
Method II (2.74 + 0.47)	3.21	
Total current cost, 1972, ETV and teacher retraining, per pupil, 40,000 pupils		
Method I	66	
Method II	80	

*Note: It is assumed that foreign loans are used entirely for transmission facilities, while grants are used for transmission, reception, and startup costs.

The main savings of the system, if it were to be extended to a
much larger number of students (there are about 70, 000 primary school
students in Niger, representing 7-8 percent of the school age population), would be realized through lower salaries paid to monitors instead
of fully qualified classroom teachers. This savings would occur despite
the fact that monitors are being paid about $600 per year instead of the
anticipated $400, and despite the fact that they handle a television
class with 40 students instead of the conventional class with 80 students. [13]

Ivory Coast

The Ivory Coast project, financed with substantial assistance from
the French and Canadian governments plus the World Bank, began operation in the 1971/72 school year with about 464 first-grade classes
(about 28, 000 pupils, according to the IIEP report). This represents
approximately 22 percent of all public first-grade pupils in a primary-
school system that enrolls about 43 percent of the age group. It is
planned that by 1979/80, there will be 723, 200 pupils in all grades of
primary school receiving ETV instruction. [14] No actual cost figures are
currently available, and even if they were, the project is in such an
early state that they probably would not mean much. The International
Institute of Educational Planning (IIEP) has, however, produced a fairly
complete documentation of planned costs of the ETV system and we shall
work from these.

Table 2.5 shows planned "capital" costs of ETV in Ivory Coast. To
get true capital costs we should add capital costs of transmission.
These are omitted because in 1967 the Ivory Coast television system
had three stations, covering about two-thirds of the country. Before
the introduction of ETV, the stations broadcast only four hours daily,
so they had large excess capacity. But two booster stations will have
to be built to bring the programs to the northern third of the country, and
these are not included in the capital costs shown. If we depreciate
construction at 4 percent, production equipment at 10 percent, and
classroom equipment and maintenance service equipment at 20 percent
(this corresponds to the depreciation on classroom equipment used by
capital estimates in Ivory Coast), and use an implicit interest cost of
10 percent, we get depreciation plus interest charges on accumulated
investment in 1972 of 193 million CFA francs. By 1976, depreciation
plus interest rises to 454 million CFA francs annually. Total capital
cost, not including transmission capital, teacher training, or supporting classroom materials investment (all left out of these planned estimates), therefore equals 193 million CFA francs in 1972 and 454 million
CFA francs in 1976.

Table 2.6 shows planned current, or operating, costs of ETV in
Ivory Coast between 1971/72 and 1979/80. If we add the 495 million
CFA francs current cost in 1971/72 to the 193 million CFA francs capital

TABLE 2. 5

Ivory Coast: Capital Costs of School Television
(millions of CFA francs)

	1969	1970	1971	1972	1973	1974	1975	1976	1977	1978
Production										
Construction	243	—	—	—	—	—	—	—	—	—
Equipment	172	118	36	—	—	—	—	—	—	—
Transmission*	—	—	—	—	—	—	—	—	—	—
Reception										
Classroom equipment	—	130	128	152	172	232	196	192	178	160
Maintenance service	—	146	18	20	18	22	14	18	18	14
Replacement	—	—	—	—	—	—	112	112	138	156
Total	415	394	182	172	190	254	322	322	334	330

*No estimate has been made for transmission investment. The existing equipment of the Ivory Coast television system is considered adequate to handle the additional transmission of the school television programs.

Source: IIEP, "Introduction of Educational Television and Its Effect on the Cost of Primary Education in the Ivory Coast Republic, " IIEP/RP/I-C. S. 3A (Rev.), part III, Table 18.

cost, total cost equals 688 million CFA francs, or about 24, 500 CFA francs per student year, assuming that 28, 000 students are served by ETV. In 1975/76, the total cost is 765 + 454 = 1, 219 million CFA francs, or about 3, 630 CFA francs per pupil. In 1978/79, the last year for which planned capital investment is available, the total capital cost rises to 710 million CFA francs. Added to current costs, the total cost of ETV will be 1, 453 million CFA francs, or about 2, 260 CFA francs per pupil year. This should be considered a minimum figure for that year, since it does not include the items discussed above. The Action Plan of the Ivory Coast government estimates the additional cost of new school supplies for pupils at 500 CFA francs. This brings the total up to 2,760 CFA francs per pupil, * but still does not include teacher retraining, current cost of maintaining equipment, or the capital cost of additional transmission equipment. [15]

*It is assumed that this figure is in 1969 prices. In 1969, 278 CFA francs equaled U. S. $1, so the annual cost per pupil in 1978/79 is about U. S. $12. In 1971/72, 255 CFA francs = $1, so the annual cost per pupil in 1978/79 at the new exchange rate is also about $12.

TABLE 2.6

Ivory Coast: Total Costs and Unit Costs of School Television, Based on the Number of Pupils
Who Will Receive Televised Instruction (excluding depreciation and interest costs)

	1971/72	1972/73	1973/74	1974/75	1975/76	1976/77	1977/78	1978/79	1979/80
Total expenditure (thousands of CFA francs)									
Production	363,000	388,000	406,000	418,000	432,000	388,000	363,000	295,000	191,000
Transmission	44,000	50,000	57,000	63,000	72,000	77,000	77,000	77,000	80,000
Reception[a]	88,000	119,000	162,000	209,000	261,000	326,000	377,000	424,000	472,000
Total	495,000	557,000	625,000	690,000	765,000	791,000	817,000	796,000	743,000
Number of pupils	28,000[b]	70,000	140,000	224,000	336,000	447,000	551,000	641,000	723,000
Unit costs (CFA francs)									
Production	12,963	5,540	2,899	1,864	1,283	865	657	462	264
Transmission	1,571	714	407	281	214	172	139	120	110
Reception[a]	3,142	1,700	1,157	933	776	728	683	661	652
Total	17,676	7,954	4,463	3,078	2,273	1,765	1,479	1,243	1,026

[a]Not including replacement of receiving sets.

[b]It should be noted that the figures as to how many students were actually enrolled in 1971/72 were overestimated by the IIEP. See Anthony Kaye's Chapter 5 in this book for more recent data.

Source: IIEP, "Introduction of Educational Television and Its Effect on the Cost of Primary Education in the Ivory Coast Republic," IIEP/RP/I-C. S. 3A (Rev.), part III, Table 22.

Using conventional teaching, per-pupil cost of primary instruction in the Ivory Coast in 1969/70 was 13,500 CFA francs. The additional cost of ETV in 1978/79, that is, when the ETV system is nearly at capacity, therefore, represents almost a 21 percent increase over present cost. It appears that these estimates were gross underestimates: recent information coming out of Ivory Coast indicates that the actual costs of the installed system will be almost twice those shown in the planned costs of Tables 2.5 and 2.6.

Korea

The Korean ETV project represents a second large ETV effort by AID. We have no actual data as we have for El Salvador (or even planned data as in Ivory Coast) on the Korean system since it is not yet operational. As in the El Salvador project, evaluations are planned on a pilot basis, in this case before the total commitment is made. The cost figures we use here are based on estimates made by a study team from Florida State University. [16]

The investment costs of the ETV system for a pilot project in a community of 100,000 students in the one-through-nine grade range are almost entirely for software development:

The software is perhaps the most critical component of the proposed system and will range from the student learning units, complete with objectives, self-instructional material and formative tests to the ITV and radio programs with their associated support materials. [17]

The cost of software development is estimated at $5,474,000 (Morgan and Chadwick, Tables 8-1 and 8-2). Teacher training for the pilot project is $34,543, hardware costs $546,000 and developing a staff for the Korean Educational Development Laboratory (KEDL) is $390,000. Assuming that the hardware depreciates at 10 percent annually and that the implicit interest on the total investment is 10 percent annually, the annual capital cost of the hardward is $91,000 and the implicit interest on other items is $590,000 [0.10(5,474 + 34.5 + 390)]. The total capital cost per student (100,000 students) is about $7 per student per year.

Similarly, if the system were to be provided for the nation as a whole (8,200,000 pupils in grades one through nine), hardware would cost $7,258,440; teacher training $2,836,428; and software plus KEDL staff development, $5,864,000. Depreciation and interest on equipment would be $1,210,000 annually, while implicit interest on other items would equal $870,000 annually (725.8 + 283.6 + 586.4 thousand) for a total capital cost of $2,090,000 per year, or about $.25 per student.

The FSU study does not estimate operating costs of the ETV system, but they should not be very high per student with more than 8 million students taught by ETV. The key to the system proposed by FSU is that one teaching team (one master teacher, one associate teacher, and two teacher aids)—getting paid a total of about $425 monthly—will handle 300 pupils. The teaching cost per pupil is therefore estimated as $1.41 per month, and the total instructional and administrational cost per pupil (not including the cost of operating and maintaining the ETV system), about $33 annually. The present cost in the traditional system is about $43 per pupil per year.

Since the present class size in Korea is about 65-75, the FSU proposal intends to save money by increasing the number of pupils per fully trained teacher by more than twofold. Teachers will be replaced by ETV and printed programmed materials (apparently 300 pupils will view the ETV programs at the same time). Since the total resource cost of the ETV system is not projected, we have no way of knowing what the savings to the educational system will be, assuming that it can produce the same output for the same or less total cost per pupil than now exists.

Neither have any alternatives, such as retraining teachers and providing programmed materials without ETV, or using radio instead of TV, been proposed in the pilot stage. ETV seems to have been decided on without testing its feasibility and costs against other ways of improving and extending Korean education.

COSTING TEACHER TRAINING

Many cost estimates for ETV projects leave out teacher training costs. Yet all ETV systems require some training of those in the classroom to work effectively with the system. The training component of ETV brings up an important issue: what would additional training of teachers cost in a "conventional" system? If we could provide teachers with a certain set of characteristics, what would they be? and how much would they cost? Since traditional teaching is the major competitor of the media, what are the possibilities of improving the allocation of resources within traditional schools and improving the output of schools? With additional teacher training?

In most countries, teachers are paid according to national scales on the basis of academic preparation, years of experience, certification, permanent or temporary contract, urban/rural location, and sometimes whether the teacher is a man or woman. It is possible to relate all these factors to teacher salary to determine what the components of teacher salary are and the "marginal cost" of a year of experience or a year of academic preparation. In Puerto Rico, for example, the "cost" in terms of teacher salaries of raising the academic preparation of a sixth-grade urban teacher by one year (the average preparation is 4.5 years of post-high-school training) is $77 annually. An additional year of experience costs $39 annually.[18] The average salary of a sixth-grade urban teacher

(4. 5 years of university and 14 years teaching experience) in Puerto Rico is about $3, 800 annually (based on a ten-month school year, 1967-68).

In Puerto Rico, rural children are taught by teachers not as well prepared or as experienced as urban teachers. One objective of the Puerto Rican system might be to equalize the teacher inputs in rural and urban schools in an effort to reduce higher dropouts in rural schools. In 1967/68 the average rural third-grade teacher had an academic preparation 1. 7 years less than her urban counterpart* (2. 85 postsecondary years versus 4. 52) and 7. 8 years less experience teaching (6. 6 versus 14. 4). According to our estimates, it would cost between $500 and $600 annually per teacher in additional salary to have equally prepared and experienced teachers teaching in rural schools. Of course, this is based on marginal costs, so the price might be much higher if we tried to get enough more highly qualified teachers to fill all rural teaching posts, or to train present rural teachers up to urban averages. Assuming a rural class size of 30 pupils and even an additional cost of $1, 000 annually would still make the cost about $33 per pupil year.

This is just a hypothetical example of a teacher-training cost study not usually done. In other countries, where there exists a much lower percentage of trained teachers, the problem of training sufficient personnel for all the school-age population is greater. But the point of our example is that upgrading, retraining, or even training first-time teachers by conventional means is a valid and researchable alternative to educational media. It is not possible within a few years to put all children in school in countries like Niger through traditional teacher-student formal schooling. So teacher retraining or training is limited in what it can achieve. But from an efficiency point of view, is it a worthwhile expenditure of funds to give formal schooling to the entire school-age population over the next ten years in a country like Niger? There are probably much cheaper ways to provide literacy training, and much more relevant things to teach people in Niger at the moment than the overt and hidden curriculum of the Western school. For extending literacy, for example, cadres of village organizers or educational radio would probably be much cheaper and just as effective.

There are other important issues:

The technology associated with ETV saves on teachers. The Korean project proposes to keep cost low by limiting the number of teachers to each pupil. Although in Niger the number of pupils in a class was reduced for the ETV experiment, if the project goes beyond the experimental stage, class sizes would probably remain large to save on teacher costs (the traditional Niger classroom has 80 pupils to a teacher; the experimental ETV classes, 40). These are countries where labor costs are low and where skilled labor costs could drop rapidly over the

---

*Eighty percent of urban and rural third-grade teachers are women.

next ten to 15 years with systematic and specialized training programs. But introducing capital-intensive technology into such economies (run by foreigners in countries with the greatest skill shortages like Samoa, Niger, and Ivory Coast) reduces the future skilled-labor needs of non-industrialized countries. This may well exacerbate educated-unemployment problems in the future. If the laborsaving technology reduced costs of education, then the savings could be spent in other, capital savings, investments. However, in no case of ETV in actual production have there been savings in cost per pupil. So the imported technology provides education at higher cost and reduces the number of skilled jobs available (compared to a more labor-intensive expansion of schooling). This would be optimum policy in a labor-shortage economy, but not in economies with persistent unemployment. For example, in many Latin American countries, there are surpluses of qualified primary teachers in urban areas and dire shortages in rural areas. The Cubans are beginning to solve this problem with special teacher-training schools for rural teachers. These are prestigious schools and prepare men and women for the rigors of rural life as well as teaching in rural schools.

Training people to take leadership roles as teachers in the village or school—to teach people how to be self-reliant and to contribute to change—has obvious implications for motivation and development that go beyond the school. Monitors or even teachers who serve as assistants to a centrally controlled system would usually not be taking such leadership roles.

THE EFFECTIVENESS OF ETV SYSTEMS

United States

A large number of ETV experiments in the United States have been evaluated in terms of student performance. Godwin Chu and Wilber Schramm[19] reviewed 207 published studies that compared television teaching with conventional teaching. Of the 421 separate comparisons made in these studies, 308 showed no significant differences in examination score gains as a result of the different treatments, 63 showed higher gains for those students getting ETV, and 50 showed higher gains for those getting traditional teaching. From this, Chu and Schramm conclude that

all these summaries show that in the great majority of comparative studies, there is no significant difference between learning from conventional teaching, and that where there is

a significant difference, it is a bit more likely to be in
favor of television than of conventional instruction. [20]

But then they find a reason for pushing ETV anyway:

> Furthermore, the research seems to suggest that there are
> a number of areas in which televised instruction has brought
> about more learning than the existing level of classroom
> teaching. The number of these cases seems to be greater
> than chance. Now, if we can identify the qualities of tele-
> vision teaching that make for maximum learning, perhaps
> schools can hope to use televised instruction more effec-
> tively even in existing classrooms. [21]

The first conclusion that there is generally no significant difference
between the ETV treatment and the traditional treatment is statistically
sounder and, based on the data, more reasonable. Of course, adding
ETV to the classroom is expensive, so we might expect it to yield some
positive effect. In Hagerstown, the annual cost of $31 per pupil for
ETV translates into $930 for a class of 30. This means that each teach-
er in the Washington County school district could get $930 of training
every year as an alternative to ETV.

As we pointed out in the beginning of the chapter, the comparisons
that were made in the United States did not evaluate ETV against alternatives that cost approximately the same; rather, they compared students
using ETV against no increase in cost per pupil.

The data which Chu and Schramm present for Hagerstown, for example, show that large mathematics-test-score gains were recorded at
all school levels for students using ETV; however, these are gains for
ETV as compared to the old curriculum. In other words, the math-test-
score gains correspond to a method that cost Hagerstown $31 per pupil
per year. How do the gains from ETV compare to gains from other curricular or teaching innovations? How do gains from alternative innovations compare on a per-dollar cost basis? We don't know, since the
nature of the Hagerstown data does not allow for cost-effectiveness
analysis. No experiments were made with retrained teachers or alternative teaching techniques. Thus, no comparisons can be made between
increases in student performance and costs associated with these alternatives and those associated with ETV. Claiming that ETV raises math
scores does not per se tell us whether ETV is better or worse than other
improvements in teaching math, improvements that might be much less
costly to the school system.

Nevertheless, some attempt can be made to assess the gains by
cost-benefit analysis. The table on page 58 shows the gains in arith-
metic of rural school students in the Hagerstown (Washington County)

district. From these data it appears that over the three years between grade three and grade six, pupils gained 0. 7-0. 8 school-year equivalents over what they would have gained if ETV had not been introduced. This translates into a math gain of 0. 25 school-year equivalents each year that students are exposed to ETV, assuming that these gains continue over the entire school experience. The gain cost $31 per year.

In order to assess the economic benefits of the test score gains, we would ideally want to know how much more Hagerstown graduates with higher math test scores earn when they enter the labor force. We could then determine how much a point of math score gain is worth in additional income for people with the same number of years of schooling.

These data are not available. But to show how the method would work if we had better data, we can use Zvi Griliches' and William Mason's estimates of test-score effect on income for a sample of male veterans. [22] The results of their analysis show that a one-point increase in the Air Force Qualifying Test (AFQT), holding constant the effect of other variables such as race, age, and years of schooling, translates into a $6. 34 increase in annual income. One point on the AFQT test is equivalent to approximately one school year, so a one school year equivalent increase in ability is worth $6. 34 in annual income.

This means that a man 29 years old and with 12. 3 years of schooling (the average age and schooling in the Griliches-Mason sample) earns $6. 34 more annually for each point higher of AFQT score. Assuming that this gain in average income will be earned over the entire working life and that the student's implicit discount rate is 10 percent,* an approximate present value of the increase in earnings is $P = Y/r$, or $P = \$6. 34/0. 10 = \$63. 40$. These are the benefits of a one-point increase in test score, or a one-school-year equivalent of test-score increase. The increase in math score by Hagerstown pupils was 0. 25 school-year equivalents for each year of ETV exposure. Thus, the present value income gain for each year of ETV exposure is $63. 40 × 0. 25 = $15. 85. The cost of this exposure is $31. 00, so the benefit-cost ratio is $15. 85/31. 00 = approximately 0. 5.

This is a low ratio (since it is less than one), and in one sense, it is a minimum estimate, since it only measures the direct gain from investing in ETV. Hagerstown pupils doing better on national tests may continue further in school than before; they may have a higher probability of going to college. This would be the indirect gain of higher quality schooling (see equation 2. 4).

---

*The discount rate used here is arbitrary, but it is supposed to reflect the weight that a person attaches to earning one year from now in comparison with earnings today, and the risk involved in the investment. With a 10 percent discount rate, a person considers that, including the risk factor, earnings received today are worth 10 percent more to the person than earnings received next year.

On the other hand, the estimated benefit-cost ratio is a maximum
gain, since it assumes that there is continuous gain for these rural
students on math scores throughout the school experience. This implies
that those who began ETV in the third grade would have gained 2. 25
years in mathematics by the end of high school over what they would
have scored without ETV. It is much more likely that through ETV the
students would maintain their scores through ETV (at 0. 4-0. 5 years
above norm) once they reached that level. This would imply a gain of
one year equivalent over a nine-year period, or an average 0. 11 year
equivalents annually, and would yield a benefit-cost ratio of ($63. 40 ×
0. 11)/$31, or 0. 22. Of course, our whole analysis is very hypothetical,
since it is not possible to relate AFQT score as an ability measure to
the Iowa math test taken by the Hagerstown students.

Samoa

Evaluation of ETV as reported by Schramm et al. for other countries
is very sketchy. In American Samoa,

> an examination in mathematical achievement was given to 106
> [pupils] from one of the new consolidated schools who had
> studied with the aid of television for the major part of a year,
> and to 229 pupils for the older schools not yet reached by tele-
> vision. The television pupils scored higher than the other on
> all three parts of the test, but the difference was not quite at
> an acceptable level of statistical significance (. 08). [23]

The ETV system in American Samoa cost almost $90 per student per year,
or $2,700 per class of 30 pupils. And not all of whatever increases in
scores do occur should be attributed to ETV.

> Samoa is operating a new system of teaching and learning, in
> which the consolidated schools, the presence of a supervi-
> sory principal, and the carefully planned classroom activities
> all play a part, along with television. [24]

Colombia

Although, according to Schramm et al., as of 1966, "The most extensive studies [in developing areas] have been made on television instruction in Colombia, " the evidence there is not very encouraging
either.

At the end of the first year of televised instruction in the
district of Bogotá, a large group of pupils who had been
taught by television were tested against a comparable group
who had received only direct class-room instruction, although from the same syllabus. Altogether about 5, 000
students were included in the comparisons. Eight meaningful comparisons were possible. In three of them—grade 2
language, grade 5 mathematics, and grade 4 natural science—the television students made significantly higher
scores. In the other five—grades 3 and 5 natural science,
and grades 3, 4 and 5 social science—the differences between television and non-television scores were not statistically significant. [25]

Other tests were made using different kinds of post-ETV program
teaching techniques, and it was found that a question-answer session
based on the ETV program produced better results in two out of four
subjects.

Again, it is impossible to do a cost-effectiveness analysis of the
Colombian product, because no experiments were set up whereby any
alternative to ETV besides the traditional methods was explored. However, since the Colombian system appears to be very inexpensive—
about U.S. $4 per pupil reported costs (see Table 2.1)—almost any
gains in score or increased school attendance may be worthwhile from
a cost-benefit standpoint.

El Salvador

The best evaluation data available now are from the El Salvador
project. We can summarize the first three years evaluation results as
follows: [26]

1. Although the third year of evaluation of the project was affected
by a teacher strike, both the second- and third-year reports show that
the gains on the tests decline for each cohort as they move from the
seventh to the ninth grade, whether they are in "traditional" classes
(those with reformed materials and retrained teacher but no ETV) or in
ETV classes. The gains for ETV classes are significantly higher than
non-ETV classes in the seventh grade, but in both 1970 and 1971 the
eighth-grade differences are not significantly different between ETV and
non-ETV classes. The ninth grade differences are particularly confounded by the teacher strike, but they also do not show significant
differences across subjects between ETV and non-ETV classes.

The largest gains of ETV over non-ETV classrooms were in the
1969 seventh grade. But, as the second-year report points out, the
non-ETV classrooms in 1969 were the prereform classrooms, which

neither had television nor new materials and pretrained teachers. In the 1970 and 1971 seventh grades, the ETV classrooms have been compared with reformed classes without ETV, so these later gain scores are more representative of the effect of television. The 1971 seventh-grade ETV/non-ETV differences are also smaller than the 1970 differences, although this result may be confounded by the strike (which apparently affected ETV classes more than non-ETV classes) and by the lower ability of the students entering the greatly expanded seventh grade in 1971.

2. There do not appear to be significant differences between the scores of urban and rural students in the seventh and eighth grades and between students who have fathers with more than primary education and those who have fathers with primary or less education. Male students score slightly higher than females in both ETV and non-ETV classes, and higher-ability students do much better on the tests than lower-ability students in the same year. Gain scores in each year are similar within traditional classes and ETV classes for urban/rural, male/female, high/low father's education and high/low ability.

In the seventh grade, ability explains about the same amount of variance in test scores in ETV and non-ETV classes, but in the eighth grade ability is more important in non-ETV classes.

The fact that there do not seem to be significant differences between the gain scores of high and low ability, high and low socio-economic background, and urban and rural children (in both ETV and non-ETV classrooms), can be taken as an indicator that the reform was neutral in its effect on different levels of pupils in each grade. The fact that ability differences had more effect on test scores in non-ETV than in ETV classes in the eighth grade (although not in the seventh) was taken as evidence that

> we can say with some confidence that there is a trend in the data indicating that television and other elements of the new system do tend to equalize opportunities rather than contributing to greater inequalities. [27]

Yet in the 1971 seventh grade, the average ability of the seventh graders was lower than in previous years, and this is given as one of the reasons that the gain scores in the ETV classes were lower than in previous years (the gains in non-ETV classes were higher than in previous years). "Students were less bright in 1971 and could not take the same advantage of the reform system with television."[28] This seems to contradict the previous "confidence" that ETV tends to equalize opportunities.

There is a more serious difficulty here. The junior-high-school students sampled—even 1971 seventh graders—probably represent a much higher average ability level than for the school-age population as a whole. Seventh-grade entrants in 1971 still represented less than

25 percent of the school-age population relevant to the seventh grade. The differential gains by ability grouping do not cover the gains of much lower levels of ability (those we might be particularly concerned about when considering equity effects). Furthermore, the rural children in the Third Cycle (junior high) are such a select group—probably representing less than 5 percent of rural children in that age level—that any statements about gains of that group as compared to the urban group tell us nothing about how well rural children as a whole would do with or without ETV. It is surprising that such a select and undoubtedly very motivated group does not have much higher gains than the much more average urban children in the Third Cycle.

The question we have to ask is: Are the gains in the seventh grade for ETV over non-ETV classrooms worth the cost of providing ETV in all three years of the Third Cycle? Given the data from El Salvador, we cannot assess the benefits to students in their future income or social life as a result of the few points test-score gain attributed to ETV. However, we can make some cost-effectiveness approximations for the educational reform aspects of junior high (retraining teachers plus new curriculum) versus the reform including ETV. We assume that all the capital costs of educational reform other than construction costs go to the Plan Básico (grades seven through nine). In Table 2.4, point E, we summarized these costs. Imputed interest cost of the capital investment in teacher retraining, supervision, and technical assistance in the reform is, by Method I, $232,000 (this does not include teacher retirement and replacement cost or textbook depreciation). In addition, we assume that the total increase in the operating cost of Plan Básico (Table 2.7) from 1968 to 1970 ($427,000) is for upgrading the quality of teaching and classroom activity in the seventh and eighth grades (after 1970), the number of students in Plan Básico increased substantially). This all totals $660,000 current costs for non-ETV reform. The cost of ETV alone in 1972, not including teacher retraining costs (see Table 2.4, point D), using Method I, is $865,000 annually. Using 40,000 students as our base, the annual cost per student of the reform not including ETV is $16 and the cost of ETV alone not including teacher retraining or other possible costs is $22.*

We have two experiments to compare with these costs. The first are taken from the First Year Report. [29] They show that in the 1969

---

*It is difficult to separate out teacher retraining costs associated with ETV and those which are part of the other reforms. In our previous estimate of ETV costs (see above, Table 2.4), we included teacher retraining costs. Here we have separated them out. The cost per pupil used here can be considered a "low"-cost cost of ETV, and the cost per pupil of the Plan Básico upgrading only can be considered a "high" estimate of the educational reform alone.

TABLE 2.7

El Salvador: Recurring Costs for the Education Sector,* 1968-72
(thousands of dollars)

	1968	1969	1970	1971	1972	Annual Growth 1968-72 (in percent)
Primary (grades 1-6)	$14,500	$15,100	$15,700	$16,750	$17,750	5.1
Plan Básico (grades 7-9)	993	1,150	1,420	1,940	2,780	23.8
Secondary (grades 10-12)	767	825	900	1,068	1,288	12.7
Normal (teacher training)	546	560	640	640	640	4.0
Fundamental (literacy)	260	273	287	301	322	8.7
Educational television						
Production and distribution	0	320	448	608	791	—
School supervision	292	360	505	577	648	18.9
General services	2,690	2,950	3,280	3,440	3,630	7.4
Current transfers (debt service, etc.)	4,220	4,800	5,370	5,780	6,140	9.2
TOTAL	$24,268	$26,339	$28,550	$31,104	$33,989	9.0

*Excluding Higher Education.

Source: Calculated from Plan Quinquenal 1968-1972 Sector Educación, CONAPLAN, El Salvador, August 1968.

57

sample, gain scores of seventh graders in reformed ETV classrooms as compared to traditional classrooms with no reforms and no ETV are not significantly different from gain scores of seventh graders in reformed classrooms without ETV compared to traditional classrooms. The gains are approximately the following:

	Gain (Feb.-Oct.)	Gain Over Traditional
Mathematics		
(1) Gain for traditional classes	1.95	—
(2) Gain for experiment ETV class	5.70	3.7
(3) Gain for experiment control group (reform but no ETV)	5.20	3.2
Science		
(1) Gain for traditional classes	1.34	—
(2) Gain for experiment ETV class	4.20	2.9
(3) Gain for experiment control group (reform but no ETV)	5.10	3.8
Social Studies		
(1) Gain for traditional classes	2.61	—
(2) Gain for experiment ETV class	6.40	3.8
(3) Gain for experiment control group (reform but no ETV)	3.10	1.5

The cost-effectiveness ratios for the different subjects are the following:

	ETV	Reform Only
Math	3.7/$22 = .17	3.2/$16 = .20
Science	2.9/$22 = .13	3.8/$16 = .24
Social Studies	3.8/$22 = .17	1.5/$16 = .10

Only in social studies is the cost-effectiveness ratio for ETV larger than for reform only. These results can be questioned in light of the experiment itself, which used highly motivated teachers in the non-ETV control group (and highly motivated teachers in the ETV group as well). But further experiments in the seventh and eighth grades in 1970 corroborate these results: there is no significant difference in gain score between the ETV and non-ETV reformed classes. [30] Therefore, the cost-effectiveness ratios argue for investing in the curriculum and teaching reforms and not installing ETV. The main rationale for installing ETV in El Salvador is that it was a necessary "lever" to achieve the reform in the face of resistance from teachers and the educational bureaucracy. But this does not explain why the ETV system is being expanded (with more fixed investment) or why it would be replaced once original equipment is depreciated.

THE BENEFITS OF MORE AND BETTER SCHOOLING

Ultimately, all educational investment projects have to stand or fall on whether they serve the society in terms of the goals and objectives of the whole society. Alternatively, educational investments may stand or fall on whether they satisfy the needs of the most powerful economic and political groups in a society. None of the educational projects we have discussed in this chapter significantly change the distribution of education within the society, nor are they designed to effect fundamental economic and social change. They do not promote rural education at the expense of urban; they do not serve those children from lower socioeconomic backgrounds at the expense of middle- and higher-class children. They do not emanate from an economic and social plan to redistribute income and wealth, although there is some hope by foreign agencies providing funds that they may redistribute income.

The main objective of the ETV projects is to produce more schooling and better schooling, primarily for children. Teachers are also trained by ETV in many of the projects, but this is part of the objective of reaching children. (Adult education generally was neglected in past showcase ETV projects.) ETV is used to achieve these objectives because it is believed in the long run to be cheaper than traditional teaching. Yet from most of the results presented above, the cost of ETV schooling is much higher per pupil than classroom-teacher schooling and the performance of pupils is not significantly or consistently better when ETV is used than when teachers are simply retrained to use more effective curricula. Teacher retraining costs are usually a small fraction of the cost of operating an ETV system.

The most persuasive argument for ETV occurs in situations where there is a long-run shortage of qualified teachers needed to reach a significant fraction of the school-age population. On the grounds that it is important to put all children in school as rapidly as possible, it is argued that educational media are the only way to achieve this objective at acceptable cost. The importation of foreign teachers in large numbers is regarded as prohibitive. So in cases where the objective is rapid educational expansion, and it is not possible to train enough local qualified teachers in the short run, educational media are an important alternative to consider. Even so, it usually takes ten years or more to make the ETV system operational at intended capacity.

On what basis, therefore, is the decision for rapid educational expansion made? The decision may be a political one: marginal groups, seeing that those in socially prestigious and economically rewarding positions have high levels of schooling, demand more schooling so that their children can have access to those positions. If the political pressure of these groups is great enough, the government will provide schooling to satisfy them. The decision may be an economic one: it is now widely held that an educated population is a key to sustained

TABLE 2.8

Social Rates of Return to Schooling, Enrollment Rates, Gross Domestic
Product Per Capita, and Economic Growth Rates, by Country for
Various Years, Primary, Secondary, and University
Levels of Schooling

Country	(1) Year	(2) Primary Rate of Return	(3) Primary Enrollment Rate	(4) Sec. Rate of Return	(5) Sec. Enrollment Rate	(6) Univ. Rate of Return	(7) Univ. Enrollment Rate	(8) GDP/Capita	(9) Economic Growth Rate
United States	1959	18	98	14	82	10	1576	2361	0.4
Canada	1961	—	—	14[a]	56	15[a]	725	1774	0.6
Puerto Rico	1960	21	70	22	46	16	1186	661	4.6
Mexico	1963	25	50	17	12	23	337	374	1.6
Venezuela	1957	82[b]	42	17	10	23	230	730	3.8
Colombia	1965	40	56	24	19	8	307	320	1.4
Chile	1959	12	68	12	23	9[c]	364	365	0.8
Brazil	1962	11	46	17	12	14	182	261	4.0
S. Korea	1967	12	66	9	33	5	760	146	6.6
Israel	1958	16	63	7	36	7	625	704	4.4
India	1960	20	20	13	31	13	281	73	1.8
Malaysia[d]	1967	9	56	12	28	11	142	280	2.8
Philippines	1966	8	56	21	34	11	1931	250	1.4
Japan	1961	—	—	7	79	6	510	464	5.8
Ghana	1967	18	35	11	34	16	70	233	-0.8
Kenya	1968	22	48	20	6	9	59	118	4.4
Uganda	1965	66	32	50	7	12	19	84	1.4

Zambia	1960	12	28	—	—	—	—	144	4.8
Great Britain	1966	—	—	5	96	8	382	1660	2.4
Germany	1964	—	—	—	—	5	396	1420	3.5
Denmark	1964	—	—	—	—	8	545	1651	4.2
Norway	1966	—	—	7	69	5	375	1831	4.2
Sweden	1967	—	—	10	44	9	647	2500	4.0
Belgium	1967	—	—	—	—	9	384	1777	3.4
Netherlands	1965	—	—	6	91	6	902	1490	3.2
Greece	1964	—	—	3	38	8	374	478	3.8
New Zealand[e]	1966	—	—	20	71	13	1005	1931	3.0

[a]The rates for Canada as reported are private rates. The rates as shown here have been lowered in accordance with the difference between private and social rates as estimated in W. L. Hansen, "Total and Private Returns to Investment in Schooling," Journal of Political Economy, 71, No. 2 (April 1963): 128-140.

[b]The 82 percent rate represents the return between illiterates and six years of schooling. Income foregone is assumed to be zero. Both facts imply that the rate is seriously overestimated.

[c]The rate as reported in Harberger and Selowsky is 12 percent, but as shown in Carnoy, "Rates of Return to Schooling in Latin America," op. cit., this is an overestimate. The 9 percent rate is approximate.

[d]Rates shown here are underestimates of unadjusted rates, since they have been corrected for nonschooling factors.

[e]Ogilvy uses an alpha-coefficient of 0.5, but he probably overestimates unadjusted rates, since he also uses starting salaries of government employees as his base for estimates.

(continued)

(Table 2.8 continued)

Sources:

Columns (1), (2), (4), and (6)—general source: George Psacharapoulos, "Rates of Return: International Comparison," Comparative Education Review 16, no. 1 (February 1972): 54-67.

United States: Fred Hines, et al., "Private and Social Rates of Return to Investment in Schooling," Journal of Human Resources V, no. 3 (Summer 1970): 318-340.

Canada: J.R. Podoluk, Earnings and Education (Canada Dominion Bureau of Statistics, 1965).

Puerto Rico: Martin Carnoy, "The Rate of Return to Schooling and the Increase in Human Resources in Puerto Rico," Comparative Education Review 16, no. 1 (February 1972): 68-84.

Mexico, Venezuela, and Chile: Martin Carnoy, "Rates of Return to Schooling in Latin America," Journal of Human Resources II, no. 3 (Summer 1967). For Chilean rates shown here, see footnote 11, adjusting rates shown in Table 7 of that article.

Colombia: M. Selowsky, "The Effect of Unemployment and Growth on the Rate of Return to Education: The Case of Colombia," Harvard University, Economic Development Report No. 116, November 1968.

Brazil: S.A. Hewlett, "Rate of Return Analysis: Role in Determining the Significance of Education in the Development of Brazil," 1970 (mimeo).

South Korea: Kim Kwang Suk, "Rates of Return on Education in Korea," USAID, 1968 (mimeo).

Israel: Ruth Klinow-Malul, "The Profitability of Investment in Education in Israel," The Maurice Falk Institute for Economic Research in Israel, Jerusalem, April 1966.

India: M. Blaug, R. Layard, and M. Woodhall, The Causes of Graduate Unemployment in India (London: The Penguin Press, 1969).

Malaysia: O.D. Hoerr, "Rates of Return: International Comparison," Development advisory Service, Harvard University (unpublished), reported in Psacharapoulos; and K. Hinchliffe, "Educational Planning Techniques for Developing Countries with Special Reference to Ghana and Nigeria," M. Phil. dissertation, University of Leicester, 1969.

Philippines: D. Devoretz, "Alternative Planning Models for Philippine Educational Investment," The Philippine Economic Journal, no. 16 (1969).

Japan: M.J. Brown, "Mass Elites at the Threshold of the Seventies," Comparative Education (London), forthcoming.

Ghana: K. Hinchliffe, "Educational Planning Techniques for Developing Countries with Special Reference to Ghana and Nigeria," unpublished M. Phil. dissertation, University of Leicester, 1969.

Kenya: Hans Heinrich Thias and Martin Carnoy, Cost-Benefit Analysis in Education: A Case Study on Kenya (Washington: IBRD and Johns Hopkins Press, 1972).

Uganda: John Smyth and Nicholas Bennett, "Rates of Return on Investment in Education: A Tool for Short Term Educational Planning Illustrated with Ugandan Data," The World Yearbook of Education (London: Evans Brothers, 1967).

Zambia (Northern Rhodesia): R.E. Baldwin, Economic Development and Export Growth (Berkeley: University of California Press, 1966).

The following European and New Zealand rates are all reported in Psacharapoulos, "Rates of Return: International Comparison."

Great Britain: L. Magler and R. Layard, "How Profitable is Engineering?" Higher Education Review 2, no. 2 (Spring 1970).

Germany: Klaus-Dieter Schmidt and Peter Baumgarten, "Berufliche Ausbildung und Einkommen," in A. E. Ott, ed., Theoretische und Empirische Beiträge zur Wirtschaftsforschung, Tubingen, Motz, 1967.

Denmark: N. B. Hansen, "Uddannelsesinvesteringernes Rentabilitet," Nationaløkonomisk Tidsakrift, No. 5-6, Copenhagen, 1969.

Norway: J. Aarrestad, On Urbyttet av a Investere i Utdanning i Norge, Norges Handelsøyskole Samfunnsøkonomisk Institutt, Bergen, 1967.

Sweden: Leif Magnuson, Department of Economics, University of Stockholm (unpublished).

Belgium: W. Desaeyere, "Een Onderwijsmodel voor Belgie, Deel 2, " Katholieke Universitaet te Leuven, Centrum voor Economische Studien, 1969 (mimeo).

Netherlands: P. de Wolff and R. Ruiter, De Economie vay het Onderwijs (Gravenhage: Montinus Nijhoff, 1968).

Greece: H. Leibenstein, "Rates of Return to Education in Greece," Harvard University, Economic Development Report No. 94, September 1967.

New Zealand: B.J. Ogilvy, "Investment in New Zealand Education and its Economic Value, 1951-1966," unpublished M. Com. dissertation, University of Auckland, 1968.
(continued)

63

(Table 2.8 continued)

Column (3): UNESCO, Statistical Yearbook, 1966 and 1967. Enrollment rates taken from Table 2.5 for year five years previous to column (1) year. The rationale for this is that the average person with primary-school training is assumed not to enter the labor force for five years after he leaves primary school. So the effect of enrollment rates on rate of return would be lagged by at least five years. The enrollment rate for column (1) minus five years is corrected to a six-year-length primary-school program, so that all ratios represent a six-equivalent primary enrollment as a percentage of five- to 14-year-olds in the country. Length of primary school in each country is taken from Table 2.1.

Column (5) Ibid. General secondary education only. The enrollment rate is taken for year three years previous to column (1) year. Enrollment rate is corrected to a four-year-length secondary-school program, so that all ratios represent a four-year equivalent secondary enrollment as a percentage of 15- to 19-year-olds in the country.

Column (7): Ibid. University enrollment is estimated as the number of university students in the population 15 years old and older. The enrollment rates are taken from Table 2.10. The correction for population 15 years old and older is based on population data from United Nations, Demographic Yearbook, 1960-69.

Column (8): George Psacharapoulos, "The Economic Returns to Higher Education in Twenty-five Countries," London School of Economics, Higher Education Unit, 1970, Table 1.

Column (9): United Nations, Statistical Yearbook, 1968. Economic growth rate is taken as the average percentage change in gross domestic product per capita in the period t-5 to t, where t is the year shown in Column (1).

64

economic growth and industrialization. If this were true, we should observe high rates of return to total investment in schooling (as compared to other possible public investments) across countries and over time. It is also widely held that increasing the average level of schooling will improve the distribution of income, increase social mobility, and make the political structure more democratic. [31]

Does an increased average level of schooling increase economic growth and redistribute income? Table 2.8 shows social rates of return, enrollment rates, gross domestic product (GDP) per capita, and GDP growth rate to various levels of schooling in 27 countries. *

The rates are generally high, averaging in the underdeveloped countries about 17 percent for primary schooling, 15 percent for secondary, and 13 percent for university. In the developed countries, the rates are somewhat lower: 10 percent to secondary school and 8 percent to university. The rates are interpreted to mean that the total invested resources in primary schooling would be expected to earn 17 percent per annum, or $17 annually on each $100 invested in primary schooling. The way these rates are estimated, all earnings differences among people with different levels of schooling are attributed to the fact that the people took different amounts of schooling. If people were assigned randomly to get varying amounts of schooling, it would be valid to assume that the reason that they earn more is primarily because they went to school. But we know that children are not randomly assigned to take more or less schooling. Those with more schooling have better-educated and higher-income parents; they generally have higher ability (nonverbal and verbal), and they come from an urban rather than a rural environment. In countries where there is racial or sexual discrimination, those discriminated against get less schooling than those who are not.

---

*The social rate of return to investment in schooling is defined as the solution to the equation

$$0 = \sum_{i=1}^{n} \frac{-C_i}{(1+r)^i} + \frac{Y_i}{(1+r)^i}$$

See equation (2.3) for the definition of the terms in this equation. C_i in the social rate case equals the sum of public expenditures per pupil on schooling and the private costs (including income foregone) of going to school. Benefits are usually defined as the difference in earnings of those in the labor force who have taken a given level of schooling (for example, primary schooling) and those who have not (for example, no schooling).

The higher income we observe for those with more schooling is
therefore not just the result of their additional schooling but of other
factors as well. If we decided to give primary education to all those
children now not in school and even if the labor market could "absorb"
them into the same kinds of jobs now given to primary graduates, they
probably would not have the same average income as today's primary
graduates. Although it is difficult (if not impossible) to separate out
the supply-demand effect on wages from the quality of graduate effect,
we would expect that for the same expenditures per pupil, those from
lower socioeconomic background and from rural areas will not do as
well incomewise as those with the same amount of schooling from
higher social background and urban areas. Rates of return to schooling
unadjusted for other factors are misleading indicators of the rates of
return to investment in those currently not in that level of schooling. [32]

The rates can be adjusted for other factors and are lower than the
unadjusted ones. Based on work by Denison, Blaug, Carnoy, and
Thias, [33] we can make some hypothetical adjustments in the underdeveloped countries of 0.4 on the primary rate, 0.8 on the secondary
rate, and 0.9 on the university rate. In the developed countries, the
adjustments we use are 0.6 for secondary, and 0.8 for university. This
leaves us with a 7 percent rate on primary, 12 percent on secondary,
11 percent on higher education investment in the underdeveloped countries, and about a 6 percent rate on both secondary and higher education
investment in developed countries. These rates are not particularly high,
and although hypothetical, they warn us that the economic payoff to
expanding schooling may be lower than we had thought. Of course, the
estimates are made without taking account of the nonpecuniary rewards
of being educated, but most underdeveloped governments are not ra-
tionalizing schooling investment in terms of providing nonpecuniary
rewards of education. These estimates are also made on the basis of
present costs of schooling and the present wage structure. Lower costs
of schooling per pupil would raise rates of return; higher costs per
pupil, like those introduced by ETV and rising teacher salaries, would
lower rates. Large increases in the number of primary- and secondary-
school graduates may lower teacher salaries, but they would also
probably lower the probability of employment in the same kinds of jobs
graduates from those levels do now, so that the rates of return could
fall rapidly over time. [34]

What about investments in improving student performance? Although there is little evidence that ETV does improve the student
performance more effectively than improved curriculum and teacher
retraining, is even this latter alternative worth the investment? We
have little data to estimate the economic returns to better schooling.
As an approximation to measuring the effects of better schooling, we
would use equation (3) to estimate the direct and indirect effects of
increasing student performance. Student performance can be measured
by various tests of verbal or nonverbal ability or attitude measures,

such as "modernity," "alienation," and so on. Estimates for the United States, Tunisia, Puerto Rico, and Kenya, indicate that the economic payoff to increased student performance is higher at lower levels of schooling than at higher levels, since ability seems to play a more important role in determining salary at lower school levels, where there is a higher percentage of the labor force employed. Therefore, investment in improved student performance would be more economically justifiable (in terms of higher future earnings of those performing better) in primary school than secondary school. [35] Other data for the United States, based on increased expenditures on schooling rather than improved student performance, indicate that for low-cost schools, the payoff to spending more per pupil (on, for example, better teachers or materials) is higher than the payoff to expenditures on additional years of schooling for pupils in such low-cost schools. [36] All these results are based on less than adequate data and cannot be considered conclusive.

But even if the economic return to increasing the quantity or quality of graduates in a particular country is not high, does not increasing the average level of schooling and learning improve the distribution of income? There is no evidence that supports this claim for schooling. [37] In the United States, for example, where average schooling has risen in the last generation from nine to more than 12 years, income distribution has not improved, and the distribution of expenditures on schooling has improved somewhat. [38] In a period of rapidly increasing average schooling in the population—1945-1969—there was little improvement in the distribution of income, and only some improvement in the distribution of schooling expenditures, whether public or total (including income foregone). Over a shorter period, Barkin reports similar results for Mexico. [39]

Theoretically, we could well expect that whether the educational system is expanding or not, it will maintain rather than change the social and economic structure unless the economic and social structure is intended to be changed. Yet the change in structure usually occurs independently of increased schooling; schooling is used to reinforce and to speed the change. * If the social and economic structure is to

---

*European influence in Africa is a good example of the change from African structures to capitalism. The European trade (slavery, and then other goods) gradually created a reorientation of power toward those tribes that traded with the Europeans and had the most contact with them. When Europeans conquered Africa in the late nineteenth century, capitalist organizations run by Europeans and Europeanized Africans began to dominate urban and then rural economic and social life in Africa. Schooling was a means of transforming Africans to fit into this form of organization.

be maintained, schooling will be used to maintain it. It can hardly be
regarded as a problem of inefficiency that those with little power in a
market economy (the income-poor) get less of what is needed to obtain
more income (human and physical capital) for their children than the
income-rich. Those in power organize institutions and the distribution
of access to them in ways that maintain their position. Usually only
drastic changes, such as the taking of power by a group that imposes
a different economic and social order, can affect these institutions.

ECONOMIC BENEFITS OF EDUCATIONAL TELEVISION: SOME EMPIRICAL EVIDENCE

Expanding schooling rapidly through ETV is more expensive than
expanding schooling through traditional means over a longer period of
time. There could nevertheless be an economic growth rationale for
such a rapid expansion if the rate of return to investment in those
levels of schooling were high enough to warrant it. If there were a
shortage of skilled labor, and it is felt that schooling children (as opposed to training young people on the job) is the most efficient way of
preparing those skills, increasing the number of graduates of primary
and secondary schools could have a high economic benefit, both for
those who take the schooling and for a society trying to improve its
productive capacity. The fact that ETV raises the costs of schooling
still might not lower the economic rate of return sufficiently to make
schooling a worse investment than other government projects. Thus,
expanding schooling by high-cost means such as ETV may still leave
schooling as a worthwhile investment in terms of cost-benefit criteria.

But there is little evidence that the ETV projects to date have taken
account of the benefits and costs of expanding schooling. The Samoan
project raised costs per pupil by an average of $90. The prospective
economic return to this investment is to prepare Samoans for work or
university (and then work) in Hawaii and the mainland United States.
This has little to do with improving the local economy.

For all the evaluational work on the El Salvador project, no study
is available on the relationship of education to conditions in the labor
force. The educational reform is designed to expand greatly the number
of junior- and senior-high schools, but there is no evidence that the
graduates of secondary schools will be able to find jobs suited to their
aspirations or that the labor force requires large numbers of secondary-
school graduates. The evaluators are apprehensive, though, about the
very high educational and occupational aspirations of junior high
schoolers getting ETV instruction. The World Bank recommended turning
down Niger's request to finance an expanded ETV system (Niger wanted
to apply for funds to AID) on the grounds that the ETV project does not
appear to be a solution to Niger's needs for "cultural" (IBRD terminology)

development, and that even the primary schooling now supplied does not square with the economic reality of the country: 14 percent of those leaving primary school go to secondary school and only 12 percent are employed in the wage sector. [40] However, with even less data, the World Bank approved its own loan to Ivory Coast for a massive ETV project.

One of the primary purposes of ETV in Ivory Coast (and Niger) is to increase the yield of the primary-school system; that is, to reduce dropouts. According to the IIEP report cited above, the "yield" of the primary-school system in Ivory Coast at the beginning of the 1970s was low—21 pupil years required to produce a primary-school graduate and seven pupil years needed to produce one school leaver who has completed the first four grades of school. [41] Although no data are yet available for Ivory Coast on the improvement of this "yield" with ETV, we do have data from the Niger experiment: the traditional schools required 10.25 student years for completing primary school, while the television schools required five years. [42] If the objective of the educational system and the society is to maximize the number of primary-school completers, then the ETV system could be twice as expensive per pupil as traditional school in Niger and have the same cost-effectiveness ratio. But if the objective of the system is to put the maximum number of children in primary school, the per pupil cost of ETV would have to be lower than the traditional system to make it more cost-effective.

The number of years required to bring a child to primary-school completion as a measure of "yield" assumes that all those who get less schooling than completion have no social value. A dropout is considered as being lost to the society—he or she is assigned a zero value in the calculation. * Unless it can be shown that those who finish fewer than the total years of primary school earn no more than those who never went to school, this calculation greatly underestimates the "yield" of the investment in schooling when dropouts occur.

The evidence on this point indicates that there is a positive earnings increase to even two or three years of primary schooling over none, although it is not as high as the last two years of primary school. [43] To make a correct estimate of the "yield" of primary schools, the (adjusted) rate of return should be used directly, or an estimate of equivalent years made where the output of each year is weighted by the earnings relative to finishing primary school. For example, if those

---

*The calculation of equivalent student years for completion is made by adding the number of students in each grade of primary school and dividing by the number of graduates. Thus, if 100 pupils start primary school and 100 pupils finish the sixth grade, the equivalent years equals 100 × 6/100, or 6. If the dropout rate is high, the denominator is small, and the equivalent years rise.

with one year of schooling earn $100 per month, those with two years
$110 per month, and so on, up to six years earning $150 per month, we
could say that those who drop out with one year of schooling are "worth"
two-thirds of those with six years of schooling; those with three years
80 percent of those with six years; and so on. The total number of students in the six years could be divided by the sum of these "six-year
equivalents" to get a truer yield of primary school before and after
investment in ETV.

The proposed Korean ETV system has the advantage of being able
to draw on several studies of rates of return to investment in schooling.
According to a study done for USAID by Kim Kwang Suk (see Table 2.8),
the social rates in 1967 were 12 percent to primary school investment,
9 percent to secondary, and 5 percent to university. These rates are
unadjusted for socioeconomic background or ability differences between
people who took different amounts of schooling, so we would expect
adjusted rates to be even lower, particularly at the primary level.
According to the proposal, costs of schooling would fall as a result of
ETV and the revised curriculum, but these estimates do not include ETV
operating costs and they propose a reduction of the teaching force,
which may reduce the rate of return to secondary school and university
in the longer run.

In both the Hagerstown and El Salvador project evaluations, an
effort is made to show that the gains in student performance are as
great for "disadvantaged" groups, such as rural origin, low socioeconomic background, and female children. We have already discussed
these scores, so shall concentrate here on their implications for income
distribution. The fact that a highly select group of rural children and
a much less select group of urban children in junior high school get the
same scores and the same gains on an examination does not mean that
they will have equal opportunities or equal jobs or even take the same
amount of schooling. For example, the El Salvador evaluation reports
that students from San Salvador had the highest educational aspirations
in the seventh and eighth grades, students from other urban areas and
semirural areas the next highest, and students from rural areas the
lowest. [44] It is likely, then, that although exam scores are not significantly different between these groups, the organization of the economic
and social structure creates a much lower probability of aspiration and
expectation of higher education for those from lower socioeconomic and
rural backgrounds and hence a lower average education (even with the
same ability), and a lower status and lower-paying occupation. The
educational system alone cannot solve this problem; if the motivation
to reach higher status levels for presently marginal groups is not built
into new economic and social organizations, even equalizing exam
scores of two groups will not provide equal opportunity. [45]

NOTES

1. See, for example, Dean Jamison, "Alternative Strategies for Primary Education in Indonesia: A Cost-Effectiveness Analysis," Stanford Graduate School of Business, September 1971.

2. Schramm et al., The New Media: Memo to Educational Planners (Paris: UNESCO, IIEP, 1967), p. 149.

3. Mark Blaug, An Introduction to the Economics of Education (London: The Penguin Press, 1970). Blaug defines cost-benefit analysis as a "technique evaluating public investment projects that compete actually or potentially with similar projects in the private sector" (p. 121).

4. Blaug, op. cit., p. 124.

5. See Martin Carnoy, "Class Analysis and investment in Human Resources: A Dynamic Model," The Review of Radical Political Economics 3, no. 4 (Fall-Winter 1971): 56-81. These data are presented in Table 2.8 of this chapter.

6. For more detail on this model, see Martin Carnoy, "The Social Benefits of More and Better Schooling," Papers in the Economics and Politics of Education, Stanford University School of Education, March 1972.

7. See, for example, Donald Holsinger, "The Elementary School as an Early Socializer of Modern Values: A Brazilian Study," Unpublished Ph.D. dissertation, Stanford School of Education, 1972.

8. The formula that combines depreciation and interest cost into annual cost of capital can be expressed as $A = [r(1+r)^n/(1+r)^n - 1]P$, where A = annual cost of capital, r = implicit interest cost of capital, n = capital life in years, and P = original cost of capital. See J.G. Kemeny et al., Finite Mathematics with Business Applications (Englewood Cliffs, New Jersey: Prentice-Hall, 1962).

9. Ta Ngoc Chau, "Ivory Coast: The Cost of Introducing a Reform in Primary Education," in Educational Cost Analysis in Action: Case Studies for Planners, vol. II (Paris: UNESCO, IIEP, 1972.)

10. IDET-CEGOS, "La Télévision Scolaire au Niger," Report No. 4669 (April 1971): 6.

11. Schramm et al., op. cit.

12. The most comprehensive of these is Richard E. Speagle, "Educational Reform and Instructional Television in El Salvador: Costs, Pay-off and Benefits," AID, October 1971.

13. For these figures and comments, see AID, op. cit.

14. IIEP, "Introduction of Educational Teievision and its Effect on the Cost of Primary Education in the Ivory Coast Republic," IIEP/RP/I-C.S. 3A (Rev.), part III.

15. Ibid., p. 50.

16. Robert Morgan and Clifton Chadwick, eds., Systems Analysis for Educational Change: The Republic of Korea (Tallahassee: Florida State University, Dept. of Educational Research, April 1971).

17. Ibid., p. 134.

18. Martin Carnoy, "Un enfoque de sistemas para evaluar la educación, ilustrado con datos de Puerto Rico," Revista del Centrol de Estudios Educativos, Vol. I, no. 3 (1971), Table 2.

19. Godwin Chu and Wilber Schramm, "Learning from Television: What the Research Says," Institute of Communication Research, Stanford, 1967 (mimeograph report).

20. Ibid., p. 10.

21. Ibid., p. 11.

22. Zvi Griliches and William Mason, "Education, Income, and Ability," Journal of Political Economy 80, no. 3, part II (May/June 1972): S74-S103 (see equation (4), p. 3).

23. Schramm et al., op. cit., p. 75.

24. Ibid.

25. Ibid., pp. 72-73.

26. These results are taken from three reports covering the first, second, and third years of research on the El Salvador ETV project proposed by members of the Institute of Communication Research at Stanford University. See Television and Educational Reform in El Salvador, Research Reports 4, 7, and 10.

27. Report 7, op. cit., p. 61.

28. Report 10, op. cit., p. 18.

29. Report 4, pp. 95, 99.

30. Report 7, op. cit., p. 46.

31. In 1961, then Secretary of State Dean Rusk said, "Democratic institutions cannot exist without education, for democracy functions only when the people are informed and are aware, thirsting for knowledge and exchanging ideas. Education makes possible the economic democracy that raises social mobility, for it is education that insures that classes are not frozen and that an elite of whatever kind does not perpetuate itself. And in the underdeveloped economies education itself stimulates development by . . . demonstrating that tomorrow need not be the same as yesterday, that change can take place, that the outlook is hopeful." (quoted in James S. Coleman, Education and Political Development (Princeton University Press, 1965), pp. 522-23.

32. The calculations of rates for Korea by John Chang in Morgan and Chadwick, op. cit., Appendix B, are a blatant example of not correcting for these factors and attempting policy recommendations on the basis of unadjusted and very crudely estimated rates of return.

33. See Carnoy, op. cit., for these references.

34. This is what is happening in Kenya. See Hans Thias and Martin Carnoy, Cost-Benefit Analysis in Education: A Case Study of Kenya (Johns Hopkins/World Bank, 1972).

35. See Carnoy, "The Social Benefits of More and Better Schooling," op. cit.

36. See George Johnson and Frank Stafford, "Social Returns to Quantity and Quality of Schooling," paper presented at the Econometric Society Meetings, December 1970.

37. See Robinson Hollister, "The Relationship Between Education and the Distribution of Income: Some Forays," University of Wisconsin (mimeo).

38. Martin Carnoy, "Notes on Schooling and Income Distribution," paper prepared for the Annual Meeting of the Latin American Studies Association, Madison, Wisconsin, 1973. See also Barry Chiswick and Jacob Mincer, "Time Series Changes in Personal Income Inequality in the U.S. from 1939, with Projections to 1985," Journal of Political Economy 80, no. 3, part II: 534-66.

39. David Barkin, "Acceso a la Educación Superior y Beneficios que Reportan en Mexico," Revista del Centro de Estudios Educativos (Mexico), 1, no. 3: 47-74.

40. IDET-CEGOS, op. cit., p. 11.

41. IIEP, op. cit., p. 52.

42. IDET-CEGOS, op. cit., p. 8.

43. See my estimates for Mexico and Puerto Rico, and Thias's and my estimates for Kenya (citations in Table 2.8).

44. Research Report No. 7, op. cit., March 1971, p. 121.

45. See Martin Carnoy, "Is Compensatory Education Possible?" in Martin Carnoy, ed., Schooling in a Corporate Society (New York: David McKay, 1972). See also Christopher Jencks et al., Inequality (New York: Basic Books, 1972).

ADDITIONAL BIBLIOGRAPHY

Girling, R.K., "A Cost-Effectiveness Evaluation of Alternative Technologies for Teaching Mathematics in Jamaica," Social and Economic Issues 21 (March 1972): 72-89.

Layard, Richard, "The Cost-Effectiveness of the New Media in Higher Education," Higher Education Research Unit, London School of Economics, 1972 (mimeo).

3

ORGANIZATIONAL AND
ADMINISTRATIVE
CONSIDERATIONS
William Perron
Michael Kirst

This chapter analyzes administrative and organizational factors associated with the introduction of a new teaching medium—television—into the educational structure of a country. According to Rene Maheu, Director-General of UNESCO, the effectiveness of new instructional technologies "depends to a large extent on the manner in which they are organized as an integral part of the overall educational efforts and on the way in which reception and utilization are controlled, guided, and organized."[1]

We have selected specific areas to illuminate the key issues involved in formulating a sound policy for the implementation and operation of educational television. These are (1) planning considerations: the preliminary decision-making process; (2) management control considerations: the necessary organizational and managerial characteristics, the overall financial picture and cost implications, and facility and equipment needs; and (3) operational control considerations: delivery and reception of the educational "product" (the televised lessons), specific staffing requirements and general personnel administration, and the administrative coordination of a research and evaluation unit.

Conceptually, there is considerable overlap between the three general headings selected for ordering the discussion. Yet certain useful distinctions can be drawn. For instance, while "planning" in the broadest sense permeates all three areas, we have isolated that portion of the planning process that is preliminary to the introduction of educational television. The first section, then, deals primarily with a process of need identification, goal setting, and initial policy formulation. Planning beyond the preliminary stages is carried over into the second general area where it is combined with overall administrative control features. Here the concern is directed toward activities that are properly designated as coming under the management rubric. Operational control issues comprise the third general section and are distinguished from management control issues in that they relate to the efficient performance of specified tasks necessary for carrying out the plans and achieving the goals of the organization. [2]

In this context, then, we emphasize the vital importance of a coordinated effort at the planning level in our discussion of the first general area. And in the second and third areas our emphasis might be best summarized as an exploration of "the grouping of activities necessary to appropriate departments, and the provision for authority delegation and coordination. "[3]

In addition to a familiarity with administrative issues likely to accompany the introduction of system-wide educational innovations, decision makers must be conversant with the particular properties of television. They must know what the media can and cannot do, and what is necessary for its operation.

Critically important, decision makers must also understand the cultural, social, and political milieu into which this technology is being introduced; and be aware of the environmental constraints and resistances that are likely to arise and limit "administrative rationality. "* At the same time they must endeavor to anticipate probable

---

*Administrative rationality, as used here, refers to "consistent, value-maximizing choice within specified constraints. "[4] Such a view captures the basic notions that people generally impute to human purposiveness in both individual and organized group behavior. These notions are: (1) that individuals are goal-directed, that is, they prefer some things to others and, correspondingly, are able to elucidate that preference; (2) that their decisions are intentional in that they choose particular actions on the basis of their perceived contribution toward the achievement of goals; (3) that decision makers act on the basis of the best available knowledge and make decisions that conform to the rules of logic and rationality; (4) that a central feature of administrative rationality is calculability—in the ETV area this means the decision maker will search out numerous alternatives and attempt as much quantitative calculation of their comparative effects as possible; and (5) administrative rationality implies some feedback in order to monitor progress toward goals.

In the discussion ahead, however, while this definition is useful, we do not intend to proceed exclusively in the context of the rational mode; for, quite obviously, in most instances of organizational life processes, such a restricted and perhaps idealistic view is directly challenged by political and bureaucratic realities (and especially so with reference to educational issues). Thus we will seek a more expansive perspective as we proceed. Still, the reader might find it useful to think of these realities as comprising, at a given point in time, the "specified constraints" mentioned in the definition above.

In less technical terms, then when we speak of administrative rationality, we refer to reasonable and sensible choice processes executed within the boundaries erected by existing environmental constraints and resistances.

and perhaps deleterious consequences that decisions in this specific
area will have on other systems—for example, the impact of new educational content and technologies on traditional belief systems.

PLANNING CONSIDERATIONS

In this section we examine the planning function as it relates to
the assessment of television as a viable and working solution to the
nation's educational problems. We also examine the formulation of a
strategic plan with both short- and long-run perspectives, as well as
the requisite policies and operating procedures for the achievement of
the new system's stated objectives.

Heuristically, we divide the preliminary decision-making process
into three stages:

1. the Needs-Assessment Stage, which includes the identification
of the most urgent educational problems and the gathering of information
relevant to, and the analysis of, the nature of these problems;

2. the Solution-Selection Stage, which includes the determination
of suitable and available alternatives and the evaluation of these alternatives in order to select the ones most appropriate for solving the
problems;

3. the Strategic Planning Stage, which includes the formulation of
explicit system objectives and educational goals, the determination of
a specific course of action or plan to utilize the alternative(s) chosen,
and the necessary follow-up requirements to prepare for implementing
the decision plan.

These three stages will be treated in the sequence provided above
since we believe their order to be of prime concern to the decision
maker. The discussion will be supplemented with specific examples
drawn from case studies of educational television endeavors.

The Needs-Assessment Stage

There is no universally applicable procedure for the identification
and analysis of educational needs, for too many other variables intervene depending upon the given situation. Instead, this process is left
to the local planners. These individuals are better able to assess educational planning areas and to set priorities when operating within the
framework and customary procedures of their own planning agencies,
ministries, or commissions.

As a guide to planners, we wish to raise the following considerations:

First, the critical appraisal of a country's educational needs and the subsequent assignment of a priority ranking to those needs represent the crucial input to the overall educational planning function. This process cannot successfully occur in the absence of clear policy orientations provided by societal priorities. The fact that it often does occur in the absence of such orientations should not mislead us. Rather, if the needs assessment is to be truly useful, it must be tied to the overriding development philosophy and goals of a country.

Ideally, the philosophy and goals of a country would be contained within a comprehensive development plan. Such a plan would define the function of education in the society—for instance, whether it is to be an instrument for social change, an agency providing needed manpower, or an institution for developing the potential of each individual. Hopefully, within this development plan there would be some fundamental choices concerning various societal needs (economic, political, cultural, social, and educational) and the trade-offs between them.

In the absence of national plans, decision makers must still attempt to check their assessment of educational problems and needs against the overall problems confronting a country and the specific different problems of subpopulations comprising it. Defining educational problems without taking into account the context out of which they arise and the target populations to be served will lead to a fiasco.

A case in point is provided by the early experience in American Samoa. Although the Samoan experience with ETV is in many ways probably more atypical than typical of other less developed countries (if only because the country is governed as a territory of the United States) it does demonstrate what can result when insufficient attention is paid to the people's intrinsic needs during the assessment stage. According to Lynne and Grant Masland, the overall educational objective of English language training and general American acculturation of the Samoan people did not in the end serve the real needs of the people. As they point out in Chapter 6:

> At best the TV curriculum in Samoa prepared young people
> for a clerical job in government, bank, or local store.
> The value to the Samoan of village life and roles foreign
> to the Western mind was not understood. . . .

American Samoa provides an example of how the wrong interpretation of needs can erroneously commit a country to large-scale use of educational television.

In this respect, however, it would appear from the information available that the most fundamental error common to almost all ETV projects is not a sin of commission, but one of omission. That is, the error lies not in an inaccurate, incomplete, or analytically faulty needs assessment but rather in the bypassing or near-total neglect of a needs assessment itself.

In addition, it is only after formulating what educational needs must be served that the planner should proceed to the Solution-Selection Stage. That is, the selection of a particular alternative or "answer," be it a technological medium like television or not, must stand as a means to an end. Too often technology selection has preceded the examination of a country's educational needs (and, further, as we will point out, the selection of educational television itself usually occurred with, at best, only a cursory and inconsequential look at other possible approaches for meeting the educational problem). In essence, then, the "solution" to the problem was chosen before the nature of the problem was properly identified or at least subjected to critical scrutiny.

This procedure has been prevalent in the history of educational television. To cite but a few instances:

In Niger

The initiative to adopt ETV in Niger was taken by President Diori of the Republic of the Niger. As a mission sponsored by UNESCO has reported:

> the French Government was a partner in the endeavor from
> the outset. It appears that the latter was willing to respond
> to President Diori's request for assistance for several rea-
> sons, including (1) to help a newly independent French-
> speaking country that had great development needs; (2) to
> compensate in some way for its policy of not making French
> teachers available to newly independent countries; and
> (3) to test the potential of radio and television to help meet
> the needs of developing countries. These objectives seem
> to be fully compatible with those held by Niger. [5]

Here, then, the primary concern was oriented toward ETV specifically and how it might best meet the needs of the country instead of oriented toward specific needs and how best they might be overcome.

In El Salvador

Although the decision to utilize educational television in El Salvador was not taken precipitously but evolved over a number of years, it does appear the concept itself preceded determination of a specific need for which it could be adapted. The country's small size, its excellent topographical conditions, and its citizens' use of virtually one language, all contributed to the planning thrust in the early and mid-1960s, which centered on the use of television alone. The first Educational Television Commission established in 1963 by former President Rivera was asked to evaluate alternate uses of television. While its progress was sporadic and its contribution small, an administrative history of the project recounts:

The Commission remained firm in its belief that television could make an important contribution to the
development of El Salvador, but the nature of that
contribution and the methods for bringing it about
were not crystallized. [6]

In 1965, after the commission was revitalized under the chairmanship
of Walter Béneke, the debate was again concentrated on "alternative
ways in which educational television might meet the country's educational needs."[7] Thus, the needs assessment that was conducted
only came after the basic concept of utilizing television had been
accepted by the country's leadership. While the ETV experience in
El Salvador has been largely successful in comparison to that of other
countries, we cannot recommend as good practice the method of starting
first with a given technology and then proceeding to locate the most
beneficial place to apply it.

In Israel

In Israel, too, the utilization of television to meet the country's
educational problems preceded their assessment. As the Lord Evans
Commission (to study the future of educational television in Israel)
reported:

In 1962, the philanthropic foundation of the Rothschild
family, known as Hanadiv, conceived the idea of
introducing instructional television in Israel. The
authorities in Israel were informed of this scheme and
welcomed it. [8]

Accordingly, Hanadiv conducted a needs assessment for their pilot
project in the context of a specific solution.

General Pattern

The pattern has been to start with the technology and find situations
where it might be applied. There is undoubtedly prestige associated
with use of the new technology. And the last decade has seen the ready
availability of large-scale funding for technological innovation in
education.

The basic lesson to be gained here is that the technology itself
becomes the formative force behind the change. The educational needs
are geared to the technology, not the technology to the needs. For the
sake of efficiency, the process of meeting educational needs is predicated on the technology's capabilities alone and, simultaneously, is
constrained by its limitations. We suggest this approach is very similar
to placing the cart before the horse; and, while there might well be some

political payoff in going about the task in this manner, we see very
little payoff in an educational sense.

The Solution-Selection Stage

It would appear that the basic element of the Solution-Selection
Stage—that of considering and evaluating a range of alternatives for
meeting particular educational needs—has been largely neglected in
the field experience with educational television to date. For whatever
specific reason or combination of reasons, many countries have chosen
to proceed with ETV without attempting to assess formally other possible
means of achieving the desired end. We have already recounted the
experiences in Niger, El Salvador, and Israel. Additionally, in the
Philippines, the impetus for establishing a pilot ETV project in Quezon
City to serve as the basis for a national system originated with a
Jesuit priest who was convinced the technology held much promise for
the country. [9] In Arequipa, Peru, the development of La Telescuela
Popular Americana was, in the UNESCO case writer's words:

> the story of a group of civic-minded, church-connected
> persons who were concerned about educational problems
> in their home community and decided to try to do something
> about it, using the medium of television. [10]

These experiences are typical of the origins of ETV in most countries.
Only in American Samoa were alternative considerations reported to
have been an integral part of the preliminary decision-making process;[11] yet even in this instance, a UNESCO mission has raised some
questions of how serious an analysis was attempted during Governor
Lee's administration. [12]

The foregoing is not meant to imply that other alternatives were
not available or considered—if only in an informal sense. In a number
of countries, the more obvious alternatives did receive formal expression and sometimes elementary evaluation; however, this typically
occurred after the initial commitment to educational television and,
therefore, did not represent an input to the decision process. Rather,
such expression is usually found in the "background" section of a
project's history or else in the "foreword" of a proposal for securing
further outside funding, where it stands as a justification for continuing the ETV project. When alternatives are considered, the tendency
has been to present them in a biased manner, as requiring efforts and
expenditures beyond the capacity of a country—without taking into
account realistically the substantial sacrifices and costs of television.

Our point simply is that these alternatives were not subjected to
a formal feasibility study with the projected cost implications of each

included and made available to the decision maker. In addition, and
perhaps of greater significance, it does not appear that other technology
media were assessed for their potential applicability in a given situation. (Probably the best example would be educational radio. A less
glamorous approach, radio is less likely to attract local political support and is probably more difficult to entice outside agencies or funding
sources to participate in than educational television. However, it does
require less initial investment, is less costly to operate, and reaches
wide audiences in rural and isolated areas not easily reached by conventional television transmission systems.)

Conversely, once the initial interest in educational television was
expressed and the other alternatives dismissed, field experience demonstrates the subsequent abundance of feasibility studies. In El Salvador,
for example, separate studies were conducted by the Japan Broadcasting
Corporation, the World Bank, and USAID;[13] while in American Samoa,
Governor Lee utilized studies by the National Association of Education
Broadcasters (NAEB) and a special survey committee of experts.[14] And
so the list proceeds from country to country, although not all had the
benefit of multiple studies. Since the "hard" financing for most projects
originates largely outside the countries, and because the various loan
or aid agencies generally predicate their investment on the successful
assessment of the project's projected worthiness, this should not be
surprising.

These studies examined educational television with respect to the
particular countries, and, it should be said, seldom concluded that it
was not feasible—Niger being one country where the World Bank turned
down a proposal for wide-scale use of ETV to expand schooling. One
plausible reason for this lies in the constituency of these study teams.
They were typically comprised of university ETV research people and/or
employees of ETV hardware manufacturers or sellers, international development agencies, and the like; as such, we believe the general orientation of the study teams can be honestly characterized as one of
propagating the concept and use of educational television. And for some
of the participants there was a personal stake in the success of the
venture. It is perhaps for this reason that these studies, in addition
to representing an important part of an investment decision for some external organization, took the form more of determining how the educational television system should be implemented, organized, and oper-
ationalized, than of assessing whether it was practicable or not. That
decision supposedly had already been reached via sound methods. Perhaps this point is best illustrated in the words of UNESCO's case writer
when describing the feasibility study/plan of the NAEB in American
Samoa. The NAEB

> concluded that the use of television would be technically
> feasible, but went far beyond technical questions. It

> summarized and documented the deficiencies of the existing
> school system. . . . Then the report recommended far-
> reaching changes built around the use of television. [15]

This type of approach would seem to be typical of the feasibility
studies carried out. As such, they made no contribution to the Solution-
Selection Stage as we have defined it; that is, the intent of these
studies was not to determine the best possible alternative for meeting
a specific need but rather to determine the best possible way to utilize
television. Given this, the studies represent an input only to the Strategic Planning Stage, to which we will shortly direct our attention.

First, however, we offer two reminders: when only one possible
alternative solution is examined critically, the effectiveness of the
educational planner is being severely hampered; and since almost any
task is possible or capable of being accomplished by means of modern
technology, we suggest that the ultimate test of "feasibility" should
center more on the question of "practicability" given the existing circumstances in a particular country.

The Strategic Planning Stage

The following statement serves both to highlight the general experience with ETV and to exemplify the frustrations encountered when
thoughtful and systematic planning is foregone at the expense of immediate system implementation. It is presented as an introduction to
the final stage of the preliminary decision-making process:

> Although the introduction of an expensive and technically
> complex educational innovation such as television would
> seem to require considerable forethought and planning be-
> fore it could be applied successfully to a school system,
> the history of instructional television projects throughout
> the world has often been one of inadequate planning and
> undue haste.
>
> Educational reformers are often impatient to get a new
> television system underway, and there is a tendency to
> rush through the planning stage in order to get studios con-
> structed and programs on the air.
>
> As a result of this haste, the needs of teachers and the
> conditions in their classrooms are often neglected or given
> insufficient attention, and corresponding weaknesses are
> built into the system from the outset. These oversights
> have often returned to haunt the managers of new television
> systems and undermine the effectiveness of their programs.[16]

The point stressed here is the need for planners to bring into the decision-making process those groups affected by the new media and those groups whose support is essential to the success of the project. At the upper echelons of an educational system, planning activities may be concentrated in the hands of a small, cohesive group or they may be dispersed throughout a number of governmental offices and agencies.[17] Not infrequently, the authority of a planning group to formulate plans is separated from the authority and mechanisms to implement a policy. Whatever the case may be, the administrator of an ETV project must mobilize commitment to the goals and processes involved in the new reform—once it is decided that television will help alleviate pressing educational problems.

In The New Media: Memo to Educational Planners, this commitment was posited as the most important prerequisite for success and was explained as follows:

> everyone who will have an important role in the undertaking must be really serious about it. By this we mean that the key educational, financial, and other officials who will decide on the project or who will later direct its destiny should have clearly in mind an important educational problem (or problems) which they wish the new media to help them solve, and should be seriously committed to making a substantial and sustained effort to this end.
>
> They must not simply be enamoured of a new fashion or of toying with a new gadget. If the project is to be undertaken at all it should be viewed as a priority and not as a marginal activity. This commitment should be sufficiently broad-based so that support for the project will continue even if one or several of its initial proponents should later leave the scene, as so often happens.[18]

If such a commitment is not sufficiently present at the time of selection, the planning stage offers a good opportunity to develop one. By integrating into this stage the relevant groups and/or individuals, realistic and effective planning can result; and, just as important, a form of "insurance" for the effort will be created. By this, we mean the granting of an input channel into the decision-making process can provide for the participants a stake in the outcome of the project, and, correspondingly, can guarantee among often multiple and competing groups a common commitment to educational television.

The gaining of support is not an easy task, nor will it positively ensure harmony of effort. The decision maker, however, must recognize all possible points of resistance and attempt to incorporate them into the planning process at an early stage. One such very crucial resistance point obviously is the teacher, and about this we will have more to say in the section on personnel administration. For the present, though, it

would seem to be common not to give teachers or their representatives
a voice in the planning process. [19] And, although there is no pretense
here that the mere act of bringing teachers into the process at this point
will entirely eliminate teacher resistance to television (for the teachers
may feel they are being manipulated and, if so, the situation must be
coped with), we do suggest that an early concentrated effort toward
securing the teachers' active participation can ease their problems in
adopting and relating to a new technology that seems threatening.

The planning group, whatever its particular constitution, must devote its initial efforts to the formulation of explicit system objectives
and educational goals for the use of instructional television. This task
involves careful delineation of the overall purpose of the project and
of matters concerning what specific audiences are to be served, in what
areas of instructional content the effort is to be concentrated, and what
the desired amount of educational progress is to be gained in these
learning areas. It cannot be overemphasized that the goals set must be
both realistic and attainable.

The essence of objective setting, then, is that the final choices
regarding the purpose of the technology's use (and there is a wide range
represented in the literature on educational television) should be well
thought out and discriminating. It would be disappointing, indeed, if
objectives and goals were not so determined, or worse, if they were
borrowed from or imitative of projects in other countries. Although some
educational problems are universal in a general sense, their specific
manifestation varies considerably. One country's most urgent need,
while perhaps similar to its neighbor's most urgent need, is in actuality
quite different. Each exhibits its own peculiar nuances; therefore no
two solutions should be expected to be exactly the same. We have
progressed far beyond the stage where we can say only that television
will be utilized to upgrade the educational system or to improve the
quality of teaching. Rather, the educational goal must be more explicit.
For instance, the specific goal assumed by Israeli ITV during its early
history was to raise the level of achievement among disadvantaged students in three subject areas: English, mathematics, and biology. [20]
(This goal, however, changed with increasing utilization of television
to enrich the standard curriculum for children and youth who were not
disadvantaged.)

Additionally, when system goals have been precisely set forward,
it provides an effective framework for the future analysis of how the
system is developing and what it is accomplishing in regard to original
expectations. On the other hand, if these goals are ill-defined in the
beginning, evaluating system preformance and taking specific corrective
action downrange becomes a terribly difficult task.

The second major decision facing the planning group is the determination of what form the project should take. We refer here specifically
to the issue of whether a pilot test or demonstration project should be
executed or whether a direct foray into full-scale television usage

should be attempted. To many, this decision implies a choice between a qualitative production approach, as with small-scale experimental projects, and a quantitative production approach, as with large-scale immediate system implementations. Whatever the case, the decision does represent, as USAID contends, "the most fundamental strategic choice that a nation interested in making changes through educational technology must face."[21] In this sense, then, we must direct our attention to the advantages and disadvantages inherent in each approach.

Experimental Pilot Project

Perhaps the greatest advantage of utilizing a pilot test is that it does provide a period of time under actual production situations during which a "reservoir of skills"[22] may be built up and data useful for the eventual expansion of the system can be obtained. Among such skills would be the training of system personnel, the development of high-quality programs or software, and the management requirements for administering a television system; while among the types of information hopefully obtained would be pupil performance data from the classrooms to assess the learning effectiveness of the programming, and pertinent cost data for projecting the financial load to be borne under a more expanded system.[23]

On the other hand, the decision to proceed with some type of experimental project carries with it a definite price to be paid in the high unit cost per pupil because of the small audience. It also necessitates continuing substantial support in both human resources and monetary resources; and if for some reason a decision not to continue with television results, this support can represent an irreversible expenditure of resources. Simultaneously, such a project requires that a "commitment to use the end result for an operational program must be maintained over a long period."[24] (The experience in Niger, although considered highly creative and a learning success, has suffered from a change in national objectives and the resulting wavering commitment to television.[25] Also, pilot projects can and do suffer from the fact that they do not always reveal specific problems inherent in large-scale applications. The successful replication of a pilot project is difficult and should be expected to be so. Small administrative and maintenance problems, tolerable because of the small size of the pilot, can become intolerable with the size magnification. Yet the most basic lesson for the educational planner to keep in mind is that "a country must work as hard to expand a pilot project as on the initial project itself."[26]

Immediate Total Saturation of Television

For a number of reasons basically of a political nature, once a commitment to the new technology is obtained, it may be imperative for a country to bring the system "up" quickly in an effort to demonstrate immediate results on a broad scale. In these instances, then, the saturation approach holds a definite advantage over the pilot-test approach. A related advantage, of course, would be the more reasonable unit cost per student. The basic philosophy operating here is one of "improve as you go."

On the other hand, while saturation does present at times a more politically or economically feasible plan, it has certain disadvantages, which on the whole are the reverse of the pilot-project advantages. That is, system personnel are compelled to learn on the job, a fact which is not necessarily bad in itself except that under these circumstances mistakes are magnified and become much harder to correct. Haphazard and inconsistent responses to problems, both of a technical and administrative nature, must be expected. Additionally, there is serious question as to whether a firm commitment to quality programming can accompany a total saturation approach to educational television. The system group is forced to spend so much time on immediate production needs that the quality of the "product" must inevitably suffer. The experience in American Samoa stands as adequate testimony to this fact. Faced with full programming for eight grades in the first year and the remaining four grades in the second year, the extremely heavy load on the production team "overshadowed optimal professional quality in broadcasting."[27] In the midst of such production requirements, it is quite difficult to incorporate changes either in content or technique. In another area of concern, it is often the case that insufficient attention is devoted to preparing the classroom teachers for use of the innovation.[28] And, finally, there is always the danger of becoming locked in with an inadequate system because of the initial heavy investment required.[29]

On the other hand, this does not have to be an either/or proposition. The ETV experience in El Salvador is a good example of a compromise between an experimental pilot project and immediate total saturation. Perhaps the most useful question for the planner to consider when deciding upon a particular approach is this: do we have sufficient time and willingness to profit from our own mistakes?

A final major thrust of the planning group should be directed to the necessary follow-up requirements for implementing the decision plan. If attended to prior to actual implementation, a well-organized effort here can contribute greatly to the success of the project, whether it involves the pilot-testing or total-saturation approach. Such requirements for consideration would include the following. First, technical preparation plans must be evaluated before delivery of the particular technological hardware selected. Sites must be prepared, and they must be suitable for the proper operation of the hardware. Second, organizing plans must be initiated. The composition and location of the television work group must be dealt with and the interrelationships between ministries defined. Third, staffing preparation plans require immediate attention in order that a trained work force can begin program preparation as soon as possible. The role of the classroom teacher also must be

clearly defined, and training initiated. And, finally, plans for evaluating the progress of the overall effort must be laid. These concerns,
among others, will be the substance of the following sections of this
chapter.

Summary

Quite obviously, the most tangible product of the preliminary decision-making process is the implementation plan itself. Determined
on the basis of a thoughtful needs assessment and on evaluation of
suitable alternatives, and characterized by an explicit statement of the
objectives and goals, the plan represents the desired end of this procedure irrespective of the specific form it takes. Nevertheless, there
are some crucial intangibles that should also emerge from this effort.

Responsible leaders should realize that perhaps the single most
important factor arising from this preliminary process is their own serious involvement in and commitment to educational television. One cannot overemphasize the importance of strong leadership at the top. We
urge these leaders to realize that their active support can go a long way
toward securing the necessary cooperation from, and overcoming resistance in, the departmental groups affected by the decision to use television.

In addition, one would hope to find among the individuals responsible for implementation of the plan a unity of purpose toward the new
technology and the educational objectives designated for it. The effort
will require as much bureaucratic harmony as possible, and, hopefully,
a common goal orientation can be shared.

MANAGEMENT CONTROL CONSIDERATIONS

In the preceding pages we have argued that one of the most fundamental administrative decisions involves whether or not ETV represents
a viable and feasible alternative for a given country in a given circumstance. We have also presented a framework for how that decision
ought to be taken. For future discussion, we will accept the premise
that educational television is to be used and explore the ramifications
of that decision.

Our treatment of management control considerations deals primarily
with the ETV organization—its location in the bureaucracy and its requisite structural interactions and interrelationships with other operational
groups in the school system—and the requirements for obtaining and
using the physical resources necessary to accomplish system goals in
an effective manner. We first focus on the organizational implications
characteristic of implementing television systems then turn our attention
to the financial as well as the facility and equipment resource needs.

Organization and Management Characteristics

The question of structuring the new educational television work group in the overall organization and in a manner conducive to accomplishing system goals represents a crucial issue to the planner or system designer. Often the search for a solution to this issue is bent on discovery of the best possible structure for administering educational television in specific. We believe such an effort to be misdirected for the following reasons.

There is within each country a certain administrative infrastructure within which the educational television system group must eventually function or, at least, with which it must be prepared to cooperate. This is usually a ministry of education or some higher authority with the final responsibility for educating the nation's young; how it is administratively constituted will vary considerably from country to country. The pattern of interactions and practices and the management philosophy that contributed to the development of this infrastructure will also differ widely. That is, over the years various political agreements among and between different departments or bureaus concerning the extent of their authority in certain areas and their standard operating procedures will have come into existence. To be effective, the ETV planner must recognize these intrabureaucratic coalitions and bargains.

In designing the new system, although a complete organizational overhaul of the education system may appear to represent the direction in which "success" lies, such a major reorientation or reconstitution of a typically large bureaucracy is usually not feasible for a variety of reasons. Politically, it may be unwise. From a very practical standpoint, there are influential groups in each nation who have vested interests in maintaining the organizational status quo and most likely the traditional mode of education. Under these circumstances, it would be foolhardy to doom the technological innovation from the beginning by tying it to an organizational reform that may not prove to be essential. Accordingly, existing organizational relationships may have to be accepted as given in formulating the introduction of educational television.

Due to tremendous cross-national differences in traditional administrative machinery, we believe that a universal "best possible" structure for educational television simply does not exist. Nor do we think one should be sought, for the "ideal" can contribute little when confronted by often unique administrative circumstances. Our recommendation is that the planner will find the actual implementation of educational television, and the problems it will generate, to be difficult enough without being hampered by unfounded guidance that such-and-such a structure is the best and therefore should be utilized. Rather, we would much prefer to see the planner's interest in this area focused on how television can be organized logically given the existing administrative surroundings. If part of these surroundings can be reorganized to the benefit of the new technology, all well and good; where it cannot be so treated, however, the planner must concentrate on how to take advantage of whatever strengths may be present, while at the same time attempting to devise a method of either bypassing or coping with those portions of the structure that stand as obstacles. Our advice is to change what you can, adapt to what you cannot change, and ignore what is irrelevant or has no bearing on eventual success.

In this respect, organizational change seems to be espoused by all as the key to success; but its achievement in a large organization very seldom lies with a unilateral decree originating from the top of the hierarchy. Rather change must be approached as a process of adaptation and accommodation, a process oriented toward (1) altering the organization's level of adaptation to its environment, and (2) inducing change in the internal behavioral patterns of employees. In general, a useful framework for characterizing the approaches to such organizational "change" has been presented as involving structure, technology, and people:

"Structural" approaches introduce change through new formal guidelines and procedures, such as the organization chart, budgeting methods, and rules and regulations.

"Technological" approaches emphasize rearrangements in work flow, as achieved through new physical layouts, work methods, job descriptions, and work standards.

"People" approaches stress alterations in attitudes, motivation, and behavioral skills, which are accomplished through such techniques as new training programs, selection procedures, and performance appraisal schemes. [30]

By drawing upon the experience with educational television in the field, we hope to demonstrate how a technological innovation of this order can and does affect nearly every component of the education system and, correspondingly, how other countries have attempted to respond to the systematic change and adaptation/accommodation processes required.

Before proceeding with discussion of these considerations, it should be noted that informal ways or methods of getting tasks done in an organization are of practical importance and should not be ignored. The informal network of relations can and does impinge heavily on the formal organizational structure and its administrative processes. The problem is that the particular configuration of informal arrangements is dependent upon the particular personnel involved and the special working relationships that exist between different sets of people. When the particular mix of individuals and their relationships are gone, the informal means of influence disappear or cease to function with predictable regularity. Since we believe educational television implementation will inevitably suffer if dependent upon shifting and

unidentifiable bases, we believe it more prudent to focus on the formal
or visible structures where authorization for certain specified actions
is explicit.

Organizational Placement or Location of the New Media Group

There have been a wide variety of approaches to the issue of organizational placement, a few of which we will summarize here. The
range extends from small autonomous working groups to groups completely integrated into existing educational systems.

The media group in American Samoa was placed in the Department
of Education. However, because of the special nature of the effort—
the total utilization of television in the curriculum throughout all school
grades—the American-based television group functioned as an autonomous control unit for the entire educational system. The tight centralization of the decision-making apparatus stands as the obvious advantage
to this approach. On the other hand, the most apparent disadvantage
lay in that the decision-making routines and procedures were not institutionalized into the existing bureaucracy. Rather the National Association of Educational Broadcasters' project team created its own bureaucratic structure within the Department of Education and operated with
vast powers. In the process, competing

> educational bureaucracies, such as those of the pre-existing
> Samoan Department of Education have been swept aside or
> made impotent. . . . All have been made to conform to the
> central programme of televised instruction, and groups or in-
> dividuals who were dissident have been eliminated or neutral-
> ized. [31]

In contrast to this experience is the joint French-Nigerois effort,
established by statutory agreement, in which the television group was
originally placed "directly under the Ministry of Education."[32] A
UNESCO mission has reported this placement was in fact only nominal,[33]
and the project director has characterized the history of the effort as
"a closed operation, institutionally isolated from the traditional education authorities."[34] Under these circumstances the management and
production team was certainly far from outside interference while con-
ducting the experimental pilot project; yet it was in part a consequence
of this freedom that sufficient support for expanding the project was not
generated among the existing educational bureaucracy.

An additional perspective is gained by the direction taken in El Salvador. Although the original planning committee desired some type of
semiautonomous institute for operating instructional television, and one
removed from the bureaucracy of the Ministry of Education, the new
media group was placed within that ministry upon the insistence of for-

eign advisors and the subsequent appointment of a new minister favorably disposed to television. The USAID representatives believed

> that while freedom in the areas of equipment purchases and
> personnel recruitment would be desirable, close collabora-
> tion with the Ministry of Education was absolutely essential
> if ITV was to be integrated into the formal school system.
> For this reason, they argued that ITV should be developed
> within the Ministry of Education where planning could be
> done in concert with those Ministry officials who had juris-
> diction over Salvadoran schools. [35]

In the end, operating with strong government backing, the group was
able to function as a separate division within the existing structure and
was allowed "freedom and flexibility to develop in its own way." [36]

In Colombia, after earlier abortive efforts to get instructional television off the ground, [37] a semiautonomous institute (INRAVISION) was
formed to coordinate all television production, commercial as well as
educational. The basic intent of this approach was to alleviate one of
the predominant problems manifest during previous attempts at installing educational television—that is, the divided responsibilities that
existed between the Ministries of Education and Communication. Representatives of these ministries served on an advisory committee to the
new institute along with representatives of the general public. [38] To
date, rivalries still persist between the different ministries and
INRAVISION over responsibility for different aspects of programming,
supervision, and evaluation.

The particular approach taken in Israel provides yet another model.
The Instructional Television Center was first operated and funded by a
private trust under agreement with the government. After a three-year
pilot project, responsibility for educational television was transferred
to the Ministry of Education and Culture in 1969 for a two-year trial
period. At the close of this interim, the Israeli Parliament chose to
continue the effort as an integral part of the Ministry. [39] It is of interest to note that this decision to incorporate television into the existing
structure was reached despite strong urging from an international committee of experts to set up instead a national center to administer both
in-school and out-of-school uses of educational television and related
media. [40]

With the foregoing, a range of possible alternative placements for
the new media group have been provided. While we are reluctant to
state that one or another represents the best method for all countries
interested in implementing educational television, we conclude with a
very relevant comment drawn from a UNESCO report:

> In designing administrative machinery for the ETV program,
> a balance should be struck between a quick-reacting,

autonomous agency on the one hand, and a structure that is completely integrated into the existing administration on the other. The former, although probably more efficient and expeditious, runs the risk of not allowing the required new patterns of decision-making to be institutionalized and regularized. [41]

Control Over, Responsibility to, and Authority of the New Media Group

There is a broad array of approaches to the issue of control. A complicating factor is that organizational charts depicting assignations of authority and responsibility often fail to reveal the actual distribution and exercise of power that occurs in an institution or program. Thus we are able to provide summaries only in the broadest sense.

It would appear the most absolute control exercised by a media group on a broad scale occurred in American Samoa. The consultant team was granted almost unlimited powers over the integration of television in the school system. Although it has been said these broad powers were on occasion used in an autocratic manner, the role played by the consultants certainly has to stand as a key factor facilitating the total transformation of schooling in American Samoa. As an interim report commented, the consultants

> designed the system, determined the specifications for equipment, and supervised purchasing. They are fully responsible for technical personnel. While their role in administration is advisory by definition, with administrative responsibility lying with the governor's office, Governor Lee made the observation that as a rule the recommendations of the NAEB are supported by the governor.
>
> Thus the chief NAEB advisor, Vernon Bronson, has had very broad powers. Bronson's influence becomes rather awesome when one considers the fact that the governor's influence on Samoan policy is almost unlimited . . . and in the field of education, this influence has been delegated to Bronson and the NAEB. [42]

And, on a small scale at least, limited to the schools participating in the pilot project, the French-Nigerois media team exhibited a degree of control very similar to that exercised in American Samoa. This was evidenced by their complete domination over the curriculum content and the scheduling in the experimental schools. [43]

By the same right, we characterize the effort in El Salvador as one endowed with a high degree of control and responsibility. Perhaps, because of the intense commitment to television as the only possible solution, this should not be surprising. However, we do not mean to imply that difficulties over final responsibility for given actions did not arise. One area where sharp conflict was encountered on occasion was between the reform curriculum planners in the Ministry of Education and the television division's subject matter specialists. Resolution of the two factions' differences required continual direct intervention of the Minister of Education. [44] An example of the problems generated by this particular conflict occurred in 1969 with the preparation of the new eighth-grade curriculum, which

> occasioned renewed disputes between ITV personnel and Ministry curriculum writers. A draft of the new 8th grade program was sent to the Division of ITV for review, where it was rejected as inadequate by ITV's subject matter specialists, who then prepared their own version of an 8th grade curriculum. This was rejected, in turn, by the Ministry curriculum writers. The Minister was forced to intervene, and in October of 1969 the curriculum writers began from scratch to prepare an acceptable 8th grade curriculum.
>
> This situation, and a further delay caused by the need to seek approval of the program from the Curriculum Commission, meant that for a second time a new curriculum was not available for ITV until the eleventh hour, a circumstance which kept the inexperienced 8th grade production teams under enormous time pressure throughout 1970. [45]

In Israel, at least during the pilot project, we are presented with the clearest delineation of shared powers. The media group was operated and managed independently, while the Ministry of Education and Culture assumed responsibility for educational priorities, content, and liaison with the schools. [46] Nevertheless, under the new institutional arrangements, the "experimental approach which characterized early production has been sacrificed or limited in recognition of the needs for support and coordination from the Ministry. "[47]

And, finally, in Colombia at the initiation of the project in 1963, there were apparently two distinct organizational groups operating in tandem, the indigenous media group and the Peace Corps Volunteer group as advisors. It would appear that in what began as a partnership, many of the operational activities were, in fact, initiated and carried out by the Peace Corps[48] (a fact which undoubtedly played a significant role in the general deterioration of the project after the Peace Corps' departure). Additionally, the implementation problems were accentuated by the need to obtain legislative approval from each individual state (departamento). This action was necessary because, despite a national curriculum, it was the departments that controlled disbursement of funds, use of facilities, and commitment of local human resources. [49]

Availability of Existing Educational System Resources to the New Media Group

Our concern is with the commitments, if any, of the existing educational authorities to developmental and implementation efforts in the area of television. For example, in American Samoa, because the new media effort itself constituted the new education system, all resources of the old system were available.

However, Niger presents an altogether different picture. Because the new media group was operationally segregated, and very likely due to its innovation and far-from-traditional production work in curriculum areas, the group functioned only in a marginal sense as part of the larger system; there were few if any real ties with the instructional materials, teacher-training programs, or general administrative apparatus of the education system. [50] There are conflicting views as to why this happened. One view maintains that the official school system "never made room for the 'media,' nor would it accept a system of tele-education that so diminished its distinguishing characteristics of a traditional education."[51] The other view relates that the education establishment was given no "opportunity to acquire a commitment to ETV."[52] There is probably a great deal of truth in both statements.

Thus, if we view American Samoa and Niger as the extreme points in relation to this issue, the majority of case examples fall in between. Certainly the effort in El Salvador has been marked with the resources of the traditional structure from the beginning. Its integral link with the general education reform at the Plán Básico level is but one reason for this. Perhaps the best example of the commitment to educational television is contained in the observation that "Ministry of Education officials were justly credited with the project's successes but also held strictly accountable for its shortcomings."[53] In Israel, the entire effort has been characterized by a good working relationship with the Ministry of Education and Culture. In the words of one case writer:

> In most cases, the need to obtain ministerial approval for series as well as individual telecasts turned out to be a formality. Although Ministry officials could and did decide on priorities for new series, they have proved willing to accept suggestions and initiatives from the ITV staff.[54]

Although the instructional television team is no longer the independent agency of its early years, and is now quartered in a typical government bureaucracy and confronted by the administrative problems such presents, this same case writer feels that the good working relationship has endured.[55]

In Colombia, on the other hand, while the Ministry of Education has assured its firm commitment to the project in the agreements that led to Peace Corps and USAID support, it has been reported that the program

still had to do a certain amount of "missionary work" within
the established structure of the education system.

Studies by the evaluation team reported that the general
inertia within the system—reluctance to change schedules,
teaching methods, etc. —was one of the more serious obstacles to the program. [56]

This report reaches the conclusion that these factors contributed in part
to the Colombians' very conservative use of educational television for
formal schooling.

Summary

Our primary emphasis in this section has been that educational
planners should concentrate on developing an organizational plan for
implementing educational television, a plan uniquely suited to their
country's needs and to the particular administrative machinery within
which the new media group must operate. We have provided examples
of a variety of approaches to this issue, approaches that have had a
variety of consequences. What general conclusions, then, can be extracted from these examples?

In locating the new media group, the planner's aim should be to
provide it with sufficient flexibility for it to generate effective responses
to system goals and objectives. Such an aim usually requires that the
planner consider the projected relationship of the new media group to
the existing education structure and assess how best to begin integrating
the new with the old. A successful effort here can generally be characterized as one that is marked at an early stage by a definite commitment
to the project on the part of existing education authorities. This commitment, almost inevitably, must be manifest in something more than
just tacit approval or benign neglect; rather, resources, both physical
and human, must be made available by the education system. The total
integration of the new media will not be easily achieved. It represents
an intensive change process throughout the existing organization.
Nevertheless, by adapting and accommodating the old to the new, and,
just as important, the new to the old during the initial stages, this
change process can be facilitated.

Financial and Costing Characteristics

Costing characteristics are probably the most acute resource requirement related to the effective introduction of educational television.
The importance of this concern to the strength and vitality of the management team and its critical relevance to the "life" of the project are
undeniable. For, certainly, if the preliminary decision-making process

serves to establish the focal point of the project, then this consideration provides the "means" by which one is able to focus on meeting
system goals and objectives.

These financial characteristics require emphasis, despite the
abundance of external financing arrangements and the relative ease of
obtaining such funds that has marked the early history of educational
television in developing countries. Although these funding sources
have begun to tighten their purse strings as well as their criteria for
qualifying for financial support, it is still largely true that if you have
a demonstrated need and a carefully developed plan for attacking its
problems, some type of foreign financial assistance will most likely be
forthcoming. Thus our purpose here does not relate to the means of obtaining such funds; but rather to pointing out that, irrespective of the
actual source of initial funding, the educational decision maker can ill
afford to play down the short- and long-term financial implications generated by and accompanying a commitment to educational television.
Instead, we suggest that the planner who ignores these implications and
fails to make adequate preparation for coping with them, courts disaster
or, at best, ensures only a very low probability of success for the project.

How then might we characterize the pertinent factors in this area?
Perhaps the most beneficial starting point lies in stating unequivocally
that educational television itself is not likely to bring about a reduction in educational expenditures; rather as its use is expanded it will
typically yield a rising spiral of costs. [57] (Readers seeking a hard assessment of the "economic costs and returns to educational television"
are referred to Chapter 2 by Martin Carnoy.) Indeed, a Rand study of
Colombian ETV has reported a fact that is very probably universal to
all ETV applications. The report demonstrated that

> the cost of the technology is overwhelmed by the cost of the
> facilities and personnel needed to support the innovation
> throughout the system. In other words, the cost of the tech-
> nological innovation itself is low compared to the cost of
> upgrading the educational establishment to the degree needed
> to support the technology. . . . [58]

Consequently, it can be said there is an element of financial or
economic risk involved in an educational television venture. This risk
is directly associated with the software development and operating costs
as opposed to hardware costs. While the latter tend to be easy to identify and thus present known dollar quantities for the decision maker,
the former costs are very difficult to pin down, for there is a degree of
unpredictability inherent in them. And therein lies the risk. It cannot
be completely eliminated but it can be reduced if proper attention is
directed to these cost areas early in the project development stage.
Typically, external funds are channeled for hardware expenditures, but

the burden of meeting these associated costs is carried by the local resource mix. For example, in the case of Singapore, the UNDP invested
$2 million in hardware. Approximately 40 people are required to main-
tain and run the production and transmission facilities. Once external
funding ends, the question that arises is whether the country by itself
can afford to operate the ETV program.

Therefore, budgeting plans must be prepared to meet expenditures
created by specific needs related to the following:

Personnel Assignments

Expenditures for personnel include not only the salaries of individuals while they are operationally employed in the project, but also their
salaries when they are required to participate in-service training for
their new job roles. [59] As the El Salvador experience indicates, for instance, extensive teacher-training programs can represent a costly
decision, especially when classroom substitutes must be hired to replace teaching personnel being retrained for television. [60]

Supporting Study Materials

Education via television necessitates a large quantity of supporting
study materials for the students. (Israel, for example, produces and
prints 540,000 guides and workbooks annually. [61]) These costs are
associated with producing and printing, and also with disseminating
this related classroom material on a regular basis. As the project is
expanded, and the quality of the televised lessons is upgraded, these
costs should be expected to climb.

School Facility Changes

Although the construction of completely new school facilities that
accompanies the television effort in American Samoa[62] is probably not
typical, accommodating television in the classroom will most likely
necessitate some remodeling that has a definite cost. Cost requirements for providing an effective maintenance and repair unit for the
equipment in the field must also be taken into consideration.

In addition, and from a more expansive perspective of television
financial characteristics, decision makers must be concerned with the
adequacy of the funding sources, both internal and external, available
to educational television. Will these sources enable an efficient operation at the level of stated expectations? Decision makers must be
concerned with the solidity of these funding sources, especially those
external. How much is actually being committed from the outside? And
how long will it be available? Alternatively, they must be concerned
about the time when foreign participation ends and total funding of educational television derives from local resources.

In this respect, decision makers must ask if these local resources can ensure successful project continuation. If the answer to this question is "yes," they should seek to maintain and strengthen existing financial commitments. If it is "maybe," they should seek alternative funding from private or other governmental sources and perhaps consider various means of generating new income from the system itself (for example, in Israel, lesson guides and workbooks are sold to the local schools and students, program schedules are sold to the general public, television facilities are rented to commercial or private producers, and programs are produced for export). [63] If the answer is "no," decision makers should very likely begin reconsidering their country's commitment to educational television.

Facility and Equipment Characteristics

Our concern in this section is directed to the planning and administrative issues related to the facility and need characteristics exhibited by educational television systems. In general, our intentions are quite basic. We explore those particular considerations that merit attention prior to the decision to implement a television-based project, and we examine factors relative to that implementation. It should be noted beforehand that our discussion has two significant omissions. First, the relative merits of specific hardware configurations available for television production and transmission are not included. Except to point out the need for ensuring system technical compatibility during the acquisition of additional resources, this is not the place for an engineering excursion. And, second, the discussion of those facility and equipment needs inherent to establishing adequate on-site receiving centers or stations is delayed until the section on system delivery and reception characteristics; for we believe these matters fall properly within the area of operational control of system resources.

With respect to the preliminary facility and equipment concerns, USAID has suggested some minimum requirements that should exist prior to the new technology's introduction. Among these are reliable transmission facilities, adequate studio equipment to meet the planned levels of production quantity and quality, and enough television receivers to reach the designated audience of interest. [64]

The planning perspective provided by these minimum requirements is greatly facilitated if there are existing transmission facilities in the country. Here, information may be available to decision makers on the technical problems connected with broadcasting in a particular locale or region with certain environmental conditions (matters such as the existence of geographical limitations on obstacles, the power and technical service requirements for reliable equipment operation, and reception quality throughout the existing transmission range). This type of data yields a valuable insight into the limitations and feasibility of prospective reforms based on use of this technology.

Correspondingly, in areas where there are no existing facilities to serve as a model, obtaining a firm grasp of just what these minimum requirements entail can be difficult; for the planner must break his own ground. Such a process is typically initiated by contracting for a technical feasibility study. If the intended effort is deemed feasible, the planner must concentrate on what it will take—in money, manpower, and engineering skills—to create a reliable broadcasting capability.

If, however, existing broadcast facilities do exist and are utilized for educational television transmission (as in Colombia where because of its location in the Instituto Nacional de Radio y Televisión, the media team enjoyed access to the facilities), [65] the minimum requirements are usually met without great difficulty. On the other hand, where a reliable facility must be developed, the crucial factor other than the equipment itself is adequate site preparation. This is true whether an existing building is renovated or a specially designed building constructed. The key decision involves selecting the most suitable location for the facility and should be predicated on transmission requirements and the availability of adequate power supplies for proper equipment operation. If special equipment like air conditioners or cable-protection devices are necessary, they should be provided. Also, this site preparation effort might include the addition of some form of fire and theft protection.

All of this sounds simple enough, but ideals are often hard to attain. The problems encountered with the first site utilized in El Salvador demonstrate the difficulties that can result. The San Andre site suffered from inadequate power and water services, and loss of power was frequent. The severe maintenance problems created by the humidity necessitated the full-time operation of the air conditioner. On the whole, the work environment was poor. These were some of the factors that contributed to a site change early in the project. [66]

Finally, in returning to matters more specifically equipment oriented, we would recommend that some type of local control be present in this area as soon as possible. Traditionally, it has been left to the foreign adviser; but the necessity for future effective management in this area requires that local experience be developed. Such experience would not only bring with it a general awareness of equipment reliability, durability, and compatibility characteristics, but also knowledge of equipment and spare-parts purchasing procedures. In concluding, then, it is interesting to note that in El Salvador, where the training of local counterparts and their assumption of responsibility has been the rule and sets a standard for other projects, the results in this specific management area were apparently disappointing. [67]

OPERATIONAL CONTROL CONSIDERATIONS

The process by which the new media group utilizes available resources to attain system goals and objectives is an important area of
operational control. This area involves a day-to-day process of scheduling and controlling clearly designated individual tasks, and of ensuring that they are executed effectively and efficiently. Such coordination and control activities exert strain on the organization as a whole
and, more specifically, place a great deal of pressure on the project's
chief administrator. Accordingly, some degree of preparedness for responding to relatively straightforward, but time-consuming "emergen-
cies of the moment" as well as problems of deeper origin should hopefully be present in the management team.

The concerns of this section are presented in the belief that knowledge of key operating issues associated with the use of educational
television can contribute in part to building such preparedness. The
three general areas of discussion include specific characteristics related to delivery and reception of the educational "product," personnel
administration, and research and evaluation administration.

Delivery and Reception Characteristics

Among the important considerations affecting the successful delivery and reception of educational messages via this medium are the
following: physical and instructional logistics support of the study
centers; receiving equipment; maintenance requirements; and contact
with and effective use of teachers and/or monitors in the classroom.

Supporting the Study Center in the Field

In general, there must be systematic planning for adequate provision of services to schools or study centers. The goal should be to
establish truly functional learning centers. This requires, in addition
to television sets, the regular supply of any supplementary materials
related to the educational efforts, such as teaching guides and student
workbooks.

In relation to equipment needs, some remodeling of classrooms
might be necessary as in El Salvador,[68] or even total construction of
new facilities as in American Samoa. A further requirement for distant,
hard-to-reach sites might be the provision of spare receivers which
was done in Niger (although the replacement sets were not always in
working condition).[69] Additionally, if reliable electrical power is not
available, receivers might have to be operated on battery power; this
was necessary in Niger[70] and in the Ivory Coast.[71]

Equally important, the distribution of printed materials should be looked upon as a "subsidiary network of the total ETV system."[72] In some countries, this can be a very difficult task. However, the American Samoa experience has demonstrated that despite most "unusual problems of delivery," they can be conquered with the application of money and dedicated effort.[73]

Maintenance of Receiving Equipment

If the television equipment in the classroom operates only occasionally or not at all, the entire effort is, in effect, being undermined from within. Part of this problem can be alleviated by carefully instructing the classroom supervisors on how to properly handle the equipment. Yet its major significance lies in the need for an effective maintenance team operating in the field. This, in turn, necessitates trained technicians, available spare parts, and, if the area to be covered is large, some means of transportation. Most projects have attempted to provide this service through their own staffing arrangements working with a regular schedule for on-site maintenance checks; on the other hand, the government in the Ivory Coast contracted with a private company for field maintenance and repair.[74] Additionally, if direct communication channels between the media center and reception points are not available, it might be feasible to install some type of two-way radio link as was done in American Samoa.[75] This would enable immediate notification of special problems being encountered in the field (breakdowns, fire, theft, picture quality, and so on) to the national maintenance office and would also prove a valuable administrative tool.

Guidance for the Classroom Teacher

This concern also is of paramount importance if an effective learning context is to be created within the educational television system. The teacher or monitor cannot be left alone to cope with the new media. Rather, some type of link must be established with these individuals in order to provide them with sufficient preparation for using the new technology, to help them adapt to it, and above all, ensure their cooperation in the venture.

Accordingly, a thorough preliminary training process is desirable. The experience in the field in this regard covers a wide variety of approaches, from the project in Israel where teachers were carefully trained and shown televised lessons prior to their introduction in the classroom,[76] to Niger where "very little training was provided the classroom monitors."[77] Whatever the procedure utilized for preliminary training, it is imperative to maintain contact with the teacher once televised lessons are being transmitted. This has been recognized in principle in most projects. How it was attempted and with what degree of success, again varies widely. Peace Corps volunteers initially assumed

this role in Colombia although not as extensively as was planned. [78]
In Niger a member of the experimental team visited the classroom monthly to observe, to help the monitor, and to serve as a feedback channel.[79]

After the pilot project in Israel was taken over by the Ministry of Education and Culture, the task of working with the classroom teacher fell to the traditional "inspector" system of that ministry. Compared with the close attention paid the teachers in the early years, the result was not satisfactory. Inspectors often simply avoided the television classrooms. A new counselor system utilizing teachers with ETV experience was instituted to replace the inspectors. With this method of contact, because the counselors are more concerned with helping the individual teachers than with evaluating their performance and reporting such to the ministry, a more functional teacher-counselor relationship has been obtained. [80]

This same type of approach, that is, one oriented toward helping the teacher solve problems, was attempted in El Salvador. When the supervisory unit functioned out of the educational television group, matters proceeded quite well. However, when the unit was integrated into the existing educational supervisory system, problems arose. Overall, the switch in the supervisor's role from that of an inspector to a counselor proved very difficult and still remains to be fully achieved. [81]

Summary

In order to establish an environment conducive to learning at the system reception points, the educational decision maker must:
● adequately prepare site facilities,
● supply these facilities with receiving equipment,
● provide a reliable maintenance capability for that equipment,
● establish a reliable distribution system for supplementary television materials,
● provide preliminary training for the teachers who must use the system, and,
● maintain an ongoing "helping" relationship with those teachers.

Personnel Characteristics

The issue of personnel administration deserves a special section because of the very real problems it presents for those instituting educational television systems. Our intentions in this regard are three-fold:

First, to explore the various components of the production and management teams operating from the central production facility. Also provided will be some general commentary on the coordination needs of this central group.

Second, and closely related to the first, to assess the role of the foreign expert in the planning, operating, and management of the new media group, and most important of all, in training local counterparts for positions of responsibility.

Third, to analyze a typical manifestation of organizational stress that experience indicates might accompany the introduction of educational television. In general, difficulties relating to employee resistance and competence are common in any organizational change. Such difficulties can take on more substance if they occur among teachers in a national school system. We will try to demonstrate through a case study ways of dealing with this strain-producing issue.

On a general introductory level, however, there is a point that must receive some emphasis. As the technology of education progresses from blackboards to radio to television, not only is it accompanied by substantial cost increases, but its managerial complexity is magnified many times over. Human resources with sufficient managerial capacity to cope with this increasing intensification must be available. The most urgent need with regard to educational television is for sophisticated management personnel.

The New Media Team

Initially, the histories of new media projects demonstrate some common factors in this regard, one of which is that technical personnel alone seldom constitute an adequate staff for educational television. In trying to correct this situation, there are primarily two organizational responses. The first would be the assignment of at least one trained individual who has both operating experience with the existing educational structure and a highly developed understanding of the country's educational needs and overall development concerns. The alternative response would be to set up a project team staffed by individuals from other operating departments involved in the educational television effort.

In whatever way this is accomplished, it is extremely important to make careful selection of the project leader. Experience would seem to indicate that this individual's effectiveness will probably be more dependent upon his or her own reputation, professional skills, and the confidence he or she commands, than upon the particular location of the project team in the organizational hierarchy.

The organization within the project team itself is usually marked by a high degree of centralization. The group is typically small enough, despite the diversity of job characteristics, for this to prove the most feasible approach, especially in the beginning stages. Audiovisual personnel, production and support technicians, television teachers, subject-matter specialists, and sometimes educational psychologists, all must be coordinated to join efforts toward a common goal—the development, production, and transmission of high-quality media content. In general, management problems of varying significance should be expected if final control over any particular group of individuals on the team lies outside the new media group.

Utilization of the Foreign Expert

Perhaps the most pressing problem in developing a smooth and efficient organization revolves around the necessary level of expertise required of individuals who must function in certain job roles. Accordingly, the development of local talent, a factor crucial to the continuing success of the instructional television endeavor, is often espoused; and, unfortunately, almost as often, neglected. While most countries must depend heavily upon external expertise during the initial stages, such assistance must eventually end. When that day arrives there should be an indigenous staff available to assume effective control of the project. Except for the Salvadoran and Israeli experiences, the results from the field have been both disappointing and discouraging—disappointing in the sense that this issue is always a stated objective of foreign advising groups or agencies; and discouraging in the sense that so little movement in the direction of achieving this objective has been accomplished.

In establishing a national ETV system, a country may pursue a policy of "do-it-yourself" with minimal reliance on outside expertise. The opposite extreme would be those cases where a country invites international technical assistance agencies and more technologically advanced countries to set up the system, put it in operating condition, and then turn over a "completed product." One danger of the first option ("do-it-yourself") is that the quality of the programs will be so low as to negate positive educational outcomes—although this is not necessarily the case, as the strong commitment to achievement of program quality in Israel deomonstrates. The second option entails perhaps the more real dangers: (a) that local staff will not be sufficiently trained to run the system at any time in the near future—unless specific measures are undertaken to build up competencies in all areas with deadlines to be met; and (b) that a technological system out of tune with the general technological level and skills of a country has been unnaturally engrafted from abroad.

The general tendency has been to take the approach of letting foreigners establish and run the ETV system. The results have not been good. In American Samoa, as indicated previously, the consultant team was the dominant force in all areas of ETV implementation. Except in technical areas, there was a definite lack of qualified Samoan personnel.[82] In Niger, members of the French aid team held all positions of responsibility and there was no attempt to train Nigerois to assume these positions.[83] And in Colombia, although there were claims that the Peace Corps effort did develop self-sufficiency among the Colombians,[84] subsequent events made it difficult to give credence to this view.

Standing in direct contrast to these experiences is the project in El Salvador where the implementation process resided largely in local hands from the beginning. [85] Local counterparts were placed in operational roles as quickly as possible. This is not to deny the extensive use of foreign advisors; but it does appear that their use was confined more to the areas of advising and training than of actually operating or managing.

A prudent policy for systematic build-up of personnel competency at all levels from programming through production to maintenance and evaluation would consist of defining the skills, knowledge, and behaviors necessary to perform successfully in the different roles required to operate the ETV system. The ETV administrators then would determine where and how these competencies could be acquired—on-the-job through a variety of training activities, in different training programs within the country (outside the production facilities), through study and internship abroad, or, if commercial television facilities are available, through some arrangement for "practice" production as was done in El Salvador. [86] Prolonged formal study in an educational institution abroad in many cases may be less feasible and useful than a combined program of supervised internship and short-intensive courses designed to equip personnel with specific skills and knowledge.

Although outside technical assistance may be required for some time, foreign advisors' functions should be carefully defined and related to developing a high-quality ETV team of nationals. We strongly recommend that foreign technical assistance personnel should be utilized, if not required, to undertake training functions for host country nationals who will assume full responsibility for all major tasks within a reasonable period of time. In this regard, the host country ETV management team should not lose sight of the fact that it is these individuals—the native counterparts—who represent the greatest resource in the long run and, correspondingly, that the ultimate test of a successful educational television effort lies in their hands.

Teacher Resistance

By and large the predominant factor creating organizational stress in regard to the implementation of educational television has been teacher resistance. Whether this resentment or hostility results from fear and the job insecurity it creates or from a genuine inability to cope with a nontraditional teaching tool is immaterial; it is an issue to be confronted wherever instructional television is attempted. The touting of the new media as a "teacher replacement" certainly does not contribute to the search for a solution. Even if the media does replace teachers in the formal sense, there still must be a degree of cooperation from the supervisor or monitor in the classroom if effective learning is to occur. In this sense, it might be useful to point out that a hostile monitor is just as capable of sabotaging the endeavor as a hostile teacher.

An integral component of any plan to alleviate this problem and thereby minimize the stress it generates must include the adequate training and preparation of the teacher for use of television, a topic discussed in the previous section on delivery and reception. Often, however, this alone is insufficient, as the experience in El Salvador demonstrates. (There, despite extensive teacher training and preparation as part of the reform, teacher resistance increased. [87]) The reason for this is that there is more to organizational change than just the obvious technical aspect. There is also a social aspect. In this case, it involves the way in which teachers think television will affect their existing relationships to the school and to classroom learning.

Accordingly, this indicates that coping with teacher resistance will require more than simply providing technical instruction on how to use the new media in the classroom. Under existing conditions, teachers are not yet replaceable, and their role should be recognized as an integral factor in the success of the change process itself. The typical remedy offered the educational planner is to involve the teacher in the decision-making process as early as possible. When this prescription is followed, however, it is not always successful—for sometimes forgotten is the fact that participation consists of more than the mechanical act of being present; it is also a state of mind. Consequently, when a project is successful in limiting teacher resistance, it invites examination. And so we direct our attention to the Israeli ITV experience.

One of the reasons posited for Israel's relative success in minimizing teacher resistance to their program has been their "for the student . . . by the teacher" approach. An Instructional Television Centre document explains this procedure in the following manner:

> This stress on thoughtful utilization has become one of the strengths of ITC's [Instructional Television Centre's] "systems approach" to instructional television. Teachers are carefully trained and must see each TV lesson before using it in their classroom. Teachers are involved in all stages of program development, production, and evaluation (as are students), and as a result there is a high degree of acceptance for ITC's product. [88]

While this teacher participation could possibly have been a contributing factor to the low teacher resistance, its usefulness has been questioned by an independent case writer who found on occasion that:

> Telecasts already deemed inadequate may be shown at the training sessions in order to allow the teachers to "rip them apart" and feel gratified when they are changed or discarded. [89]

On the other hand, it seems likely the instructional objective underlying the implementation of television in the schools played an
equally important, if not larger, role in keeping teacher hostility at
tolerable levels. Under this objective television was never seen as
nor purported to be a means of replacing the teacher. Rather, the effort
has been characterized by a more modest intention of integrating televised instruction into the classroom in a manner that allowed both the
classroom and television teachers to do what they could do best. [90]
A reflection of this particular philosophy, and undoubtedly an additional
reason for the low level of teacher resistance engendered, can be seen
in the selection of the initial subject areas where television was to be
introduced. Concentration was first centered on those subjects where
teachers exhibited less expertise and encountered the most teaching
difficulties. [91]

Research and Evaluation Characteristics

We limit our comments in this section to general observations on
how research and evaluation relates to the overall administration framework of educational television systems. Perhaps the most important
point is that evaluation constitutes a basic tool in the decision-making
process. Its essence and purpose have been described in an Urban
Institute (Washington, D. C.) study as follows:

> The essence of evaluation is the comparison of both outcome—
> what happened that would not have happened in the absence
> of the program?—and relative effectiveness—what strategies
> or projects within programs work best?
>   The purpose of evaluation is to provide objective informa-
> tion to program managers and policy makers on the costs and
> effects of national programs and local projects, thereby as-
> sisting in effective management and efficient allocation of
> limited resources. [92]

Accordingly, we view a system effort in this direction as one primarily concerned with "control" (albeit control of things related to
learning). That is, within our administrative framework, we see research and evaluation as a necessary follow-up to the planning process
and as a logical corollary of the management control process: it exists
as a "check" on both past and current system performance, as a "gen-
erator" for future system performance standards, and as a "beacon" for
providing general direction to the project. As a control function, it
utilizes the educational objectives that should have emerged from the
planning process as the primary point of reference; it devises means

of obtaining accurate and timely measurement of system output; and it
contrasts current system performance in meeting those objectives with
a definite look to the future. From an administrative standpoint, the
salient concerns then become questions of how the administrative structure receives this information, how it reacts to it, how it proceeds to
formulate a response, and how it incorporates that response into its
programming.

The results reached by the research and evaluation team may indicate a variety of variables or problems for management's attention, but
for our purposes we can categorize them into ones pointing out either
favorable or unfavorable system performance. If the measurements indicate a favorable operation, we recognize the new media group's right
to a certain degree of self-satisfaction; yet, simultaneously, we would
issue a sobering note not to slacken the effort.

On the other hand, if the field measurements indicate something
is amiss, plausible reasons are many; therefore, the specific factors
contributing to the problem must be isolated before correction or revision is possible or attempted. One cause of an unfavorable performance report can lie with how realistic the measurement standard is.
Specifically, can that standard be reached? If not, perhaps the criteria
for measuring success need revision.

The negative rating usually implies the need for some alteration in
the actual method of producing the instructional television product. It
might even indicate problems more intrinsic to the learning process itself—that is, the inherent quality and purpose of the subject presentation. Just as teachers must reassess their methods of instruction if
students fail to learn, so must educational television. A typical solution might call for more personnel, or a reorganization of work loads,
or something further. Yet the common strand that runs through the organization reaction and response to this research and evaluation feedback is the importance of planning the indicated change as opposed to
responding to the feedback in a haphazard and unclear manner.

This is a costly, difficult, and sometimes frustrating process; and
it should be understood as such. Perhaps the best example of an operating and supposedly effective research and evaluation unit is found in
Israel. Its stated purpose is to provide data that is both "practical and
timely," while its goal of being "involved at every stage of development" has been generally met. [93] Yet there are problems that serve to
highlight the administrative difficulties that can plague even a well-
organized and efficient research and evaluation system. These difficulties are best described in an Instructional Television document, and
their statement stands as a very relevant note of conclusion to this
section:

> However, the pressures of production typically receive
> priority over the more measured and time consuming re-
> quirements of research and evaluation. R/E recommenda-

tions are not always acted upon and in some instances are
frustrated by lack of personnel and facilities—again a question of priorities. 94

In summary, we have attempted to emphasize the importance of
providing for and maintaining an evaluation unit as an integral part of
the administrative structure managing the educational television system. This is a need commonly recognized and often expressed and almost as often neglected during the start-up and implementation phases
of ETV. Yet, while we have suggested it is fundamental to the success
of the venture, it does not of itself guarantee success. In this respect,
it is useful to conclude with a comment drawn from the Urban Institute
study on federal evaluation policy:

Evaluation, of course, is no panacea. Formal evaluation
studies are and will continue to be only a part of the process of getting information relevant and necessary to decision making. Even if we had sound information on the
effectiveness of existing programs and projects in achieving a variety of public objectives, there would still remain
differences of opinion over how much effort to assign each
of the objectives. Nevertheless, more enlightened decisions can be made by those who get good information on
program effectiveness. 95

CONCLUSION

The purpose of this chapter has been to provide the present or potential ETV administrator with a broad administrative orientation to the
implementation of educational television systems. In developing this
orientation or frame of reference for viewing ETV, three general areas
for consideration were identified: planning, management control, and
operational control. Further, within each of these areas key issues
were illuminated. Related to planning considerations, the absolute
need for a coordinated and concentrated preliminary decision-making
approach was emphasized; while related to the management and operational control considerations, administrative and organizational characteristics of especially pertinent ETV issues were explored.

It is not our intent to close this chapter by reiterating the specific
points made or conclusions reached in the preceding pages. It might,
however, prove beneficial to give additional emphasis to the common
posture that has governed our examination of those issues presented—
that is, our attention has been directed to the sometimes unique administrative and organizational needs that these selected ETV issues generate for the educational decision maker. Our ultimate concern has been

with providing a basis for improving the rationality of the ETV administrative decision-making machinery. Simultaneously, since educational decisions are not reached independently but rather as a part of some larger scheme, we have recognized that political and bureaucratic decisions can often overwhelm or at least greatly constrain administrative rationality with respect to educational television systems.

We make no pretense of having presented an all-inclusive discussion. We do feel, however, that the administrative fundamentals inherent to the formulation of a sound policy encompassing the design, implementation, and operation of ETV have been presented. Yet, we hasten to point out, these fundamentals alone will prove insufficient in the end. Therefore, we would expect our readers to add their own particular knowledge about and experience with the educational situation in their countries. The resulting mix of general fundamentals utilized in concert with specific awareness of local conditions hopefully will enable the educational administrator interested in ETV to explore more extensively and to assess more accurately the applicability of the new media in a given circumstance.

NOTES

1. From the Foreword to Wilbur Schramm et al. (eds.), The New Media: Memo to Educational Planners. (Paris: UNESCO, IIEP, 1967).

2. For a more extensive treatment of this framework, see: Robert N. Anthony, Planning and Control Systems: A Framework for Analysis (Boston: Division of Research, Graduate School of Business Administration, Harvard University, 1965).

3. Harold Koontz and Cyril O'Donnell, Principles of Management, 3rd ed. (New York: McGraw-Hill, 1964), p. 205.

4. Graham T. Allison, Essence of Decision: Explaining the Cuban Missile Crisis (Boston: Little, Brown and Company, 1971), p. 30.

5. The Ivory Coast Republic, Education by Television, 1968-1980, Vol. 3 (Ministry of National Education, 1968), p. 5.

6. John K. Mayo and Judith A. Mayo, An Administrative History of El Salvador's Educational Reform, Research Report No. 8 (Stanford, California: Institute for Communication Research, Stanford University, 1971), p. 7.

7. Ibid., p. 8.

8. Lord Evans et al., The Future of Instructional Television and Related Media in Israel, A Proposal Submitted to Hanadiv by the Committee Set up to Enquire into the Continuation of the Instructional Television Trust (ITT) Project (London: 1967), p. 7.

9. From a copy of a speech delivered by Leo H. Larkin, S.J., Director of the Center for Educational Television, on February 24, 1971, at Radio Veritas in Quezon City, Philippines, to the representatives of UNDA in Southeast Asia, p. 3.

10. Jack Lyle, "La Telescuela Popular Americana of Arequipa, Peru, " in Schramm et al. , eds. , New Educational Media in Action: Case Studies for Planners, Vol. 1 (Paris: UNESCO, IIEP, 1967), p. 79.
11. Wilbur Schramm, "Educational Television in American Samoa, " in Schramm et al. , eds. , New Educational Media in Action: Case Studies for Planners, Vol. 1, op. cit. , p. 16.
12. The Ivory Coast Republic, op. cit. , p. 65.
13. Mayo and Mayo, op. cit. , pp. 6-12.
14. Schramm, "Educational Television in American Samoa, " op. cit. , pp. 14-16.
15. Ibid. , pp. 14-15.
16. Mayo and Mayo, op. cit. , pp. 4-5.
17. Harold Goldstein, "Manpower Requirements and Educational Organization, " Organizational Problems in Planning Educational Development (Paris: OECD, 1966), p. 49.
18. Schramm et al. , The New Media: Memo to Educational Planners op. cit. , p. 161.
19. The Ivory Coast Republic, op. cit. , pp. 62-63.
20. Naomi E. Kies, "Instructional Television in Israel, " in Paul Kimmel et al. , ITV and Education of Children of Migrant Farm Workers, Indians, and Inner-City Poor: Cross-Cultural Comparisons of International Uses of Media, Vol. II--Case Studies (Washington, D. C. : U. S. Department of Health, Education and Welfare, 1971), p. 62.
21. USAID, "Draft Working Paper on Educational Technology, " (Washington, D. C. : 1971), p. 12.
22. Schramm et al. , The New Media: Memo to Educational Planners, op. cit. , p. 101.
23. Kimmel et al. , op. cit. , p. iv.
24. USAID, op. cit. , p. 12.
25. The Ivory Coast Republic, op. cit. , p. 19.
26. Wilbur Schramm and John K. Mayo, "Notes on Case Studies of Instructional Media Projects—A Working Paper" (Stanford, California: Institute for Communication Research, Stanford University, 1971), p. 39.
27. Academy for Educational Development, Educational Technology and the Developing Countries (Washington, D. C. : Agency for International Development, 1972), p. 85.
28. The Ivory Coast Republic, op. cit. , p. 60.
29. USAID, op. cit. , p. 13.
30. Gene W. Dalton et al. , Organizational Change and Development (Georgetown, Ontario: Irwin-Dorsey Limited, 1970), p. 3.
31. Schramm, "Educational Television in American Samoa, " op. cit. , p. 21, quoting from Block report.
32. Robert LeFranc, "Educational Television in Niger, " in Schramm et al. , New Educational Media in Action: Case Studies for Planners, Vol. 2 (Paris: UNESCO, IIEP, 1967), pp. 16-17.
33. The Ivory Coast Republic, op. cit. , p. 20.

34. Max Egly, "The End of a Period for Tele-Niger (1964-1971): Some Observations for Future Projects" (Paris: Director of Télé-Niger Project, 1972), pp. 11-12. Mimeographed.

35. Mayo and Mayo, op. cit., p. 15.

36. Academy for Educational Development, op. cit., p. 66.

37. See Jack Lyle, "Colombia's National Programme for Primary-Level Television Instruction," in Schramm et al., New Educational Media in Action: Case Studies for Planners, Vol. 2 (Paris: UNESCO, IIEP, 1967), pp. 51-54.

38. Margaret B. Carpenter et al., Analyzing the Use of Technology to Upgrade Education in a Developing Country (Santa Monica, California: The Rand Corporation, 1970), p. 45.

39. Instructional Television Centre, "Instructional Television in Israel: Some Facts and Figures" (Ramat Aviv: 1971), pp. 1-24.

40. Evans et al., op. cit., p. 12.

41. The Ivory Coast Republic, op. cit., p. 94.

42. Schramm, "Educational Television in American Samoa," op. cit., p. 36, quoting from the Block report.

43. The Ivory Coast Republic, op. cit., p. 8.

44. Mayo and Mayo, op. cit., pp. 42-45.

45. Ibid., pp. 42-43.

46. Instructional Television Centre, op. cit., p. 1.

47. Kies, op. cit., p. 67.

48. George Comstock, The Peace Corps Volunteer and Achieving Educational Change with the New Media (Santa Monica, California: The Rand Corporation, 1969), p. 5.

49. Carpenter et al., op. cit., p. 46.

50. The Ivory Coast Republic, op. cit., p. 20.

51. Egly, op. cit., p. 12.

52. The Ivory Coast Republic, op. cit., p. 20.

53. Mayo and Mayo, op. cit., p. 73.

54. Kies, op. cit., p. 66.

55. Ibid., p. 68.

56. Lyle, op. cit., pp. 72-78.

57. Academy for Educational Development, op. cit., p. 20.

58. Carpenter et al., op. cit., p. v.

59. The Ivory Coast Republic, op. cit., p. 95.

60. Mayo and Mayo, op. cit., p. 59.

61. Instructional Television Centre, op. cit., p. 12.

62. Schramm, "Educational Television in American Samoa," op. cit., p. 17.

63. Kies, op. cit., p. 74.

64. Academy for Educational Development, op. cit., pp. 27-28.

65. Lyle, op. cit., p. 68.

66. Mayo and Mayo, op. cit., p. 22.

67. Ibid., p. 21.

68. Ibid., p. 48.

69. The Ivory Coast Republic, op. cit., p. 14.

70. Ibid.

71. Emile G. McAnany, "Ivory Coast ETV Project: Consultation Report" (Institute for Communication Research, Stanford University, 1972), p. 4.

72. The Ivory Coast Republic, op. cit., p. 97.

73. Ibid., p. 60.

74. McAnany, op. cit., p. 3.

75. The Ivory Coast Republic, op. cit., p. 63.

76. Instructional Television Centre, op. cit., p. 7.

77. The Ivory Coast Republic, op. cit., p. 62.

78. Comstock, op. cit., pp. 13-17.

79. The Ivory Coast Republic, op. cit., p. 63.

80. Instructional Television Centre, op. cit., p. 7.

81. Mayo and Mayo, op. cit., pp. 51-58.

82. The Ivory Coast Republic, op. cit., p. 65.

83. Ibid., pp. 65-66.

84. Comstock, op. cit., p. 21.

85. Mayo and Mayo, op. cit., p. 24.

86. Ibid., p. 11.

87. Academy for Educational Development, op. cit., p. 66.

88. Instructional Television Centre, op. cit., p. 7.

89. Kies, op. cit., p. 66.

90. Instructional Television Centre, op. cit., p. 8.

91. Ibid., p. 16.

92. Joseph S. Wholey et al., Federal Evaluation Policy: Analyzing the Effects of Public Programs (Washington, D.C.: The Urban Institute, 1970), pp. 19-20.

93. Instructional Television Centre, op. cit., p. 8.

94. Ibid., p. 19.

95. Wholey et al., op. cit., pp. 22-23.

4

RECONSIDERING THE USE
OF TELEVISION FOR
EDUCATIONAL REFORM:
THE CASE OF EL SALVADOR
Henry Ingle

Over the past two decades, education increasingly has become the largest item in the national budgets of many countries. Government officials and policy makers emphasize educational reform, both in the formal and nonformal sectors, as a key to national development. Lack of trained manpower, it is argued, constitutes the critical bottleneck to industrialization and modernization. Demand for education also has been sparked by societal pressures for better employment opportunities. The widespread expectation exists that more years of schooling will increase an individual's income-earning capacity and life chances. Thus, whatever the economic arguments against the allocation of scarce resources to education, the political and social forces in favor of such extension are overwhelming.

International funding agencies have both responded to and stimulated the demand for education by providing countries with varying types of loans, grants, and technical assistance. In recent years, a number of these efforts have involved the use of broadcast communication media to reach not only in-school populations but to provide alternative and continuing learning opportunities to out-of-school populations. One such example of the introduction of a new educational technology, television, is to be found in the Central American country of El Salvador.

This chapter will examine the Salvadoran Educational Reform and the changes, both expected and unexpected, which the use of instructional television (ITV) appears to have effected. First, I will review the distinctive features of the ITV project, the history and background of the Reform and its major elements. Then, I shall briefly present the major findings of the extensive research and evaluation effort that was undertaken from 1968 through 1973 on the project's use of instructional television. Concomitantly, I shall examine the expectations of societal change envisioned by the leaders of the Salvadoran Reform as a result of setting in motion basic changes in the educational system with the

introduction of television. I shall argue that the expected outcomes of
the Reform—linking the education sector with the socioeconomic development thrust of the country—largely were left to chance on the assumption that things would take their natural course. It was assumed graduates from the Reform program would form a pool of technically trained
manpower that would quickly stimulate needed growth in the economic
and job-market sectors. Unfortunately, this has not happened. I believe this can be attributed to the fact that the intensive effort for
reform in the educational sector was not paralleled by similar attention to complementary social-service and employment sectors of the
society. Although television was applied in a systematic way as part
of a larger effort for change, integrating the best theory and practice
to bring about qualitative changes and quantitative expansion in the
educational system, the social and economic sectors of El Salvador
were left largely unaltered. The agricultural, labor, health, and nutrition sectors of the Salvadoran nation were neither given adequate attention nor related in an integral way to the Educational Reform. These
were the sectors most in need of alteration—the sectors that television
and the Reform jointly were supposed to affect. To date, changes in
the educational system have not greatly affected life outside the classroom. Thus, rather than bringing about one of the government's principal goals, the restructuring of the existing economic and social structures of the country, the Reform appears, instead, to be reinforcing the
status quo.

The Salvadoran experience demonstrates the need to give closer
attention to the relationship between an educational system and the
society it serves and the effects of schooling on individual achievement
and national development. Otherwise, educational change isolated from
the mainstream of development can adversely affect both the individual
and the collective advancement of the most disadvantaged sectors of
the society.

THE DISTINCTIVE FEATURES OF ITV
IN EL SALVADOR

El Salvador's use of television for education is unique in many ways
from the experience of other developing nations.[1] Unlike other major
experiences with instructional television, the El Salvador project grew
out of development problems diagnosed by the country's own educational
planners. That is, before television was advanced as an element of the
Reform, Salvadoran educational planners already were grappling with
possible solutions to the expansion and upgrading of their educational
system. Thus, educational problems that seemingly defied the conventional solution of more teachers and more classrooms had been identified
and alternative nonconventional solutions were being advanced prior to
the use of television technology.

Another feature of the Reform was the systematic and controlled manner in which television technology was introduced and developed as one element in a comprehensive national plan for educational improvement. In addition to the use of television, the Reform involved virtually all major aspects of instruction: curriculum, teaching methodologies, evaluation and promotion policies. Particular attention was given to in-service training of teachers so that they could work with these changes. All of these activities were carefully timed and set in motion within the short span of five years, under the administration of one government.

Commitment to educational reform and the use of instructional television has been a salient feature of the past two governments. Although many of the individuals who pioneered the Reform have left government service, the basic program continues. Such continuity is unique among national programs for educational reform based on television.

Televised instruction—unlike the case in many other counties— was carried out in the country's own national language (Spanish) and within the country's own educational perspectives. Furthermore, El Salvador relied on foreign experts to a lesser extent than have other countries using educational television, and the advisers functioned as advisers—they never assumed decision-making positions as happened in Niger, American Samoa, Colombia, and the Ivory Coast. Thus major decisions for planning and operating the television project (and indeed the Reform itself) were in the hands of Salvadorans. Over the past eight years, some 50 advisers have been associated with the Reform in areas such as school supervision, curriculum development, teacher training, testing and measurements, program production, graphics, film, instructional materials, and research and evaluation. Their stay in the country varied from two weeks to as long as 4.5 years, with the average tour of duty being 18 months.

In addition, the project in El Salvador profited from extensive empirical research over the first five years of its life. Research and evaluation were institutionalized as integral aspects of the educational process. As a result, the El Salvador experience is perhaps the best documented and studied effort to date on the use of educational television in a developing country. *

---

*The research was completed under the general supervision of Dr. Wilbur Schramm in cooperation with four staff members of the Institute for Communication Research during the years 1968-73. The four staff members were Emile G. McAnany, John Mayo, Robert Hornik, and Henry T. Ingle. Yolanda Rodriquez Ingle and Judith A. Mayo also were members of the team and conducted specialized observation studies.

BACKGROUND AND DEVELOPMENT OF THE REFORM

Problems

El Salvador is the smallest and most densely populated mainland country in the Western Hemisphere. It has a land area of about 150 by 75 miles, 95 percent of which already is under cultivation, and a rapidly expanding population of about 400 inhabitants per square mile. [2]
Mainly an agrarian society, with a severly limited supply of natural resources, El Salvador faces a broad range of development problems common to other countries: widespread poverty, malnutrition, poor health care, a high population growth rate estimated at 3.3 percent per year, limited arable land, concentration of wealth in relatively few hands, and a dwindling market for its agricultural and manufactured goods. Faced with these conditions, Salvadoran planners in the mid-1960s realized that they could not continue to rely on the agrarian economy, with coffee as a main cash crop, if the country were to progress and provide a better life-style for all its people.
These factors prompted the government of El Salvador to concentrate its efforts on improving its greatest single resource—its people. Educationally El Salvador faced difficulties that were not unlike those of other countries. These included a high rate of illiteracy (56 percent); a high dropout rate (70 to 90 percent); an outdated, rote-learning curriculum; and poorly trained teachers. In the 1960s, only one child in six who entered primary school ever completed basic education.
Educational reform was at the heart of El Salvador's development policy. One of the chief assumptions behind the entire Reform was that the country's major bottleneck to development was the lack of a middle-level technical manpower. A readily available pool of middle-level trained manpower became the government's objective. With such a labor pool, government planners felt that foreign industry and related commercial enterprises would be attracted to El Salvador. The ensuing industrial development would help to alleviate some of the socioeconomic problems faced by the country's growing population and the almost total dependence on an agrarian source of livelihood.

Educational Policies

In July 1967, President Sánchez Hernández appointed a new minister of education, Walter Béneke. The new minister (a former diplomat and businessman) launched into a five-year educational reform program by proposing the reorganization of nearly every educational function, beginning with the Ministry of Education itself. [3]

Under the motto "Efficiency, Quality, Sufficiency, " program objectives were spelled out and phases of program development were identified and arranged in a timetable. Top priorities were the reorganization of the Ministry of Education; the strengthening of teacher training; the development of a modernized curriculum; and the creation of a Division of Instructional Television within the Ministry. These four major projects were to form the base from which the educational reform program would proceed.

Educational television had been under serious consideration in El Salvador ever since 1960. Prior to assuming the leadership of the Ministry of Education, Walter Béneke had been El Salvador's ambassador to Japan. He was impressed by the use of television within that country's educational system. At Béneke's urging, a team of engineers from the Japan Broadcasting Corporation (NHK) visited El Salvador in 1962 to investigate the feasibility of using educational television in El Salvador. The Japanese confirmed the Salvadorans' belief that the small size, the topographical conditions, and the linguistic unity of the country made educational television highly feasible. The well-developed highway system and the high degree of rural electrification, both unusual for a developing country, facilitated national coverage. However, the investment needed for equipment, production, transmission, and reception of ETV seemed very high. The project was temporarily set aside as uneconomic. Nonetheless, late in 1963, the then president, Julio Adalberto Rivera, established a National Educational Television Commission to recommend a national plan for ITV by 1964. The Commission met sporadically and little progress was made until late 1964. At that time, a Department of Educational Television was created in the Ministry of Education, and over the next two years, when Ambassador Béneke returned from his stay in Japan and was appointed chairman of the Commission, the group began to act in defining the role ITV might play in El Salvador. [4]

By the end of 1966, the Television Commission had debated the possible uses of television and had reached some important decisions. A case was made for extending education with television to those adults and children who had never finished primary school. But the scheme that attracted most support was to use television to upgrade the quality of instruction and to increase enrollments in grades seven through nine, later known as the Third Cycle. Inadequate education at this level was seen as the major bottleneck to development, since it restricted the quantity and quality of middle-level personnel for industry. Fewer than 35 percent of the students in the sixth grade continued into the following year. While there were a number of factors associated with this low continuation rate, the principal reason appears to have been the limited capacity of the education system to absorb more students. In addition to this quantitative problem, inadequately trained teachers at this level contributed to poor quality of instruction.

While serious, these problems paled in comparison with those of primary education. The amount of resources required to combat the high dropout rates and other difficulties in the elementary grades (grades one through six) exceeded the capacity of the Salvadoran economy. El Salvador's leaders felt that the problems at grades seven through nine could be approached more easily. The smaller number of students and schools provided more favorable conditions for controlled experimentation. Reforms successfully tested at this level could then be transferred on a step-by-step basis to the more numerous population of elementary-school students if circumstances permitted.

A second point of consensus was the fact that the country had neither the economic resources nor the trained technicians to embark upon a massive ITV project. Foreign technical and financial assistance was to be sought for the project from the outset.

During this period, contact was made with the Japanese, the U. S. Agency for International Development (USAID), UNESCO, and the World Bank. A breakthrough in the planning came at the conference of Western Hemisphere presidents at Punta del Este in 1967. At this conference, President Lyndon Johnson invited a Latin American country to participate with United States assistance in an educational reform program in which television would be a major component for spreading the process of educational change. Further, he suggested that this project might serve as a model for other Latin American nations. Salvadoran leaders seized the opportunity. Thus it was the possibility of technical assistance for a television project that finally determined the decision to embark on the Educational Reform.

By April of 1967, a team of American experts under contract to the National Association of Educational Broadcasters (NAEB) and USAID was in El Salvador to conduct another feasibility study. It should be noted that no systematic "needs assessment," as described by Perron and Kirst in Chapter 3, was undertaken. And there was little, if any, consideration of the use of alternative media such as radio. Foreign experts simply confirmed previous opinions on the suitability of educational television for El Salvador. They recommended that El Salvador apply educational television on a large scale. The NAEB team felt that television should be aimed at primary education, reasoning that there were 13. 9 times as many students in the primary grades as there were in the Third Cycle. The Salvadorans, however, still advocated using television in the Third Cycle in the belief that better education in these grades would quickly lead to a better-trained labor force, which, in turn, would attract foreign investment.

What followed in El Salvador is now history. While touching all levels of the school system (grades one through nine), the Reform's primary emphasis was on the seventh, eighth, and ninth grades, as the Salvadorans had wished.

The Reform was introduced on a pilot basis to about 32 seventh-grade classrooms in 1969 and expanded yearly so that by 1973 virtually all seventh-, eighth- and ninth-grade classes in the country were participating in the Reform and receiving televised instruction. In 1966, before the Reform, there were fewer than 22,000 students enrolled in public seventh, eighth, and ninth grades. These students, plus some 23,000 other private-school students, constituted only 22 percent of the relevant age group (age 13-15).

By 1973, more than 65,000 students were enrolled in public junior high schools. Counting an additional 26,000 students from the private schools who also were touched by the Reform and ITV, the seventh-through-ninth-grade enrollment was 34 percent of the total number of school-age children. It should be noted that the expanded enrollments were largely accounted for by students from poorer and rural homes coming to junior high school for the first time, and by an increasing proportion of girls who previously stayed at home after finishing grade six, rather than continuing to grades seven through nine.

In 1973, the Ministry of Education issued a new five-year educational plan, which included the extension of the use of television to the Second Cycle of the primary grades (four, five, and six); the use of TV for teacher in-service training at the primary grade level; and TV for educational programs directed to out-of-school populations.

Since 1974, educational television services have been expanded to reach grades four and five, teaching four subject areas (Spanish, mathematics, science, and social studies) to roughly 50,000 students. These estimated 50,000 students along with the 65,000 now receiving televised instruction at grades seven, eight, and nine form a sizable audience.

The same experimental format used in the introduction of television for grades seven through nine has been used in grades four through five; that is, a sample of experimental classrooms (40) were selected at the fourth grade in 1974 to receive televised instruction. After one year of experimentation, TV was extended to all fourth grades and the experimental 40 classrooms were followed into fifth grade. In 1976 they will be followed into the sixth grade as TV is extended to this level.

ELEMENTS OF THE REFORM

The technology of instructional television was perhaps the most visible and highly publicized element of El Salvador's educational reform. Television, however, represented but one part of a more fundamental and comprehensive program of change affecting nearly every aspect of the elementary and secondary school system in the country.

Under the Reform the curriculum was completely revised and modernized for grades one through nine, and for grades ten through twelve (the new diversified technical career studies, Bachillerato Diversificado). The bureaucracy and administrative structures of the Ministry of Education were reorganized and centralized; and a planning office was established within the Ministry to undertake long-term planning of the Reform and to monitor the current efforts. The system of school supervision was reformed, making the supervisor less of an inspector and more of a pedagogical resource person to the teacher. Tuition was eliminated for grades seven to nine where the Reform initially was concentrated, and double sessions (morning and afternoon) were instituted to handle the flood of new students. A liberalized student-evaluation system established new, relevant criteria for student grading; and revised promotion practices helped decrease the number of student repeaters and dropouts.

As a major component, and as the catalyst for the rest of the Reform, television was introduced to carry the core of the curriculum. Each week in each of five subject areas (English, math, Spanish, social science, and natural science) from two to four 20-minute programs were broadcast. Each ITV lesson was designed to be preceded by ten minutes of motivation and followed by 20 minutes of reinforcement; these activities to be conducted by the classroom teacher. To enhance further the effective utilization of the telelesson, each television production team prepared printed classroom teacher guides and individual student workbooks, which stated the specific behavioral objectives of the lessons and the criteria to be applied in determining successful mastery.

The successful implementation of the Reform hinged upon the motivation and competencies of teachers. Substantial training was given to each teacher before he or she was assigned to a classroom receiving televised instruction. In the first year of the program, this training consisted of an intensive three-month course at the Alberto Masferrer Normal School at San Andres, on the outskirts of the capital city of San Salvador. The first retraining course began in November 1968, and ended just before the new school year began in February 1969. Thereafter, annually 250 teachers undertook a full year's retraining course at San Andres prior to being assigned to classrooms during the second, third, fourth, and fifth years of the Reform program. Most of these were experienced teachers who were withdrawn from classroom service for a year to study the substance of the new curriculum, the methods of teaching with television and new teaching-learning and evaluation methodologies in their subject area. As far as is known, no other instructional television project has ever put so much emphasis on retraining its classroom teachers in advance of their new assignment.

Finally, it also should be noted that the entire ITV production-programming staff in El Salvador—from the cameraman to the producer, director, and lesson preparation specialist—were retrained in-service to assume the new responsibility of operating an ITV facility.

In summary, the Reform's major components were a new curricula, retrained teachers, student workbooks, teacher guides, and instructional television—all combined within the context of a system for educational improvement. The technology of television, therefore, was not

introduced as an appendage to the existing system; the system was
revamped along with the introduction of television.

In order to assess the impact of the technological changes that
were taking place, a resident research-evaluation team from the Institute for Communication Research at Stanford University, working with
Salvadoran counterparts, undertook to monitor the overall Reform and,
in particular, the use of television. [5] The research was funded by the
Bureau for Technical Assistance of USAID, which in combination with
UNESCO, the World Bank, and the Organization of American States,
were the principal donor agencies supporting the Reform program.

The research data gathered by the evaluation team served the
twofold purpose of (1) providing feedback to the leaders of the Reform
so that they could better understand what was happening and quickly
readjust the system when necessary; and (2) providing important information to international donor agencies and to planners in other countries with interest in the use of technology to improve education.

Stanford's participation in the evaluation of the El Salvador ITV
system began in 1968—six months before the Reform actually went into
the classrooms—and ended in August 1973 with the publication of the
last of 20 research reports.

While it is still premature to talk about the total impact and effectiveness of the Reform, and to say that television has revolutionized
the educational system, there is evidence of considerable change in
important sectors of the system. The following section serves to highlight the relevant findings and policy implications of the project during
the period 1969-73. The section covers the economic costs of the reform, student learning and attitudes, teacher opinions and reactions,
and the overall effects of the changes introduced into the educational
system.

Economic Costs of the Reform

The introduction of instructional television as part of the Reform
has been accompanied by an increase in the number of students in each
class and an increase in teacher classroom hours, with a less than
proportional increase in teacher pay. This effectively has lowered the
cost per student of the classroom teacher. Thus, ITV has been essentially an add-on cost. That is, ITV has been used along with teachers
in the classroom, which requires the expense of maintaining a school
building and paying a classroom teacher's salary as well as the expense

of operating and transmitting televised instruction. However, when enough students are enrolled, the total per-student cost of classroom teaching plus television actually will be lower than what the cost would have been within the traditional system. In a year in which 60, 000 students were using ITV, the per-student cost of ITV plus the classroom teacher was estimated to be U. S. $47. This was lower than the $52 estimated per pupil if ITV had not been used, class size not increased, and teacher load not enlarged. Using some rough enrollment estimates of the rate of expansion over the first 25 years of the project, the average yearly cost per student over that period has been estimated at about $13. 50. [6] And assuming that on the average, each student watches 13 ITV programs a week for 38 weeks, this works out to a cost of about 8. 2 cents per student per hour of ITV. The average annual production cost of an ITV program (including the cost of videotape) has been calculated at $283. [7] Since the average audience size for any program is approximately 11, 000 students, the production cost of putting one hour of ITV in front of one student is approximately 7. 7 cents. These figures compare favorable with the per hour operating cost of Third Cycle education without television, which is 10. 7 cents, if one assumes an average of 25 hours of class each week for 38 weeks.

However, under present procedures in El Salvador, the classroom teacher forms an integral part of the instructional process and is not doing something else while the television lesson is in progress. Therefore, the cost of instructional television, no matter how economically the ITV is operated, will always constitute an add-on cost. And as long as instructional television is treated as an add-on cost, it must be defended as a part of the mix of learning opportunities, along with the classroom teacher, the textbooks, programmed instruction, films, or whatever is used. As such, it is worth 8 cents per student per hour. [8] It also should be noted that the costs of ITV in El Salvador have never surpassed 5 percent of the Ministry of Education's budget. And at present, the costs of ITV amount to less than one-quarter of the total costs of the Educational Reform, which, as of 1973, totaled almost $30 million, or 75 million Salvadoran colones.

Over its first ten years of life, the television project in El Salvador has been calculated by the Stanford research group at a total cost of $10. 8 million. Of that money, 73 percent will have gone into program production costs, 7 percent into transmission, and 20 percent into reception. [9]

In other countries, the percentage of money spent on transmission and reception costs has been much higher in relation to production costs. However, because of the small land area of El Salvador, its territory can be covered with less transmission expense than would be the case in any of the other American republics, and most of the other countries in the world. In addition, El Salvador has an unusually well-developed road system and degree of rural electrification for a developing country. Both of these factors contribute to lower receiver

installation and maintenance costs. Any school in the country can be
reached by three hours' automobile travel. With electricity present,
there is no need for costly generators or batteries, which have affected
reception costs in other developing country educational television
projects.

The major questions lingering on with respect to the use of television in the El Salvador Reform program concern the cost of attempting
a national reform and its effects on the country's development.

Most of the major national ETV projects involving core instruction
have relied on substantial financial resources from outside. In the
case of El Salvador, total outside funding and assistance has been
valued at about $5 million, [10] the bulk of which came from USAID for
technical advisory assistance and the initial equipment investment
costs.

It is important to note, however, that in spite of large contributions
from abroad, the Salvadorans will have paid the majority of the costs
of the educational television project in their country. Through 1973, the
Salvadoran government will have paid outright for over 50 percent of
the costs of the ITV system. In addition, El Salvador will shoulder the
burden of an additional 30 percent of the ITV costs through foreign loans.
Only one-fifth of the costs of ITV in El Salvador, therefore, can be accounted for in terms of foreign grants and donations. Indeed, over the
first five years, when total foreign financial contributions have been
$3,790,000, the Salvadoran government will have paid $7,052,000 or
nearly 1.9 times as much as the foreign donors. Furthermore, in the
years after 1976, the entire costs will be born by the Salvadorans. In
1980, repayments of loans to foreign agencies must begin. In short,
therefore, the financing of ITV in El Salvador, like its planning and
programming, has been very much a Salvadoran endeavor.

The Salvadoran expense in the ITV project, however, does not
totally represent new expenditures, which would not have been made
otherwise. For example, the 200 people in the ITV Division of the
Ministry of Education were drawn from existing personnel on the Ministry payroll. This avoided the expense of creating all new positions.
Nonetheless, there is an opportunity cost associated with allocating
Ministry personnel to the ITV projcet. Had television not been undertaken, these people could have been assigned to other jobs.

Although another, even technological approach, might have been
less costly, no other alternative media were considered because of
the longstanding interest in television on the part of the Salvadorans
and because of the availability of large-scale U.S. assistance for a
television project. In spite of such assistance, it is important to
realize that the decision to use television was not without substantial
long-term costs to El Salvador, as the preceding paragraphs have
indicated.

Concerning the future, the extension of televised instruction to
grades four through six and, eventually, to grades one through three

will most likely lower per-student costs. Leaders of the El Salvador Project hope to improve the cost-benefit ratio of television by using the existing facilities to reach a larger number of students and thereby make optimum use of the initial investment in the broadcast facilities, installations, and programming.

Furthermore, the television programs used for in-school instruction in grades seven through nine are being retransmitted in the evening hours on an open-broadcast basis to those adults wishing to complete their basic education. This too will reduce the initial per-pupil investment in programming. Plans also are underway to make the services of the television facility available to other ministries—for example, agriculture, health, tourism. Besides the in-school instructional applications of television, other departments and divisions of the Ministry of Education are making use of the system. For example, the Guidance and Vocational Programs of the Ministry of Education are being transmitted over the ITV system to acquaint students with the various study and career options available to them in the Diversified Technical Career Program (Bachillerato Diversificado) at grades 10 through 12. In addition, programs on the new student evaluation, grading, and promotion system were aired to parents, students, and teachers over the television system. All of these complementary uses of the television system are designed to expand the system and to lower the cost of maintaining and operating it.

Student Learning

A primary goal of El Salvador's Educational Reform was to improve student learning. Graduates of the new system would be critical thinkers, capable of scientific inquiry, and able to deal with abstraction in a more sophisticated way. Thus they would be able to function in the industrial and technical business sectors that would be developing in El Salvador.

To measure student learning, the most influential cognitive effects of schooling were not conceptualized as being the specific content learned in the classroom but rather the verbal and numerical skills and general reasoning capacity of the student. Student development in these skill areas was measured with general ability and reading tests. It was hypothesized that if the Educational Reform and its television component were to make an important qualitative difference, improvement would have to be reflected on these tests. Complementary indicators of learning quality were provided by achievement tests geared to the curriculum content of each course. These tests made it possible to evaluate the success of the televised instruction in teaching specific content.

On a regular basis throughout 1969-72, the evaluation team administered general ability and reading tests as well as mathematics, science, and social-studies achievement tests to three cohorts of Third Cycle students. Cohort A, which began seventh grade in 1969, included students studying with television and other elements of the Reform and students learning in the traditional way. Cohorts B and C, which started seventh grade in 1970 and 1971, respectively, included only students from Reform classes; these groups were divided into ITV and non-ITV subsamples.

In general, the analysis of the general ability, reading, and subject-matter achievement tests showed striking results. Different kinds of schooling (traditional, Reform with ITV, and Reform without ITV) were found to be related to varying rates of change in general ability. However, substantial transformations did not occur in individual students' general abilities. That is, although overall group increases were large, the rankings of students on the basic skills tests were quite similar at the beginning and at the end of their Third Cycle careers. This basically means that the skills which Salvadoran students brought to seventh grade generally determined the skills that they graduated with at the end of the ninth grade. Overall improvement did not greatly change the pecking order.

More specifically, the learning results, as reported by the research-evaluation team, [11] indicated the following:

1. In all three cohorts (A, B, and C), the ITV students gained from 15 to 25 percent more on the general ability tests than did their non-ITV peers. These results remained constant even when socioeconomic status and individual student characteristics were taken into consideration. On reading tests, the ITV and non-ITV students gained about the same.

2. Students in ITV classrooms in each cohort also gained more than non-ITV students on the achievement tests administered in seventh grade. The ITV advantage in mathematics was particularly noticeable, and this advantage was maintained through ninth grade. In social studies, eighth- and ninth-grade achievement results were mixed; sometimes ITV students gained more, and sometimes non-ITV students gained more. In science, non-ITV students gained more in both eighth and ninth grades. Overall, ITV students in all three cohorts completed ninth grade with an achievement advantage over non-ITV students.

Reform classrooms with ITV, retrained teachers, a revised curriculum, and new printed materials proved to be a better learning environment than either traditional classrooms or classrooms with all elements of the Reform except for television. The major effort to integrate ITV into classroom instruction, therefore, appears to be largely responsible for the students' learning gains. Because the teaching materials were designed to accompany the telelessons, because teachers were retrained with the specific understanding that future instruction would involve television, ITV was well integrated in Salvadoran classrooms.

3. Despite a cumulative advantage in favor of the ITV classrooms, the overall level of learning in specific courses was not satisfactory. Only in seventh grade did students consistently gain as much as 20 percent over the course of a year—perhaps due to the novelty of televised instruction. In eighth and ninth grades, learning in science and social studies, and sometimes in mathematics, was particularly poor. A principal reason was the poor quality of telelessons for these upper grades.

Recognizing this problem, El Salvador invested considerable resources in remaking programs and improving the teaching capabilities of its production staff. Such difficulties are stressed here both to endorse the ongoing effort in El Slavador to improve program quality and also to forewarn future investors in ITV systems.

4. Older children within a cohort (those who had started school late, repeated a grade, or for some other reason interrupted their education) gained less on the general ability and reading tests than did younger children in the same cohort. Also, boys gained more than girls. These two variables (age and sex), as well as father's level of education, family economic capabilities, and level of urbanization, were substantially associated with students' scores on the basic skills tests at the beginning of seventh grade.

5. In the final analysis, television and the other reform programs did not overcome the effects of background characteristics on basic skills test performance. There was some evidence, however, that the learning advantage of urban over rural children was smaller in the ITV subsamples. In general, rural classrooms had poorer facilities than those in urban areas and their teachers were less well trained and less experienced. Television may have been the only resource that was apportioned equally to rural and urban classrooms. As a result, while non-ITV rural classrooms continued to lose ground to urban classrooms, rural ITV classrooms achieved about the same as urban ITV classrooms. This offers hope that where unequal performance among classrooms is the result of unequal provision of resources, ITV can help to equalize student performance.

Student Attitudes

The information collected on student learning was complemented with information on student attitudes toward ITV and toward particular subject matter in the telelessons. Students also were asked their opinion about various elements in the Reform and their plans for the future. Only students in ITV classes responded to questions in the first two categories while all students answered questions in the third category. The major findings are as follows:[12]

1. High initial enthusiasm for ITV declined as students progressed through the Third Cycle, although a majority of students remained favorable toward ITV in every survey. When asked if they would prefer to do

without one or more specific televised courses, the overwhelming response from the students was no. However, at the last measurement wave in 1973, one-third of the eighth- and ninth-grade ITV students said they would like to eliminate the math teleseries.

2. Attitudes toward science and social studies were positive from both ITV and non-ITV students. Spanish and math were disliked by both subsamples, although math was particularly ill-regarded by ITV students. English was very well liked by ITV students and little liked by non-ITV students.

3. Socially disadvantaged children and children with low general ability were more favorably disposed toward televised instruction than their more advantaged peers. Only science was equally well liked by all strata of students.

4. Sex influenced the choice of favorite subject with boys leaning toward science, social studies, and math, and girls toward English and Spanish.

5. Choice of math, science, or social studies as a student's favorite subject positively influenced his or her gain on achievement tests in the subject.

The relationship of motivation and attitude to learning is a complex one. Most educators assume that without a strong desire to learn, students will become bored and obtain little from classroom instruction. In El Salvador, as in other developing countries, the strongest motivation to stay in school may well be extrinsic: the belief that a diploma is the best guarantee of eventually finding a good job. However, if what students are studying is of little or no intrinsic interest to them, their ability to take advantage of schooling is likely to diminish. That is, long-range employment goals probably do not provide sufficient motivation for students on a day-to-day basis in school activities.

One of the attractive aspects of ITV, therefore, is its potential as a motivator, and in El Salvador this certainly was the case. Salvadoran students were excited by its introduction in their classroom, as the following excerpt from a classroom observation study indicates:

> On May 12, the TV set from the Ministry arrived, two months late . . . but it arrived. The set had been placed in the classroom the night before; the students caught their first glimpse of it as soon as they entered the room at 7AM. The reactions were varied but enthusiastic. Que galan! . . . Que Chulo! . . . Que bonito! . . . Some students simply stood in front of the set and stared. Others touched it, and one went so far as to put his arms around it lovingly. Another wrote on the board in bold letters, "DO NOT TOUCH THE TELEVISION SET." The rest of the students walked around the room selecting the best seating position to view their first lesson. [13]

It was assumed that such enthusiasm about the medium of instruction would carry over to learning the content of the instruction. The investigation confirmed the motivating force of television; and it is quite possible that the higher achievement in seventh-grade television classes may be related to this initial enthusiasm. Unfortunately, the motivating role of television was not long-lasting. Enthusiasm within each of the cohorts of students waned when the mere presence of ITV ceased to be exciting.

When the teleseries were lively and imaginative, they continued to motivate students. The positive regard of ITV students for English, in contrast to the dislike for the subject among non-ITV students, indicated that the initial attractiveness of television need not diminish over time. The continuing success of the English teleseries confirmed what many advocates of instructional television have suggested: that television can be particularly effective in carrying the instructional burden in subjects for which classroom teachers have not been appropriately prepared. Subjects like music and foreign languages are often beyond the scope of the average developing-country classroom teacher and most of these countries cannot afford to hire specialists to teach them. Thus, ITV can fulfill a vital role in such subjects, a role that can continue long after classroom teachers have stopped relying upon television in other subjects.

The enthusiasm of socially disadvantaged students for the teleseries reflected several possible influences. As was mentioned above, instructional television was particularly exciting for poor students who had the least exposure to commercial television. These students were also concentrated in rural communities where schools often had minimal resources and the least prepared and experienced teaching staffs. As a result, television loomed larger for them than it did for their counterparts in richer urban schools. This finding was encouraging because, as enrollment in Third Cycle increases and instructional television is extended to the primary level, a growing portion of its school audience will be poor children. Instructional television's potential as a motivator for this group may well continue to be quite large.

No consistent pattern of evidence was found linking students' attitudes toward ITV with learning. The lack of such a link may have resulted from the fact that the least able students were the most enthusiastic about ITV. When student attitudes toward specific subjects (as opposed to teleseries) were analyzed, a link with learning was established. And while the influence of liking a subject and learning varied, its existence was generally confirmed. Therefore, one priority for the producers of a teleseries should be to design quality programs that stimulate interest in particular subjects.

A general cautionary note: an investment in ITV is not only an investment in hardware. Adequate production facilities are certainly essential. But a more important investment is in programming and in the training of good production and programming personnel. Producers must

be carefully recruited and thoroughly trained. They must receive adequate salaries so that they are not tempted to leave for better jobs.
They also must be given sufficient time to make good programs. It also
may be better to produce fewer programs and to be on the air for a reduced number of hours, thereby ensuring the quality of the televised
materials, than to produce large quantities of low-quality programs
merely to fill an overambitious programming schedule.

Reactions of the Classroom Teachers

As part of the Educational Reform in El Salvador, a serious effort
was made to retrain all Third Cycle teachers so that they could work
effectively with the proposed new innovations. Teachers' attitudes toward the Reform therefore became an important aspect of the research
and evaluation activities. Briefly, the findings are as follows:
1. Not unlike the student findings, there was a decline from high
levels of enthusiasm in 1969 for ITV to less positive attitudes in 1971
and 1972. That is, teachers were more willing to be critical several
years after the introduction of ITV and the Reform program. Problems
other than the presence of instructional television or the basic thrust
of the Reform, however, were behind the teachers' negative attitudes.
2. In particular, teachers were not happy with their everyday working conditions because of increases in enrollment and the corresponding
increases in teaching loads, with morning and afternoon classes from
7 a. m. to 6 p. m. becoming the norm. Despite this extra work, teachers'
salary levels were not adequately improved and remained unattractive.
Given these conditions, it was not surprising that two major teachers'
strikes occurred within the initial years of the Reform.
3. There was also a general misunderstanding of the part played
by the classroom teacher in the new system of student grading and promotion, and a sense of being inadequately prepared to use such a system well. This new system required classroom teachers to be better
prepared for their classes and to invest precious out-of-class time in
various evaluation activities. At the same time, the new grading system diminished the possibility that a student could be flunked for failure to perform adequately on a single end-of-year exam.
The new evaluation system emphasized continuous and varied
evaluation of the student throughout the entire nine years of basic education. [14] The previous promotion system had been based on an end-
of-year written examination that determined whether the student passed
or failed the school year. The exam was heavily oriented toward memo-
rization. A high rate of students generally failed the exam and had to
repeat the school year. It was a common practice among some teachers
to flunk the majority of their students and then have them retake the
test three months later for a fee that was paid to the teacher. This fee,

an extra source of income to the teacher, was eliminated by the new grading and promotion system. This situation no doubt contributed to the antagonism of many teachers.

With the new grading and promotion system, the end-of-year "do or die" exam gave way to a series of short tests and observation activities undertaken throughout each teaching unit. For purposes of grading, these tests were weighted more lightly than the activities undertaken by the students throughout the teaching unit, such as experiments, individual reading assignments, investigation of aspects of the community, classroom participation, scrapbooks, and oral reports. The students' fear of failure was diminished as they were promoted throughout the nine years of basic education, relatively free of punitive barriers inhibiting the completion of their education. Only in extreme cases or poor performance or continued periods of absenteeism was the student not promoted to the next grade.

Teachers felt that such a liberal promotion system would weaken the quality of instruction. They failed to see that the student's promotion to each succeeding grade level would be followed by an appropriate period of review and remedial activities at the beginning of each grade and that the curriculum had been revised to emphasize the concentric nature of the subject matter. According to the new system, students study the same material in varying amounts and detail over the nine years of basic education. Thus they have a yearly opportunity to improve their mastery of areas in which they are weakest. In addition, the new promotion system called for diagnostic and orientation tests to be given at three critical periods in the child's nine years of basic education—at the end of the third, sixth, and ninth grades. Aptitude and occupational interests tests also are a special aspect of these diagnostic measures administered at the end of the ninth grade. The results are used to direct the student into appropriate levels of higher and/or technical education levels.

Despite its merits, the teachers resented the new promotion system. It has taken the Ministry of Education much effort to introduce this system and to train the classroom teacher in its use.

4. In addition to the above concerns, the teachers also were negative in their attitudes toward the Reform because of the not uncommon difficulties involved in its administration: lack of communication and coordination with the various agencies of the Ministry spearheading the Reform, late arrival or shortage of materials for the classroom, and indiscriminate methods of assigning teachers to schools. Obviously, there were multiple causes for the discouragement reflected in the teachers' attitudes.

5. Teachers also were not very satisfied with the quality of the televised materials and the prevailing tendency to fill the 20-minute television lessons with too much content and new concepts.

Teacher ratings of ITV courses over the four years showed a changing pattern of preferences: mathematics declined for all three grades;

Spanish and social studies improved. When asked how much televised instruction they wanted in the different subjects, 25 percent of math teachers but very few other teachers favored cutting back television. Most teachers wanted about the same number of classes as before (three per week) and 50 percent of the English teachers wanted all classes with television. But they wanted less of a content orientation and more concept emphasis on the lessons.

6. A project was undertaken to develop and validate a form for observing classroom teaching behavior. [15] Based on Beeby's theory of development stages in teaching, the form enabled researchers and school supervisors to distinguish modern from traditional teaching behaviors.[16] A sample of 16 teachers was observed. Results showed that whereas years of formal training did not seem to affect classroom behavior, teachers retrained under the reform employed more modern pedagogical techniques as manifested by inquiry-oriented and student-initiated activities.

7. An intensive year-long observation of two classrooms concluded that teacher self-confidence had increased and that classroom teachers had become more demanding critics of televised instruction in the course of the Reform. [17] Furthermore, the study revealed that teacher attitudes toward television were a key determinant of how much children learned from the medium.

These results permit some generalizations about Salvadoran teachers and their reactions to television. Generally, the teacher studies indicate that the program of teacher retraining was crucial to the success of ITV in the classroom and to the introduction of some modern pedagogy into the Salvadoran school system. The observational evidence further indicates that Salvadoran teachers were in Beeby's "transitional" stage. They were beginning to rely less on lecturing or rote drill and more on student activity; they were asking more "thought" questions (that is, questions with more than one correct answer); and they were encouraging students to ask their own questions, state their own opinions, and work on individual projects. These characteristics were all observed frequently enough to suggest that El Salvador's classroom teachers are changing, but also that they have far to go if the Reform's ambitious goals are to be achieved.

The year's retraining unquestionably sharpened the teachers' skills; it also may have raised their consciousness to the point where they were able to criticize ITV and the other reforms when the latter were not of sufficient quality or did not serve their purposes. In the final analysis, the teachers did not fear or resent ITV, but they did become increasingly aware of its shortcomings. Insofar as the teachers were critical of specific television series, their criticisms were often justified.

The results should also be seen as evidence that if teachers are expected to use modern methods in their daily teaching, they first must be instructed in those methods and allowed to practice them. The effectiveness of televised instruction in the classroom largely depends on the cooperation and resourcefulness of the classroom teacher. A less than ideal TV lesson can be made effective through good classroom utilization, just as the effects of a good television lesson can be weakened by poor classroom utilization. No one medium of instruction—be it the classroom teacher or television—can maintain a consistently high level of performance. Each has good and bad days, but, in combination, ITV and the classroom teacher can reinforce each other and increase the quality of instruction.

Overall Effects of the Reform

Overall, the research findings on teacher attitudes, student learning, and student attitudes suggest that the changes in the Salvadoran system have not been as dramatic as might have been expected. While there has been incremental, and occasionally substantial change in relation to what previously existed, the Reform cannot be classified as having radically changed the nature and societal functioning of the educational system.

A 1973 socioanthropological study of two groups of seventh-grade Salvadoran students (one rural, the other urban), prior to and during their experience with television, identified a few of the major difficulties that still await resolution.[18] For example, there is the problem of making televised instruction more visually appealing, less laden with informational content, and more geared to emphasizing critical reasoning.

Because of heavy programming schedules that had to be met, often requiring the production of 20 to 25 20-minute programs per week, not enough attention was given to the preplanning, instructional design, and pretesting aspects of the television lessons; as a result, program quality suffered. In the rush to get something on the air at the scheduled time, television lessons often included no more than a few graphic visuals, a blackboard, some superimpositions and a teacher lecturing in front of the camera. These defects were particularly evident in the mathematics and social-studies programs. Also, with such a rushed production schedule, little if any effort was made to leave the confines of the television studio to record programs in real-life settings and to bring into the classroom experiences and information relevant to the students' immediate interests and future roles in Salvadoran society. Television's potential to acquaint students with experiences beyond their everyday reality was not capitalized upon. The solution perhaps is to produce fewer lessons, thus allowing more free time to give detailed attention to pedagogical and production aspects, as well as to the relevancy of the materials to the lives of the students and the goals of the Educational Reform.

In addition to the problems of producing quality televised instruction, there is another difficulty. Repetitive, memoristic teaching still

continues to be practiced in Salvadoran classrooms more often than one
would care to admit. This is particularly the case in rural areas where,
because of the lack of transportation, supervisors do not visit classroom teachers as often as they should. There is an inconsistency in
the use of new teaching approaches by the retrained teachers; many tend
to revert to rote lecture and blackboard dictation more often than they
should. Also, incidents still prevail where teachers either fail to meet
their classes or do not arrive on time. Teachers often come unprepared
for the day's assignment, and they occasionally leave the classroom
while the televised lesson is being aired. In these ways, they fail to
integrate the classroom activity with the televised materials. Teachers,
therefore, need to be consistently reinforced in the new teaching meth-
odology of the Reform and encouraged to eschew dull, repetitive, and
disorganized classroom performance.

   Conversely, the situation also exists where students skip classes
or are engrossed in other activities in the classroom while the teacher
is trying to conduct class. To a certain extent, the new grading and
promotion system has contributed to this attitude on the part of the students because they know it is almost impossible for a teacher to flunk
them. Thus there is a need to instill a more mature and responsible
attitude in the students toward their studies; and there is a need to help
them to understand the implications of the new grading and promotion
system over the long run.

   In addition to the poor classroom teaching they encountered, many
of the most severe difficulties faced by students participating in the
Reform were outside of the classroom environment. The socioanthropological study documents factors that troubled students from low-
income families throughout the three years of their Third Cycle education. These students, more likely than not, came from a household
where there was no father, and the mother was forced to work outside
of the home. They lived in cramped, noisy, one-room quarters. Quite
frequently they came to school without any breakfast and in some instances had no lunch. They traveled, on the average, two to three
miles on foot to get to school. They had little spending money and
lacked even the barest material goods. Furthermore, these students
varied in age from 12 to 22 at the seventh-grade level, with 15 to 16
being the average age. On the average, students had repeated at least
two grades before entering the seventh grade.

   On the positive side, the graduates credited their Third Cycle
education with being particularly helpful to them in instilling a desire
to achieve and to better themselves, as well as giving them a spirit
of independence and self-confidence. At the same time, there was an
almost unanimous feeling among graduates that the Reform helped develop their reasoning abilities, increased their intellectual curiosity
about the world, and provided them with knowledge they otherwise
would not have received. School activities most valued by students
were individual or group research and investigation projects. Over

half of the graduates cited these activities as being the most useful
and relevant aspects of their own schooling. More than three-fourths
of the graduates interviewed felt that more attention should be given
to these types of activities under the Reform. Unfortunately, many students felt that not enough time was given to these types of activities
in the school schedule.

With respect to the broader question of the effects of television
and the Educational Reform on the country's socioeconomic development,
the results to date indicate a need for some rethinking.

Over 85 percent of the ninth-grade graduates in 1971 (the first to
complete three full years under the Reform) were interviewed nine months
after their graduation. The results of the interview study[19] conform
closely to the aspirations students expressed in a survey while they
were still in junior high school. Over 90 percent of the students were
continuing their education beyond the ninth grade. The Reform was to
some extent achieving its objective of stimulating more students into
diversified technical career programs for grades 10 through 12. Also,
a significantly higher proportion of the students who had been educated
under the Reform system, as opposed to those who had come through
the traditional classes, were enrolled in the technical career-oriented
secondary-education programs. To this extent, then, the Reform appears
to be moving toward fulfilling its objectives.

Below the surface the results are less encouraging. Most students
surveyed wished to continue their studies beyond the ninth grade. Indeed, when the first group of graduates had completed their Third Cycle
education in 1973, the number satisfied with jobs requiring only a ninth-
grade education had fallen to 2 percent; the number aspiring to jobs requiring additional secondary education had remained steady, hovering
in the mid-50th percentile, while the number aspiring to jobs requiring
post-secondary or professional training had risen from 34 to 44 percent.
These high expectations cannot presently, or in the foreseeable future,
be met by the Salvadoran educational system or the economy.

While many of these first graduates were able to find places in
high school, it is unlikely that there will be sufficient space in the
universities for all those who hope to attend. And as ever larger numbers of students complete ninth grade, it is unlikely there will be sufficient places in high school for all of the junior-high-school graduates.
The Ministry of Education already has decided that only 60 percent of
the graduates from the ninth grade will be allowed to continue their
education. And the majority of these students will be steered into terminal technical high schools. It is the Ministry's expectation that the
other 40 percent will change their perception of Third Cycle education
and see it as a valid termination point for entry into the labor market.

It should be noted, however, that in 1973 relatively few technical
jobs were available for the graduates of the Reform, and students were
inclined to continue schooling rather than enter the job market. The
economic situation was not good, but the first group of Reform graduates

also believed that their schooling had not helped them develop market-
able job skills. The country's unemployment rate was then 12 to 15 percent, and the underemployment rate was 60 to 70 percent. If there is
no economic expansion to match the large increase in school enrollments, students may be forced to reconsider the kinds of middle-level
jobs they currently consider unsuitable. For example, instead of studying to be medical technicians, they may come to be satisfied to work
as assistants to a pharmacist. Also, as the demand for employment increases, the jobs themselves may be reevaluated vis-a-vis the academic
credentials necessary to hold them, and over time all but the lowest-
level positions may be held by ninth-grade graduates.

Another finding of this study suggests that conditions are set for a
migration of Third Cycle graduates to the more important towns, cities,
and the capital. Because most high schools are located in large cities,
almost 50 percent of all graduates interviewed had to commute or change
residence in order to continue studying. This exodus of talented rural
youth could adversely affect the development of rural areas and further
aggravate overcrowded conditions in urban areas.

To counteract such migration, the Ministry should consider a greater
decentralization of schools away from urban areas and/or the development of viable out-of-school educational opportunities in the various
geographic localities of the country. There is a need for more such opportunities as evidenced by these findings: the considerably higher proportion of graduates from the rural areas identified in the study who were
neither working nor studying, and the lower proportion of rural students
among full-time students in grades 10 through 12.

While conceding that employment is likely to be a problem for students in the immediate future, Salvadoran planners believe that, in the
long run, the economy will expand sufficiently to absorb them. By investing in education, they believe El Salvador will create a labor pool
of adequate size and quality to attract outside industrial investment to
the country. This, in turn, will create new technical-job opportunities.
But such an expectation could lead to an unsatisfactory pattern of external political and economic dependency, possibly harming the long-
term national development interests of the country.

It also has been emphasized that the rationale for mounting such a
comprehensive educational reform in El Salvador was not limited solely
to the economic argument that it would help generate more jobs. There
was a belief that nine years of basic education should be the right of
every child regardless of the costs of such a policy to the society as
a whole. But here again, this may be unrealistic. Given the current
3.6 percent annual population growth in the country and the limited resources available to the government for social development programs,
such as education, this goal is not likely to be met.

CONCLUSIONS AND IMPLICATIONS

This chapter has underscored El Salvador's comprehensive approach to the use of educational television. Salvadoran leaders saw ITV as something more than a relatively inexpensive substitute for well-trained teachers. They recognized that television, regardless of its quality, could not by itself effect far-reaching educational reform. While ITV constituted but one element of a total reform program, it is unlikely that such change would have occurred without the impetus of ITV. Television served as a catalytic agent for inducing and speeding up the needed changes. Few developing countries have understood so well the role of technology in a program of educational reform and acted accordingly. Nonetheless, the Salvadoran experience must be viewed with reservation and caution. The evidence herein reviewed suggests that the causal relationship between more or better schooling and socioeconomic development remains problematic.

Student aspirations for higher education opportunities and the most prestigious professional jobs, which are apparently being nurtured by the schooling innovations in El Salvador, may lead to serious problems in the near future. Salvadoran educational planners will be caught in the uncomfortable position of convincing students to make adjustments between their personal aspirations and the realities of the marketplace.[20] Through their ambitious Educational Reform program the Salvadorans have expanded educational opportunities. But they have not yet instituted the desperately needed socioeconomic changes that were to accompany educational reform.

Therefore, the questions now are these: education for what purpose? and education for whom? Also: what investment strategy should the government pursue to achieve rapid and sustained socioeconomic growth? Concentration on educational improvement and expansion of education opportunities alone appears not to be the answer. El Salvador has taken a one-sector approach to development instead of an integrated approach. More attention must be given to employment opportunities, land reform, nutrition, and health care. Providing individuals with increased skills and knowledge and increased amounts of schooling will not automatically increase their chances in life nor reduce existing societal inequities. This is the inescapable conclusion of the El Salvador case.

NOTES

1. Wilbur Schramm, The Use of Television in The El Salvador Program of Educational Reform: Differences Between This Project and Some Others (Stanford, California: Institute for Communication Research, Stanford University, 1969).

        2. Henry T. Ingle, "Technology and Educational Reform: The Case
of El Salvador, " in Instructional Technology Report (Washington, D. C.:
Information Center on Instructional Technology, January 1974).
        3. Eugene M. Nuss and Emile G. NcAnany, "The Role of Instruc-
tional Television in the Educational Reform of El Salvador, " Educational
Broadcasting International 5 (September 1971): 179-88.
        4. John K. Mayo and Judith A. Mayo, An Administrative History of
El Salvador's Educational Reform, Research Report No. 8 (Stanford,
California: Institute for Communication Research, Stanford University,
1971).
        5. A series of 20 research reports and memoranda were generated
by the Staff of the Institute for Communication Research in the period
of October 1968 to August 1973. Research Report No. 14, Television
and Educational Reform in El Salvador: Final Report, by R. C. Hornik,
H. T. Ingle, J. K. Mayo, E. G. McAnany, and W. Schramm (August
1973), encapsulates the principal research findings.
        6. Cost data for the El Salvador project were collected by Dr. Rich-
ard Speagle and are the subject of a summary publication released by
the Information Center on Instructional Technology in Washington, D. C.,
Educational Reform and Instructional Television in El Salvador: Costs,
Benefits and Payoffs. Dr. Dean Jamison of the Educational Testing
Service at Princeton, New Jersey, also assisted in certain aspects of
the final analysis of the El Salvador ITV cost data. See also Wilbur
Schramm, Instructional Television in the Educational Reform of El Salvador, Bulletin no. 3 (Washington, D. C.: Information Center on
Instructional Technology, March 1973). It should be noted that cost
estimates for the El Salvador ETV Project are generally lower in this
chapter than those in Chapter 2 by Martin Carnoy. The differences occur because my estimates are based on more recent data pertaining to
larger student enrollments and therefore lower unit costs.
        7. Schramm, ibid., p. 37.
        8. Ibid.
        9. Hornik et al., op. cit.
        10. Schramm, Instructional Television in the Educational Reform of
El Salvador, op. cit., pp. 39-39.
        11. Hornik et al., op. cit., pp. 63-69.
        12. Ibid., pp. 98-101.
        13. Yolanda R. Ingle, "An Observational Study of Two Classrooms, "
in Henry T. Ingle et al., Television and Educational Reform in El Salvador: Report on the Fourth Year of Research (Stanford, California: Institute for Communication Research, Stanford University, 1973), pp. 64-
103.
        14. Henry T. Ingle, "Behavioral Objectives and the Evaluation of
Educational Reform in El Salvador" in Educational Broadcasting International 6 (June 1973): 91-97.

15. Judith A. Mayo, Teacher Observation in El Salvador, Research Report No. 5 (Stanford, California: Institute for Communication Research, Stanford University, 1971).

16. C. E. Beeby, The Quality of Education in Developing Countries (Cambridge, Massachusetts: Harvard University Press, 1966).

17. Yolanda R. Ingle, "Los Cipotes": The Children of El Salvador, Washington, D. C., November 1973 (mimeo.).

18. Ibid., pp. 1-70.

19. Henry T. Ingle with Jose R. Velasco and Victor M. Zelada, Television and Educational Reform in El Salvador: Follow-up Study on the First Group of Ninth Grade Graduates (Stanford, California: Institute for Communication Research, Stanford University, 1973).

20. Ibid.

5

**THE IVORY COAST
EDUCATIONAL
TELEVISION PROJECT**
Anthony Kaye

Most West African countries, and indeed the majority of developing countries, share a number of serious problems that impede educational, social, and economic development. These problems are well documented in a wide range of publications, and it is unnecessary and inappropriate to discuss them to any great extent in this chapter. However, to allow the reader to put this case study in context when reading it in conjunction with the studies of El Salvador and American Samoa, it is important to list briefly the main problems in the area of educational development in West Africa in general, and then in the Ivory Coast in particular.

THE WEST AFRICAN CONTEXT

The following ten points are critical in considering the general economic, social, and educational situation in West Africa:

1. West Africa has a low average per capita Gross National Product (GNP)—in only six West African countries does this exceed U. S. $200, in 11 it is less than $100. In many cases, this situation is combined with one of extreme inequality in income distribution—salary ratios of over 100:1 between highest- and lowest-paid groups are not uncommon. (These discrepancies are compensated for to some extent by the highly supportive nature of traditional family networks.)

2. Average population growth rates that are between 2.2 and 2.7 percent per year have not yet reached their peak values, and include a concomitantly high proportion of the population below adult age.

3. The population is predominantly rural and dispersed, although in the relatively more prosperous countries such as the Ivory Coast, this situation is changing rapidly as migration from rural areas increases.

4. There is a relatively poor communications infrastructure in rural zones (to varying degrees in different countries) and unequal development of different regions within a given country.

140

5. A variety of ethnic groups and hence of languages exists within a given country (although again, with significant variation from country to country), coupled with an almost total lack of correlation between the geographical spread of different ethnic groups and the delimination of state frontiers created by the colonial powers.

6. The adult population is literate in either French or English (depending on the country) only about 15 percent on average. The proportion of adults who are fluent speakers of one of these languages is not much greater. This poses evident problems in countries (like the Ivory Coast) where the excolonial language is used exclusively from the first grade of primary school.

7. Average school enrollment rates (for the whole of West Africa) are on the order of 45 percent at the primary level, 5 percent at the secondary level, and less than 1 percent at the tertiary level.

8. High dropout and repeater rates are apparent at all levels of the formal schooling system, creating a high unit cost per student (student input/output ratios average 2. 0, with a range of 1. 25-3. 50). In many West African countries public expenditure already devoted to education is of the order of 25 percent of total public revenues, which means that significant proportional increases in educational spending are unlikely to be possible.

9. An increasing belief exists in many cases that the output of existing school systems does not correspond to current or future societal needs. School curricula and methods are still often traditionally oriented, resembling closely those installed by the excolonial powers, and are often geared more to criteria set by the higher levels in the educational system than to employment needs. Unemployment levels among primary- and secondary-school graduates, especially in rapidly growing urban areas, have increased seriously in the last few years, in parallel with both increases in total numbers attending school and with rural migration rates.

10. There is little realization among parents and children that formal schooling no longer leads automatically to a salaried white-collar job. The social demand for schooling is in general extremely high. Outside the public sector, and the traditional Koranic schools in Muslim areas, there is a wide variety of private and semiprivate fee-paying educational facilities, ranging from the écoles-boutique set up by individual entrepreneurs to correspondence colleges of varying degrees of efficiency.

CHARACTERISTICS OF THE IVORY COAST

Although sharing common characteristics with them, Ivory Coast differs from many of its neighboring countries on several critical dimensions. For a start, its population is extremely heterogeneous: of the current estimated population of about 6 million, about 1 million are non-Ivorian African immigrants, about 100, 000 are of Syrian or Libyan origin, and about 50, 000 are European, mainly French.[1] Furthermore, the population growth rate is higher than average for West Africa, on the order of 3. 8 percent per year (of which about 1 percent per year. represents immigration from neighboring countries); consequently, the present population is a young one, with around 53 percent under 20 years of age.[2] Within the Ivorian population there exists a multitude of different ethnic groups (normally estimated at about 60, depending on the criteria of classification adopted) with different language and social structures. These ethnic groups can be classified into four main culture circles, but even within these circles, language and customs can vary significantly. And the geographical boundaries of these culture circles do not necessarily correspond to the national state frontiers. The people of the southeast have strong family and ethnic links with their neighbors on the other side of the Ghanaian frontier; the Mande groups of the north have far more in common (including their Islamic traditions) with their neighbors in Mali and Guinea than with their fellow Ivorians from the south, who, traditionally animist, have to a large extent been converted to Christianity during the course of this century.

Historically, Ivory Coast came under European colonial influence at a much later date than many of its neighbors. Although some, not very successful, trading posts had been established along the coast during the nineteenth century, there was very little French penetration into the interior during this period and military pacification of the territory was not completed until 1917. The French imposed a system of direct rule with the help of African auxiliaries recruited from among the Southern tribes and from more "advanced" colonies such as Senegal (Senegal had already elected a deputy to the French National Assembly in 1916). The period since the end of World War II, when the French began to take a serious interest in exploiting the timber and agricultural potential of the country, has been one of very rapid change in terms of economic and social development. Since Independence in 1960, the country has had a stable government, mainly through the influence of President Félix Houphouet-Boigny (a one-time minister in the French government), and has enjoyed a spectacular growth rate of around 8 percent per year in real terms—the origin of the expression, "the Ivorian miracle." This is perhaps the factor that distinguishes the Ivory Coast most clearly from all other West African states. The GNP of the Ivory Coast has tripled in real terms (inflation discounted) during the 14 years since Independence.[3]

This high economic growth rate has been extensively documented and analyzed and it is sufficient here simply to list some of the main factors to which it can be attributed:
• a stable government since Independence;
• the deliberate adoption of an unbalanced growth model in the first decade since Independence;
• the extremely liberal policy toward foreign investment; for example, in 1968, 95 percent of companies operating in the country were foreign owned, and 60-70 percent of all private investment was foreign;[4]

- the financial and trading advantages that can be attributed to Ivory Coast's adherence to the Franc zone: in 1968, France bought 35 percent of all Ivorian exports and provided 50 percent of all imports;[5]
- the relatively late date (early 1950s) at which the intensive exploitation of the agricultural and timber potential of the country really got under way;
- the rapid and effective development of basic infrastructures (such as roads, telecommunications, and ports).

Concomitant with this growth rate has been the development of a certain dependence, not only on foreign capital, but also on highly paid foreign (mainly European) management and technical-assistance staff. This is evident not only in classical areas such as postprimary-level teaching, but in all the major sectors of the economy as well, and at the highest levels. For example, a significant proportion of the technical staff in the Planning Ministry is expatriates.

That this state of affairs represents a serious concern for the Ivorian government is evident from the following quote from the abridged version of the current five-year plan:

> As for employment, the (following data) show that:
> - expatriates hold nearly all executive and management training positions and half of the overseeing jobs;
> - nationals are in competition with non-Ivorian Africans for skilled labour jobs;
> - most unskilled labour is assured by non-Ivorian Africans.
> This employment framework means that top decision-making and, to a certain extent, pressure from the bottom, by-pass nationals. Its influence on the distribution of mass wage-earnings is evident since expatriates receive 41 per cent of wage-earnings, although they account for only 6.3 per cent of all employment. As for the Ivorians, who represent 47.5 per cent of the working population, they receive only 32.5 per cent of wage-earnings. [The data for the late sixties mentioned above] show that 89.3 per cent of all management personnel were non-African, and 80.2 per cent of all executives and technicians.[6]

At the lower end of the employment spectrum, there is a high proportion of poorly paid African immigrant labor, mainly from the neighboring countries of Upper Volta and Mali, working in agriculture, industry, and domestic service. In 1965, for example, African immigrants represented one-quarter of the total population of about 5 million, and over one-third of the total active male labor force.

The combination of a rapid economic development in certain sectors and the relative neglect of the rural population in the 1960s has contributed to a massive increase in population movement from rural to urban zones. The population of the capital city, Abidjan, has grown

from around 20, 000 in 1938 to an estimated 900, 000 by 1975. Thirty-
five percent of the country's inhabitants are now living in an urban environment and it is estimated that this proportion will have reached 42
percent by 1980.

The imbalance that has been created by the changes mentioned
above is obvious to even the most casual visitor. The accelerated
growth of Abidjan in recent years has given rise to "the appearance of
vastly different types of housing, ranging from multi-story buildings
. . . to shacks built out of planks and waste material. . . ."[7]

Despite noble efforts by the government to assist in the construction of low-cost housing, it is proving very difficult to keep up with
the immigration into Abidjan of both rural Ivorians and non-Ivorians in
search of employment. The problem is to some extent exacerbated by
the resources, both private and public, that are invested in catering
to the needs of the elite Ivorian and expatriate population of the city
(luxury shops, hotels, and office buildings, daily flights to and from
Paris, and so on).

It is difficult to predict for how much longer the economic growth
of the last 15 years can be maintained, especially in the light of recent
developments in many commodity prices throughout the world, and the
strict dependence of the Ivorian economy on outside factors (such as
the very high proportion of foreign-owned investments, and membership
in the Franc zone. Samir Amin, in his extensive analysis of the situation, compares the growth due to the rapid exploitation of the country's
resources to that already experienced in much older established colonies
such as Senegal, Ghana, Southwest Nigeria, over a longer period, at a
much earlier time.[8] He points out the limits to this type of growth, and
notes clearly in a 1970 postscript to his book, that the moment of economic "takeoff" as an autonomous economy seems to be getting further
and further away, as foreign influence seems to increase.

The government is obviously not unaware of the existing and potential problems that are associated with the country's recent growth,
and with its unbalanced nature. The current five-year plan puts a great
deal of emphasis on rural development, and a special government body
within the Planning Ministry (the Office Nationale de Promotion Rurale)
has been created to coordinate activities in the areas of information
and education for the rural population. Other government organizations
have been set up to promote rural enterprises (such as cooperatives)
and to supply banking and loan facilities to farmers. At the same time,
serious efforts are being made to diversify agricultural production. Such
efforts, if they prove in the long term to be fruitful, could, along with
the development of universal primary education through the ETV system,
help significantly in reducing gaps in living standards both between
different regions of the country and between the rural and urban populations.

EDUCATIONAL ENROLLMENTS IN THE IVORY COAST

The general structure of the educational system is modeled fairly
closely on the French one. It has six grades of primary education, sanc-
tioned by a competitive examination for entry into secondary education.
The secondary program is divided into a four-year first cycle and a
three-year second cycle, the latter terminating in the baccalaureat examination. Tertiary education covers university programs, technical
studies, agricultural studies, teacher training, and so on.

During the period before World War II, little progress was made in
setting up schools in Ivory Coast. Overall enrollment rates in 1922 and
1935 respectively were only 1 and 2 percent. In 1940, post-primary-
school enrollments in the Ivory Coast numbered only 200, although there
were some Ivorians at the Normal School (Ecole William Ponty) in Dakar.
In 1945 Ivory Coast boasted only four university graduates, and a com-
parably small number of university students (in French universities).
The next 15 years, however, showed dramatic changes. Overall school
enrollment rates were around 20 percent in 1957, and 1959 saw about
1,000 Ivorian students in France and a further 200 at the University of
Dakar. [9] In 1958 a Center for Higher Education was founded, to be
transformed into the University of Abidjan in 1964.

The years since Independence have seen steady increases in enrollment in all sectors, as Table 5.1 illustrates.

TABLE 5.1

Total Enrollments in Each Major Educational Sector[a]

	Primary[b]	Secondary[b]	University
1960/61	238,772	11,455	147 (Center H.E.)
1965/66	253,745	28,166	1,147
1970/71	502,865	63,978	3,092
1973/74	606,185	91,000	4,734

[a]The figures include both Ivorian and non-Ivorian students.
[b]The figures for primary and secondary enrollments include both
public and private schools.
Source: La Côte d'Ivoire en Chiffres and the Rector's Office,
University of Abidjan.

The marked increases in number of students at postprimary level has been accompanied by a parallel increase in the numbers of expatriate teaching staff, for the most part French: numbers of teachers supplied under French government technical assistance programs have increased steadily from 405 in 1960 to 2,462 in 1972.[10] The French government pays less than one-third of the total salary bill for this staff; the rest is paid by the Ivory Coast. Ivory Coast, in fact, employs over a quarter of all French technical assistance staff working in black Africa and Madagascar.

Table 5.1 indicates that enrollments in secondary education have expanded substantially. However, the proportion of primary-school children, even of those who actually complete all six grades, who can find a place in a secondary school remains relatively limited. At the moment, about 25 percent of any given sixth-grade primary-school group can be accommodated in secondary schools.

Enrollment rates for primary education in 1970 (the year before the introduction of ETV) stood at about 54 percent, as opposed to about 33 percent in 1960 and only 6 percent in 1950. However, the raw figures for this dramatic evolution in overall numbers and rates in the primary sector conceal a certain number of factors that are far from positive.[11] Dropout and repeater rates were high in traditional public primary school: for the period from 1965 to 1970, the number of pupil-years necessary to produce a given number of terminal sixth-grade pupils was 2.7 times greater than it should have been, assuming no repeaters or dropouts. There were regional disparities in enrollment rates, varying from less than 20 percent to over 70 percent in different parts of the country, with the northern regions being the least favored. There were also urban/rural disparities in enrollments, and male/female disparities, with girls representing slightly more than one-third of all primary school enrollments. In addition, there were great discrepancies in the quality of teaching and in pupil achievement between different schools and different areas—factors often overlooked due to the pressure to increase overall numbers at all costs and as quickly as possible.

There is also evidence from demographic data, collected between 1965 and 1970, of a major differential emigration of primary-school leavers from rural to urban zones, which, if not checked, could lead to a condition in which literacy rates in rural areas remain at their existing low levels as children who have been to village schools move to the towns.[12]

The decision to reform the educational system, and to use television as a component of this reform, must be seen against the background briefly sketched above. To summarize, this is a background of very rapid change in the country's economy; an apparently increasing reliance on expatriate staff and advisers in many areas; a traditionally modeled system of primary education, which inevitably had to sacrifice quality to rapidly increasing enrollment rates; differential exodus of school youngsters to urban areas; and limited opportunities for further education after the primary level.

EDUCATIONAL TELEVISION IN THE IVORY COAST—
THE ORIGINAL PLAN

It is difficult, now in 1976, to go back ten years in time and
imagine oneself in the place of Ivorian educational planners and decision makers faced with the problems briefly outlined above. The
gravity of the educational situation in many developing countries that
had recently gained independence was becoming more and more evident.
The 1963 Pan-African Congress at Addis Ababa had assigned an urgent
priority to increased primary-school enrollment throughout the continent.
There was, in the mid-1960s, a faith in the power of the mass media,
and especially television, to provide a solution to a wide range of educational problems. UNESCO had just sponsored Wilbur Schramm's survey of the use of the media in education, which listed a wide range of
promising-looking media-based projects, many of a small-scale experimental nature. [13] There was a strong desire on the part of planners in
the developed world and in the international aid agencies to do something concrete and visible toward assisting educational reform in the
developing world. There was undoubtedly also an interest in trying out
a large-scale application of ETV in the primary-school sector, given
the commitment of many developing-country governments to a policy of
universal primary education.

In the case of the Ivory Coast, various experimental and often un-
coordinated projects had been mounted during the 1960s in an attempt
to improve the quality of classroom instruction. These included programmed instruction applications, correspondence courses for teachers,
audiovisual "modules" (tapes, slides, and illustrated brochures), and
occasional cinema, radio, and TV programs for teacher updating. [14]
Many of these projects were based on underlying assumptions concerning the efficacy per se of an audiovisual approach. Early costings
demonstrated, however, that to apply such methods universally without
having recourse to a centralized production and distribution system
would be ruinously expensive. Furthermore, the experimental ETV
primary-school project in neighboring Niger, which, although only on
a small scale, was showing promising initial results, was being followed with interest by both the Ivorian and French governments. Factors conducive to large-scale adoption of ETV in the Ivory Coast included the existence of a TV transmission network and the relatively
favorable economic conditions of the country. In fact, Ivory Coast had
already itself experimented with ETV during the 1960s, both for adult
literacy training and for a Télé-Bac operation designed as a preexami-
nation revision exercise for final-year secondary-school pupils.

There is little evidence, in the initial planning documents for the
project, that alternatives to the introduction of TV into primary-school
classrooms (for example, use of radio) were seriously considered.
During the planning phase of the project, evaluation teams were sent

to Niger, American Samoa, and El Salvador to look at progress in these schemes. The evaluation teams were asked to study what alternatives to ETV had been considered in the planning stages of these three projects, but in fact no reference to the question is found in the final report prepared by the teams. [15] It would seem, in any case, that the decision to go ahead with the Ivory Coast scheme had been taken before these evaluation missions were carried out. It is obvious, however, that the decision was not taken without any consideration of less costly alternatives. As instructional radio combined with printed support materials diffused in a weekly newspaper had already been used for in-service teacher training in Ivory Coast, it would appear that an extension to this much less costly approach had been considered and then rejected.

The studies carried out during the planning stage of the project were extremely comprehensive. The role of television, although major, is nevertheless conceived as part of a total educational reform that included the following: adaptation of the curriculum (up to that time very largely inspired by the French primary-school syllabus), in-service teacher training, establishment of new teacher-training institutions, conception and preparation of printed support materials, and development of out-of-school postprimary education schemes for primary-school graduates who would not be continuing into secondary education and for rural adults.

An important element of the argument presented in the planning studies concerned costs. Unit costs in the traditional system were extremely high because of the high repeater rates (around 30 percent) and dropout rates (around 8 percent) in any given year. These rates lead to a 2.7(x) increase in average student-years necessary for a pupil to reach the end of sixth grade (CM2) and a 4.8(x) increase for a student gaining the certificate of primary studies (the CEPE)—this due to the higher-than-average repeater rate in the final grade. (These figures are based on a study carried out on the 1958/59-1965/66 cohort.) Thus the actual cost for obtaining a noncertificated primary-school graduate was 2.7 times the theoretical six-year cost, and for a certificated graduate, 4.8 times the theoretical cost. [16]

In 1967 unit running costs for public primary education—including teacher-training costs, but excluding school-construction and maintenance costs (borne by local communities except in Abidjan)—were 13,500 CFA francs per pupil (about U.S. $53 at that time). Thus total costs for producing one final grade noncertificated graduate could be estimated on such a basis as $6 \times 13,500 \times 2.7 = 218,700$ CFA francs. Costs for producing a certificated graduate were of course nearly double ($6 \times 13,500 \times 4.8 = 388,800$ CFA francs). Costs with zero repetition and dropout rates would have been only 81,000 CFA francs.

The fundamental argument underlying the introduction of an educational reform using ETV was that the increased quality of teaching that would result, combined with a more adapted curriculum, would permit a policy of automatic promotion from one grade to another and would more or less eliminate the dropout problem. Thus the add-on costs of introducing TV (estimated at 930 CFA francs per pupil-year on the basis of a total pupil number in excess of 500, 000) and of improving both qualitatively and quantitatively the teacher training output (estimated at 3, 000 CFA francs) would be insignificant in relation to the savings in unit costs gained by automatic promotion. These add-on costs were thus estimated at 3, 930 CFA francs per pupil year, hence 23, 580 CFA francs per six-year graduate cycle. This would bring the total notional cost of producing a primary school noncertificated graduate from the 81, 000 CFA francs quoted above to 104, 580 CFA francs, less than half the existing per graduate cost under the traditional system.[17]

It should be noted that, contrary to the practice adopted in the Niger ETV project of using relatively low-paid monitors instead of more expensive, trained teachers, the Ivory Coast government insisted on a policy of enhancing the quality of teacher training and the number of more highly trained teachers in conjunction with the development of the ETV Project.

The arguments that were put forward for using television, as quoted in the government Five-Year Plan,[18] included the following: the pedagogical advantages (presentation of concrete and not merely verbal elements, good visual and auditory models, an opening to the outside world, constant updating of content and methods); the advantages of a centralized production system (the need for a limited number of expert staff, the unifying quality of the teaching, the integration of the different subjects taught); the advantages of a modern telecommunications system (rapid delivery, a theoretically infinite number of reception sites); its role in the permanent education and updating of teachers; its role in reducing regional disparities in the quality of teaching, and in increasing a sense of national unity.

Arguments for the efficacy of television as a teaching medium were based in part on promising early achievement test results in French (expression and reading) from the Niger Project. Arguments also stressed the reports of much increased participation and interest on the part of both teachers and pupils in that project.[19]

Initial plans for TV programming included a daily session for teachers between seven and eight o'clock each morning to prepare them for their day's work; and then four 15-to-20-minute programs a day at each of the first four grade levels, which the teacher would develop during the remainder of each class period. The remaining two grade levels would have a reduced TV input and a different overall orientation from the first four "fundamental" grades. Daily postprimary programs were also envisaged for youngsters who had left school as part of an overall out-of-school education project (see below). Great importance was to be attached to integrating TV programming content with overall development options, to use of constant reference to the students' milieu (both rural and urban), to stimulation of active involvement by the children

in their learning, and to encouraging self-expression. Teaching of
French was to be restructured radically in the light of what is now known
about the principles of second-language teaching to young children.
The vocabulary and basic language structures would be revised in the
light of the Ivorian situation, priority would be given to understanding
and learning spoken French before teaching reading and writing. Mathematics, the other main subject matter, was to be revised in accordance
with modern thinking so as to be beneficial to pupils going on to secondary education. But modern mathematics was considered of questionable value for children who would later only need to use their math
knowledge for simple costing and accounting purposes. All references
to French history and geography would be removed from the syllabus
and replaced with more relevant material based on Ivorian needs and
priorities. Manual activities in school gardens and workshops would
be integrated into the curriculum.

Curriculum development was planned in conjunction with improvement of teacher qualifications. The strategy called for accelerated replacement of monitors and assistant monitors by trained teachers, as
well as the rapid expansion of teacher-training facilities.

The implementation plans for the project envisaged the following
main stages: (1) a preparatory phase involving development of teacher-
training facilities, creation of the necessary infrastructure, setting up
of the production complex (the TV and printed materials production facilities and associated teacher- and staff-training facilities); (2) start-
up of broadcasting at grade-one level (CP1) in autumn 1971 with 21,000
first-grade pupils, then addition of one grade per year so that all six
grades would be "covered" by the school year 1976/77; and (3) achievement of total enrollment of the entire 6-to-12-year age group in ETV
schools by 1986; this would represent a total estimated enrollment of
about 1.5 million pupils by that time and, with a target figure of 44
pupils per class, a total need for about 34,000 teachers and the same
number of TV classes. It was planned that the ETV system and curriculum would be made available to the private schools (numbers of pupils
in private primary schools being expected to remain constant at the 1971
level of around 110,000).

Basically then, this plan implied, over a 15-year period, considerably revising the traditional curriculum; tripling the number of pupils,
teachers, and classes in the primary school system; making TV receivers
and printed materials available to all those classes; and substantially
improving teacher qualifications (in 1967, only 612 out of the 6,409
practicing teachers were fully qualified instituteurs).

To complement the reform at the primary level, two further orientations were developed in the original proposals. One concerned the
introduction of television and other audiovisual methods into secondary
schools in time to receive the first cohort of ETV primary school graduates for the school year 1977/78. The other concerned the use of the
TV reception network and the production facilities to provide an out-of-

school, vocationally based, part-time education for primary-school leavers who would not continue in the formal educational system, and for rural and urban disadvantaged adults.

The objectives of postprimary out-of-school education, as outlined in the Five-Year Plan for the period 1971-75 were the following: to assure a means of personal development for young school-leavers in their own milieu, and thus to promote the society of which they form a part; to facilitate their integration into their milieu; to direct the ambitions of a larger number of people toward the construction of the rural environment and the development of modern agriculture.

The preoccupation with the rural exodus of young school-leavers already mentioned is apparent. There is, however, a certain irony in the idea of using one of the main elements of the primary school system—television—to persuade youngsters to remain in an environment from which the primary school is seen as one of the main means of escape. But it was hoped that the program would provide general training aimed at applying the skills taught during the primary-school years to everyday life. The proposals made in the Plan for implementing this out-of-school system included the formation of groups of 20 or 30 youngsters in village "educational centers." A full-time specially trained <u>animateur</u> ("animator") would take charge of these groups and help organize them into self-sufficient economic units. With the aid of TV programs in the evenings and during the school vacations, the animators would train the youngsters in modern agricultural techniques. This particular element of the proposed out-of-school program has not in fact been adopted as yet: the costs of providing and training the animators would have been high; the urgency of getting the primary-school reform off the ground was the main priority; and, in any case, many aspects of the proposal were far from realistic. However, limited experiments in the use of ETV with local teachers as animators have been mounted for urban and rural adult audiences. We will return to a discussion of these efforts later in the chapter. The original proposals have been mentioned here mainly to underline the thoroughness of the overall planning approach adopted and to demonstrate how the dual objectives of providing a basic education for both a future educated elite and/or a rural and urban "working" majority were envisaged in practical terms.

ETV IN THE IVORY COAST—THE FIRST FOUR YEARS

The effectiveness of an operation such as the Ivory Coast ETV Project can be looked at, in general terms, on three levels. First, one might ask if the objectives set by the government for educational, social, and economic development could have been met more effectively, and at less cost, by a completely different type of approach within the educational sector. It is questionable whether the teaching of French and modern mathematics using television and attractively designed printed materials, even with a certain amount of "environmental studies" added on, is going to help persuade primary-school leavers unable to continue to secondary education to happily accept their lot as future agricultural workers. Even in the schools that do have vegetable gardens in the grounds, it is difficult to believe that the few hours a week that some pupils devote to tending them outside class hours really represent anything more than lip service paid to the idea of involving the school in rural agricultural activities. And in the rapidly growing urban centers, where the benefits of a continued education are visibly evident in the competition for white-collar jobs, it is even more difficult to see how primary-school leavers are going to accept entry into the lower end of the labor market. These problems are shared, of course, by a large number of developing countries, and very few of these countries have attempted reforms at the primary-school level that are very much more than local adaptations (with or without a technological input) of the educational model inherited from colonial times. In a few African countries, such as Tanzania, where an attempt has been made at a serious rethinking of educational strategy, the political and economic orientation of the government is quite different from that of the Ivory Coast's. It is not the purpose of this chapter to indulge in speculation about whether a more radical reform of the primary-school system (such as raising the entry age, teaching in local languages, really adapting the curriculum to agricultural and industrial development needs, and so on) would have been more effective. This is manifestly an impossible question to answer. It is important, however, to realize the difficulties any such major restructuring would have encountered. As pointed out at the beginning of this chapter, Ivory Coast's economy is very closely linked with the French economy, the social demand from the population for increased educational facilities of a "traditional" kind is extremely high, and the case for the unifying role of a single language—French—can be made very forcefully in a country possessing so many different ethnic groups. Finally, the president has been from the start an enthusiastic promoter of the ETV Project.

A second level of analysis, accepting the design of the reform as a given, would concern itself with the actual output of the reformed system. Specific questions would be addressed to the skills of the system's graduates (numeracy, fluency in French, knowledge of their country and its social and political structures), to their future careers (how well they perform in entrance examinations to secondary school, how adequately the other graduates fit into the employment sector), and to the overall costs of the reform in its "steady state." Unfortunately, at the present time it is too early to answer any of these questions, nor is it the purpose of this chapter to speculate on what the answers might turn out to be. One can only say that the procedures that will provide some of these answers have been built into the system, and that ac-

curate scientific data, at least in the fields of knowledge testing and
cost analysis, will be available in a few years.

A third level of analysis would concern itself with evaluation of
the operation of the system in different areas during the first few years
of its implementation, and with a comparison of original plans with what
has actually happened. This is the purpose of the concluding section.

Initial Implementation

Implementation of the primary-school reform started on schedule
in autumn 1971 with the introduction of the revised curriculum, of
specially prepared and printed documents for teachers and children, and
of ETV programs in 447 first-grade (CP1) classes, covering 20,500
pupils. Enrollment data, as of late 1975, are shown below in Table 5.2.

Extension of the reform to sixth- (final-) grade classes will be completed by the beginning of the 1976/77 school year. From then on it is
simply a matter of carrying the reform through to the schools not yet
brought into the ETV system, and of putting the final touches to the extension of the TV transmission network to the few regions of the country
not as yet covered (notably the southwest). In such regions, the reform
will be implemented as from this year in the first and second grades by
using the revised curriculum but without the TV transmissions (that is,
on the basis of the printed documents and visiting teacher support
alone).

TABLE 5.2

Numbers of TV Classes and Pupils
by Grade (Autumn 1975)*

Grade	No. Classes	No. Pupils
1st (CP1)	1,707	75,108
2nd (CP2)	1,325	58,318
3rd (CE1)	1,105	48,626
4th (CE2)	801	35,265
5th (CM1)	415	18,276
Total	5,353	235,593

Note: Numbers of children in non-ETV classes, public and private
= 448,994.

*Estimations based on projections of 1974 numbers and assuming
an average of 44 children in each class.

The current figures for total numbers of children in ETV classes are about 100, 000 less than the projections in the original planning documents; nevertheless, the progress made over the last four years represents a remarkable achievement in terms of production and distribution of hardware and software for the reform. The probability is, then, that the target of total enrollment of all primary-school-age children in ETV classes by 1986 has a good chance of being reached, with only a few years' delay in the original plan. This is assuming, of course, that output of trained teachers is maintained at a satisfactory level, and that the funds earmarked for equipping the schools with reception equipment and printed materials are made available.

In addition to the progress made in the primary-school sector, developments have occurred in the out-of-school education field using ETV. During the 1974/75 school year, 38 programs aimed at adult audiences were broadcast to reception groups in classes of ETV schools throughout the country, after experimentation with pilot programs during the previous year. These transmissions, generally broadcast on Wednesday evenings during school terms, relied on a local primary-school teacher acting as unpaid animator, translating the French sound track into the local dialect and running a discussion session after the program. It is estimated that during the last year, about 600 viewing groups, with an average number of 57 in each group, more or less regularly attended these broadcasts. Programs, designed in conjunction with technical advisory staff from various government ministries and departments, covered such subjects as health care, infant nutrition, formation of agricultural cooperatives, crop protection, sanitation, use of banking facilities, collaboration on the 1975 census, and so on.

Production of the programs and of associated printed documents, posters, and newspaper supplements, was the responsibility of the staff of the out-of-school education unit in the ETV Project, which also handled feedback from the animators and requests for further information. In 1975/76, it is estimated that about 1, 000 regular viewing groups will be in operation. Special attention will be focused on urban viewing groups, which formed a significantly low proportion of the audience during the first year.

The progress made since the beginning of the ETV reform in both the primary and out-of-school sectors, briefly outlined above, will now be considered under several main headings, in an attempt to provide a brief overview. The reader should, however, bear in mind two limitations on the thoroughness of the analysis: the difficulty of condensing into a few pages the enormous amount of information that could be presented, and the fact that the author participated in the Project for a limited period (1973-75).

The ETV Project (both primary and out-of-school sectors) will be looked at below under the following headings: Overall Organization, Administration, and Financing; Production of Course Materials; Delivery Systems; Use of the Media in the Teaching Situation; Evaluation, Feedback, and Control Mechanisms.

Differences that have arisen between the original plans and the actual situation will be noted when they occur, but it must be stressed that such differences do not necessarily imply a criticism of the way the Project has developed: original plans always need to be adjusted to reality; and large and complex projects that do not overshoot original manpower and financial estimates are the exception rather than the rule.

OVERALL ORGANIZATION, ADMINISTRATION, AND FINANCING

Organizational Structure

Before the introduction of ETV, primary education was the responsibility of a director, who reported via a general Directorate of Education to the minister. The director of primary education controlled, through his secretariat, teacher training, the primary-school inspectors (and through them the teachers), the payment and promotion of teachers, authorizations for opening of new schools, and the supervision of private schools. This was a straightforward, well-organized system with a clear definition of functions and responsibilities. With the exception of a few administrative advisers, some teacher-training staff, and a few inspectors, it was also an entirely "Ivorized" system.

Introduction of ETV involved addition of large numbers of expatriate staff from several different sources (mainly France, Canada, and UNESCO) and the setting up of control and distribution systems for which the existing administration was ill-adapted. With the best will in the world, it would have proved difficult to effect the required changes over such a short time without some problems arising. A pressing immediate priority concerned the procedures for installation and maintenance of receivers, batteries, and aerials in the ETV schools. This was resolved very successfully by the creation of a private company charged with the entire operation, working to schedules prepared by the Directorate of Primary Education (see section on Delivery Systems below).

To assume overall responsibility for the project, a secretary of state for primary education and educational television was appointed in 1972, reporting directly to the minister of education, and to whom the existing director of primary education would be responsible for all pedagogical matters concerning the reform. The secretary of state's cabinet includes the three senior expatriate administrators (UNESCO, France, Canada) responsible for day-to-day coordination of all external aid to the program. This is not always a simple matter, as, apart from the three sources already cited, UNICEF, the World Bank, Italy, Belgium, the Federal Republic of Germany, and the United States are all involved to varying degrees (see Table 5.3 for the main responsibilities of each external aid contributor). Overall coordination at a

TABLE 5. 3

Main External Contributions to the Ivory Coast ETV Project

Source	No. of Expatriates in Project (1975)	Main Sector(s) of Activity
UNESCO UNDP[a] UNICEF	17	Technical assistance in administration, teacher training, data processing, evaluation and out-of-school education. Funding of some initial studio facilities, of various studies, some training courses and equipment, and of study grants for Ivorians.
World Bank (IBRD)[b]	1	Technical assistance for evaluation and management. Loans for about half the cost of the new TV complex (and for construction of some new teacher-training schools). Funding of various studies.
France (FAC)[c]	137	Technical assistance in TV production, maintenance, evaluation, library, out-of-school education, and administration. Financing of various technical and pedagogical studies, of some initial production equipment, and of initial receiver installation; provision of study grants for Ivorians.
Canada (CIDA)[d]	27	Technical assistance in written materials development, editing, and printing; and in administration. Funding of some equipment and operation expenses; provision of study grants for Ivorians.
United States (AID) Belgium Federal Republic of Germany	2 1 2	Technical assistance in evaluation. Provision of study grants for Ivorians and backup academic support (United States, Belgium).

[a]United Nations Development Program.
[b]International Bank for Reconstruction and Development.
[c]Fund for Cooperative Assistance.
[d]Canadian International Development Agency.
Note: All expatriate staff have national counterparts. Majority of external aid is planned to terminate in 1978-80.

senior level of all external aid is handled by a top-level committee presided over by the secretary of state (the "Abidjan Club"), which meets annually.

Organizational matters are further complicated by the fact that the secretary of state and his cabinet, as well as the Directorate of Primary Education, are based in Abidjan, while the ETV production complex (responsible for TV and printed support material production and some teacher training) is sited 300 miles away in the center of the country at Bouaké. This, in the author's opinion, has contributed to the creation of a structure that is very difficult to manage effectively and economically, and where to some extent, the staff in Bouaké feel divorced from certain important decision-making functions. Informally at least, there are potentially several different management hierarchies in operation within the system. These are the original Directorate of Primary Education, controlling both the traditional and ETV schools through the network of inspectors; the Directorate of the ETV complex in Bouaké, controlling the different functional sous-directions (divisions), each headed by an Ivorian; the UNESCO, French, and Canadian groups, with the majority of the staff based in Bouaké under the control of their Ivorian directors, but for whom most important decisions concerning functions, salaries, promotions, and so on, are made in Abidjan, if not in Paris or Montreal; the secretary of state's cabinet in Abidjan, with several Abidjan-based units directly attached to it: the Architectural Unit, the Information Processing Unit, the Out-of-School Education Unit, and an Evaluation Unit.*

The relationships between the various services that make up the ETV Program, and their links with other government bodies involved, are shown schematically in Figure 5.1.

The fact that this unwieldy structure works (programs and printed materials are produced and distributed to the schools) is more a tribute to the good sense and adaptability of the senior staff involved, both expatriate and Ivorian, than to the design of the system. At least, however, it is flexible enough to adapt to continual structural changes and modifications, which leaves open the possibility of a much simpler organization evolving as expatriate assistance is withdrawn over the next few years.

The TV Production Complex

The production complex in Bouaké was set up initially in a "provisional" location (a teacher-training college) while awaiting the construction of a tailor-made building to be financed jointly by the Ivory

---

*Now directly attached to the Directorate of Primary Education.

FIGURE 5.1

Schematic Organizational Chart of the ETV Project

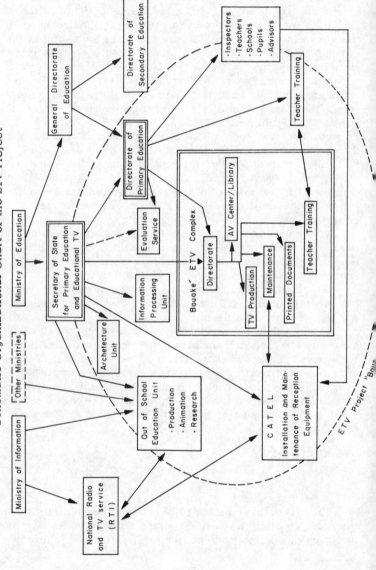

Coast and the World Bank. Work on the construction of this new complex has only just started and it will not in fact be ready until most of
the production for the six primary-school grades, remakes apart, is
completed. As indicated in Figure 5.1, the complex contains a separate
unit (sous-direction) for each main functional area, together with various specialized services—the library, the internal evaluation service,
and so on. The original conception of the complex as a joint production
and teacher-training establishment (the Normal School and one of the
seven other teacher-training institutions are located inside the complex) is a sound one in that it provides for a potential direct integration
of some trainee teachers into the ETV operation, even though it somewhat complicates the organization of the system. And it has also permitted an important recent innovation—specialist training in production
methods, combined with on-the-job practice, for future Ivorian teacher-
producers who will eventually take over from the expatriate production
staff.

     In the limited space available here, it is not possible to go into
all aspects of the organization of the complex. Some specific aspects
of course production are dealt with in the next section, and only two
out of many possible general points will be made here. The first concerns the problem of training of national staff and eventual withdrawal
of expatriates. The number of expatriate staff now working on the project is well above that proposed in the original planning document and,
with a few exceptions, the actual conception of most printed and televised material is still effectively in the hands of expatriates. This is
despite the fact that the project has been in operation for over five
years, and that each expatriate is "doubled" by a national. The reasons for this situation are many. In the first place, the pressure on
expatriate staff to produce learning materials on schedule, and at the
same time to be responsible for on-the-job training of their Ivorian
counterparts, has proved too demanding for many people. As a result,
each unit within the complex has managed, with varying degrees of
success, to increase its staff in response to the pressures imposed
by production deadlines.

     The problem is exacerbated by what are perceived by some ex-
patriate staff as poor working conditions (cramped offices, a slow-
moving bureaucracy, uncertain management, low morale),[20] and a lack
of adequate preparation of some technical assistants prior to their arrival in Bouaké. And, of course the differences in salary levels and
life-styles between expatriate and local staff, let alone cultural differences, provide a potential barrier to good working relationships. The
great strength, and yet at the same time the great weakness of the on-
the-job training approach adopted is that it rests almost entirely on
the dynamics of individual working groups of expatriates and nationals;
some of these groups have been extremely successful, mainly because
of the personalities and attitudes of the individuals involved; other
groups have been less successful.

On-the-job training is supplemented by more formal training periods for some staff, either abroad or within the Ivory Coast, and now a specialized training course for Ivorian producers is being built into the curriculum of the Normal School at Bouaké. Plans made at the 1975 meeting of the Abidjan Club envisage a much greater effort in the training of nationals, even if this should mean a slowing down in production of sixth-grade materials. These factors may go some way toward alleviating the problem.

Difficulties encountered in the combined training/production role of technical assistants are not, of course, special to the Ivory Coast Project—even in the small-scale and much less recent Télé-Niger Project, nearly one half of the current staff of 120 are expatriates, and Nigerois occupy mainly technical posts. [21]

The second general point to be made concerning the organization of the production complex has to do with the role of printed course materials in the teaching situation. The original planning document envisaged a relatively minor role for "accompanying texts" and the unit responsible was to be a branch of the main TV production service, with a total personnel of only eight—including typists and printing staff. Before actual implementation of the Project in 1971, it was realized that a more important place would need to be assigned to this area, and aid from the Canadian government was solicited for equipment and technical assistance. A sous-direction of Printed Support Materials was created, jointly staffed by French-speaking Canadians and their Ivorian counterparts (total staff in this service was 91 in 1975). The pedagogues in the service are responsible for planning of course content and progressions in collaboration with those in the TV Production Service, and for detailed elaboration, production, and printing of the accompanying documents. The offices and printing shops for the service were unfortunately located, however, in a different part of the town from the main complex, and this, in the early years at least, contributed to a lack of effective collaboration between the Canadians and the French TV production staff in the joint planning of TV and printed materials. In fact it has taken several years for a joint team approach to develop between the two groups. Despite these early difficulties, it is now evident that the attractively produced printed support materials for teachers and pupils play a very important role in the teaching situation— some would say a more important role than television. Concomitantly, their production costs—directly proportional to pupil numbers unlike those of TV—are taking up an increasingly important part of the Project's recurrent budget.

Overall Planning of the Primary-School Reform

With the benefit of hindsight, a few general points can be made concerning the overall planning of the educational reform in the primary

sector. First, most people involved would probably agree now that insufficient attention was given at the beginning to the training of local
staff to take crucial decisions on implementation policy and on curriculum conception. It may well have been wiser to have delayed introduction of ETV into the classrooms for a few years until this was done.
Once the decision was made to go ahead, however, immediate pressures
for production of first-grade programs and printed materials became the
priority, and insufficient thought was given to what the profile of the
primary-school graduate at the end of the sixth grade should be. As a
result, course material for each subsequent grade after the first tended
to be based more on what had been taught in the previous grade than on
a set of clearly defined terminal objectives.

Secondly, insufficient attention was paid to informing the public
(both parents and teachers) of the intentions and mechanisms of the reform. A particularly sensitive point has been the initial plan to delay
introduction of teaching of reading and writing until pupils had an adequate grasp of spoken French. In the traditional school system, reading
and writing is introduced at the beginning of first grade, and both parents and teachers have put such pressure on ETV authorities that the
first-grade ETV French curriculum has had to be modified several times
to introduce these subjects at an earlier stage than was originally intended. It is quite possible that a well-informed public would have
accepted the pedagogical advantages of giving priority to the spoken
language, had the reasons been explained to them adequately in the
first place.

Another sore point has been the abolition of homework, of regular
reports to parents, and of end-of-year tests, which are used in the
traditional system to decide whether a child should go on to the next
grade or repeat. In fact, once again, pressure from parents on this
last point has been such that the proposed policy of automatic promotion
from one grade to another has been officially modified to allow for a
5-10 percent repeater rate, should individual teachers judge this necessary. This decision is liable to have serious "knock-on" effects on
original cost and enrollment estimates. At the present time, however,
it is too early to say what effects this policy change will have on per
capita pupil costs, and hence on the whole economic argument for the
introduction of ETV discussed earlier in this chapter.

Organization of the Out-of-School Education Sector

The unit responsible for out-of-school education started off in 1972
as a part of the in-service teacher-training unit at the Bouaké complex,
and on a purely experimental basis in the first instance. However, as
the scale of the operation increased, it became evident that a continued
attachment to the complex could only hinder further development—partly

because most of the other ministries with whom the unit works are
Abidjan-based and partly because the unit needed greater autonomy
and flexibility in its management. Accordingly, the entire unit was
moved to Abidjan in 1974 and administratively directly attached to the
secretary of state's cabinet.

The unit works essentially as a production and animation service
at the disposal of the various ministries and other government bodies
who want to put across particular messages to the adult public; program
planning for each year is the responsibility of a joint interministerial
committee.

The working principles on which the use of TV in out-of-school
education is based (in some sense the "charter" of the out-of-school
ETV unit) are the following:

● that out-of-school education covers a variety of different areas
concerning the various different ministries, and is thus not a preroga-
tive of the Ministry of Education;

● that neither TV nor the mass media in general are the only means
of providing out-of-school education;

● that the ETV Project should be subject to the different ministries
concerned in both the choice and conception of programs and in the organization and "animation" of viewing groups;

● that the ETV Project is to be considered as a tool at the disposal
of the interested ministries and other parties, but as a tool whose role
is to guarantee the educational and televisual quality of the programs,
and to provide an organized reception structure in the TV schools
throughout the country;

● that official working groups should be set up within each ministry to act as a permanent link with the ETV Project. [22]

These working principles represent a valiant attempt to put TV in
its place as part of an overall system of out-of-school education, and
to create a vehicle for coordination of educational efforts between different ministries and other government organizations.

Programs are received in both an organized manner by adult viewing groups in ETV classrooms throughout the country, with a local
teacher acting as animator and translator and, of course, by individual
members of the public who possess their own receivers. The Abidjan
unit maintains the network of teacher/animators by providing them with
printed support materials for each program, by running a feedback service, and by attempting to deal with queries and requests for help. All
this is the responsibility of the "animation" service in the out-of-school
unit.

Financing of production is shared by the ETV Project and the ministries concerned in individual programs; expatriate technical assistance
in production is provided by France and UNESCO. The national radio
and television service, in addition to providing prime evening viewing
time, also provides some production assistance.

In general, it is too soon to say at this stage how this aspect of the ETV Project will develop. There are certain problems inherent to the interministerial collaboration involved, and it would seem that the government will need to think seriously about providing supplementary payment to hundreds of primary-school teachers who, at the moment, are "animating" rural and urban viewing groups on an entirely voluntary and unpaid basis. Most important, however, is the question as to the effectiveness of this type of action (centrally produced rural and urban development programs transmitted on TV) unless the necessary specialist technical advice can be provided as a follow-up. Telecasts aimed, for example, at pointing out the benefits of agricultural production cooperatives can lead to a feeling of frustration among the target audience if an agricultural extension worker is not at hand to give specific advice. And the number of such field workers (in the areas of health, agriculture, commerce, and so on) employed by the relevant ministries is at the moment inadequate to cover the needs.

PRODUCTION OF COURSE MATERIALS

Several points concerning course materials production have already been mentioned, notably the problems associated with the joint responsibility of technical assistants for production and for training, the importance of backup printed materials, and the effect that starting off production with first-grade materials has had on development of curricula for subsequent grades.

Only two of the many points that could be discussed will be mentioned here. The first concerns the actual production scheme adopted in preparation of both televisual and printed materials at the Bouaké complex. It is evident that production of materials of this sort relies on the skills of three different types of people: pedagogues, who, on the basis of a general curriculum outline, can prepare the detailed objectives and content of the printed materials, TV scenarios, and assessment instruments; creative staff experienced in matters such as page design and layout, illustration, and visualization and sequencing of film and TV products; technical staff able to print the supporting documents and produce the television programs.

It is also evident that the pedagogues and the creative staff need to work closely together and that, ideally, the latter should have a pedagogical background, and be familiar with the subject matter on which they are to work, and with the psychological principles underlying the design of the teaching materials.

An organization that facilitates the effective functioning of these three groups of people should reflect the structure shown in Figure 5.2.

FIGURE 5. 2

Production Functions

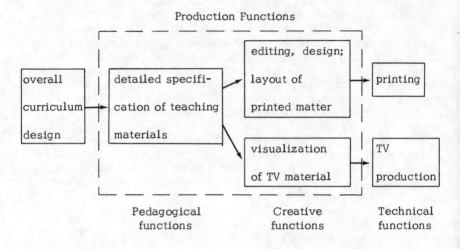

| Pedagogical | Creative | Technical |
| functions | functions | functions |

In the author's opinion, a major reason for the difficulties experienced at the Bouaké complex is that the organizational and functional structures do not correspond to each other. The particular pattern of external aid has in fact created an unnecessarily elaborate structure (see Figure 5. 3) with actual physical separation of people who should be working together and with three separate sous-directions where two would have sufficed (a pedagogical-creative unit and a technical unit).

FIGURE 5. 3

Production at the Bouaké Complex

Sous-direction Printed Documents (Canadian Aid)

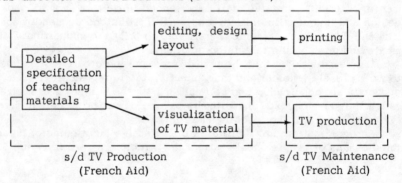

s/d TV Production   s/d TV Maintenance
   (French Aid)   (French Aid)

In such a scheme, it is easy to see how the extremely important phase of initial conception and specification, which ideally should be the responsibility of a single unit of nationals (advised by technical assistants in this case) is liable to go wrong. In the early years, a tendency rapidly appeared for the French pedagogues in the production unit to send over draft scenarios to their Canadian colleagues on which the latter were supposed to base their printed materials. Only recently has a joint group approach evolved. Matters were, and still are, complicated by the fact that the latest possible deadlines for finalization of printed materials are several months earlier than the corresponding deadlines for final TV production. Printed materials require in any case more lead time for production (printing, cutting, binding, packaging) than TV materials, and are delivered to the schools in bulk only three or four times a year. A significant part of the complex's TV production, however, is not finalized until a week or two before transmission. This factor increases the likelihood of a mismatch between the final TV and printed materials.

It would, theoretically, be possible to avoid this problem without advancing TV production deadlines—were the TV programs conceived as enrichment or accompanying material for the printed documents, to be produced only after finalization of the latter. Such an approach, of formally attributing a priority to printed materials, would, however, be contrary to the whole basis of the Project.

The general situation cannot in fact undergo any fundamental change until external aid in course production is withdrawn or reorganized, until all the staff are on the same site on the new complex, and professionally trained Ivorian pedagogue-producers are available. The intention is that these staff will be able to combine the functions undertaken separately at the moment by the expatriate pedagogues and the producers (réalisateurs). If at the time of such a change, the technical production side ("manufacture" of printed and TV materials) could be brought under joint control as a semiautonomous unit with its own recruitment and promotion policy, considerable improvements could be made in the level of professionalism of the TV material. At the moment the complex finds it difficult to recruit and promote good technical staff (such as cameramen, soundmen, maintenance technicians) because of the rather inflexible employment norms of the Ministry of Education to which it is subject.

The second general point to be made here concerns specifically the quantity and scheduling of TV production. In 1975, after five years of operation, the number of pedagogues working in TV production was 55 (of whom 25 were expatriates); and the number of producers, 17 (of whom eight were expatriates). On the technical side, out of a total staff of 120, the great majority of staff (101) were nationals. In the original plans, each primary-school TV program was to be 15 to 20 minutes long, and maximum use was to be made of material shot outside the studios. Reference has already been made to the problems in keeping up with deadlines, and to the difficulties encountered by expatriate staff in taking on both production and training roles. Furthermore, the number of producers has not really been adequate for the amount of work involved (for the school year 1973/74, for example, over 340 hours of programming was broadcast, of which the great majority was film production). In addition, administrative procedures for financing and arranging filming on location (vehicles, fuel, expense allowances, petty cash funds) have never functioned adequately, based as they are on rules laid down for the traditional educational administration. All of these factors have contributed to actual average program lengths of only five to ten minutes, to the great majority of production being studio based, and to an important use of "stock shot" and archive material.

Again, an early emphasis on film equipment and techniques, combined with technical problems in processing exposed films (films had to be sent to Abidjan for development), has contributed to a general slowness of production. Only in the last year or two has significant progress been made in video production, which is inherently a more time-efficient and flexible medium than film.

In the author's opinion, many of the problems encountered in TV production could (on the basis of hindsight) have been avoided if these principles had been adopted from the origin of the ETV Project: (1) a commitment to maximum use of video equipment and techniques, rather than film; (2) initiation, at the earliest possible stage, of the training of Ivorian pedagogues in video production techniques, thus abolishing the pedagogue-producer distinction; and (3) joint organizational collaboration of pedagogues responsible for conception of TV and printed materials.

It is salutory to see, in fact, that the Project is currently developing along these lines, for it is only in this way that a successful total transfer of production to national staff will be effected.

DELIVERY SYSTEMS

Overall Structure

Although the main emphasis in the design of the Project was on the use of television as the major "delivery system," it is by no means the only method used for transmission of information and learning materials. The list below shows the complete range:

• Television broadcasts. Currently there are about 20 broadcasts daily for the primary-school sector and one or two weekly for out-of-school education, representing an annual total of about 500 hours air time when sixth-grade classes are included in 1976.

● Weekly radio broadcasts. These are used mainly for providing some in-service training to teachers in non-ETV schools to prepare them for their eventual incorporation in the ETV system. Radio information bulletins are also extensively used for announcing meetings, training courses, examination sessions, and so on.

● Printed teacher guides and pupil texts. These are prepared as supporting documents for the primary-school TV programs, and are delivered by truck at the beginning of each term to the primary-school inspectorates, from which teachers have to collect them individually; this presents problems in some parts of the country, but delivery to individual schools would be too costly (in 1974 over 200 tons weight of such printed documents were produced and distributed).

● A biweekly 24-page supplement for ETV teachers in the weekly government-controlled paper Fraternité-Hebdo. It is mailed to the schools, but not always received in time in many of the outlying parts of the country. This supplement, entitled L'Ecole Permanente, carries articles of general interest concerning the development of the Project, answers to readers' letters, additional explanatory material on curriculum subjects, and material on the psychology of teaching.

● Printed animation guides and wall charts for the teachers involved in assisting out-of-school programs. The texts include not only backup and preparatory material for each broadcast, but also summaries of feedback data and answers to questions and problems raised by individual animators. These materials are either sent directly to the teachers or delivered to the schools involved by the TV maintenance vehicles. (Use of these vehicles for delivery of primary-school teaching materials directly to the schools is not possible because of the volume and weight of the documents).

Television Installation and Maintenance

The problems posed by the use of a television on a wide scale, in a humid tropical country, with inadequate existing maintenance facilities and only partial electrification, were fully explored in the original planning documents. [23] It was recommended that the receivers should be transistorized, low-voltage sets with adequate protection against damp and insects, that the circuitry should be contained in a small number of removable subunits or modules to facilitate speedy repairs (by exchange of a defective module for a new one), and that teachers should have access only to the brightness and volume controls. Installation and maintenance of receivers, it was suggested, would be assumed by a special service attached to the national broadcasting network, Radio-Télévision Ivorien (RTI) and each school would be visited once a month by a TV maintenance team. Repair of faulty subunits would be the responsibility of a central workshop in Abidjan.

As a final precaution, it was recommended that each first-grade class in 1971/72 (the first year of broadcasting) should be equipped with two receivers so that a spare would be available in case of breakdown. The following year, this receiver would be used by second-grade classes, and then a new receiver would be added for each grade year by year.

The majority of the technical recommendations have in practice been followed. However, the suggestion for the organization of installation and maintenance under the control of the national broadcasting authorities has not been adopted, partly because time did not allow for the necessary administrative arrangements to be made. In fact, a private company has been created to fulfill these functions, the Compagnie Africaine de Télévision (CATEL). The activities of this company include measurement of transmitter field strength; installation of receivers, aerials and batteries; maintenance and renewal of equipment (batteries are replaced after two years use, receivers are to be replaced after five years use); and research and development on equipment improvement. The company runs a fleet of maintenance vans—each van makes a monthly visit to each school in its circuit—and a number of supervisory vehicles, which are in two-way radio contact with the head office and warehouse in Abidjan. Urgent repairs can be made in response to letters and phone calls outside the monthly visits schedule. Installation of equipment in new schools is carried out during the summer vacation, when the maintenance vehicles are not otherwise in use.

The basic "reception module" installed in the majority of schools (over two-thirds of the schools have no electricity) is composed of three TV receivers (specially designed and manufactured for the Project by the Centre Electronique de France); a stand for each receiver; one aerial and mast; a 32-element alkaline battery; and a switch unit.

The standard six-classroom, six-grade school has two such modules. Each battery set has a useful life of about 2,000 hours, which corresponds to about two years of school use (theoretically more, but it appears that in many classes the teachers leave the sets switched on between broadcasts, despite directions to turn them off, and sets are probably also used for an unknown amount of evening viewing by some teachers). Battery replacement costs (each set of batteries currently costs the equivalent of about $1,000) form a significant part of the recurrent budget for the Project and the CATEL is carrying out field trials of solar-powered batteries at the moment. Initial results from these trials suggest that their wide-scale use may provide valuable cost savings.

In general the system operated by the CATEL works efficiently, and the modifications to reception equipment already introduced by their engineers have contributed significantly to both the power efficiency of the receivers and their reliability. With the exception of a handful of senior management and research staff, the company is manned entirely by nationals. The relative independence of the organization and administration of the service, which can be attributed to its status as

a private company, has undoubtedly been a major factor inherent to its
successful operation.

Direct Contact and Periphery—Center Links

The various delivery systems listed above, and television especially, can be criticized as being inherently center-to-periphery information channels providing little opportunity for communication from
teachers to the complex, or between teachers. And this orientation has
undoubtedly been reinforced by the traditional French model of heavily
centralized teaching systems that formed the basis of the Ivory Coast
Project. Nevertheless, a number of direct face-to-face links between
teachers and central production staff are built into the system. Numerous training, updating, and familiarization courses for teachers
are presented each year at the complex, both during the school year
and the summer vacation. Out-of-school animators are brought into
the complex for a two-week course before the start of each school year.
Project officials as well as evaluation staff get to visit a number of
schools each year in the course of their work, and at an intermediary
level each school has access to the advice of the two or three pedagogical advisors based in each of the 60 or so primary-school inspectorates. Problems of an administrative nature can also be discussed
at a local level with the primary-school inspector, who can then raise
them with the office of the director of primary education. Other channels
of communication from teachers to central staff include direct correspondence to relevant groups at the complex, of a solicited kind—such
as the requests for comments and views made over the TV network and
in the biweekly newspaper supplement—and, of course, unsolicited
mail. Out-of-school animators are asked to return a completed feedback
form after each program, which not only keeps central staff informed of
audience characteristics and reactions, but also acts as a vehicle for
personal comments and suggestions.

Finally, as far as communication between schools is concerned,
recent projects and plans include a regular newspaper for pupils to be
composed mainly of children's work and comments, and a weekly TV
magazine for children, to include material filmed in various urban and
rural schools.

USE OF THE MEDIA IN THE TEACHING SITUATION

Classroom Teaching in the Primary Schools

Despite the difficulties described above in the discussion on
course materials production, the degree of integration between printed

and TV materials, as perceived from the users' end, is very good in some disciplines—especially those materials prepared and/or revised in the last year or two. In general, in each main subject area, detailed teacher guides and pupil workbooks are available for each term's work, and these form the basis for utilization and development of the material presented in the 5-to-10-minute television broadcasts (see Table 5.4 below for main discipline areas and associated total class time and TV time). The printed materials, all of standard A4 format, are attractively produced and presented, well illustrated and in some disciplines (environmental studies, basic education) contain photographs and even reproductions of children's drawings and poems—all based on Ivory Coast material. There can be no doubt of the superiority of thest texts compared with those used in the traditional public primary schools or in the French-oriented private primary schools.

The general scheme for classroom activities in the early grade lessons is the following: [24]

1. Prebroadcast Preparation (five minutes). The children settle down and the teacher prepares the lesson.

2. Viewing of Broadcast. The teacher watches pupil reactions.

3. Postbroadcast Evaluation (ten minutes). The teacher questions the pupils on reactions to the broadcast.

4. Follow-up. The pupils, in groups or individually, carry out exercises based on the guidelines in the teacher's manual or those included in the pupil workbooks.

As a specific example of the way in which the materials are planned, one can cite the pattern used for math teaching in first-grade classes. The printed materials for the third term include a 40-page teacher manual and a 32-page pupil workbook containing exercises on set theory and basic calculation. The teacher manual, for each of the 64 math lessons of this term, contains notes on the objectives of the lesson; the content of the TV program; any materials needed (such as bottle tops or seeds for counting and classification exercises); lesson activities (to be carried out in groups or individually in the classroom or in the school playground).

In the higher grades, and in some disciplines, the classroom time is more flexible, and greater liberty is given to the teachers to adapt teaching to the individual requirements of their pupils and the local milieu. In addition, in grade three, for example, time allocations for lessons for some subjects are longer (for example, 1/2-hour blocks for French language)—thus permitting the teacher to develop his work at greater length without changing subjects every 45 minutes. Use of TV also tends to be more innovative and milieu-related in the higher grades—language teaching is built around a TV serial (one installment a week), which is a dramatized version of the day-to-day life of a group of village children.

Use of milieu-related material is particularly evident in some areas of the basic education curriculum (which includes singing, music,

TABLE 5.4

Total Class Time for Each Discipline Each Week, Including
Average Weekly TV Broadcasting Time,
for Grades One Through Three

Subject	Grade 1 (CP1)*		Grade 2 (CP2)		Grade 3 (CE1)	
	Total	TV	Total	TV	Total	TV
French language	6'40"	1'40"	6'10"	1'40"	5'55"	1'00"
Reading	6'10"	0'25"	7'00"	0'15"	4'40"	0'40"
Writing	2'25"	—	0'30"	—	0'45"	—
Mathematics	4'00"	0'30"	4'00"	0'30"	4'50"	0'30"
Hygiene, morals, civics, serial	0'30"	—	0'50"	—	1'55"	0'20"
Basic education	3'30"	0'40"	3'00"	0'35"	2'15"	0'35"
Environmental studies	—	—	—	—	2'40"	0'25"
Physical education	2'00"	—	1'45"	—	2'15"	—
Recreation	2'00"	—	2'00"	—	2'00"	—
Total	27'15"	3'15"	27'15"	3'00"	27'15"	3'30"

*Figures for grade one are those for the second and third terms.

bodily expression, art, poetry, and physical education). The opportunities for using Ivorian music, dance, and crafts as a basis for pupil
activities have been fully exploited here, with detailed illustrative
material on TV and in the printed texts. In the environmental-studies
curriculum introduced in third grade, great attention is paid to illustrating scientific and geographical principles by using material relevant
to the Ivory Coast—agricultural practices, seasonal climatic changes,
different zones of vegetation, and so on. The television programs here
play an obviously important role. In general, the proportion of TV time
devoted to this and other locally relevant material increases significantly as one passes from the lower to higher grades. Such material—
as opposed to that associated with basic teaching of trends and math—
passes from about one-tenth of total transmission time in grade one
in 1971 to one-half of total time in grade three in 1974. This change
is no doubt due to a number of factors not necessarily associated with
conscious curriculum design. These factors include the increasing
experience of expatriate staff, the increasing influence of nationals,
and the gradual overcoming of practical difficulties associated with
outside filming.

In-Service Teacher Training and Support

The original plans for the project foresaw one hour being reserved
at the start of each day (from 7 to 8 a. m.) for TV programs aimed at the
teachers, to help them plan their day's work. [25] In reality, this plan
was never adopted as such, but on Monday, Tuesday, Thrusday, and
Friday evenings (at 5:15 p. m.) there is a short live broadcast for
teachers after the children have left school. These broadcasts, called
Le Journal des Maîtres, serve a number of purposes inherent to their
"live" quality—including announcements, last-minute program changes,
feedback reports, and discussions of problems raised by individual
teachers.

Each Wednesday afternoon (when there are no regular classes) is
devoted to more formal in-service training (Ecole Normale Permanente).
In some cases, teachers from different schools meet together at the
Inspectorate where they receive face-to-face teaching from a more
knowledgeable colleague in conjunction with the programs broadcast
from the complex. These Wednesday afternoon sessions have proved
particularly valuable in "converting" teachers to modern mathematics;
the newspaper supplements already mentioned provide the necessary
supporting material for the broadcasts and the face-to-face sessions.
Teacher groups are encouraged to submit reports on their reactions to
this training and send them in to the complex to form a basis for subsequent modifications and adjustments.

The Impact of Primary School ETV

As has already been pointed out, it is too early at this stage to
make any conclusive judgments about the effects of the ETV Project on
pupil learning in the main discipline areas—such test data will not be
available for several years. It would, however, be reasonable to
assume that implementation of the Project is having a significant effect
on equalizing the quality of primary-school education in the different
parts of the country—one of the major overall objectives. The framework
provided by the schedule of broadcasts, the quality of the printed materials, and the efforts devoted to in-service training, spread throughout all the ETV schools, together represent an enormous improvement
on the situation that used to prevail in the traditional schools, especially those in the less favored parts of the country. And there appears
to be an increasing agreement, on the part of both ETV and non-ETV
teachers, that children in the ETV schools are more active, more questioning, and express themselves better than those in the traditional
schools. However, accurate information on this very important point
will have to await the conclusion of a number of tests and surveys that
are currently under way.

Impact of Out-of-School Education Viewing Groups

Even more so than for the primary-school sector, it is too early at this stage to measure the behavioral and attitudinal effects of the out-of-school broadcasts. However, a description of the typical rural viewing group and the reception its members give to the programs can be derived from information collected on a wide-scale and regular basis in 1975. Such a "typical" group has 60 to 80 spectators, of whom about one-half will be more or less regular members, and will include several of the village notables. Reception conditions are generally good during the transmission, and the French sound track will be translated into one of about 30 local languages (depending on the region of the country and the main ethnic groups represented in the audience). In about half the groups, the translation is done by the teacher, in other groups, another member of the community will assume this task. On average, the discussion following the broadcast lasts about 40 minutes. In about half the centers, some form of decision for action is taken by the group concerning the proposals made in the program.

In the urban centers, however, it is proving very difficult to stimulate the formation of such viewing groups. This is due to the combination of a number of factors—the widespread ownership of private TV receivers in electrified areas, the competing distractions of town life, and the fact that, in the towns, the teachers often do not live on or near the school premises.

Current areas of research in the out-of-school sector include follow-up studies of decisions for action taken by specific viewing groups and tests of visual comprehension of TV images. In many rural areas, these telecasts represent the first exposure many adults have had to moving (TV) images, and program producers are having to take special care over the use of techniques such as rapid zoom-ins, close-ups, and voice-offs, which are not necessarily readily comprehensible to their target audience.

EVALUATION, FEEDBACK, SERVICES AND CONTROL MECHANISMS

The necessity of installing a unit to monitor the effectiveness of the ETV Project was recognized from the beginning. The original planning document proposed the creation of an evaluation and research unit attached to what became the TV production service of the Bouaké complex. [26] Its functions were only vaguely defined, although mention was made of diagnostic evaluation, global evaluation, cost-effectiveness evaluation, management evaluation, and so on. All this with a proposed team of three or four specialists. The main concrete proposal made concerned systematic comparative achievement testing between the traditional and reformed system, with test development to start in 1969.

What in reality has happened is somewhat different from this initial scheme. A small feedback service was set up in the Bouaké complex (1971) staffed by three French technical assistants and their Ivorian counterparts, the latter mainly recruited at the primary-school-teacher level. The function of this service, which was directly attached to the directorate of the complex, was to provide rapid feedback of a formative nature to the TV and printed materials production staff. Data collection in the field was carried out with the help of the pedagogical advisers attached to each primary-school inspection. A panel of 50 such advisors would be sent periodic classroom observation schedules and test materials to administer in a selected sample of classrooms within their area, the results being mailed back directly to the feedback service in Bouaké. In addition, occasional experiments in administering test materials via the TV network were attempted.

The problems encountered in organizing this type of formative data collection and especially in reinvesting the information culled will be familiar to those readers who have any experience in this field. For example, the production process did not allow sufficient time for adequate design and pretesting of test instruments between the stage at which objectives were clearly formulated for specific course materials (and of course, in many cases such clear statements of objectives did not exist) and the time at which materials were being presented. Furthermore, the use of the pedagogical advisers as regular testers and data gatherers was not always successful (the return rates of completed test schedules and questionnaires were usually too low to be representative). This was in part due to the fact that such tasks did not form an official part of the advisers' job descriptions, and tended to be perceived as extra, unpaid chores. Finally, even in the cases where feedback activities led to reasonably clear prescriptions for improvements in specific printed and TV course materials, the changes could in theory only be effected for the subsequent year's cohort of pupils, and that only on the assumption that adequate staff and resources were available for "remakes." As a general rule, however, such resources would be totally committed to planning and producing materials for a higher grade level. Attempts at rapid corrective feedback to teachers and classes, such as using spare TV transmission time, were limited by delays inherent in returning and processing data from the pedagogical advisors—a minimum of three weeks would be necessary for this if the postal system was used. The alternative—to base such rapid corrective advice on classrooms readily accessible within the Bouaké area, using the central feedback staff as data gatherers—was of course open to the criticism of being nonrepresentative of the country as a whole, especially when the variations among different ethnic groups are taken into account. Thus any program producer hostile to evaluation findings from such a source could readily discount them.

Over the years, improvements have nevertheless been made in this system at several levels. For example, central feedback service staff are now integrated into the different discipline groups of pedagogues and producers preparing course materials. They can thus help not only in involving all members of the groups in feedback and evaluation schemes, but also in elaborating teaching objectives in a testable form. Feedback activities now tend to be oriented more toward specific and manageable priority areas, tackled on a thorough basis, rather than in attempting to obtain regular weekly data from a standard questionnaire format. And a small team of motivated pedagogical advisers, who come to the complex for training in the use of specific instruments, is being formed. These changes are already having positive effects on the quality and amount of data being received.

In late 1972, an external evaluation unit was created, directly attached to the secretary of state's cabinet in Abidjan, and charged with overall summative project evaluation in several critical areas (pedagogical testing, economic evaluation, and technical and management evaluation). This unit is staffed and financed jointly by three countries not otherwise involved in the project (the United States, Belgium, and the Federal Republic of Germany). Specialized academic aid is provided for evaluation and for associated training of graduate-level Ivorian staff by two universities (Liège, in Belgium, for testing work and Stanford, California, for out-of-school evaluation and eventual cost-effectiveness analysis).

More recently, in 1975, the external evaluation unit and the feedback service at the complex have been reorganized into a single evaluation service, under the charge of an Ivorian graduate who reports to the director of primary education. This should ensure more comprehensive planning of evaluation activities, and facilitate reinvestment of test results in the process of curriculum planning and revision, this being the responsibility of the Directorate of Primary Education. The service is now adequately staffed, including at the moment eight expatriates, and about 12 Ivorians—half of whom are graduates in social sciences or educational sciences. Most of the expatriates are on loan for a limited period from their home institution or university and have a well-defined training role incorporated into their contracts. A long-term comprehensive program of criterion testing in French and mathematics, at each grade level, and for teacher training, together with teacher behavior and attitude measures, was initiated in 1973 with the assistance of the University of Liège's Laboratory of Experimental Pedagogy. This program, while of little immediate value in providing formative evaluation data (preparation of instruments for each grade level involves a three-year cycle of pretest, dry run, and final representative testing) will, however, furnish an accurate global evaluation of pupil achievement for the ETV system throughout the country and for each grade level.

Evaluation in the out-of-school education sector, where the parameters of the system (for example, audience characteristics, specification of learning objectives) are much less controlled than for the primary sector, and where surveys and tests must be carried out via interpreters, is much more problematic. Current projects are concentrating on two major points: collection of base-line data on viewing groups on a regular basis, using the animators as information gatherers, and detailed follow-up surveys of the eventual impact of specific programs on small samples of viewing groups.

Project Control Functions

During the early years of the ETV Project, it rapidly became evident that the traditional structures for collection of data for management and control purposes were ill-adapted to the needs of the ETV system. In the traditional primary school organization, two services under the control of the director of primary education were responsible respectively for collection of statistical data on schools, pupils, and teachers (Service de la Carte Scolaire) and for planning and processing all budgetary matters, including salaries, purchasing, investment, and loan (Direction des Affaires Administratives et Financières). The procedures and methods of analysis that functioned quite adequately under the old system came under great strain with the addition of all the new components involved in the ETV Project (budgetary control of the Bouaké complex, receiver installation and maintenance, provision of printed materials, coordination of external aid resources). Accurate base-line data for cost-effectiveness analysis and personnel and resources management were difficult to establish given the constraints of the existing system.

These problems are now being resolved to some extent by the development of the original data-processing unit, established in late 1972, into a specialized service charged with collecting and analyzing all information necessary for the effective management and control of the ETV Project. For example, recently installed budgetary control procedures, involving computer storage and analysis of data, are at last beginning to provide detailed information on expenditure within different sectors of the system. This new system should not only permit a much closer control of resources, but also provide a sound basis for subsequent cost-effectiveness analysis.

However, these improvements in project control procedures are being obtained not only at the expense of a certain reliance on computer-based technology, but also at the cost of an increase in foreign personnel. In 1975 there were 13 expatriates in this service, and with two exceptions national staff occupied technical posts only (as coders, card-punchers, and so on). Recruitment and training of graduate-level national staff to take over these crucial control posts in the Project must be considered an urgent priority.

One important, though obvious point, can be made in concluding this brief overview of some aspects of data collection and analysis for both evaluation and control of the ETV Project. This is that adequately specified systems to serve these functions should have been set up before the Project became operational and not three or four years later. The original planning document, although specifying in great detail the technical equipment and personnel needed for TV production, is very vague about the functions of, and need for, specialized evaluation and control systems. As a result, accurate data on project development in the first few years, which would have been an invaluable aid to more effective project management, was not available when it was needed.

CONCLUDING REMARKS

It must be stressed again that it is too early at the present time to make any definitive judgment on the ETV Project, even in terms of pupil achievement and unit costs. It is even more impossible to judge to what extent the output of the reformed system will correspond to the basic social, political, and economic objectives for development as laid down in the current Five Year Plan.

As far as the questions of pupil achievement and unit costs are concerned, the important point centers on the real reduction in repeater and dropout rates under the reformed system. If repeater rates are kept to around 5 percent per year, then unit cost for each graduating pupil will still be lower than under the traditional system. But at the moment, accurate countrywide data on actual repeater rates is very difficult to obtain—perhaps partly because some teachers may feel that they will risk official disapproval by making children repeat, even though the automatic promotion policy has now been modified. It remains to be seen whether a low average repeater rate can be maintained, however, especially in the final grade of the primary cycle. In the present situation, only about one-quarter of graduating pupils will be able to find places in secondary schools in any one year. Traditionally, pupils who failed to enter a secondary school the first time around would re-peat the last primary grade and take the exam again 12 months later. If such a policy is permitted under the ETV system, it will have serious implications for the whole cost basis of the project. It would imply an increased delay in achievement of universal primary education by the mid-1980s target date. And it is here that the real problems start to appear. Questions concerning the relative merits of different strategies of ETV utilization and in-service teacher training pale into insignificance when compared with these issues: the total cost of universal primary education, the corresponding increase in social demand for secondary and higher education, the lack of employment opportunities for the qualified school-leavers, and all the related difficulties that beset any country in a comparable situation and with comparable social and political structures.

In 1972 President Houphouet-Boigny set up a National Commission for Educational Reform with a representative from each of the ministries, from the private sector, from teachers' unions, from agricultural organizations, and from other important national agencies, to study the whole area of educational policy in the Ivory Coast. Students at the University of Abidjan were also involved. And in a survey conducted by the university's Institute of Ethno-Sociology and presented to the Commission, it was apparent that many students felt the current system was unadapted to Ivorian social and political realities. The students believed the education system tends to create an isolated intellectual elite, and that it needs reforming from top to bottom. According to Paul-Henri Siriex, [27] the conclusions of the Commission, presented in mid-1974 to the president, are of a similar nature. It would appear that the Commission is recommending a nine-year basic compulsory primary cycle, followed by employment, job-related training, or a relatively conventional secondary cycle. There would be strong technical, scientific, and rural orientations to both the revised primary and secondary cycles.

Should the recommendations of this Commission be accepted by the government, it would then seem evident that the ETV curriculum will have to be radically modified, as will current plans for introducing ETV into the existing secondary system.

NOTES

1. The Ivory Coast Republic, La Côte d'Ivoire en Chiffres (Abidjan: Ministry of Planning, 1975), p. 9.

2. Ibid., p. 12.

3. Ibid., p. 27.

4. Perspectives Maghrebines, La Côte d'Ivoire (Casablanca, 1971), p. 15.

5. Ibid.

6. The Ivory Coast Republic, Five Year Plan for Social, Economic and Cultural Development, 1971-1975, abridged English version (Paris, 1972), p. 25.

7. J. M. Gibbal, Citadins et Villageois dans la Ville Africaine—l'exemple d'Abidjan (Grenoble, France: Presses Universitaires de Grenoble, François Maspero, 1974), p. 22.

8. Samir Amin, Le Développement du Capitalisme en Côte d'Ivoire (Paris: Editions du Minuit, 1967).

9. Figures quoted in this paragraph are cited in R. Z. Zolberg, One Party Government in the Ivory Coast (Princeton, N. J.: Princeton University Press, 1962), pp. 29-30.

10. The Ivory Coast Republic, La Côte d'Ivoire en Chiffres, op. cit., p. 53.

11. The Ivory Coast Republic, Programme d'Education Télévisuelle, vol. 1 (Abidjan: Ministry of Education, 1968), chapter 1.

12. Ibid., p. 31.

13. Wilbur Schramm et al., eds., New Educational Media in Action: Case Studies for Planners (Paris: UNESCO, IIEP, 1967).

14. The Ivory Coast Republic, Programme d'Education Télévisuelle, vol. 1, op. cit., pp. 44-50.

15. Ibid., vol. 3.

16. Ibid., vol. 1, pp. 35-40.

17. Ibid., p. 284.

18. The Ivory Coast Republic, Plan Quinquennal de Développement Economique, Social, et Culturel—1971-1975 (Abidjan: Ministry of Planning, 1972).

19. The Ivory Coast Republic, Programme d'Education Télévisuelle, vol 1, op. cit., p. 88.

20. Y. Durandeau, La Coopération en Pratique, in Recherches no. 15 (Paris: CERFI, June 1974).

21. L'Agence de Coopération Culturelle et Technique, Télé-Niger Douze Ans Après (Paris: Centre d'Information et d'Echanges Télévision, September 1975, VII-65).

22. The Ivory Coast Republic, "Document d'Actualisation du PETV" (Abidjan: Ministry of Education, 1973).

23. The Ivory Coast Republic, Programme d'Education Télévisuelle, vol. 1, op. cit., chapter 5.

24. Secretary of State for Primary Education and Educational Television, Television in the Modernisation of Education in the Ivory Coast (Abidjan: Ministry of Education, 1972).

25. The Ivory Coast Republic, Programme d'Education Télévisuelle, vol. 1, op. cit., p. 95.

26. Ibid., p. 147.

27. Paul-Henri Siriex, Félix Houphouet-Boigny, l'Homme de la Paix (Paris: Seghers, Nouvelles Editions Africaines, 1975), p. 268.

6

SOME CROSS-CULTURAL IMPLICATIONS OF EDUCATIONAL TELEVISION: THE SAMOAN ETV PROJECT

Lynne Masland
with Grant Masland

When the South Pacific Commission announced plans to hold its annual conference for 1962 in American Samoa, U. S. government officials, already concerned about the U. S. image in Southeast Asia and realizing that regional, if not world, attention would be focused on Pago Pago, felt this could be an opportunity to make the Samoan territory a showcase for the benefits of American influence.

Until the 1960s, American rule of Samoa had been rather laissez faire. The island group had been administered since 1951 by the U. S. Department of the Interior, which appointed a governor; previously, the U. S. Navy had provided medical services and administration. The public school system, languishing under the supervision of the Naval Commandant, changed little when the Department of the Interior took over. American Samoa was still known as the "Tobacco Road of the South Pacific."

> Observers of the school system at that time report that
> Samoa had no acceptable school plant, organization,
> teaching staff, nor administrative structure; no dis-
> cernible educational goals; and only the vaguest form
> of curriculum. The 43 village elementary schools,
> scattered throughout the islands were dilapidated. The
> Samoan classroom teachers, themselves products of
> Samoa's public schools, averaged only a fifth-grade
> education. . . . English was the medium of instruction
> in the schools; yet the Samoan teachers understood and
> spoke it poorly. [1]

A project to dramatically improve public education seemed suitable.

One should not assume uncritically that the generally accepted description of Samoan education was accurate in all respects. There are indications that the actual situation was somewhat more favorable to overall Samoan standards and goals and that the negative descriptions were, to some extent at least, influenced by American inclinations toward "manifest destiny. " In his 1960 Annual Report, Samoa's only Samoan-born governor, Peter Tali Coleman, states:

> The objectives and policies of the American Samoan educational system are to provide training which will enable the people to serve more effectively within their social, economic, professional, and political structure. At the same time, education must provide suitable background for those who will find it possible to take advantage of opportunities for education in the United States or other countries. Proficiency in the English language must not be the sole subject goal, but proficiency in basic skills related to science, medicine, business, the arts and other varied fields must also be accomplished. Therefore, it becomes the responsibility of the government, as the Samoans are influenced more and more by contact with Western civilization, to conserve the best of Samoan culture, and at the same time to guide them in developing changes which are to their advantage. 2

English was considered the "international language" of Samoa; therefore, it was important that children be trained in this language, while maintaining proficiency in Samoan. In addition to language arts, science and health, and social studies emphasizing Samoan culture and values, the pre-TV curriculum included vocational training in such skills as carpentry, electricity, plumbing, and boat repair. Elementary-school buildings and teachers' accommodations, built in traditional Samoan fashion, were provided by each village; secondary schools were furnished by the government, with plans made to extend these facilities. Education, at the onset of the 1960s, was to be strengthened at the elementary level by improving the teaching staff and directing attention to the teacher-training college. This pattern was similar to the educational systems in the neighboring island groups: Western Samoa, Tonga, and Fiji.

Nevertheless, in 1961 the alternatives considered by the newly appointed governor, H. Rex Lee, were, according to Wilbur Schramm, the following:

> (a) to use television to carry the core of the teaching, and for adult education (this would require teachers and administrators to adapt quickly to a radical change in school procedures); (b) to recruit several hundred fully qualified teachers from the United States (this would have had an immediate effect on standards, but would have been very expensive . . . and would have required

the dismissal of several hundred Samoan teachers, many
of whom had twenty years or more of service); (c) to
recruit a smaller number of teachers, say, 100, in the
United States, and spread them throughout the system
(this would also have had a quick effect on standards
and would have been less expensive than the previous
alternative, but would have been counter to the Samoan
norm of everyone moving forward together); (d) to initiate
an extensive and long-term plan for training future Samoan
teachers in the United States, introducing these new
teachers into the system as vacancies appeared (this would
have had little effect on standards for ten years or so). [3]

Governor Lee proposed the installation of an instructional television network through which the core teaching for all public schools
would be broadcast. In October 1964 the first three channels of KVZK-TV
began broadcasting to a limited number of elementary classrooms; and a
year later, three additional channels began broadcasting to secondary
schools. [4] The Pago Pago television studio, by the end of the 1960s,
produced as many as 200 class programs a week for all primary and
secondary grades. ETV carried the basic curriculum in the elementary
grades (one through eight)—language arts, mathematics, science, art,
and physical education. At the secondary level (grades nine through
12), it carried instruction in home economics, general shop, and business courses. [5]
    Accompanying the development and dissemination of the new cur-
ricula was a quantitative expansion of the school system, involving a
large-scale school construction program. By 1970 approximately 9,000
students were enrolled in public schools through the 12th grade, with
another 1,800 in church schools. (The estimated population of Samoa
at the time was 28,000.)
    The objectives of the Samoan educational television project were
to equal, through what Governor Lee described as "explosive upgrading,"* the educational standards of schools in the continental
United States, and to improve rapidly the Samoans' ability to speak
English. In practice, ability to speak and understand English had become equated with the upgrading of the school system. The main thrust

---

    *Here is the rest of the statement: "It was a technique that we
blatantly burgled from the advertising methods of Madison Avenue.
In fact, we call much of our instruction in letters and numbers commercials. From the technical viewpoint, commercials are among the
most effective moments on American television today. So our decision
to adapt the technique was an easy one to make, except we are selling
some basic skills of early education instead of cereal, toys or tooth-
pastes. "[6]

of the ETV project became the teaching of the English language. In
1969 a UNESCO team surveying ETV systems in Niger, El Salvador, and
American Samoa reported:

> In both primary and secondary education in Samoa there
> is reflected a preoccupation with gaining English language
> proficiency. This preoccupation or emphasis is so dominant
> that it appears that education in Samoa is virtually equated
> with attaining some level of precision in the use of English
> language. 7*

The ability to read and speak English competently was believed important for every Samoan, whether he remained in Samoa or moved to
Hawaii or the United States mainland.
    To achieve this "upgrading," the Samoan ETV network was set up
to provide centralized control of all material taught in every public
school classroom. Overall planning and curriculum coordination,
teaching and lesson plan research, production, scheduling, and broadcasting of the TV lessons took place in the production studio. Most
studio personnel were Americans, hired in the United States by the
National Association of Educational Broadcasters, which managed the
project. There were some Samoans in training.
    Lesson plans, to be followed by the Samoan classroom teacher,
student worksheets, and supplemental materials were written and
printed at the production studio and distributed weekly to the schools.
The Samoan classroom teacher, supervised by an American principal,
facilitated and complemented the TV lessons by following the lesson
plans. Each lesson was structured in the following manner:
    Preparation: Done by the classroom teacher in accordance with
lesson-plan instructions.
    TV lesson: Core teaching. Televised.

_____

*I have seen studies or reports of studies that analyzed test results
rendered by overseas samples of children in Puerto Rico, Mexico, Chile,
and West Germany. Only one as yet unpublished study runs counter to
the general trend, showing that children exposed to the program score
higher on achievement tests than their counterparts who have not been
equivalently exposed; or exceed their own scores before exposure. The
maverick study is the work of investigators at the Mexican Instituto
Nacional de Ciencias del Comportamiento y de la Actitud Pública,
"INCCAPAC." A preliminary report on this research claims that rural
Mexican preschool children register no discernible gains after exposure
to the programs. This is in contrast to children from nonrural areas
among whom gains were registered. See Rogelio Diaz Guerrero and
Wayne H. Holtzman, "Learning by Televised 'Plaza Sesamo' in Mexico,"
Journal of Educational Psychology 66 (October 1974): 632-43.

Follow-up: Done by the classroom teacher in accordance with
lesson-plan instructions.

Feedback: Teachers were often instructed to send selected papers
back to the television teacher. Television teachers periodically
visited classrooms.

In this manner, the unit of teaching—the TV lesson—was standardized and made uniform for every class, with control of lesson content,
teaching methods, and curriculum remaining centralized at the production studio.

Since English language instruction was a main concern, its teaching
was closely supervised and thoroughly carried out. The Tate-Pittman
method, in which all elements of language—sounds, vocabulary, syn-
tax, and so on—are introduced in a highly structured, systematic way,
was employed. In American Samoa, the Tate-Pittman method was used
not only for the formal English lessons but also was incorporated into
all teaching materials: TV lesson vocabularies, worksheets, and reading
materials. Supplemental reading outside of prepared materials was dis-
couraged.

A school for training new teachers was set up, while workshops
and in-service programs helped retrain and upgrade already employed
Samoan teachers.

Feedback was considered important. Samoan teachers often sent
student papers back to the TV teacher at the production studio. American teachers and researchers were required to visit schools and observe
pupil response to telecasts regularly. Generally enthused about visiting
the schools, American teachers often undertook real physical risk and
hardship hiking over mountain trails or going by longboat to remote
villages. The sight of three or four middle-aged American women in
bright-colored muumuus and sandals jauntily setting forth to climb the
steep, muddy mountain trail to Afono—a three-hour hike in hot, humid
jungle—was not unusual.

Yet despite the installation of the educational television network
and centralized control of public school education which it made possible, despite strict adherence by the American personnel to the overall
program for upgrading education as outlined by the planners of the
Samoan ETV Project, [8] despite the initial cooperation and good will of
the Samoans, educational levels and standards in Samoa are still not
those of American public schools. Although English language instruction has received the maximum efforts of the entire system; has, indeed,
been equated with "education," the quality and quantity of English
spoken and understood does not reflect the degree of effort. * Some

---

*"Teaching is more difficult than learning. . . . Not because the
teacher must have a larger store of information. . . . What teaching
calls for is this: to let learn. The real teacher, in fact, lets nothing

observers have noted that the Tate-Pittman language instruction method, in which there is one correct pattern and one correct sequence in which this pattern may be learned, does not encourage confidence in the free use of the language. Further, while English may be the language of the classroom, Samoan is used at home and throughout the community. In our opinion, however, another reason for the difference between efforts and results stems from growing Samoan apathy and hostility as it became apparent to them that the American planners considered their society picturesquely primitive, but essentially inferior.

It is true that the Americans made efforts to change lesson materials and content to be more relevant to the Samoan environment. Stories were written about Sua and Tuna in the village instead of Dick and Jane on the farm. Shells, leaves, and stones were used to teach mathematical concepts such as sets and grouping. Samoan was allowed to be spoken in the classroom if necessary, particularly with younger children. Many American teachers and researchers tried to learn something about Samoan customs and life; there were also a few Samoan television teachers and a twice-weekly program about the Samoan way of life.

Nevertheless, the UNESCO group, commenting upon the local relevance of education content, noted:

> In American Samoa, local patterns are reflected in a course on Samoan life, but in little of the other programming is there skillful and sensitive integration of the local environment into the instruction. The mission thought that some of the . . . efforts were insensitive on this score and probably counterproductive. For example, in one of the telecasts we observed, the stateside teacher used a Samoan adult as a prop, asking him to touch his nose, to go to the door, and so on. All the talking was done by the stateside teacher. This sequence may have implied an ethnic superior-subordinate relationship. 10

Again, the Samoan counterpart to the American assistant director of elementary education, a man who had been elected chief of half the island of Tutuila and certainly a skilled diplomat and administrator, was given a desk in the outer office with the secretaries.

---

else be learned than—learning. His conduct, therefore, often produces the impression that we properly learn nothing from him, if by 'learning' we now suddenly understand merely the procurement of useful information. The teacher . . . has to learn to let them learn. . . . We must keep our eyes fixed firmly on the true relation between the teacher and the taught. "9

Although initially the Fono (Samoan Senate) had allowed the governor complete freedom to reorganize the Department of Education for
the ETV Project—the Department of Education was autonomous, responsible only to the governor and the National Association of Educational
Broadcasters—by 1969 the Fono was trying to gain control and to exercise some voice in the workings of the Department of Education because of the indiscriminate introduction of American ideas and tendency
to ignore or undervalue the Samoan way of life.

It must be remembered that the ETV system provides compulsory,
universal education to school-age children throughout the islands of
American Samoa. These schools are not private church schools where
students more or less choose, by their presence, to learn the European
language and way of life. The Samoan ETV teaching reached all Samoan
children, in theory at least; its stated aim was to rapidly acculturate
them to the American language and patterns of life.

The appeals to Samoan culture were being used, in the end, to
bring about American acculturation. Not only was American acculturation the theme of the Project's stated objectives, it was the implicit
criterion, the cultural bias by which all lesson plans, TV lesson scripts,
and curriculum guides were approved, by which all feedback was judged
and by which results were tested and evaluated.

In order to survive, every culture must have some means of resisting unqualified rapid change. When culture is considered to include the deep, underlying patterns for arranging time, space, inter-
personal communications, and the details of daily life as well as for
ordering public and national life, it becomes apparent that culture is
not just a few different customs, rituals, behavior patterns, and language. Culture determines to a great extent one's perception of an
relationship to oneself, other people, and the environment as well as
one's definition of reality.

This does not mean that rapid, or slow, change cannot take place
within a culture, nor that cross-cultural learning and borrowing is not
beneficial. Many changes have been taking place at various rates in
the Samoan culture since the arrival of the European 200 years ago.
Such diverse borrowings as cloth, tinned corned beef, buses, and
money have been fully incorporated into fa'a Samoa, the Samoan way
way of life. The point is that the culture itself, the people comprising
that cultural group, must make the changes, incorporating and adapting
some new patterns, rejecting others. Most Samoans were indeed
willing, even eager, to learn English and the American way of doing
things in order to have the contacts with Europeans that increased their
well-being and prestige—but as a foreign language and a foreign way
of doing things. The Samoans readily adopted such American ways
and thinking as suited them; otherwise, they preferred their language,
their patterns, their culture.

CROSS-CULTURAL DISSONANCE

Culture is learned; it must be taught. All education involves in-
duction into a culture; a primary function of schools is to teach what
members of a particular cultural frame of reference deem to be true and
important. But what is taught as fact in one culture is nonsense for
another, and men are seldom aware of the ground rules of their own
environmental system.

In all cultures, language is one of the dominant threads, both as
a shaper of cultural thoughts and patterns and as a means of teaching
and passing on cultural knowledge and ideas. Thus the domination of
the educational system in Samoa by the Americans, with the teaching
emphasis on their language, their cultural ideas, and methods of
ordering information, had far-reaching implications for the Samoans.
By resisting the compulsory training in English and the American viewpoint, the Samoans were resisting the reshaping of their culture and
the imposition of another.

Often overlooked, on the other hand, is the acculturation, although
to a lesser degree, of the representative of the teaching culture. In
order to teach anything at all, the teacher must usually make some
accommodation, however small, to the patterns of the receiving culture.
The Americans, in their efforts to develop materials to facilitate the
teaching of English, had to learn something about Samoan culture. This
cross-cultural enrichment took place by "accident" in the Samoan
Project, but its possibilities should be more thoroughly and consciously
explored.

The problems experienced by the Americans and Samoans in the
Samoan ETV Project were marked by cross-cultural dissonance. First,
the two cultures often did not understand each other's communications.
Second, many Samoans were hesitant about change—how much and why.
The need for and goals of change had been decided upon by the American administrators. The goals of change to be brought about must be
consistent with the values of the local culture—in this case values
and incentives within the Samoan culture. Goals imposed by a foreign
culture, such as a certain level of proficiency in English in case a
Samoan wishes to move to the United States, do not have meaning to
the local people and do not generate any energy among them.

As another example, the Samoan schools were criticized in 1961
by Governor Lee and American educators because "there was little
encouragement of discussion, investigation, or discovery. . . . Most
of the classroom activity . . . was taken up by the class chanting in
unison a set of responses learned by rote. "[11]

Visiting the same schools, operating eight years later under the
ETV system, the UNESCO survey group criticized American teaching
methods for the same faults. Chanting is, however, the traditional
Samoan way of passing down cultural information.

Investigation, discovery, and individuality are Western values. [12] The Samoan culture emphasizes hierarchical relationships determined by age and rank. Precociousness and cultivation of individual differences are not encouraged as they tend to upset ordering by age and rank. The family group or aiga is the important unit, and individuals are expected to contribute to the prestige of the aiga rather than to seek individual praise and recognition. In the spring of 1972, disturbances occurred at Samoan High School. The difficulties were due, in part, to resentment by the regular students toward the "accelerated" students, those who are accorded special attention because they are considered brighter.

CULTURAL PATTERNS

Misinterpretations and misunderstandings frequently arose because of lack of awareness. Each culture had patterns that the people took so much for granted that they couldn't imagine or understand how things could be structured otherwise. One example of differing patterns for organizing spatial relationships took place during the taping of a news program. The set for the newscast included a large map tacked to the wall behind the newscaster. During the making of the program, the videotape was stopped because the map had been attached to the wall crookedly. The American director of the newscast had been trained in a cultural system in which geometric regularity is valued, in which crookedness indicates carelessness, negligence, poor workmanship, and a lack of order. The Samoan crew, however, could not understand stopping the tape to straighten the map; to them it was not important that the map was hung crookedly. It did not alter the meaning and usefulness of the map itself. The irregularity apparently was not disturbing to the Samoan, whereas it was to the American.

Another difference in handling spatial relationships had widespread implications for education in Samoa. Americans in the Department of Education began to suspect that the Samoans had difficulty in grasping abstract spatial concepts; testing tended to prove the Americans right. Samoans' spatial conceptualization seemed erratic, to say the least, to Americans who would sigh exasperatedly as one Samoan girl indicated the distance between two buildings about 50 feet apart to be a mile, while another Samoan boy waved vaguely in the direction of a village on the other side of the island and said it was about a mile away. One American psychologist even discoursed learnedly, if obscurely, about protein-deficiency brain damage in relation to inability to grasp abstract concepts.

Actually, the problem was probably more cultural than physiological. Americans tend to handle spatial relationships abstractly and technically. They have a system of abstract rules and measurements—

inches, feet, miles, degrees of longitude—by which they order and
relate objects in space. Samoans, on the other hand, tend to handle
space informally, by feel and assimilated experience rather than by
an abstract standardized unit of measurement. Sitting cross-legged on
the floor of her <u>fale</u> (a traditional Samoan home or building), a Samoan
woman could take a pair of scissors, a piece of cloth, and cut out by
eye and feel, the pieces for a dress, which, when assembled, would
fit her or the person for whom she was making it quite comfortably.
This is a complex bit of spatial visualization; the pieces of a blouse
with darts, for example, look very different in their two-dimensional
cut-out form from their assembled three-dimensional shape. Few American women would think of cutting out a dress without a pattern.

The informal organization of spatial relationships also worked when
used cooperatively within a group. A few years ago, the Samoans decided to build a large ceremonial fale to house the Women's Health
Committee; construction was to be done in the traditional Samoan
fashion. The structure was about 30 feet wide and twice as long, with
the roofline formed by a series of curved arches. Each arch was made
in several segments; each segment was carved by hand out of wood,
using only an adze and a knife as shaping tools. The task was parceled
out in such a way that several men would work on one arch. Each man
took his particular segment of the arch, sat on the ground, carved, and
chatted with friends. Few attempts were made to measure or compare
work, yet when the task was finished, the segments fitted together
exactly. When joined, they formed the continuous curve needed for
the arch.

Samoans navigate across the ocean by relating their position not
to an abstract grid system of longitude and latitude but to the physical
environment around them. Sailing chants contain navigational directions: seasonal positions of stars, direction of the seas, wind, types
of clouds, fish, birds, colors, and smells tell the Polynesian helmsman
his position and direct his course on the ocean.

Some Americans might argue that while the Samoan way of relating
objects in space is fine for organizing the familiar, the routine, it
gives no basis for organizing and relating the unfamiliar, the unknown,
the different. There would be much trial-and-error before a group of
men could get together to build an automobile without measurements.
A standardized unit of measurement—an inch equals an inch in Detroit
or Pago—gives a basis for relating and comparing parts. This argument
focuses on classifying many different items according to a few abstrac-
tions they may have in common. The Western methods of using abstract
measurements, concepts, of structuring time, space, and materials
make possible many things, including technological developments, but
it is a cultural framework. Other cultural frameworks may make possible
other developments, other realities, of which the West is unaware.

Samoans and Americans also differ in their treatment of time.
Marshall McLuhan writes in <u>Understanding Media</u> that to native

cultures, Western lives seem to be one long series of preparations for
living. Perhaps cultural differences in time patterns help to give this
feeling. Westerners tend to think of time as fixed in nature, inflexible,
an ever-present part of their environment. They cannot imagine being
without time, not knowing or being able to ask the time. Time for
Westerners is linear, a line or road stretching from the past, through
the present, and into the future. On this time line, Americans, particularly, are oriented toward the future. The present is regarded as
a stepping stone to the future, while the past is usually of little interest except to examine occasionally for "know-how" clues with which
to influence and plan the future. "Future," to the American, however,
is only the short-term future—tomorrow, a month, a year, five years;
it is not the future of a thousand, a hundred, or even ten years.

Along this time line, events are discrete, separate. The basic
unit of time is the second, which can be arranged into blocks of varying
sizes: minutes, hours, days, years. Each unit can always be fixed in
place on the time line, pinpointed by the coordinates of date and hour,
in much the same way as positions in space can be pinpointed by the
coordinates of longitude and latitude.

Westerners segment and schedule the discrete modules of time,
carving out a block of future time, labeling it carefully by date, hour,
and minute, and deciding that during that block of time, they will perform such-and-such a task. Americans, especially, tightly schedule
their future time and seldom "waste time" or have unscheduled time
blocks. Thus in American Samoa, curriculum planners could know that
on every school day, for the next nine months, every level-3 pupil
in every elementary school would be receiving a 15-minute English
lesson beginning at exactly 10:45 a.m. Precise scheduling of future
time was felt to be essential for the functioning of the instructional
television system.

In contrast to the Americans, the Samoans are oriented toward the
past and present, which merge imperceptibly into one. A Samoan describes the driving-out of the Tongans from Samoa, a World War II
experience, or a great debate between the high chiefs of Samoa and
Fiji as vividly as if all were yesterday's news items, with names, details, and dialogue. Placing these events on his own segmented, classified historical timeline, the American realizes, with a jolt, that the
driving-out of the Tongans took place around 1300, the war experience
some 30 years ago, and the great debate at some indeterminable time
50 to 200 years ago. To the Samoan, the past is not finished, dead,
receding out of memory, but is a very real part of the living present.
In this cultural frame of reference, it is the future which is indefinite
and unimportant.

One of the problems in the Samoan Project, closely connected with
differing time patterns, concerned the rate of change to take place
through the introduction of ETV into the school system. Governor Lee,
appearing before the United States Congress in 1961, spoke of "explosive change" as desirable. Wilbur Schramm writes,

The most striking feature of the rapid educational development in American Samoa is the heavy responsibility
being placed on television. It is . . . counted upon to
serve as prime mover in a very swift reconstruction of
the entire educational system. [13]

While different cultures probably have different rates at which
they can assimilate various changes, a change that occurs too rapidly
can break apart any culture. In Samoa, the pace of change, as well as
the content, was being set by the Americans, who are more oriented
toward the future and who culturally value change over the preservation
of traditional ways. The Samoan culture, however, merges the past into
the pool of the present, and deeply values its roots and traditions. It
is a very stable, cohesive, pelagic society, in which rituals, genealog-
ical ties, and routine daily living patterns emphasize the value of preserving old ways.

CULTURAL CHANGE

Another aspect of the difficulty in cross-cultural communications
was that the Samoans were not sure where they wanted to change their
culture, how much, and why. The decision to install the ETV system
was made by the Americans; the Samoans had little say in its use or in
the educational content which it transmitted.

There is a distinction to be made between change brought about by
the introduction of a technological process, such as television, and
change brought about by the educational content that television trans-
mits. If a country accepts Western technology, it also receives something of that society's culture and values.

Even teaching the simple act of hammering a nail connotes certain
cultural patterns. The use of tools carries with it the value of tools,
the value of making something, the idea of constructing a complex
structure from simpler parts. A nail fastening implies a certain value
given to rigidity, material permanence, whereas a bound fastening,
such as the braided sennet (coconut fibers) lashings used in traditional
Samoan construction, gives a feeling of flexibility, of blending with
natural materials, rhythms, and forces. When one chooses between a
nail and a bound lashing, one chooses to a subtle degree between different values and ideas.

Television is only a more complex tool than the hammer and nail.
Both are technological processes, and there is no form of technical
entry free of acculturation. Technical support presupposes teaching,
training, learning how to do something that was not done before. Acculturation by the technical instrument itself occurs in addition to whatever
educational content is programmed through it. It may well be that the

values and ideas behind the technological process also were not present in the receiving culture before. These new values and ideas may or may not be congenial or congruent with previously held ideas and values.

Cultural change through the adoption of a technological process may be unavoidable (even the Western industrialized societies do not know yet to what extent and how their cultures will be affected by television). Yet the imparting and receiving of technology is a cross-cultural transaction. Technological developments bring in part of Western culture, but the ways in which these developments are used must be allowed to change, adapt, become different within the context of the receiving culture. The use to which the process is put—its content—should be determined by the receiving culture.

In the case of the Samoans, the American educational content and values may have been made more emphatic by the use of the television medium; the subliminal "selling" capabilities of TV, utilized so successfully in the United States in commercial advertising and in educational programs such as "Sesame Street," are still a matter of controversy (see, for example, Chapter 7 by Rose K. Goldsen). At any rate, American educational content and values were certainly made more pervasive and far-reaching through the introduction of television into the schools. Every Samoan school child received exactly the same lessons—lessons whose content and method of presentation had been closely screened by American supervisors at the production studio.

American social values encourage self-sufficiency through the ability to earn money rather than to directly produce or grow what is needed. People are seen in terms of their jobs, what they do, rather than who they are. In American society, with its nuclear family structure and competitive economic values, individuals are alone, surviving against the others only in relation to their ability to compete successfully in order to secure the necessities for themselves and their dependents. American education curricula generally train for salaried jobs, emphasize economic self-sufficiency in a money-oriented, communal society. At best the TV curriculum in Samoa prepared young people for a clerical job in government, bank, or local store.[14] The value to the Samoan of village life and of roles foreign to the Western mind was not understood by the American curriculum writers and so not integrated into the lessons.

The Samoans stress cooperation between individuals for the good of the extended family group (the aiga), which is the basic unit of the society. Possessions and services are shared freely among extended families; no person owns anything. Private property as such does not exist, and it is a matter of shame to deny a relative food or anything he needs. Usually no one lacks because he can always visit some member of his aiga who has what he needs. The sheer size of the Samoan aiga means that there are bound to be influential, well-off members as well as needy ones. Genealogies are important because they indicate to whom one has a right to ask for or a responsibility to give help. In Samoan society, the individual rarely stands alone but is contained in a wide, complex network of duties, obligations, privileges, and relationships, all of which act flexibly to keep him both a responsible (as regards his duties and obligations to others), yet well-cared-for (as regards others' duties and responsibilities to him) member of the family and of society. American educational values of individualism, competition, and economic motivations mitigated against this intricate network.

To Americans, with their sense of individualism, the authority of the matai, the head of the extended family group, is oppressive. The matai decides the daily tasks of those of his family living with him, collects salaries or portions of salaries for use in family matters, and generally regulates the lives of his dependents. Often foreigners do not take into account that in Samoan society a skilled matai can maneuver so as to increase the power and authority of his whole family vis-a-vis other families and that, should dissatisfaction with a matai be widespread, he can be deposed through a family council.

Through the Department of Education changes began to occur in Samoan life. In the belief that Samoan children were not getting a good breakfast, and that local foods and eating habits were not nutritionally sound, school breakfast and lunch programs were instituted. The children were introduced to the foods which Americans feel are essential to good nutrition; foods that were considered more appealing, that provided variety in the diet, and that were available under U.S. government food programs. Unwittingly, the Americans were changing the food tastes of the Samoan children, to the consternation of older Samoans. The Samoans do not look for variety in foods, but expect to eat relatively few kinds of goods regularly. Certain foods, such as taro, have a cultural, emotional significance, much as bread does in some Western cultures. Many Samoans were concerned to find their children getting away from the traditional Samoan foods and developing a desire for European foods. They saw this as a weakening of Samoan cultural identity. In addition, the taste for European foods made the Samoans dependent upon imported tinned goods, sold at high prices. Money was needed for such foods, which meant leaving the traditional Samoan way of life to enter the money economy of the Europeans and half-caste traders. To find work and to be near the stores, Samoans often left their villages to live with relatives near town.

The overt rationale of the planners of the Samoan ETV Project was to prepare Samoans for life in the United States, should the Samoan choose to leave the island to go to the United States to live and work. The out-of-awareness urge was to supplant Samoan ways with American ways in areas where there were conflicting values. This was not necessarily intentional but came as part of the Americans' cultural preferences. Cultural patterns are as encompassing and as essential for life as air and, for the most part, as completely unnoticed. It is only in cross-cultural situations that differences in cultural patterns and values begin to show up, and then individuals tend to feel vaguely but strongly that their familiar way is "better" or "right" and that the unfamiliar way is puzzling, incomprehensible, or even "uncivilized."

The emphasis on American acculturation encouraged the local society to become dependent upon Western life-style needs, to become a part of a society organized along bureaucratic, industrialized lines, in which a person performs one specialized job but is dependent for other survival needs upon a complex chain of supply and labor, which, if broken, makes vulnerable most of the population.

Education of the Samoan was seen in relation to American education in the United States, not in relation to the needs of a people living on a small island surrounded by thousands of miles of ocean. Local cultural values and outlooks, important for the psychological health of the individual and for the preservation of local society, which acts as a matrix within which individuals function were disregarded.

Just as individual development, growth, and differences give meaning to the individual human experience, so do different cultural developments, patterns, rituals, and traditions give meaning and depth to the human communal experience. Ultimately, different values and ways of ordering the environment are not only welcome but necessary for the well-being of the species.

Both the metropolitan and the local cultures can learn and be enriched by interaction. But as Arnold Toynbee notes, when a tribal society sits next to a civilization, the high-energy psychic output of the industrial society disintegrates the institutions of the less complex society. The local culture should try to maintain the important cultural values and patterns that give it stability; these should not be quickly abandoned under the pressure of Western technology and values.

SOME ORGANIZATIONAL AND TRAINING CONSIDERATIONS

The planning, installation, and maintenance of an ETV system involve cross-cultural contact, if not conflict. Some considerations: Will the ETV system be used to provide education for all school-age children or will it be installed only in large cities and towns? If the latter, will it increase the tendency of people to leave villages to crowd into the cities? (Careful planning in the location of schools could encourage people to remain in their villages; rural concerns can also be part of the educational content.) Also: Does a philosophy of maintenance exist in the local cultural make-up? Will importation of foreign maintenance specialists be necessary or can local people be trained to maintain and repair equipment?

Similarly, problems are likely to arise over the capability of local people to administer the new system. Is competence developed in the recipient country by donors?

If it is decided to train local personnel to administer and run the ETV system—the most desirable goal for most countries—there is the choice of sending local people abroad for training or of importing Westerners to train locally. In American Samoa, it was decided to recruit personnel from the United States who would reside in Samoa and organize and run the ETV system while training local Samoans to take their places. Some of the frictions that occurred could have been lessened had the Americans been more informed about Samoan culture and had the overall goals and objectives of the Project been more in accord with the interest of the Samoans.

There was a decided lack of sufficient orientation for Americans into Samoan culture. While most Americans were curious, even sympathetic toward the Samoan people and their way of life, they could find little information about it other than a few books, trial-and-error guesses, and hearsay. The training and cultural orientation programs for Americans coming to Samoa were minimal; after arrival, they were nonexistent.

Learning the Samoan language was not encouraged. There were sporadic, but on the whole unsuccessful, private attempts to learn the language. No formal classes or instruction were provided. This seems to have been a combination of American linguistic laziness and cultural bias, justified because the Samoans were supposed to be learning English, not Americans Samoan. Not knowing the language well increased cultural dissonance for the Americans, particularly for American principals living in remote villages.

The Americans required constant and expensive care to keep them from disintegrating under the pressure of being surrounded by a very different culture whose language they couldn't understand. This was especially noticeable in the case of those principals and their families who were isolated from the rest of the American colony on the small island of the Manu'a group or in outlying villages on Tutuila, accessible only by sea. These homes had to have radio contact with the Americans in Pago possible at all times in order for the family to feel secure. Isolation of the principal in a completely different culture often brought out strengths and adaptive abilities in both the person and family; occasionally fissures and crumblings of the personality developed. That few Americans spoke or understood Samoan, other than simple phrases, increased the sense of isolation, proclivity to clannishness, and underlying apprehension and fear.

Logistics of supply—transportation of the family's household goods, installation and maintenance of electric lights, refrigeration, plumbing, supplying imported European foods, providing transportation into town— were additional problems.

As a result of the emphasis on American acculturation in the educational goals of the Project as well as cross-cultural misunderstandings, the Americans rarely thought that a Samoan had reached the point of being able to carry on the system, or his part in the system, according to American standards. During the period we observed the ETV Project (1966-68), Samoans in the Department of Education were confined to lower positions, supervised by American personnel, or were given equal rank but little power in the Samoan bureaucracy that developed parallel to the American one. Each American had a "counterpart"; the American assistant director of elementary education, for example, was paralleled by a Samoan assistant director of elementary education. Training seemed to stabilize, however, at a point at which the Samoan director interpreted Samoan ways and customs to the Americans, proofread Samoan language when it had to be used in lesson plans, and smoothed ruffled feathers in a village if misunderstandings arose between the villagers and the residing American principal. The American director continued to decide what was taught and how.

Some sections of the Education Department were more effective in turning over authority and some measure of control to the Samoans than others. The Maintenance Section seemed somewhat more willing to allow the Samoans full participation. This may hinge on the nature of the responsibility turned over. Maintenance was concerned with the technical and mechanical aspects of the system—with installing and repairing TV sets and production and transmission equipment. What was required was a technical knowledge of the equipment. Americans can analyze procedure and teach technical information well. Overall instructional methods and curriculum planning in the schools, on the other hand, go much deeper into out-of-awareness cultural biases; it is not simply a repair technique which is being taught but a whole cultural way of life—in this case, the American way of life. The Americans seldom felt the Samoans were ready to take over—that is, until a rising sense of cultural awareness on the part of Samoans in the 1970s pressured an American reassessment of the U.S. neocolonial position in the territory. The emergent awareness and pressure for change was stimulated in large part through Samoan interaction with other South Pacific territories that gained independence in the 1960s.

AFTERMATH AND RECENT DEVELOPMENTS

This chapter has focused on ETV in American Samoa during the 1960s, the period of the Project's inception and initial development. By the mid-1970s, the deficiencies and deleterious aspects of the ETV Project were becoming obvious to both Americans and Samoans.

One important change has been the recent devolution of important decision-making roles to native-born Samoans. In 1973 the first native Samoan Director of Education was appointed. Simultaneously, the number of high-level American personnel has been reduced substantially.

Another important change has been the reduction of television utilization in the classroom, particularly at the high-school level.

Students were bored by the overuse of rigid teaching telecasts and felt that television teachers were often not aware of the level of understanding of students, that the level of televised instruction was either too easy or too difficult. Teachers, particularly high-school teachers, resented the arbitrary structure of the lessons and thought the TV format did not allow them enough freedom to use their own ideas and training, to respond to individual needs of the students, and to expand upon the material presented. Some teachers wanted the option of deciding whether or not to use the television lessons regularly or as enrichment only. (Elementary teachers generally felt language arts to be their most helpful program, while high-school teachers favored social studies and science programs.)

In 1974 telecasts were curtailed by a series of power shortages and difficulties that lasted well into 1975. By August of 1974, KVZK-TV was operating on a shortened schedule and on only one channel instead of six. Instructional television was off the air during the last month of school. These technological breakdowns patently exposed the vulnerability of an education system based on advanced systems of television production and transmission.

In 1974 there also was a significant change in the virtually exclusive emphasis on English language proficiency. At the elementary level, the first three years of instruction are now primarily in Samoan with English introduced as a foreign language. Gradually English instruction will be increased until, at the high-school level, English becomes the primary language of instruction. This pattern is similar to that of Western Samoa, in which the first seven years of schooling are taught in Samoan; English is studied as a foreign language, becoming the language of instruction in the eighth year. *

Reflecting upon this shift in educational policy, the present native-born director of education, Mere T. Betham, has stated:

> In the past our leaders have come out strongly about the
> need to be proficient in English. We have emphasized
> English teaching for proficiency en masse to the extent
> that we have become insensitive to the individual needs
> of many Samoan children and thus contributed to the
> retardation of those children's conceptual learning in
> both Samoan and English. . . . Perhaps we have failed

---

*As part of this shift in language policy, the territory's only totally English-language public school, Fia Iloa, was closed in 1974. Fia Iloa was attended by children who already spoke English, usually children of Samoans who have returned to the islands from the United States or New Zealand.

to recognize the importance of putting some emphasis, if
not equal emphasis, on proficiency in our native Samoan
language. *

A result of the emphasis on English during the 1960s and early 1970s
was that many students went through the educational system without
mastering either Samoan or English.

These developments indicate that Samoans are presently attempting
to regain control of their educational system and redefine its policies
and goals. In this process, they are examing the effects of past instructional policies and priorities upon Samoan children. In formulating
a more indigenous strategy for educational advancement, Samoans also
are beginning to look at the experiences and policies of neighboring
South Pacific countries such as independent and culturally proximate
Western Samoa. The problems of maintaining a complex technological
system are likely to become an increasingly important factor in determining the character and continued use of ETV in Samoa. Future changes
in Samoan education, however, are more likely to be influenced to a
significant degree by the reassertion of Samoan cultural independence.

----

*Proctor and Gamble, Bristol-Myers, Colgate-Palmolive, Coca-
Cola, Pepsi-Cola, Ford, and General Motors for years have sponsored
American programs abroad ever since the Esso Corporation (now Exxon)
began experimenting with television advertising in Cuba in 1951. When
a TV campaign launched by the oil company a few years later increased
sales by over 20 percent in a period of only 12 days, a huge advertising
surge abroad followed, with other firms enjoying similar successes
elsewhere. As one Max Factor executive put it in 1959, the year his
company sponsored 39 U.S. programs in Brazil, "to ignore the power
of television is to ignore the most powerful advertising force the world
has ever known."

The ABC corporation has cornered the market in Latin America,
owning stock in five Central American television stations, three
Japanese stations, and one each in Australia and the Philippines; and
in program production companies in Mexico, Great Britain, and West
Germany. In addition, ABC maintains minor holdings among some 54
other television stations around the world, to which over the years it
has supplied assistance in the areas of administration, sales promotion, and programming. CBS and NBC do the same. All three companies
have been active in developing foreign broadcast systems. In 1960,
ABC built Ecuador's first television station, and later assisted both in
the creation of the Philippines' Republic Broadcasting System and in
the formation of the Arab Middle East Television Network, which includes stations in Syria, Lebanon, Kuwait, Iraq, and Jordan. [15]

SUMMARY: SAMOA AND ETV

The following points sum up some of the cross-cultural aspects of the Samoan ETV experience:

Planning and Goals

1. The need for change, goals of change, and pace of change were decided upon by the Americans rather than the Samoans.
2. Education of the Samoans was seen in relation to American education in the United States, not in relation to the needs of an isolated, pelagic people.

Curriculum and Telecasts

1. Curriculum and telecast content was not related to Samoan cultural values. Although special lesson plans and reading materials were written using characters with Samoan names and familiar materials such as banana leaves and shells, these efforts were superficial.
2. The lecture-type, "stand-up" teaching telecasts were monotonous. The medium was not used imaginatively to stimulate active participation of students.
3. On the plus side, there were frequent opportunities for exchange of information and sharing between individual American and Samoan teachers through school visitations and workshops. Arrangements were made for feedback to evaluate lesson effectiveness. Teacher training and in-service training were provided.

Resistance

1. The underlying attitude or belief that Samoan culture is deficient, primitive, inferior seems to have blocked effective cooperation between American planners and Samoan leaders and people.
2. The compulsory pervasiveness of TV education, dominated by American cultural values, language, and ideas, may have severely damaged Samoan cultural integrity and social equilibrium.

GENERAL CROSS-CULTURAL CONSIDERATIONS
REGARDING THE USE OF ETV

How can television be used in developing countries without posing
a threat to the cultural integrity and relative equilibrium of the community? How can cross-cultural transactions be carried out to the advantage of all? Philosophers on technology such as Marshall McLuhan
and Buckminster Fuller foresee global interchanges and tribalization,
free of all racial, religious and political considerations, made possible
by the electromagnetic media. [16]
Within some North American communities small groups and individuals are beginning to use multichannel cable TV systems and portable
videotape recorders to look at themselves and their community, and
to exchange information they deem important. In the United States, the
advent of cable television with its potential for 40 or more channels
has brought into existence groups who are trying to create public forums
through television. Public access channels, such as those used on
cable systems in New York City, generally play videotapes made by
local citizens, dealing with social and environmental problems of sew-
age disposal, racial conflict, overcrowded hospitals, and so on. In
Canada, the "Challenge for Change" program of the Canadian National
Film Board involves community organizers and concerned citizens of
such diverse communities as Montreal, Fogo (an island off Newfound-
land), and Indian reservations who are using portable videotape equipment to develop and share fresh solutions to community problems. These
efforts are decentralized in the extreme. The equipment is operated by
people with little training but with a desire to learn about the social
organism of which they are a part. Perhaps such informal, decentralized, and indigenous uses of television may represent an interesting
direction for non-Western cultures to explore. [17]
Following are several considerations for the implementation of an
educational television system:
1. Television, when first introduced into a new locale, should
conform to and support the indigenous value system.
2. All decisions regarding the implementation of television should
be made by those people who will be most affected by it.
3. Educational goals should be relevant to the local culture; ETV
should be used to complement these goals, not to acculturate indigenous
people into a metropolitan culture.
4. Changes should not be imposed by outside cultures but must
evolve organically within the cultural context of the particular group
as a result of their own use of the medium.
5. Can the country continue to maintain the ETV system on its own,
or will its installation increase the country's dependence upon foreign
powers for parts, personnel, planning, and direction? If the country
cannot in all ways incorporate the ETV system into its own culture, be-

coming responsible for its direction, continuance, and maintenance, then the system is, to a greater or lesser degree, a superimposition of the foreign culture upon the local one.

6. Ideally television should be viewed as a major community resource and as a communication process in which many people may interact, rather than a delivery system of packaged goods.

7. Students need to release their own energies into the process of learning and discovering, not just be passively programmed.

8. Used in traditional ways to teach subjects, ETV tends to be expensive, inflexible, and manipulative. Instead, television should be a process that children and adults use to learn about themselves, their environment, and about others—for example, through the making and exchange of tapes.

9. Television, as a communication process, can act as a homeostatic device that will assist the social organism to gain information about itself and thus to effect change as needed.

In Samoa, the use of television enabled the Americans to extend their influence, and the power of their values and way of life, into the daily education of every child and many adults.

NOTES

1. Academy for Educational Development, Educational Technology and the Developing Countries (Washington, D. C.: Agency for International Development, 1972), p. 81.

2. 1960 Annual Report, the Governor of American Samoa to the Secretary of the Interior (Washington, D. C.: Department of the Interior, 1961, Document Number 5758120-61-7), p. 42.

3. Wilbur Schramm, "Educational Television in American Samoa," in Schramm et al., eds., New Educational Media in Action: Case Studies for Planners, Vol. 1 (Paris: UNESCO, IIEP, 1967), p. 16.

4. Academy for Educational Development, op. cit., p. 83.

5. Ibid.

6. Tom Kaser, "Classroom TV Comes to Samoa," Saturday Review, June 19, 1965.

7. The Ivory Coast Republic, Education by Television, vol. 3, Report of the Missions for the Evaluation of Educational Television in Niger, El Salvador, and American Samoa (Ministry of National Education, 1968), p. 26.

8. Vernon Bronson, A System Manual for the Staff and Faculty, National Association of Educational Broadcasters for the Government of American Samoa, Washington, D. C.

9. For a discussion of the rather disappointing performance of Samoan students on English proficiency tests, see Academy for Educational Development, op. cit., pp. 84-86. For a more optimistic

assessment of English-language learning in American Samoa, see Wilbur Schramm, ITV in American Samoa—After Nine Years (Washington, D. C.: Agency for International Development, Office of Education and Human Resources, 1973).

10. Ivory Coast Republic, op. cit., pp. 58-59.

11. Schramm, "Educational Television in American Samoa," op. cit., p. 13.

12. Americans, themselves, although they philosophize about the desirability of creativity and initiative, are part of a culture which stresses uniformity and standardization. According to Edward T. Hall, it was no accident that the American Henry Ford developed the standardized part and the assembly line. See Hall, The Silent Language (Greenwich, Connecticut: Fawcett, 1968), p. 159.

13. Schramm, "Educational Television in American Samoa," op. cit., p. 13.

14. A dependence on government employment was indicated by a 1974 survey of graduating high-school students: 90 percent of students interviewed wanted to work for the government rather than private employers. Of the 8,000 people in the total territory work force, more than 4,000 work for the government, an increase in government employment of over 400 percent since 1956. The survey, conducted by Peter Creevey and Eliu Paopoc for the Department of Manpower Resources, found that "the students seemed handicapped in their job finding prospects by a lack of counseling and work exposure." The researchers point out that "only 1 in 10 students taking a U.S. Navy recruiting test could score over 30%, which is the minimum score for entering the Navy." U.S. military service is one source of possible employment, and is attractive for many because of American Samoa's history as a naval base. See "Student Survey Alarms Samoans," Pacific Island Monthly, August 1974, p. 9.

15. John F. Gallien, "Tough Job for Samoa's Mrs. Betham," Pacific Island Monthly, May 1975, p. 24.

16. See, for example, R. Buckminster Fuller, Operating Manual for Spaceship Earth (New York: Pocket Books, 1971).

17. For further discussion, see Grant Masland, "Where the Masses Control the Media," occasional papers (Santa Barbara, Calif.: Center for the Study of Democratic Institutions, March 1971).

LITERACY WITHOUT BOOKS:
THE CASE OF "SESAME STREET"
Rose K. Goldsen

Riddle: What is the longest street in the world? Answer: Sesame Street—the only street that winds clear around the globe, the only street that crosses oceans on the way.

THE PROGRAM'S REACH

"Sesame Street's" programs are produced, distributed, and its products are franchised for sale, through Children's Television Workshop (CTW). The first series of "Sesame Street" programs made its debut in November 1969 in the United States and they've been going strong ever since. The year 1975 marks the seventh cycle in the domestic series. This means that over 900 of these charming programs will have been broadcast and repeated, broadcast and repeated coast to coast. One result is that "Sesame Street" characters are now entrenched in the culture of childhood in the United States for all time. Stop any three-year-old you happen to meet and ask him about traditional folk characters like Paul Bunyan or Johnny Appleseed or Bre'r Rabbit and see what kind of blank stare you'll get. Then ask him about Big Bird or Kermit the Frog and you'll see what I mean.

Overseas versions of "Sesame Street" in four different languages are now being shown in 69 countries. These spinoffs from the original version include "Plaza Sesamo," the Spanish-language version whose target audience is 22 million preschool children in Spanish-speaking countries of the Western Hemisphere and also Puerto Rico. The Portuguese version is "Villa Sesamo," targeted to 11.5 million preschool children in Brazil. "Sesamstrasse" hopes to reach 3 million West

German preschoolers and "Bonjour Sésame" is aimed at the millions of French-speaking youngsters throughout the world. *

The English-language version has found buyers in more than 50 countries, and not only English-speaking countries like Great Britain, Canada, and Australia, either. Japan national television has broadcast the original program in English. Curaçao has done the same, fading the English into the background in favor of voice-over commentary in the national language (Papiamento). Poland and Yugoslavia television do likewise. Indeed, CTW estimates that the series in English has been broadcast to several million children in iron-curtain countries and that it is adaptable with only slight modifications to almost any social system. †

---

*"Plaza Sesamo" was the first coproduction arrangement, when Taller de Televisión Infantil in Mexico began production in 1972, with Mr. John Page as producer. The first Spanish-language series was released in January 1973. The second cycle, consisting of 260 half-hour programs, is currently being shown and further cycles are planned. "Plaza Sesamo" has been bought by purchasers in 14 Latin American countries and Puerto Rico, plus several domestic Spanish-language stations.

"Villa Sesamo," the Portuguese version, is another coproduction following the pattern of the Mexican arrangement. The first cycle, 130 54-minute hours, began in October 1972. A second cycle of 260 half-hour programs, is in production.

"Sesamstrasse" is the German-language version, another coproduction arrangement. The first series consists of 260 half-hour programs. As of this writing a second series, to consist of 180 additional half-hour programs, is in production.

"Bonjour Sésame" is the French version. It consists of 65 half-hours, aired as a series of 130 15-minute programs, spliced together from the original programs maintained at the library of Children's Television Workshop under the title, "Open Sesame." This package is available for sale to any country; any language can be dubbed into the sound track. It has been bought by purchasers in France, Holland, Spain, Belgium, Sweden, and French Canada. [1]

†The head of children's programming in Poland agrees, stressing that adaptations can "give the Polish child a frame of reference which he can recognize. . . . For example, milk in Poland comes in bottles not in cartons. . . . [Still] a square is a square both in Poland and the United States and children's cognitive processes are the same the world over." [2]

Not everyone agrees that it is so easy to divorce cognitive processes from value orientations and emotional processes. "Sesame Street" was bought in England not by the BBC, which rejected it, but by Britain's Independent Television Authority. (In April 1975, however, the

The quoted population figures refer only to the present cohort of children in the appropriate age groups in the respective countries. As one cohort goes on to formal schooling, their ranks are continually replenished by a steady stream of replacements moving these days in continuous flow from the cradle to the television set. CTW and its co-production companies abroad aim to reach all these children, if possible. It is the first time in the history of civilization that so many of the world's children will have been exposed simultaneously to the identical cultural materials—images, music, sounds, laughter, body movements, facial expressions—all feeding into a child's developing sense of self, all showing him particular ways of interacting in social relations. This now goes on during the most formative years in which a huge proportion of the world's children are being clothed in their humanity, the years in which they are trying on the individual and cultural identities they will adopt throughout their lifetimes.

THE CONTENT AND FORMAT

Sunny day, keeping the clouds away
On my way to where the air is sweet,
Can you tell me how to get
How to get to Sesame Street

That's the signature song. The melody is the same the world over. On hearing that bouncy tune, preschoolers in countries in which the program has found buyers run toward the television screen. In the four coproduction arrangements, the lyrics have been translated into the appropriate national language. Since the only coproduced series I have seen is "Plaza Sesamo," I shall present a composite summary illustrating the standard format. Other coproduced versions follow essentially the same pattern.

Each program is a 54-minute episode, usually consisting of 40 segments. About eight of the videotapes of dramatic action that takes place on the Plaza are made in Mexico with advice and consultation

---

BBC was willing to buy "The Electric Company." In Peru the Ministry of Education rejected the series. The Mexican journal Siempre (August 1973) devoted an approving article to the Soviet Union's decision to reject the series. In each case, rejection is based on the claim that the programs project a particular set of values appropriate to a particular set of social relations in a particular social system.

Critical articles about "Sesame Street" and its foreign-language spinoffs that stress the values embedded in its hidden agenda are easy to find in journals of education, literary journals, and the like, both in the United States and abroad.

of a panel of Latin American experts.* About seven additional segments
are spliced- in films produced in Latin America. The remaining segments
come from the International Library CTW maintains—the animations,
puppet sequences, film clips—and constitute about two-thirds of the
program.†

The show opens with a shot of children playing in a sort of parklike
area. One tot is on a tricycle, one is swinging in a rubber tire sus-
pended from a tree branch, some are in a sandbox, others run and jump
and skip and play. This is the standard opening signature of "Plaza
Sesamo." The screen goes blank for just a moment, then a hand appears
holding a piece of chalk. It writes, letter by letter, XEROX, while a
voice- over explains, "This program has been made possible by a grant
from the Xerox Corporation."‡ This is what the television business
calls "a commercial billboard," and each program begins with the billboard acknowledging Xerox's principal sponsorship. Other "sponsors"

------

*The experts who participated in two seminars convoked to discuss
the feasibility of the Latin American version and to suggest ways in
which to guarantee the authenticity of such a version, are the following:
Pilar Santamaria de Reyes, INRAVISION (Colombia) and the Organization
of American States, Bogotá, Colombia; Susana Szulanski, Buenos Aires,
Argentina; Ana Underwood, director of Preschool Education, Department
of Public Instruction, San Juan, Puerto Rico; Rogelio Diaz Guerrero,
technical adviser to the School of Psychology, Mexico City, Mexico;
Luisa Elena Vegas Vegas, professor of Educational Pedagogy, Central
University of Venezuela, Caracas, Venezuela; Evaristo Obregon Gárces,
Department of Communication and Graphic Arts, Tadeo Lozano University, Bogotá, Colombia; Francisco Javier Seijo Gonzales, Bolivia; Vic-
toria Sanz de Waite, Costa Rica; Horacio Harris Duque, Panama; Edith
Altmann, Chile; Elivra Paredes Deza, Peru.

The seminars were held in Caracas, Venezuela, the first on
March 18, 1971, the second on March 9 and 10, 1972.

†Some of the materials the International Library circulates are done
by "retracing." The animation cells are drawn on clear plastic without
the letters and words. They can be filled in later, in the appropriate
language.

‡In 1969 the Xerox Corporation provided a special grant of $50,000
to make possible purchase of prime time on the NBC network for a 30-
minute special previewing "Sesame Street." In 1973 Xerox gave a million dollars to help fund "Plaza Sesamo." A condition of the grant was
that each program would identify Xerox as the sponsoring corporation.
The show in Latin America is often referred to as "The Xerox Show."
The expressed purpose of the grant, according to Mr. Ed Truschke of
The Xerox Corporation, was "to get us institutional visibility throughout
Latin America as a concerned business corporation" (interview, October 1, 1975).

are the letters and numbers the lesson of the day wants the children to learn; and the program ends with a billboard plugging them, as the credits roll across the screen in what the business irreverently calls "the crawl."

The segments that take place on the plaza involve the stable cast of characters, the actors and puppets ("muppets") who are continuous from program to program. In the Spanish-language version, it's a married couple, Gonzalo and Maria Luisa. The husband's sister Rosita, a public health nurse, seems to live with them. An older man, Don Ramon, is their neighbor. He runs a small candy-grocery store—the kind that in East Harlem is called a bodega—and the storefront opens onto the plaza.

There are creatures very reminiscent of the "muppets" we know in the U.S. version. Big Bird is there—but on closer look it turns out that he's a sort of crocodile, Abelardo, strongly resembling Big Bird in looks and manner, just as slow to catch on, just as prone to mix things up. Oscar, the grouch, is there, too, incarnated as Paco, a cranky parrot who lives not in a garbage can, like the original, but in a house. * There's the Cookie Monster, Ernie, and Bert—exactly the same as the originals since they come in the package of CTW library materials but with dubbed sound tracks.

The show of the day—the coproduction—tells a story about an event dramatized on the plaza. Gonzalo may star one day, Maria Luisa another; or it might be Don Ramon or Rosita in the leading role. Sometimes there are guest stars: Jose Feliciano, Bill Cosby, Julie Andrews, Judy Collins, Carol Burnett have appeared as well as other equally distinguished "personalities." Separate segments of the day's drama are spotted throughout the 54 minutes the program lasts. Whatever the problem that troubles Gonzalo or Rosita or Don Ramon or Maria Luisa or Abelardo, the conflict is stated, faced, and ultimately resolved to everyone's satisfaction before the 54-minute hour comes to a close. It's the same format the children get used to as they watch the dubbed versions of "Get Smart," "Bonanza," "Gilligan's Island," or "Bewitched" that most of these countries importing CTW productions likewise buy from U.S. sources.

The billboard advertising Xerox fades into an animated sequence featuring a little girl in a beach scene. She looks up. "Hi," she says, "My name is Olga. Olga begins with the very nice letter, 'O.' One day I went down to the beach and found a pot of gold (olla de oro) and in it were eight oysters (ocho ostras). Oh boy! Did I feel happy! But then along came a terrible ogre and he demanded my eight oysters in

---

*Since the same actor takes both roles, Abelardo and Paco never appear on the scene together. The original muppets are copyrighted by Jim Henson, their creator. The overseas approximations are look-alikes, having the advantage that royalties need not be paid to Muppets Incorporated, the company that owns the originals.

that pot of gold. " At each appropriate point as she speaks, the film
shows all the images she discusses, along with the letter "O. " It
grows tall and short, fat and thin, changes its position, its shape, its
color, moves close to the camera, then far away.

This is television show-and-tell at its best, utilizing the medium's
special advantages. Indeed, "Sesame Street" came into being precisely
because the founders of Children's Television Workshop had the insight
and imagination to see that television show-and-tell could be exploited
to the benefit of culturally deprived children in the slums of our own
inner cities. Their counterparts in other countries, where slum children
likewise need the cultural infrastructure that is prerequisite for later
acquisition of literacy, were quick to see the possibilities such a program seemed to offer and eager to take advantage of its availability by
buying the series. CTW had not initially sought an overseas market*
but when the requests came pouring in, saw no reason to reject the
overtures. When the English-language version was so enthusiastically
received even in non-English-speaking countries, the idea of coproduction was pursued as a way of achieving "cultural authenticity. "[5]

The Olga sequence takes about a minute. Note that the sponsor-
letter of the day is the featured star, dominating stage front and center,
shown from every facet—just like any real commercial the children can
watch on their own television networks. This is considered policy.
The people at CTW even refer to these sequences as "commercials, "
acknowledging that "we blatantly burgled from the advertising methods
of Madison Avenue. "[6]

Next sequence shows Rene, the frog. Rene: "We are fortunate
today to have with us Professor Pastana who will deliver a lecture on
the letter "O. " Professor . . ."

The professor, a muppet, turns out to be one of those absent-minded
professors television programs like so much to show children. He has
trouble staying awake. Now, he comes to with a start. "Young man,
what am I supposed to talk about?" he asks Rene. "O, " says the frog—
but the professor misses the answer because he has nodded off and is
again fast asleep. People in the television business call this a yuk-
yuk, and the producers of "Plaza Sesamo" rely on yuk-yuks and one-

---

*The first films in the first series of "Sesame Street" did not even
run separate voice, music, and effects tracks, would would have been
necessary to allow for dubbing into different languages. [3] When the
initial requests from overseas buyers began to arrive, the staff, aware
of fundamental differences in social systems and cultures, considered
what policy to pursue: ". . . it is not assumed that the same knowledge
and the same tools are necessarily appropriate for any other culture.
The policy has been that if educators and broadcasters outside the U.S.
feel that the original version of the show is appropriate for their audiences, then CTW will provide it, at their request. "[4]

liners just like the yuk-yuks and one-liners delivered by Ted Baxter in
the dubbed export version of "The Mary Tyler Moore Show" or those
delightfully funny Nazis in "Hogan's Heroes."

Blackout, and we're on the Plaza. Gonzalo and Don Ramon are
having an argument. Gonzalo wants to buy a newspaper, but Don Ramon
says it's his last copy and he wants to keep it for himself. The CTW
workbook explains that this day's drama will focus on compromise and
cooperation as a mode of conflict-resolution; but meanwhile, we pause
for another commercial, this time plugging the charms of the number
four. Again we're treated to television show-and-tell at its best, as
a variety of different kinds of objects in sets of four parade across the
screen, flash on and off, grow tall and short, approach and retreat,
dance and pirouette. We hear offstage children laughing delightedly
as they name the numbers and the objects. "Four cars. Four chicks."
The clincher is a waiter carrying four cream pies; he trips and falls,
ending up with pie all over his face—a pratfall, as they say in the business. Just like any of the skits the children might see on one of the
television's exported variety shows—"The Carol Burnett Show" or
"Englebert Humperdinck."

Now comes a film sequence, very short, very punchy. A lumber-
jack is cutting down a huge tree with heavy power equipment. He calls
out a warning as the tree topples and falls. The actor in the original
had called out in English, "Look out below!" In the dubbed Spanish
version, it comes out as "Abajo!"

This is followed by a sequence featuring Batman and Robin. "Holy
vocabulary, Batman!" exclaims Robin admiringly, as Batman catches
the bad guy and trusses him up for delivery to the forces of law and
order. In case there's still a preschool child who doesn't recognize
this as a curtain-line when he hears it, the curtain is definitively rung
down by still another commercial. It's the famous counting sequence:
one, two, three, four, five, six, seven, eight, NINE, ten—complete
with rock music and light show. Ten spies wearing trenchcoats and
pulled-down slouch hats (just like Maxwell Smart in "Get Smart," also
available for export).

Back to the plaza. Don Ramon and Gonzalo take up the dramatic
action just where they had left it a few minutes before, still arguing
about the newspaper as if no time had passed. Gonzalo protests that
he needs the paper to keep abreast of current events in the country.
Don Ramon counters that he needs it just as badly for the same reasons.

And so the show progresses: commercials, film clips, animations,
the scenes on the plaza. The argument between Don Ramon and Gonzalo
builds to its climax and reaches its final resolution, the compromise,
just in time for the closing commercial to drop the final curtain. It's
the Olga commercial again, the same animation we saw at the beginning; then comes the final billboard, the crawl, the music—and the
program is over. That's the format for all these programs: just like the
old "Ed Sullivan Show"; just like the new "Saturday Night Live with
Howard Cosell."

LEARNING THE LESSON

It should surprise no one to learn that test results from this country and from almost every country in which evaluation studies have been
made show with gratifying consistency that the children who watch the
programs learn the letters and numbers and concepts the charming segments in their version of "Sesame Street" try to convey. [7] After all, it
is a common enough observation that even the dullest preschoolers
recognize the characters that television features. Our children know
the Jolly Green Giant and associate him easily with the Niblets he
pushes for LeSueur Industries. They recognize Mother Nature and
Ronald McDonald and Fred Flintstone and Tony the Tiger and the White
Knight and the White Tornado and Mr. Clean and Mr. Coffee; and they
easily make the proper association with the products these mythical
creatures sell—margarine, fast foods, vitamins, prepared breakfast
foods, cleaning agents, and so on. [8] Latin American children are no
different in this regard: they recognize many of the identical characters appearing in the same associational contexts, as well as their own
home-grown varieties. In the same way, of course they come to recognize Olga and the letter "O, " just as they recognize the letter "S, "
and associate it with Superman, just as they recognize the concept
below and associate it with the tree crashing down in the forest. It's
just as easy to interest the children in the little drama enacted by
Gonzalo and Don Ramon and the puppets, as it is to interest them in
the dramas enacted on the same television screens by the Cartwrights
of "Bonanza, " or Gilligan and his friends, or Louis Erskine of "The
FBI, " or any one else in the long array of glamorous and attractive television shows that enter their lives so frequently in Latin America, just
as they do in the United States.

SHOW-AND-TELL—BUT NOT FOR BOOKS AND READING

Ah! But is it a world of reading the children are being ushered
into? Or do these charming programs usher them into a world of television watching? The children are entertained by animations; by commercials and billboards; by pratfalls, yuk-yuks and one-liners; by rock
music and light shows; by guest stars and production numbers—but
never by anything that involves books! No program, no sequence in
any of the seven cycles of "Sesame Street" in the United States, nor
in either of the two cycles of "Plaza Sesamo" that have been shown in
Latin America, has ever starred a book! No sequence in the ready-to-
buy package of "Open Sesame" focuses on a book. The daily dramas
on the street or in the Plaza never feature anyone absorbed in a book,
laughing or crying over a book, so gripped by a book that he cannot

bring himself to set it aside. No sequence has shown a child pleading
to stay up a little longer to finish a book, or sneaking a flashlight under
the covers to keep on reading after lights out. People caring enough
about a book to risk prison for possessing it or to face death for writing
it, even for reading a forbidden book—never! The incessant "commercials" sing the praises of letters and numbers, but never of books and
reading. The set itself, the familiar scene in the Plaza, doesn't even
give the children a chance to see books: Don Ramon's store sells
everything but books!

Now, at first glance, that "Sesame Street" and its overseas counterparts push literacy but not books may seem as contradictory as Coca-
Cola pushing beverages but not Coke. And yet, is it really so para-
doxical? Teachers teach not what they know but who they are, how
they think, how they learn, and how they relate to their pupils, their
special fields of study, and the whole quest of learning. [9] Scholars
teach scholarship; civil servants teach bureaucracy; and show business
wedded to advertising teaches the culture of both enterprises.

In a democratic society, literacy is not a legitimate goal in and
of itself. There is, after all, more than one kind of literacy. The literacy that goes with books can free the mind, stretch the imagination,
liberate the reader from his bondage to the present, linking him back
to all of human history, all of human culture, all of human experience
(that is why we still say "liberal education," meaning education that
liberates). There is another kind of literacy that does not have much
use for books. A work force must read to be able to read instructions
concerning the operation of equipment in a modern factory. Consumers
must read to decipher the instructions on a package of cake mix. The
citizenry must read to be able to fill out income-tax forms and use an
automated post office. Automobile drivers must read to find the right
exits off the throughway. Even a nation of television watchers must be
able to look up listings in the local equivalent of TV Guide and to follow
all the puffery about the stars, to say nothing of deciphering the stream-
er across the bottom of the screen announcing, "Mature subject matter.
Parental guidance suggested."

                          IDEOLOGICAL BAGGAGE

I have mentioned that the creators of "Sesame Street" were eager
to avail themselves of television's special capacity to show-and-tell,
aware that it is a more powerful tool for teaching and learning than
mere didactic exposition. All the programs I have seen are show-and-
tell at its best—show-and-tell for family structure and family relations,
food and table habits, household arrangements, occupational roles, age
and sex roles, rural and urban behavior patterns, economic pursuits
such as buying and selling and going to work; fashions in vehicles and

dress and hair styles; health practices and . . . well, just about everything. It is difficult to see how these repeated and repetitive images of
culture and social interaction can be divested of cultural content and
the claim that they can be has been challenged by many critics. [10]

What about that hand, printing the letters "XEROX" and the voice-
over linking the Xerox Corporation with the program's charm, beauty,
and good intentions? This is a very obvious part of the hidden curriculum, legitimizing not only the company and its officers, * but also a
commercial system of broadcasting depending for support on purchases
of time by self-interested people manning institutions with funds to
afford the investment. When those who are now children reach adult-
hood, the "normalcy" of such advertising practices is most likely to
be taken for granted, and any challenge to these policies and practices
will find itself on the defensive.

What about Gonzalo's claim that he needs the newspaper to find
out what is going on in his country? It is scarcely an ideology-free
comment in countries with a controlled press, whether that control is
exercised publicly by government censors or privately by families and
corporations so powerful they are the equivalent of private governments.
And that power saw cutting through the tree trunk—is it ideologically
neutral to feature industrial imports in countries whose currencies are
disadvantaged in the international market? To star capital-intensive
rather than labor-intensive technology in countries with vast pools of
unskilled, unemployed labor? To take for granted the destruction of
forests? All this, beamed to children who are sopping up primal impressions, not considering arguments pro and con.

MEDIA LITERACY: THE FORMAT IS THE LESSON AND THE LESSON IS THE FORMAT

It remains to be seen whether these charming programs teach the
children the fundamental skills they will later put to use to expand their
horizons by exploring the world that books and literature can open to

---

*Sol Linowitz, a former chairman of the board of the Xerox Corpo-
ration, was appointed by then President Lyndon Johnson to be Ambassador to the Organization of American States in 1966. This was just
when that organization was engaged in maintaining "peace-keeping
forces" in the Dominican Republic in a maneuver that many consider
to have been a gross interference in the domestic affairs of that country, equivalent to the Vietnam intervention.

Jack Hood Vaughan, Director of the International Department of
Children's Television Workshop, was Assistant Secretary of State for
Inter-American Affairs during the same period.

them. What is clear right now, however, is that the children are being
taught to "read" not books, but television. They learn to piece together
the day's drama on the street or in the Plaza, unifying it into a continuous story in spite of all the interruptions. This skill will stand them
in good stead, helping them to "read" the commercial television programs "Sesame Street" in all its versions imitates. The offstage laughter of the behind-the-scene audience teaches them to "read" the laugh
track that now defines humor all over the world. They even learn to
"read" what in other contexts would be puzzling statements directly
contrary to sensory experience, accepting them as television's acceptable constructions of false experience. For example, the spots in the
CTW export package often refer to colors seen on the screen; yet many
importing countries have facilities only for black-and-white reception
and their children see no colors. After their first puzzlement wears off,
the children learn to live quite comfortably with the contradiction, just
as they learn to live with television's constant claims that good guys
always thwart bad guys, the law is always on the side of justice, action is the same as drama, and using this or that brand of toothpaste
guarantees love. This is quite different from fantasy, since it requires
adjustment to unreality constructed as reality rather than fantasy's
playful moving back and forth between the world of imagination and the
world of daily experience. *

The featured stars teach the children to "read" television's star
system, so that they learn to recognize not only names and faces, but
also show-business categories, such as lead, supporting cast, and
extras. The sequences featuring Batman and Robin, Superman, and the
rest of television's syndicated heroes are an appreciation course for
beginning watchers of the original programs available for sale in international syndication, just like the CTW productions. In addition, they
teach the children to "read" the action-adventure and crime-show formulas that American businesses and their overseas imitators use as
electronic envelopes, † tucking in the commercial "messages" designed

---

*The broadcasting and advertising term is "puffery"—the kind of
hyperbole our own television idiom takes for granted. The term also
includes showing, as if it were perfectly acceptable and normal, behavior that would call down punishment and censure were the child to
engage in it: walking into someone's house unannounced, commenting
about the odors or the dinginess of the wash; frying a loaf of bread in
deep fat; discussing publicly discharges from the body's nether regions;
exclaiming rhapsodically about the color of the water in the toilet bowl,
wolfing down one's food and smacking the lips over it, and so on.

†A recent UNESCO study estimates that the total number of hours
of American television programs exported abroad each year ranges from
100,000 to 200,000 hours. [11]

to create public attitudes and consumer needs that can be linked to particular products. Indeed, the programs are themselves full-length commercials, hawking over and over again the kind of worldview that is compatible with postindustrial, privatized, consumer society, complete with the sort of pious slogans George Orwell dubbed "goodthink."[12]

And so is "Sesame Street"—domestic and international versions. Like other programs exported by American Television interests, no matter what the overt story line may be, it's all show-and-tell for the consumer society's version of the "good life"—the cars, the planes, the helicopters, the housing patterns, industrially produced foods and music, to say nothing of the electric refrigerators and blenders and mixers and household equipment, all taken for granted as standard props on "Sesame Street" as on any exported "situation comedy." These images of the "good life" are not innocuous. They pave the way for foreign subsidiaries, affiliates, clients, and imitators of American consumer-goods industries to leap into the breach, ready to provide whatever merchandise the natives may select from the offerings appearing in the glamorous showcase that now encircles the globe.[13]

SUPPORT SYSTEMS

Children are charmed by CTW's delightful programs. They approach the screen, try to pat the cheeks of the characters, try to hug those delightful muppets. The natural warmth and affection they direct toward the cast, the muppets, the animations, the songs, the music, envelops them all in an aura so real it's almost tangible—tangible enough, in any case, to be packaged and sold by CTW to companies producing a variety of products ready for sale to the children and their parents.

CTW, like so many other television production companies, links its television programs to a total support system of income-producing franchises. The CTW Products group licenses over a hundred items for production and sale, * and is continually reaching out for more custom-

---

*Earnings from nonbroadcast activities in 1972/73 were ten times higher than earnings just three years earlier, 1970/71. The figures appear in CTW Annual Report, 1973, p. 25, as:

1968-1970:	$ 123.6 thousand
1970-1971	259.0 thousand
1971-1972	369.0 thousand
1972-1973	2,436.4 thousand

Franchised products include comic books, magazines, records, stick-ons, toys, and other playthings. ". . . Behind a mask of fun . . . the media is different, the message is the same.[14]

ers. Companies producing CTW tie-in products include massive con-
glomerates encompassing our own commercial broadcasting companies
and their subsidiaries, as well as some of television's biggest adver-
tisers. An abbreviated list would feature Random House, a subsidiary
of RCA, the parent company of all the NBC interests; Columbia Records,
a subsidiary of CBS, Inc.; the Milton Bradley Company; Ideal Toys;
Quaker Oats; J. C. Penney; Burlington Industries; the Lilly Co.; and
the Elgin Watch Company.

And it is a two-way street. CTW, in its turn, has an arrangement
with Marvel Comics, publishers of Spider-Man (among other comic
books) to use that copyrighted character as a CTW regular on its television shows as Spidey-Man and again in comic book form as Spidey
Super Stories. In both roles he softens up the children not only to "buy"
the letters and numbers CTW is selling, but also to buy the original
Spider-Man series sold by Marvel, as well as the many products licensed by them to use the Spider-Man image and logo. They include
chewy multiple vitamins produced by the Hudson Pharmaceutical Corporation (owned by Marvel's parent company)* competing with other
television salesmen in the business of pushing vitamins such as the
Flintstones and Bugs Bunny (for Miles Laboratories) and Monster vitamins (for Bristol-Myers).

The stars, themselves, try to cash in on that aura and sell it to
their own advantage. Television personality Bill Cosby describes how
he makes commercials for Jello. "They get about 500 kids in a room
before I even get into the building . . . show them me in 'Electric Company' tapes and they watch . . . for the five kids who are most turned
on . . . and they grab them and give them to me for the ad. The rest
is easy. . . ."[15] Morgan Freeman, who portrays "Easy Reader" and
other characters on "Electric Company," demonstrates Procter and
Gamble's deodorant, Sure. He also appears in a John Hancock Insurance
spot singing, "We put our John Hancock on a John Hancock for our family." Harold Miller, who plays Gordon, does a commercial for Bristol-
Myers' Excedrin. Rita Moreno has done a commercial for Gabrielle
Wigs.[16] In Mexico, the "Plaza Sesamo" stars likewise appear in television commercials.

Companies that have bought the "Sesame Street" franchise are
producing products ranging from toys and games to children's clothes
and bedclothes: books, too, of course—even though most of the
"Sesame Street" books are not exactly proper books but pop-ups, comic
books, magazine formats complete with centerfold, and a "scratch and

_____

*"Try Spider-Man Vitamins from Hudson and I'll send you a free
Spider-Man poster," says the advertisement on the back cover of a
Spider-Man comic book (January 1975). "Spider-Man Vitamins are great!
They're new! They're fun! And they're really delicious! . . . No
hassle with Mom and Dad either." Cadence Industries Corp owns both
Marvel Comics Inc. and Hudson Pharmaceutical Corporation.

sniff fragrance book."* The companies producing them can and do take
advantage of the export market that overseas sales of CTW programs
open up for them, although the franchising system metastasizes overseas as well. South American, West German, Brazilian, and French
companies are offered the same opportunity to divert that aura their
children invest the program with, and reattach it to their own products.
In Colombia, South America, for example, "Sesame Street" books are
published by Norma (stationery, office supplies, and book publishing).
In Mexico the associated business firms are the Lili-Ledy Company
(toys) and Editorial Navarro (comic books). In West Germany, an initial
agreement with the Carl Herlitz Company gave way to a more lucrative
arrangement with Gunner and Jahr, the country's largest publishing company. Gunner and Jahr will not only publish for CTW, but will seek
other companies wanting to buy the franchise, profits to be split with
CTW. In France, franchising arrangements are under negotiation, aiming for a 1976 concluding date to synchronize with the opening of a
new, improved version of "Bonjour Sésame."[17]

EROSION OF LANGUAGE

There are further ways of subtly invading a culture, such as gradually eroding its language. Dubbing provides a good example of this
erosion. Translating for the dubbed sound track is a difficult task.
Choice of words is guided more by technical considerations and less
by concern for rhetorical faithfulness, with the result that the precise
term often ends up on the cutting-room floor, yielding to the approximate term with the right number of syllables. This, coupled with the

---

*The scratch-and-sniff book uses highly transparent microcapsules,
which contain microscopic droplets of fragrant oils within a polymeric
shell. The encapsulated scent is applied to paper by high-speed printing equipment, where it remains as a stable, strong, colorless, and
odorless coating until the capsules are broken. A light scratch releases
the scent. There are enough tiny encapsulated droplets in a small area
for dozen of scratches and sniffs before the scent disappears. The
process may be applied not only to paper but also to toys, games, novel-
ties, educational materials, merchandising aids, T-shirts, pajamas,
and so on. One company that specializes in the process claims that
"Micro-Scent increases sales potential by combining visual display
and fragrance," and refers to "this sweet smell of sell." "From pine
to peppermint, raspberries to roses—this is the way to sell seasons,
products, almost anything, luringly." Promotional materials issued by
NCR Appleton Papers Division, Capsular Products, 9095 Washington
Church Road, Miamisburg, Ohio 45342.

loss of acoustic faithfulness (the sound of actors reading lines while they sit motionless before a microphone is different from the sound of actors speaking as they move through space) accounts for the peculiar flatness of dubbed dialogue. In dubbing, flesh-and-blood actors on film mouth their lines in English but the words and phrases come out in Spanish. ("Look out below!" becomes "Abajo!") When lips send out one set of signals but the words signal something else, language is "out of sync"—as they say in show business.

What happens when the infrastructure that will form the basis of language appreciation and language use among children who have not yet internalized their language is laid down in this manner?

And then there are all those animations and puppets acting as speech models—creatures whose facial expressions and eye movements and even body movements do not orchestrate themselves with the emotional sense of the words they seem to be uttering, nor with the lilt and cadence of the phrases. Someone speaks, and his mouth moves but his facial expression and body movements remain unchanged. His listeners remain immobile, frozen. In show-business jargon, everything is deadpan. Someone walks, runs, gets up, sits down; his limbs move but his body does not. What does all this mean to these young learners?

In "Plaza Sesamo" as in "Sesame Street," nobody in the cast seems to have a family name, an apellido. Everyone is addressed by his or her first name—unless children are involved, in which case no names at all are mentioned. (In these programs it is only the grownups, the animated figures, and the puppets who are rescued from nameless anonymity.) The "Plaza Sesamo" cast consistently features the tú form of address.* Usted appears rarely, if at all, vos and che, never.

These practices are not unquestioningly accepted throughout the Spanish-speaking world, yet the programs present them as perfectly normal, perfectly natural, beyond question. Family name is a repository

---

*In Spanish as in many other languages, there are two versions of the second-person singular form of address; the tú form, equivalent to the French tu, and the Usted form, equivalent to the French vous. The tú form is used symmetrically among family members and other intimates. The Usted form is used asymmetrically to indicate that one member of the conversational pair pays the other the greater respect—the younger speaker to the older, the employee to the employer, the student to the professor, and so on.

The precise equivalents of tú and Usted in English would be the "thou" form of address compared with the "you" form, a distinction that is now archaic. In English, the nearest approximation to Usted is the use of Mrs., Mr., and Miss plus last name, rather than unadorned first name. This usage is now going the route of "thou," as the culture of television, including CTW productions, spreads all over the world.

of family history, of racial and ethnic tradition, and many families seek
to preserve it as a source of identity worthy of their children's pride.
Its use in address, along with the Usted form of the verb, is an easy
linguistic signal announcing that some relationships prefer to remain
at arm's length, that not all relationships are necessarily on an intimate
footing. Vos and che are customary usages in Argentina, Chile, Uru-
guay, and parts of Colombia. The program's obliteration of all these
forms now requires families adhering to them to justify their own speech
styles and the values implicit in them before their own children. Other
families whose usages conform to CTW's definitions of normal usage
are placed under no such obligation, of course.

SPACE, TIME, AND TIME SENSE[18]

Show-and-tell depends heavily on the language of time and space,
and CTW productions are outstanding examples of creative use of movement, rhythming, and pacing. This is a language that communicates a
world of information especially, perhaps, to preschool children who are
still more fluent in body language than in verbal language. One set of
spatial relations mutely signals importance or intimacy or consent; another indicates that the relationship is distant or consent is to be with-
held, or that the goings-on are unimportant, peripheral to the main
event. Children must learn the spatial codes for their own culture and
subcultures. Play-acting—their own and dramatizations they watch—
is essential to this learning. [19]

Nor is the time sense that we take so for granted inborn in human
young. Children in U.S. culture must learn to pace their internal
rhythms to mealtimes, playtimes, quiet times, nap time, and bedtime—
at least they must if they come from the subgroups that educators and
television executives come from. Children everywhere must grasp what
their culture means by long and short duration, proper synchronization
of one's reaction time to others; margins of permissible promptness and
tardiness under different conditions—all learned. Music and chants
help us synchronize these cultural rhythms and internalize them. This
is only one way in which music is no more culturally neutral than spoken
language. *

---

*The Latin American consultants advising Children's Television
Workshop on the cultural appropriateness of the Spanish language version were aware of the cultural distinctiveness of music, and strongly
recommended that "Plaza Sesamo" utilize the rich folk music so easily
available in every Latin American country. Summary of First Preparatory
Seminar for the Spanish Television Series, "Plaza Sesamo." Mimeographed, 1971. Alas! When the "Plaza Sesamo" series came out, each
54-minute program boasted at best one selection of Latin American music.
The rest: bubblegum rock!

Even standard measurements of time that we take so for granted—
a 24-hour day, a 60-minute hour, a 60-second minute—are socially defined and change from culture to culture, from one historic period to
another. Insightful writers have noted how the earliest stirrings of the
industrial system we know introduced massive changes in the way people
experienced time, and depended upon such changes in time sense to
come into its own full existence. [20] In the present historic moment,
television is introducing equally massive changes even though they are
so widely experienced that we take them for granted. Along with the
rest of American television, CTW is exporting the 54-minute hour. It
is also exporting the 60-second commercial, even the 30-second commercial as another entrenched rhythm and rhythm-marker. In that 30-
second interval, marked by the new, universal metronome, information
and images are so tightly packed that we pay only glancing attention
to any specific element, "reading" the whole simultaneously in a single,
seemingly timeless instant; and as we do, we scarcely notice the absence of opportunity to reflect and consider intellectually what we have
taken in emotionally.

IMPRINTING

Children all over the world can watch "Sesame Street" just as they
watch exported versions of the rest of U.S. television properties: "Bat-
man," "Superman," "Bonanza," "Gunsmoke," "Gilligan's Island,"
"The Carol Burnett Show," "The Mary Tyler Moore Show," several gen-
erations of "Lucy" shows, the "FBI," "Mission Impossible," "Mod
Squad," "Dragnet," "The Untouchables," "Dr. Kildare," "Medical
Center," "Marcus Welby, M.D."—the list is endless. When they turn
off the set they can sleep on "Sesame Street" sheets, cuddle up to
Sesame Street pillows, wear Sesame Street clothes, tell time with
Sesame Street watches, sing Sesame Street songs, dance to Sesame
Street music, play with Sesame Street toys and muppets, color Sesame
Street coloring books, sniff Sesame Street fragrances, all the while
chewing those delicious Spider-Man vitamins. For a change of pace
they can switch to identical products featuring Mickey Mouse and the
gang (Walt Disney Productions), the Flintstone Family (Hanna-Barbera
Productions, Inc.), Bugs Bunny (Warner Brothers Entertainment, Inc.)—
the list is endless but the merchandise is the same. *

---

*Walt Disney characters such as Mickey Mouse and the gang are
well known all over the world. The Character Merchandising Division
of Walt Disney Productions licenses about a thousand companies permitting them to attach to their products the characters produced and
created by the Disney studios. Their aura is so powerful that the U.S.

Will the children's body movements and body rhythms, their facial expressions, and their emotive use of language all converge to a sort of universal mean? Nobody knows the answer to such questions, of course; but it does not take much wisdom to see that it is a kind of imprinting that was science fiction when Huxley wrote Brave New World.[24] That was more than four decades ago, though. Today it is neither science nor fiction.

Department of State has tried to take advantage of it to promote American business interests in Latin America. An admirer of the Disney technique tells how the Disney movies, Saludos Amigos and The Three Caballeros were made explicitly to open the South American market. The State Department agreed to underwrite four short Disney films. They were later cut and spliced, documentary footage was woven in and Saludos Amigos was the first release. Two years later, The Three Caballeros, also aimed at the Latin American market, appeared. [21]

Hanna-Barbera Productions Inc. produces most of the animated cartoons shown on American television in the hours reserved for attracting children to the set, the so-called Saturday morning ghetto, then releases the cartoons for syndicated sales all over the world. They claim "the largest merchandising operation of its kind in the world. More than 1500 licensed manufacturers turn out some 4500 different products ranging from Flintstones window shades to Banana Splits bubble bath." They produce cartoons featuring Huckleberry Hound, Yogi Bear, and other talking animals. [22]

Converting children's affection for the fictional and mythic characters that command their attention into lucrative come-ons to boost sales is now a specialized business. The largest concern that does nothing but license the use of such characters is the Licensing Corporation of America. Its chief executive estimated the total take from such sales as over $400 million; that was almost a decade ago, in 1966. Since then, it has surely doubled. The Licensing Corporation grossed at least $150 million selling the aura surrounding Batman and associated props. Other characters and props whose aura they peddle include Superman, Star Trek, Aquaman, and James Bond.

The claim that the franchised items are identical, regardless of which logo they use, is not simply figurative; it can be literal. The plastic models for the dolls and equipment can be used interchangeably; leftover equipment can be repainted and renamed to conform to whatever series is currently eliciting the heaviest demand. [23]

NOTES

1. CTW '72, A Special Report From the Children's Television Workshop (New York: Children's Television Workshop, 1972); Editorial Backgrounder: Sesame Street Overseas (New York: Children's Television Workshop, April 1973); Children's Television Workshop Annual Report (1973); CTW Review 1973-1975; interview with Gretchen Bock, International Division, Children's Television Workshop, September 1975.
2. New York Times, March 20, 1973.
3. CTW '72, op. cit., p. 23.
4. Ibid., p. 21.
5. Ibid., p. 23.
6. "Remarks by David D. Connell and Dr. Edward L. Palmer, before the International Seminar on Broadcaster/Research Cooperation in Mass Communication Research" (Leicester, England: University of Leicester, December 19, 1970). Xerox copy, p. 20.
"An early conclusion of parents and experts who observed children's watching habits was the fact that the children responded most positively to commercials. They learned to recognize words and phrases long before they actually learned to read because of the simple, direct methods of rhetoric employed in the one minute product commercial. Pace, style, jingles, and repetition are key elements. At the workshop we intend to employ these same elements to 'sell'—if you will—the letters of the alphabet and numbers. . . ." Testimony of Joan Ganz Cooney, Hearings before the Subcommittee on Communications of the Committee on Commerce, U.S. Senate, April 30 and May 1, 1969 (Washington, D.C.: U.S. Government, 1969), p. 88.
7. Test results showing consistent increments among U.S. children exposed to the program are summarized succinctly in Gerald Lesser, Children and Television (New York: Random House, 1974). A critical reexamination of U.S. test results appears in Thomas D. Cook, Hilary Appleton, Ross Conner, Ann Shaffer, Gary Tamkin, and Stephen J. Weber, "Sesame Street" Revisited (New York: Russell Sage Foundation, 1975).
8. See, for example, Tom Sullenberger, "Folklure," Human Behavior 4 (June 1975): 65-69, for an interesting analysis of how commercials press into service ancient mythic figures and symbols whose charismatic aura is now bound to the products they advertise.
9. Martin Heidegger, What Is Called Thinking? (New York: Harper & Row, 1954), pp. 15-16.
10. See, for example, Armand Mattelart, "El Imperialismo en Busca de la Contrarevolución Cultural," in Comunicación y Cultura (Buenos Aires and Santiago), no. 1 (July 1973), pp. 146-224. See also his La Cultura Como Empresa Multinacional (Mexico City, 1974), pp. 84-100. See also, "Down Sesame Street," New York: The Network Project, Notebook Number Six, November 1973.

11. Tapio Varis, "The Trade in Television, " Intermedia 3 (1973).
"Superman" is distributed by Warner Brothers in 117 countries, along
with "Kung Fu, " "77 Sunset Strip, " "F Troop, " and "Maverick. "

12. See, for example, Richard Barnet and Ronald Müller, The
Global Reach (New York: Doubleday, 1975).

13. George Orwell, 1984 (New York: Harcourt Brace Jovanovich,
1949).

14. CTW advertisement in Time, December 18, 1972.

15. Andrew R. Horowitz, "The Global Bonanza of American TV, "
[More], May 1975. See also Herbert Schiller, Mass Media and Ameri-
can Empire (Boston: Beacon Press, 1971) and Herbert Schiller, The
Mind Managers (Boston: Beacon Press, 1973).

16. Advertising Age, July 14, 1975.

17. Advertising Age, July 29, 1974. "Electric Company, " produced,
distributed and exported by CTW, is a television series designed to
correct reading deficiencies among older children already in school.
Gordon is the original model for Gonzalo. Rita Moreno is a comedienne
appearing in "Electric Company" and "Sesame Street. "

18. The following sources have in common their understanding that
the power to control the way in which people experience time is a fundamental power, convertible into political and economic domination: Lewis
Mumford, The Myth of the Machine, Technics and Human Development
(New York: Harcourt, Brace Jovanovich, 1966), pp. 284-87, and also
his Interpretations and Forecasts: 1922-1972 (New York: Harcourt, Brace
Jovanovich, 1974), pp. 270-78; Warren J. Brodey, "The Clock Mani-
festo, " Annals of the New York Academy of Science 138 (February 6,
1967), pp. 895-911 and also "Biotopology 1972, " Radical Software,
no. 4 (Summer 1971), pp. 4-7; Herbert G. Reid, "American Social Science in Politics of the Time and the Crisis of Technocorporate Society,"
Politics and Society 3 (Winter 1973), pp. 201-44.

19. Sesame Street 1973, Playthings, Books and Records, promotional material issued by Children's Television Workshop. Also, interview with Carol McCabe and Jeannette Neff, of CTW Products Division,
October 20, 1975.

20. For further discussion of the concepts of space, time, and
time sense, see, for example, Edward T. Hall, The Silent Language
(Greenwich, Conn.: Fawcett Publications, 1959) and The Hidden Dimension (Garden City, New York: Anchor Books, 1966).

21. Christopher Finch, The Art of Walt Disney: From Mickey Mouse
to the Magic Kingdoms (New York: Harry N. Abrams, 1975), pp. 113-
14. See also A. Dorfman and A. Mattelart, Para Leer Al Pato Donald
(Buenos Aires, Argentina: Siglo XXI, 1972), p. xxi.

22. "History of Hanna-Barbera Productions, " Hanna-Barbera Productions, Inc., Hollywood, California. Mimeographed, undated.

23. Ron Goulart, The Assault on Childhood (Los Angeles: Sherborne
Press, Inc., 1969), pp. 102-03.

24. Aldous Huxley, Brave New World (New York: Harper Bros.,
1932).

ROBERT F. ARNOVE is Associate Professor of Education at Indiana University, Bloomington. He received his doctorate from Stanford University in 1969, in the field of International Development of Education. He returned as a visiting faculty member of the Stanford University school of education in 1972, where he directed this study of educational television in developing countries. Professor Arnove has worked extensively in Latin America as an educational adviser and researcher. He has published a number of articles on education and development, and the role of students in national politics in Latin America. Praeger Special Studies published his earlier work, Student Alienation: A Venezuelan Study.

MARTIN CARNOY is Associate Professor of Education and Economics at Stanford University and an Associate of the Center for Economic Studies in Palo Alto. He is the author of numerous articles and books on economic development and on the role of education in the development process, including Industrialization in a Latin American Common Market, Schooling in a Corporate Society, Education as Cultural Imperialism, and The Limits of Educational Reform. He has just finished a monograph on economic change and educational reform in Cuba, and is currently working on a study of the relationship between alternative forms of work organization and the educational system.

ROSE K. GOLDSEN, Associate Professor of Sociology at Cornell University, has lived and worked in South America, most recently as social science adviser to the Ford Foundation (1969-72). She specializes in studying society's opinion-forming institutions and in methods of social research. She has written numerous articles on the role of the mass media in society, and is the author of the forthcoming book Television: The Product Is You. Professor Goldsen discusses the mass media on her weekly radio program in Ithaca, New York.

HENRY INGLE was in residence in El Salvador for two years, representing the Institute for Communication Research of Stanford University, as Field Research Director of the use of television in the Salvadoran Educational Reform program. He has been a consultant to a number of communication media projects in Latin America and Asia. He currently resides in Washington, D. C., and works as a technical adviser to various international development agencies in the areas of educational policy research and evaluation. He has coauthored a series of publications on educational television in El Salvador and has recently published a monograph entitled, Communication Media and Technology: A Look at Their Role in Non-Formal Education Programs.

ANTHONY KAYE has been with the Open University in the United Kingdom since its inception in 1970. He initially worked within its Institute of Educational Technology on course development and evaluation, and is now Assistant Director of the University Consultancy Service. This unit within the University is responsible for providing technical assistance to other countries interested in the Open University model of higher education. During a two-year leave of absence from the University (1973-75), he served as Director of the External Evaluation Unit of the Ivory Coast ETV Project, while an Ivorian counterpart was undergoing training overseas. He has published articles on the Open University and educational television.

MICHAEL KIRST is Associate Professor of Education and Business Administration, Stanford University. Since 1975, he has been a Member of the California State Board of Education. Among his recent books are Federal Aid to Education, The Political Web of American Schools, and State, School, and Politics. Professor Kirst also has published books based on school finance studies in Florida and Oregon.

LYNNE AND GRANT MASLAND worked for the Department of Education in American Samoa for two years (1966-68). Lynne Masland has taught English at the University of Nebraska at Omaha. She is currently at work full-time on two books. Grant Masland is a professor in the Department of Human Communication at the University of Nebraska at Omaha. He has written on alternative uses of the mass media.

WILLIAM PERRON currently works as an analyst for the Provost's Office at Stanford University. He previously held positions in the Harvard University Central Administration. He is a graduate of Stanford's joint program between the Graduate School of Education and the Graduate School of Business.

CARRASCOLENDAS: BILINGUAL EDUCATION
THROUGH TELEVISION
>Frederick Williams
>Geraldine Van Wart

EDUCATION AND DEVELOPMENT RECONSIDERED:
The Bellagio Conference Papers
>Ford Foundation/Rockefeller Foundation
>edited by F. Champion Ward

EDUCATIONAL PLANNING AND EXPENDITURE
DECISIONS IN DEVELOPING COUNTRIES: With a
Malaysian Case Study
>Robert W. McMeekin, Jr.

TELEVISION AS A SOCIAL FORCE: New Approaches
to TV Criticism
>Douglass Cater and
>Richard Adler

DE PROPRIETATIBUS LITTERARUM

edenda curat

C. H. VAN SCHOONEVELD

Indiana University

Series Practica, 59

ILLUSION AND REALITY

A STUDY OF DESCRIPTIVE TECHNIQUES
IN THE WORKS OF GUY DE MAUPASSANT

by

JOHN RAYMOND DUGAN

University of Waterloo

1973

MOUTON

THE HAGUE · PARIS

LIBRARY OF CONGRESS CATALOG CARD NUMBER: 72-94459

Printed in Hungary

TABLE OF CONTENTS

I

THE MAUPASSANTIAN POSITION

In the most widely known of Maupassant's theoretical pieces, the so-called "preface" to *Pierre et Jean*, there occurs a statement of purpose which has given rise to much critical examination. Maupassant says: "Les grands artistes sont ceux qui imposent à l'humanité leur illusion particulière."[1] Although this problem has been examined in several critical studies,[2] a satisfactory explanation has yet to be made concerning his aesthetic aspirations and realizations.

There can be no doubt that the universe of Maupassant, like that of any other exponent of the art of fiction, is basically illusionary. The present study is certainly not an effort to prove or indeed to disprove the author's claim. Aesthetic products of necessity spring from the imagination, and are by definition bound up to a greater or lesser degree with the necessity of creating illusion.

Typical of opinions expressed by a number of critics, that Maupassant was facile, shallow, a shining example of the "artiste inconscient", is this remark by Beuchat:

Cet admirateur de la nature ne s'attarde que rarement à l'évocation d'un paysage. S'il le fait, c'est parce que la nature extérieure a pris part à la scène. Tout concourt ainsi à reproduire la vie, rien que la vie. Le style clair et limpide

---

[1] Guy de Maupassant, "Le roman", *Pierre et Jean, Oeuvres complètes* (Paris: Conard, 1907–10), p. XVI. The complete works published by Conard seem to be the standard critical edition of Maupassant in spite of certain lacunae and inaccuracies of dating. Because it is so readily available, all references to Maupassant's works will be to this edition when possible. Its twenty-nine volumes are not numbered and therefore the title of the pertinent volume will be given in each case. The fifteen volume Librairie de France edition (1934–38) is chiefly valuable for the final tables concerning theme and chronology, but this material is also to be found in René Dumesnil's *Chroniques, études, correspondance de Guy de Maupassant* (Paris: Gründ, 1938).

[2] See especially the following excellent studies: R. Dumesnil, *Guy de Maupassant* (Paris: Taillandier, 1947); E. D. Sullivan, *Maupassant the Novelist* (Princeton: Princeton University Press, 1954); André Vial, *Guy de Maupassant et l'art du roman* (Paris: Nizet, 1954).

apporte sa contribution, c'est le style le plus naturel qui soit. Jules Lemaître avait raison d'affirmer que l'écrivain produisait 'ses nouvelles comme un pommier des pommes',[3]

or the following evaluation of his style by Pierre Cogny:

Maupassant a naturellement le style qui n'est pas un style parce qu'il colle à la vie même. Sa phrase, nette et pure, est aussi difficile à analyser que celle de Voltaire, ou d'Anatole France. Les articulations, sujet, verbe, complément, y sont bien, mais le mystère qui préside à leur parfait agencement demeure entier. Il n'y fallait qu'un immense talent, et ce talent est tout.[4]

A profound thinker he certainly was not, but nevertheless, how could it have been possible for someone so closely linked with Gustave Flaubert as was Guy de Maupassant not to have seriously weighed such problems of creative writing as style, precision, documentation, form – those basic tenets of the Flaubertian aesthetic, the dogma of that most conscious of nineteenth century novelists. Maupassant's faith in his mentor's teachings burned with a bright flame throughout his creative life, and doubtless the popular conception of Maupassant the spontaneous inventor of tales, the author of brilliantly executed but essentially empty narratives, is little else but an unproven cliché of criticism.

The heir to Flaubertian "realism", the intellectual cousin of Zola's naturalism, Maupassant is often regarded as the epitome of the objective novelist, that most dispassionate observer of phenomena who seems to be a logical conclusion of a whole century of fictional tradition.

Et si, maintenant, autour de ces nouvelles de la peur et de l'angoisse, on rassemble tout le reste de l'oeuvre, toutes les pages écrites avec le goût et le sens de la vie, sans aucune vaine prétention scientifique ou documentaire, d'un style admirablement limpide, on sera tenté d'affirmer que bien plus que Zola, Maupassant, dans les parties troubles de son oeuvre, aussi bien que dans ses claires visions de la campagne normande ou de la vie parisienne, est représentatif de la génération naturaliste; il a traduit à la fois le goût du siècle finissant pour la réalité et aussi son inquiétude devant la réalité, qu'on finissait par juger bien incomplète et triste.[5]

With particular reference to the novel, Sullivan maintains that what he sees as an extension of this so-called objective technique leads Maupassant into a kind of psychological morass of subjectivity.[6] It is my contention that an analysis of objectivity in this author's work will not in itself prove

[3] Ch. Beuchat, *Histoire du naturalisme français*, 2 vols. (Paris: Corréa, 1949), II, p. 91.
[4] P. Cogny, *Le naturalisme* (Paris: Presses Universitaires de France, 1953), p. 93.
[5] P. Martino, *Le naturalisme français* (Paris: Armand Colin, 1965), p. 145.
[6] Sullivan, *Maupassant the Novelist*, ch. 9.

a great deal. Even that most "objective" of novels, Flaubert's *Salammbô* is, as everyone knows, quite revealing when viewed in the light of the author's personal sensibilities. And Maupassant's contention concerning illusion suggests that he, like his master, was well aware of the problem.

Maupassant's creation of illusion must first be approached from quite another angle – that of aesthetic resolutions of fictional problems as seen from within the works themselves. In other words, must the noticeable changes in subject matter, technique and emphasis which are visible in his later period be seen as a break, a denial of earlier concepts, or can a logical, unbroken progression be discerned? Do his early and later productions show a necessary and predictable evolution in terms of technique? These problems are of course aggravated by the fact that his creative life was unusually brief. Maupassant's writings themselves must therefore speak, and suggest some conclusion to the debate over subjectivity and objectivity.

One must of necessity then approach Maupassant's work from within. Only by viewing in some detail the methods and techniques practised in his stories, novels and travel books, is it possible to understand the writer. However significant his celebrated malady may or may not be, its much disputed influence on his creative imagination must take secondary position within the confines of the present study. A very great weakness of much critical work on Guy de Maupassant up to the present, has been the inability on the part of the critic to separate Maupassant the man from Maupassant the creative artist.[7] I would be among the first to admit that his life holds great fascination, and obviously plays its part in his artistic development, yet in terms of literary criticism, this aspect has been much over-emphasized. Critics seem almost in spite of themselves to be attracted by his biography.

With the exception of Sullivan's book[8] with which, for all its excellence I cannot always agree, and André Vial's most detailed study[9] which, in its thoroughness fails, in my estimation, to offer a clear elucidation of the author from a strictly artistic and formal point of view, there have been

---

[7] There is a vast amount of biographical material available concerning Guy de Maupassant. Among the best studies I would mention: René Dumesnil, *Guy de Maupassant*: E. Maynial, *La vie et l'oeuvre de Guy de Maupassant* (Paris: Mercure de France, 1906); F. Steegmuller, *A Lion in the Path* (New York: Random House, 1949).

For a more complete list of books and articles see the excellent bibliography in Vial's work *(Guy de Maupassant)* or A. Artinian, *Maupassant Criticism in France* (New York: King's Crown Press, 1941).

[8] Sullivan, *Maupassant the Novelist*.

[9] Vial, *Guy de Maupassant*.

few attempts to deal with these problems on anything more than a fragmentary basis. Certain astonishingly similar techniques from novel to novel, from story to story, have been noticed in the isolation of a single work.[10] Nowhere has there been, to my knowledge, an attempt to link them up into a unified view of the whole.

Maupassant's "illusion particulière" is not necessarily a reflection of his inherited neuroses if such there were, nor of the intellectual erosion effected by disease, if such there was. Disregarding the surfeit of conflicting medical evidence surrounding "le cas Maupassant", I think it is possible to explain his work satisfactorily from self-contained evidence, that is to say from the point of view of the conscious artist.

This study takes the form of a progression from the interior outward, with a view to showing a logical development in Maupassant's work. It is my hope that it may in some way contribute to a re-appraisal of this novelist's significance in the larger framework of literary history. Misjudged by his contemporaries[11] and somewhat slighted by succeeding

[10] A number of articles have dealt with imagery in a single novel with little attempt to integrate them into the totality of Maupassant's creation. The following are among the best of these: R. B. Grant, "Imagery as a Means of Psychological Realism in *Une vie*", *Studies in Philology* LX, 669–84; G. Hainsworth, "Pattern and Symbol in the Work of Guy de Maupassant", *French Studies* V (January, 1951), 1–17; R. J. Neiss, "*Pierre et Jean*: Some Symbols", *French Review* XXXII (May, 1959), 511–19; E. D. Sullivan, "Portrait of the Artist: Maupassant and *Notre coeur*", *French Review* XXI (December, 1948), 136.

[11] We have seen something of Jules Lemaître's view in Beuchat's reference to him (see note 3). Anatole France, with his usual facility dismisses Maupassant in the following manner: "J'inclinerais à croire que sa philosophie est contenue tout entière dans cette chanson si sage que les nourrices chantent à leurs nourrissons et qui résume à merveille tout ce que nous savons de la destinée des hommes sur la terre:

Les petites marionettes
   Font, font, font,
Trois petits tours
   Et puis s'en vont."

Anatole France, "M. Guy de Maupassant et les conteurs français", *La vie littéraire*, 1ère série: *Oeuvres complètes* (Paris: Calmann-Lévy, 1926), p. 61.

Only Brunetière comes anywhere close to a valid judgement: "Tous les procédés du vrai naturalisme, si l'on y veut bien faire un peu d'attention, n'ont pour objet, dans le roman, comme en peinture, que de mettre l'artiste en garde contre mille moyens qu'il a de déformer la réalité, pour un seul de la reproduire. Lisez à ce point de vue les meilleures nouvelles de M. de Maupassant: il vous semblera que tout autre que lui, que vous-même, au besoin, eussiez pu les écrire; elles sont impersonnelles comme les oeuvres classiques. ... Mais si cette fidélité de l'imitation, si la réalisation de ce caractère impersonnel et en quelque sorte éternel de l'oeuvre a été dans notre temps, en France et aussi ailleurs, l'objet du naturalisme, on peut dire encore que nul ne l'a plus pleinement atteint que M. de Maupassant" (F. Brunetière, *Le roman naturaliste* [Paris: Calmann-Lévy, 1889], p. 379).

generations, Guy de Maupassant has been perhaps the most maligned and most frequently misunderstood artist of his period.

Before we embark on this study of more precise textual material I think it is useful to review in as brief a space as possible the general lines of his thinking concerning some of the great novelists of his century.

In a form of literature as closely related to its society as is the nineteenth century novel of manners, the external world, its sights, its smells and its sounds, performs a vital function.

But the rôle of this real world varies greatly in importance from author to author. The Stendhalian view of the novel as a mirror, which furnishes a kind of point of departure for the imagination, is far removed from Zola's concepts of the real. Maupassant is well aware of the difficulties which arise out of realistic aspirations. Can literature be real? Within the bounds of nineteenth century the tradition may be considered to have its focus in the work of Honoré de Balzac, whose tendencies towards realism have been so often analyzed.

What concerns us with regard to Maupassant, the relationship between external appearances and internal make-up is a device which is very common in the nineteenth century novel. One can think of Fabrice del Dongo imprisoned in the citadel urgently needing to communicate with the outside world in the person of Clelia Conti, or of Jean Valjean and the famous loaf of bread. There is in nineteenth century fiction a constant interplay between character and environment, between interior life and external objects, rendered more complex by the function of the observer, the artist who depicts this interplay. It is especially in this regard that the work of Balzac looms so large. His "Avant-propos" succinctly suggested this when he wrote of the triple form that fiction should take: "les hommes, les femmes et les choses, c'est-à-dire les personnes et la représentation matérielle qu'ils donnent de leur pensée; enfin l'homme et la vie."[12] One has only to think for example, of the elaborate apartment of César Birotteau or of the faded yellow salon of Mademoiselle Gamard to see to what excellent use physical objects as an adjunct of character portrayal can be put in Balzac. The décor of a place of residence becomes under his pen a tangible, exteriorized manifestation of what is already established beneath the surface. The "peau de chagrin" takes on a multitude of forms. Reality in his narratives is often subservient to character, and Balzac's detailed descriptions such as that of the Pension Vauquer which opens *Le père Goriot* not only performs this same function with regard to those

[12] Honoré de Balzac, "Avant-propos", *La comédie humaine* 1 (Paris: Bibliothèque de la Pléiade), p. 5.

who dwell therein, but sets a mood and furnishes an architectural skeleton which the novel will clothe. The tangible world in Balzac's most successful works is seldom, if ever, extraneous. It is rather an illustration of, a mould for, a comment on personalities and relationships. In other words, Balzac's reality is by no means photographic, by no means independent. Detailed as it may be, it is the servant of the greater whole that is the novel. Maupassant, an admirer of the work of his illustrious predecessor is most astute in his perception of the true nature of Balzac's world. Already in 1876, that is to say, four years before he himself published anything of significance, and at a period at which he is under the direct influence of Flaubert, he senses Balzac's basic unreality. While his portrait of Balzac is based on the letters rather than the novels, Maupassant had a clear understanding of the true rôle of all the descriptive detail:

Chez lui tout est cerveau et coeur. Tout passe en dedans: les choses du dehors l'intéressent peu, et il n'a que des tendances vagues vers la beauté plastique, la forme pure, la signification des choses, cette vie dont les poètes animent la matière; ...[13]

Maupassant's interest in Balzac lies principally then in what he sees as an almost magical ability. It is a case of a basically non-realistic approach in art, which, because of the great skill of the creator, takes on a vitality unequalled in life. It transcends the bounds of the imagination to enter a world more closely identified with the real. That Maupassant criticizes Balzac because of his disregard for the material world, or to use his terminology, for the lack of poetry in his writing, is eloquent testimony of the extent to which Flaubert's training has already gone. But for Maupassant, Balzac is nevertheless a great artist, a creator, a man endowed with a special talent. The images he uses, the word paintings he constructs take on a depth of meaning which surpasses the limits of the tangible. His work moves into reality, it does not spring from it. Fictional reality has a very special sense in the Balzacian view of life, and although Maupassant would appear to have little sympathy for it here, his interest in it should be noted.

But Balzac is not of course the only novelist concerning whom Maupassant makes this kind of observation. I have already mentioned the special relationship between himself and Gustave Flaubert. The biographical facts are well known and need no further comment. But just how did Maupassant view the work of Flaubert with regard to his use of the real

[13] Maupassant, "Balzac d'après ses lettres", *Chroniques, études, correspondance de Guy de Maupassant*, ed. by René Dumesnil. This article was first published in *La Nation* (November 22, 1876).

world, and indeed what distinction did the young man make between the rôle of the perceptible in the works of Balzac and Flaubert.

Flaubert, the painstaking artisan of prose style and narrative fiction is equally particular about accuracy of detail. The physical world plays no small part in the art of Flaubert. As might be expected, his view is far more accurately documented than was that of Balzac, and in this sense, the author of *Madame Bovary* is without question a realist. But writing naturally involves choice of detail, choice of material, choice of situation. And nowhere is that choice more scrupulously controlled than in Flaubert. He too seeks to harmonize the interior world of his fiction with the exterior world, but significantly enough, in a calculated, rational manner. His constant choice is the small, but significant detail; Charles Bovary's famous cap, the description of the ball at "la Vaubyessard", Salammbô's snake, or the Seine valley in the opening chapter of *L'éducation sentimentale*.

Flaubert's ideal artistic product would have, among numerous attributes, total objectivity. The external world becomes then in his fiction not only an architectural framework on which the book can be erected, but an integral part of the narrative itself. The physical setting moves into a more active rôle, commenting on character and situation, reflecting, observing and recording. Characters become identified by material objects such as Félicité's parrot, and whole lives are commented on by setting, such as we find in *L'éducation sentimentale* with its views of Paris and surroundings. This is at least the traditional view of Flaubert, a view which, in spite of newer and equally valid interpretations of his work by such critics as Richard or Brombert, cannot be totally rejected.

In a preface to an edition of *Bouvard et Pécuchet* published in 1885 Maupassant tells us something of his conception of art in the light of Flaubertian principles. After mentioning the doctrine of "impersonnalité" which his master cultivated, he goes on to tell us something of his idea of the writer and his aims:

L'écrivain regarde, tâche de pénétrer les âmes et les coeurs, de comprendre leurs dessous leurs penchants honteux ou magnanimes, toute la mécanique compliquée des mobiles humains. Il observe ainsi suivant son tempérament d'homme et sa conscience d'artiste.[14]

Considering only this problem of the function of reality in fiction, we see here another element in Maupassant's concept. The Flaubertian struggle

[14] Maupassant, "Étude sur Gustave Flaubert", *Oeuvres complètes, Oeuvres postumes* II, p. 97. First published in *La Revue Bleue* (January 19 and 26, 1884).

to grasp what underlies the perceptible in human motivation intensely interests the younger author. The small but meaningful detail drawn from close observation of the surrounding world, such as the decoration of the china at the inn as Emma at age thirteen travels to the convent, acquires through art a depth of value which cannot be overestimated. Flaubert may hold a mirror up to nature, but it is a mirror "qui ... reproduisait les faits, en leur donnant ce reflet inexprimable, ce je ne sais quoi de presque divin qui est l'art".[15] Herein lie the roots of his restrictions concerning Balzac.

The third major figure with whom the name of Maupassant is often connected is of course Emile Zola. Again much confusion has tended to cloud the relationship between the two men. In the few years immediately prior to 1880, that is to say preceding Maupassant's meteoric rise to celebrity, the elder writer had become closely acquainted with, among others, Guy de Maupassant. The product of this relationship, the famous *Soirées de Médan*, has given rise to a general misconception of Maupassant.

Such an association tended to link his name too closely to Zola's naturalism, although Brunetière, no friend of the latter, admires the young author's work. In his study of naturalism entitled *Le roman naturaliste* (1888) he wisely associates Maupassant with the work of Flaubert rather than with Zola.

Maupassant's own explanation of the *Soirées de Médan* which appeared in defence of the work shortly after its publication is not only factually inaccurate concerning the collection's original inspiration, but obviously for the sake of propaganda adopts a literary argument which Maupassant never really espoused as his own. To see his career as an adoption of the cause of naturalism followed by a reversal and a return to more orthodox Flaubertianism is to distort literary perspective.

He states himself in this article, entitled "Les soirées de Médan", that none of the authors involved had the intention of forming a school. Their stories are reactions against romantic patriotism. A curious comment, obviously intended for Flaubert, is contained in the piece:

Quand un monsieur, qualifié de réaliste, a le souci d'écrire le mieux possible, est sans cesse poursuivi par des préoccupations d'art, c'est à mon sens un idéaliste.[16]

---

[15] Maupassant, "Étude sur Gustave Flaubert", p. 96.
[16] Maupassant, "Les soirées de Médan", *Oeuvres complètes, Boule de Suif*, p. 84. First published in *Le Gaulois* (April 17, 1880).

Does this of necessity indicate a preference for the Zola type of realism, or indeed a predilection for realism at all? He unquestionably attacks those who tend to embellish nature,[17] and designates this type of author as a charlatan or an imbecile.

Zola's personal interpretation of the real differs greatly from that of either Balzac or Flaubert. In the experimental novel the author's position is quite distinctly that of the dispassionate observer of phenomena. Reality then takes precedence over art and will determine the latter's quality, which will be in direct proportion to the accuracy of the reproduction. Such is the theory that Zola expounds, in spite of the concessive "à travers un tempérament".

Maupassant has no delusions as to Zola's ability to live up to his own theories. He has great admiration for such novels as *L'assommoir*, but little regard for the author's theories. As early as 1883 he states:

... fils des romantiques, romantique lui-même dans tous ses procédés, il porte en lui une tendance au poème, un besoin de grandir, de grossir, de faire des symboles avec les lettres et les choses. Il sent fort bien d'ailleurs cette pente de son esprit; il la combat sans cesse pour y céder toujours. Ses enseignements et ses oeuvres sont éternellement en désaccord.[18]

What is so very curious and indicative for Maupassant is his observation that the founder of naturalism has a tendency to "faire des symboles avec

[17] Maupassant sees a long line of sentimental novelists whose falseness he attacks. Among them he singles out Octave Feuillet (see especially "Les soirées de Médan" and "Réponse à Monsieur Francisque Sarcey", *Oeuvres complètes*, *Mademoiselle Fifi*, p. 277; first published in *Le Gaulois* (July 28, 1882).

George Sand does not escape criticism in the same light. In a "chronique" published in *Le Gaulois* on July 9, 1882, Maupassant observes: "Le romancier se trouve donc placé dans cette alternative: faire le monde tel qu'il le voit, lever les voiles de grâce et d'honnêteté, constater ce qui est sous ce qui paraît, montrer l'humanité toujours semblable sous ses élégances d'emprunt ou bien se résoudre à créer un monde gracieux et conventionnel comme l'ont fait George Sand, Jules Sandeau, et M. Octave Feuillet" (Maupassant, "Chronique", *Oeuvres complètes* XV [Paris: Librairie de France, 1934–38], p. 70).

Pierre Loti too is included in this group. Speaking of *Pêcheur d'Islande* in a "chronique" which appeared in *Le Gil Blas* of July 6, 1886, he remarks: "Il [Pierre Loti] nous dit aujourd'hui les amours des marins, et la détermination d'idéaliser jusqu'à l'invraisemblable apparaît de plus en plus. Nous voici en plein dans les tendresses à la Berquin, dans la sentimentalité paysannesque, dans la passion lyrico-villageoise de Mme Sand." "Cela est charmant toutefois et touchant; mais cela nous charme et nous touche par des effets littéraires trop apparents, trop visiblement faux, par l'attendrissement dure et poignante qui nous bouleverse le coeur au lieu de l'émouvoir facticement comme le fait M. Loti" (Maupassant, "L'amour dans les livres et dans la vie", *Maupassant journaliste et chroniquer*, ed. by G. Delaisement (Paris: Albin Michel, 1956], p. 185; first published in *Le Gil Blas*, July 6, 1886).

[18] Maupassant, "Étude sur Emile Zola", *Oeuvres complètes*, *Oeuvres postumes* II, p. 157. First published by Quantin in *Les célébrités contemporaines* (1883).

les lettres et les choses". One thinks immediately of such things as Félicité Rougon's yellow salon, or of Lison, the faithful locomotive of *La bête humaine*. Inanimate objects, observed in exterior reality again take on more than their surface meaning and conjure up a whole state of mind. The tangible world again is placed in communication with the world of ideas, the abstract, the general. The remarkable fact is that Maupassant attributes to the logical, factual Zola a greater poetic feeling than he does to the imaginative Balzac.

Basically, what we have seen him attracted to here is the actual relationship, in the works of Balzac, Flaubert and Zola, between the physical world in which their novels exist, and the deeper, intangible world of feeling, the idea, the inexpressible. Each of them has evolved a means well suited to his own temperament. Maupassant also seeks some personal means of identification between the two, some bond that will clearly state that they are closely interrelated, and that therefore they are really only different aspects of one universe. It is a search for unity.

In Balzac he finds a basic lack of concern for "realism" which makes use of it only to clarify those pre-ordained problems of life which do interest him – problems of the mind and heart. In Flaubert he sees the potentialities of an aesthetic approach to reality to be able to convey great depths of meaning. In Zola he admires the great evocative sweep of his descriptions. Balzac's functional description, Flaubert's significant detail, Zola's epic and symbolic exaggerations are all, in Maupassant's view, links between this physical world of sense perception and a deeper, more meaningful literary experience.

The problem we are about to examine then is by no means unique to Maupassant, and might at first glance appear obvious and naive. The relationship between fiction and life as manifested in descriptive material is a problem common to most literature.

However this dialogue between two worlds gives rise to deeper concerns than one might expect, concerns which I shall not investigate further at this particular point in the discussion. Since my general intention is to proceed, in dealing with Maupassant, from the particular to the general, I feel it will be of greater value to deal with these more abstract problems as a result of, and not as an introduction to, more precise textual analysis. We must begin this investigation with a consideration of the presence of the physical world in Maupassant's fiction. Observation of just what material he uses should lead us directly towards the deeper questions of how and why such material is meaningful.

II

THE SHORT STORIES

The short stories of Guy de Maupassant present to the critic certain rather complex problems. The two hundred and seventy odd tales which are known to be his, present such a variety of subject matter and technique that it is extremely difficult to pin him down. Some readers, judging from such well known pieces as "La parure" or "La ficelle" see him as the master of the trick ending, while others will consider "Le Horla" or "L'endormeuse" as sufficient evidence to call him an explorer of hallucination. As Sullivan so aptly points out,[1] no such sweeping generality can even hope to approximate the truth.

Added to this variety of treatment and of subject matter is of course the thorny problem of chronology. For the vast majority of stories the only means of dating which we have is based on the time of publication, which sheds little or no light on the more significant factor – date of composition. For these reasons it is virtually impossible to single out significant stories in a study of this nature. In seeking textual evidence which will offer clues as to Maupassant's view of his world we must by necessity approach the short stories as a kind of organic unit and take note of trends not with a view to chronology but rather with the intention of discovering patterns in his descriptive material.

The problem of the physical world is given a great deal of attention by Maupassant, as one might logically expect from an artist of his period and formation. By assigning to it a special function with regard to fictional problems of character and situation, he too will seek to bridge the gap. If our observations of his opinions are borne out in his own works, then reality must be developed according to some kind of discernible pattern.

On the simplest level this reality is obviously the décor in which the narrative is placed. This external world deals with a relatively small

---

[1] E. D. Sullivan, *Maupassant: The Short Stories* (= *Barron's Studies in French Literature*) (New York: Barron's Educational Series, 1962), pp. 7–8.

number of geographical locations, variations on which can be traced through his work from beginning to end. What follows here is a kind of catalogue of Maupassant's world as he presents it to us in fictional terms. Through it we may gain some insight into the relationship between these descriptive passages and the narratives they illustrate.

A child of Normandy, of that rich green countryside astride France's most important river and wedded to the sea, Maupassant exploits the area to great advantage. Landscapes, rural and maritime settings, are perhaps the richest and most varied descriptive elements in his work. Using as a basis for analysis the Conard edition of Maupassant, let us first consider the frequency with which the rural landscape appears.

It is perfectly justifiable to expect that Normandy will dominate Maupassant's interest in non-Parisian France. Out of the stories reviewed, I have found that somewhere over half the total, or about one hundred and fifty, contain some reference, direct or otherwise to this geographical area[2] -- the Norman countryside, the Seine Valley, or the principal urban centres of this region that the author knew so well, Rouen, Le Havre, Etretat or Fécamp.[3] Those essentially rural tales dealing directly with Norman peasants in their native habitat number some fifty, with considerable variety with regard to the attention devoted to the physical surroundings. One might consider as extreme cases such stories as "Le Père Judas" (1883),[4] with a panoramic view of the Seine Valley at Rouen strongly reminiscent of Georges Duval's honeymoon excursion with Madeleine to his native Cantal in Bel-Ami, and "Une vente" (1884), one of a number of courtroom tales in which references to the natural setting are completely absent. In the one case, physical exterior reality occupies at least as much of the reader's attention as the narrative itself, and in the other it is dispensed with totally. Within this range there lies a whole group of stories of various types and lengths in which the rural scene plays some rôle, major or minor. In the village scenes of "La maison Tellier" the setting is closely interwoven with the narrative, and we catch glimpses of the fields, their colours and their smells during the journey of the motley group of women, of certain aspects of the village, such as its church and street. But nowhere does the author focus our attention for any extended

---

[2] See Appendix II for a breakdown of the stories according to setting.

[3] For a complete breakdown of the short stories according to theme consult René Dumesnil, Chroniques, études, correspondance, pp. 459–503.

[4] Rather than referring to the location of individual short stories mentioned, I have included as Appendix I of the present study the table of contents of each volume of short stories in the Conard edition. Only direct quotations or those stories with identical titles will therefore need any further elucidation.

duration on this element. The characters in such stories as "Le Père Amable" (1886), "Le diable" (1886) or "Le petit fût" (1884), are closely bound up with their fields and crops, yet again Maupassant does not indulge in extensive passages of description of external nature. The farm in these three is always there, but any description of the natural setting is brought into the narrative only as an adjunct of development of plot and character. Indeed, in *Le diable*, while the harvesting of the crops is a vital and essential element in the establishment of the dramatic situation, the entire story takes place indoors with only brief reference to the sunlight and the breeze through the open window of the bedroom.

Exterior description has still another variation in these essentially rural stories. Vial points out an interesting fact concerning Maupassant's method of presentation – that in about half his stories he uses as a point of departure, or as an introduction, an incident which is only remotely connected with the main body of the tale, such as an after-dinner conversation, a train journey, or a courtroom situation, to mention only three general types. Description is often involved in this indirect introduction.[5] Sullivan quite justifiably remarks that such a "cadre" technique is as old as story-telling itself[6] and that Maupassant exploits it simply because it is well suited to his general approach to creative writing. But with regard to descriptive passages it is not without significance. In a number of rural tales this element is entirely contained within this framework, and is thus set apart from the development of plot and character. The fairy tale effect the "cadre" produces is most effective for example in "La légende du Mont-Saint-Michel" (1882), in which the description of the setting encases the narrative, thereby providing both the backdrop and the link between a timeless mythological tale and the real contemporary world of Maupassant the observer and the writer. This "cadre" description appears as well in such works as "Le fermier" (1886), in which it links people of distinct social classes, or in "Le retour" (1884), where we find an opening seascape which evokes the past life and the hardships of the principal participants in the action. By setting the description apart from the main action, Maupassant not only stresses the value of it within the story, but deepens its meaning and intensifies its relationship to the work as a whole.

These peasant or rural tales offer still another type, when one examines them from the point of view of external setting. Along with the courtroom dramas of the sort mentioned, and including such others as "Le cas de

---

[5] Vial, *Guy de Maupassant*, pp. 460–69.
[6] Sullivan, *The Short Stories*, pp. 12–19.

Madame Luneau" (1883) and "Tribunaux rustiques" (1884), we have
those that, while remaining essentially peasant in flavour, take place in an
environment which is not specifically rural. The outstanding example of
this is of course "La ficelle" (1883). Although the Goderville market is
quite logically agricultural and rural in nature, it must be regarded as
an urban concept. Its description in the story makes no mention of
nature, and Maître Hauchecorne is seen against a social backdrop, not a
specifically rural one in the descriptive sense. It is indeed his society which
establishes the lifelong conflict the tale presents, and external nature has a
minimal function to play here. Much the same can obviously be said
about others, such as "La bête à Maîtr' Belhomme" (1885), which is set
almost entirely in a coach, or "Les 25 francs de la supérieure" (1888) and
its urban, hospital milieu.

There are of course a significant number of Norman stories which do
not involve characters of peasant stock. The Norman château is also a
favorite setting for Maupassant's stories, again an atmosphere commonly
found in the short story from its earliest manifestations in European
literature. I have found over forty stories of the two hundred and seventy
which make at least some mention of this part of the author's experience.
But again, when dealing with descriptions of the exterior world, and more
specifically with nature descriptions this group contains a broad spectrum
of different types.

Many of these stories, which for the most part are predictably upper
class provincial in social background, deal with the theme of hunting,
and understandably lead the reader directly into communication with
nature. One need only consider for example the volume of stories entitled
Les contes de la bécasse[7] to realize that this background attracts Maupassant with some frequency. The opening "story" is curious since it provides,
much in the tradition of Boccaccio or Marguerite de Navarre, a kind of
framework or introduction for the collection, and is intended to have the
function for a number of stories that has been mentioned with regard to
individual ones. Again description of external nature is directly involved.
Just as we have seen with peasant tales, the "cadre" technique, so prominent throughout Maupassant's all too brief career, can be placed in a
position of prominence with regard to its presentation of nature. A short
story such as "Le fermier" (1886) for example must attract our attention
since the description of nature in the work is contained entirely in this

---

[7] Indeed Albert-Marie Schmidt uses this little piece as the initial entry into his most
useful and accurate edition of the short stories. See bibliography.

framework. The narrator, part of a hunting party, entertains the group after dinner. What is told is the tragic story of a Norman farmer's love, a farmer whom those present had recently encountered in the course of their day's activity. The immediately real, that is to say the countryside and the peasant's house, is visually presented to us as a direct experience of the narrator, while the actual events of the central story we hear second-hand, as told to the narrator by his host. Similar complex relationships between the perceptible world of nature and the fictional world of character and plot may be seen in numbers of other hunting tales, told on rainy days when the party is confined indoors, or during the course of an evening's conversation after dinner, or simply as part of a week-end visit to a friend in the country. Of such a construction are "Un réveillon" (1882), "Une veuve" (1882) or "Le père".[8] Although in each of the stories mentioned nature performs some function, it will be found that the only significant presentation of the countryside, the weather, the sky, that is to say of nature, will be found in the introductive element of the narration.

But nature descriptions in these non-peasant rural stories is by no means confined exclusively to introductions and conclusions. "Le loup" (1882), a hunting tale, has a good deal of description integrated with the narrative itself, while the framework introduction and conclusion offer us nothing but a brief outline of the basic situation which inspires the story. Similarly a work like "La rempailleuse" (1882) springs from an identical and only briefly mentioned "real" situation, and indeed contains no noteworthy description of nature either in the framework or in the central narrative.

Not all these essentially rural tales which deal with other than peasant types involve hunting, of course. Stories such as "Joseph" (1885) or "La fenêtre" (1883) are located in country homes, but in neither case is the external setting dealt with significantly. In both the action takes place exclusively indoors, and the outdoor world would have little or no contribution to make. Nor are all these Norman stories developed around the country home or hunting lodge. Tourism also appears with reference to Maupassant's native province, particularly in association with the sea-coast of his childhood at Etretat. The people seen on the beach here often become the subjects of the author's attention. Here again we will find some stories in which the descriptive talent is employed entirely in the framework of the piece, such as in "Imprudence" (1885), in which the beloved is seen in the opening paragraph against a background of sun and

---

[8] Maupassant, "Le père", *Clair de lune, Oeuvres complètes*, p. 181. First published in *Le Gil Blas* (July 26, 1887).

sea, and in which the external plays no further rôle in the deepening of their relationship once they return to Paris. In "Bombard" (1884) we discover in the opening paragraphs, a similar emphasis on the setting which is not maintained throughout the story. Still more striking is the case of "Le modèle" (1883) which launches directly into an exhaustive description of the seacoast at Etretat. This serves again as a framework into which the action is fitted.

On the other hand, a masterpiece such as "Miss Harriet" (1883), as much a rejection of "objectivity" as any work of Maupassant, depends for most of its impact on the significance of the setting. Both in the framework introduction and throughout the ensuing narrative, landscape and seascape are vitally important. The link is direct and immediate. The natural setting joins the "present" of the introductory cadre with the past of the central story by means of a visual image, a panoramic view of the coast and is complicated by the narrator's painting to which Miss Harriet reacts so strikingly.

Tourism inevitably leads us beyond the borders of Normandy to that most celebrated of seaside resort areas, the Riviera. Many of Maupassant's tales deal directly with Mediterranean settings. A fairly important number involve descriptions of this part of France, and considered as a group, they are most enlightening. It would seem that, when speaking of this region he cannot resist including some reference to the attractions of nature. Travelling through it by train, as we do in "Les soeurs Rondoli" (1884), "Idylle" (1884) or "En voyage"[9] we are treated to the smells of fruits and flowers, to glimpses of the mountains and the sea for which the coast is renowned. Even when Maupassant wishes to deal with what amounts to an essentially interior theme, in which setting is not specifically linked to situation or character, as in "Madame Parisse" (1886), we are regaled with a lengthy presentation of a Mediterranean sunset. Or again in "Julie Romain" (1886) the story opens with the coast, the sea, the physical setting of her house, when in fact the main focus of our attention will be Julie, the retired celebrity of the Paris stage – again what I would consider to be in the main an internal or interior presentation. Even in such a brief little story as "Rose" (1884) we are offered a sunset as an external framework for a tale of deception in which natural setting must be regarded as non-essential to the intrigue, save for a vague suggestion of mood.

One of Maupassant's most effective panoramas is found in "Le bon-

---

[9] Maupassant, "En voyage", *Miss Harriet, Oeuvres complètes*, p. 285. First published in *Le Gil Blas* (May 10, 1882).

heur" (1884), a story directly concerned with Corsica, which is inspired in the cadre by its appearance on the Mediterranean horizon. And the author again cannot resist returning to this immediate setting once he has completed the tale itself. The attraction for the Midi remains with Maupassant until late in his active career, where it appears vividly in "Le champ d'oliviers" (1890), one of his extremely successful short stories.

Maupassant visited many other areas besides the Côte d'Azur. "Mes 25 jours" (1885), "Le tic" (1884), "En wagon" (1885) and others provide us with descriptions of Auvergne as well. And again the beauties of the countryside with its hills, trees and enormous vistas occupy his attention with some frequency. Corsica also provides a backdrop for a number of pieces – "Une vendetta" (1883), "Un bandit corse" (1882), "La main" (1883), "Un échec" (1885), to mention only four. Algeria too is useful to him. One need only mention "Mohammed-Fripouille" (1884), "Allouma" (1889), "Maroca" (1882), or "Un soir" (1889) to see again that the physical surroundings are dealt with quite extensively.

In all these settings however, we see similar trends to those already considered in our examination of the Norman stories. In some the description is integrated with the narrative and the whole story appears as a web of interdependent threads. Of such a type are "Mes 25 jours", constructed as it is after the fashion of a diary, "Allouma", again told in the first person, and "Une vendetta", in which the setting is central to the action itself. In others the atmosphere, the setting, while mentioned, plays a very secondary rôle. Certainly "La main", and to some extent "Un échec" illustrate this type. While a third group, including "L'ermite" (1886), "Rose", and "Madame Parisse", all Riviera stories, and certainly "Un soir", an Algerian one, contain descriptions only in the cadre, albeit in the case of the last mentioned this framework occupies more of our attention than the story it introduces.

We find isolated examples of still other natural settings such as Switzerland in "L'auberge" (1886) or India in "Châli" (1884), but since these two are somewhat atypical of the author, with regard to their settings at least, they are of little value in any attempt to discern an overall pattern. They are the only two whose milieu is so far removed from the norm that it is impossible to relate them to the whole. Yet both of them depend heavily on descriptive material.

Normandy, Provence, Auvergne, Corsica, Algeria all essentially non-urban, if not in the strictest of senses rural backdrops for a very large number of Maupassant's stories, all showing similar variations in the use to which exterior description is put, and all revealing a similar concern with the sea, the sky, panoramic vistas. In the vast majority of cases the descriptive element somehow links the fictional world the author is creating to that of his own direct experience. Maupassant too is bridging a gap. This is supremely evident in the framework stories in which, by means of description, or less frequently an unexpected event, there is a sudden shift and immediate jumping of the time sequence. The framework represents the present, the story itself usually the past. But what about those stories which are basically urban in nature?

I have briefly mentioned certain works which are concerned both with the Norman seacoast and with Paris. The urban stories, mostly of course Parisian, must be regarded separately from these others. Quite logically, nature will be viewed differently in urban settings if indeed it is involved at all. In looking at the non-urban group, I have tried to distinguish between what I have called "exterior" and "interior" stories, that is to say, those which take place at least in part outdoors, and in which physical description may be given full rein if needed, and those interior stories in which outdoor references, if included, must necessarily be of a much more limited, and perhaps more detailed nature.

In terms of background, these remaining stories divide themselves conveniently into two general groups, those concerned with essentially urban centres distinct from Paris, and those involving Paris and its environs. Particularly with reference to the former and much smaller group, there will of necessity be some overlapping with other stories, since the action of several includes both country and city settings. Of such a type is of course "La maison Tellier", one of Maupassant's most celebrated pieces. But my concern is with that aspect of the story which is urban in setting, and consequently only part of that well known work is useful to us here.

Very early in his career we find Maupassant creating situations set within the confines of a town. "Le papa de Simon" (1881) for example is located in some unnamed community of very limited size, in which the child's problem is brought to the fore because of close association in school with others of his age. It would appear here that his descriptive powers are again devoted essentially to what lies beyond the confines of the village, and the story, like "La maison Tellier" represents something of a fusion of environments. The same cannot be said for "Un coup d'État" (n.d.) or "Berthe" (1884), taking place as they do, entirely in towns. In the case of the former, the author clearly defines his setting, and the town square becomes a kind of stage set in front of which the conflict of political interests is allowed to run its full comic course. With the latter we encounter again the "cadre" technique, by means of which the narrator can paint for us the depressing, grey, forbidding appearance of the streets and buildings of Riom. Reality thus acquires that same immediacy for us the readers, and provides a more profound impact for the doctor's story, especially with regard to mood. Both "Hautot père et fils" (1889) and "Divorce" (1888) provide fine illustrations of Maupassant's knowledge of Rouen, and particularly in the case of the second work, the street references tie the action very closely to its setting as the new wife proceeds towards the railway station followed by the suspicious husband. In "La maison Tellier" as well, we first catch sight of the notorious establishment from the street as certain regular customers discover the notice on the door.

Maupassant can then, if he so desires, make use of the outdoors in the urban tale if and when the need arises. But what is striking about them as a group is the fact that in relatively few do the streets and buildings occupy his attention at much length. In the majority the main action takes place by and large indoors, or if outside, with little regard for the surroundings. If they are mentioned they are rarely described. We have already seen how an essentially urban story can be contained in a highly descriptive non-urban framework, such as is the case with "Madame Parisse" for example, or "Un soir". If we are given a view of the town's appearance, it too can be contained in the introductory episode, as in "Le rosier de Madame Husson" (1887). Here again we find, as with "Un soir", that this presentation almost takes precedence over the story itself, and we are furnished with not only some description of Gisors, but a discussion of the character of its inhabitants and a résumé of its glorious history. The Limoges we see in "L'ami Patience" (1883) is restricted to a mention of a café, and the disreputable Patience's place of residence, the interior of which interests the narrator much more than does the city itself. La Rochelle displays only its arcaded streets in "Ce cochon de Morin" (1882) and we see virtually nothing of either Le Havre or Lille in "Une passion" (1882).

What we are witnessing then is an interiorization of Maupassant's descriptive interests in the urban atmosphere. Numbers of them take place almost exclusively indoors – "La chambre 11" (1884) in a hotel, "Le lit 29" (1884) in a Rouen hospital, "Le pain maudit" (1883) in a Le Havre apartment, "Madame Hermet" (1887) in an asylum and a home. Whether the name of the town is given or not, the author is not concerned here with the outdoor world to any appreciable degree.

Paris and its environs furnish us with a much larger number of urban stories, and consequently with greater variety in the treatment of external description. Particularly if one includes in this group those stories dealing with boating excursions on the Seine, an important part of Maupassant's life in his early years in the capital, one will find some striking contrasts in the treatment of the external setting, natural or other.

Although these river stories may be found almost throughout the author's years of feverish literary activity, that is to say from 1881 with "La femme de Paul" to 1889 with "L'endormeuse" they naturally appear with greatest frequency in the earlier period. What we can observe in this context is the fact that, somewhat in the fashion of his treatment of the Mediterranean coast, he cannot resist describing this most fascinating of settings. Woven into the fabric of "Yvette" (1884), for example, the trees, the water, boating activity, and that most renowned of riverside establishments "La grenouillère" draw our attention at a number of points. Similar interests are discernible in "La femme de Paul", "Une partie de campagne" (1881) and even in "Le trou" (1886). And in all these cases the central participants in the action are Parisians on holiday. There can be no doubt in our mind that, drawing heavily on his own experience, Maupassant frequently identifies this aspect of the Seine with Paris life. The rural is again closely linked with the urban, the fictional past with the real past or present. For as with other stories, here too the descriptive passages may be relegated to the introductory or concluding framework of the work, as we can see in "L'endormeuse" (1889).

These stories cannot be considered however as typical of Maupassant's scenes of Parisian life, since they do not strictly speaking deal with the city. C. Luplau-Janssen, in his study entitled *Le décor chez Guy de Maupassant* shows that the geographical references to Paris contained in his short stories and novels are restricted almost exclusively to areas of the city with which the author was intimately acquainted.[10] This can hardly be surprising if we consider the other backgrounds that he includes. Only very rarely, and I am thinking particularly of "Châli", does he deal with a setting which he himself has not experienced directly, and even there, there is a "real" cadre. Normandy, Provence, Algeria, why not the eighth and ninth *arrondissements*?

The Parisian background includes something in excess of one hundred stories, one of the largest groups in size, and comprising tales of great variety in length and development. As with other groups, I must restrict myself here too to what I deem representative examples. More exhaustive analysis would require a volume in itself.

10   Maupassant, "L'enfant", *Clair de lune, Oeuvres complètes*, p. 45. First published in *Le Gaulois* (July 24, 1882).

The Parisian atmosphere is very much in evidence in a story like "A cheval" (1888), for example, in which the main action takes place during a "promenade" on the Champs-Élysées and in the Bois du Vézinet. The procession of elegant carriages, horses and people, a subject which Maupassant will return to with surprising frequency in other stories, not to mention his novels, constitutes the environment into which the ridiculous pretension and resultant downfall of Hector de Gribelin are placed. Setting forms an integral part of the development of the plot, beginning with a reference to the drabness of the Faubourg Saint-Germain and working up to the critical scene on Paris' most fashionable avenue.

The brief little incident described so touchingly in "Menuet" (1882) is also very intimately connected with exterior surroundings, this time the "pépinière" of the Jardin du Luxembourg, inspiration as it is for the pathetic little scene of re-creation of a long dead era.

In "L'héritage" (1884), a very interesting novelette of 1884, Maupassant presents to us a panorama of the city from the balcony of the Cachelin's apartment. On more than one occasion Lesable, the potentially rich son-in-law steps out on this balcony to view Paris from above and we are presented with a reasonably detailed rendition of what lies below and beyond. And even as late as "L'inutile beauté" (1890) we catch some sight of street activity from the victoria of the count and countess de Mascaret as they proceed up the Champs-Élysées. As a matter of fact the boulevards, and particularly the Champs-Élysées, reappear with surprising frequency in his short stories. In "L'inconnue" (1885), "Tombouctou" (1883), "Promenade" (1884), and indeed even in "Le Horla" (1886) we find references to this uniquely Parisian atmosphere of crowds and activity, great vistas and fashionable elegance.

The streets of Paris are also, naturally enough, an evocative backdrop for those stories which deal specifically with loneliness and prostitutes, one of the few groups for whom Maupassant seems to have genuine sympathy. In "La nuit" (1887), "Lui?" (1883), "L'armoire" (1884), "L'Odyssée d'une fille" (1883) he uses the identical backdrop of dark damp streets in which to locate his incident. But here again the description is presented as a kind of exterior frame in which to locate a brief narrative in which little or no reference to the exterior world is required. Paris too can provide a descriptive link between the author's immediate and fictional worlds. Even with no description it can sometimes be a cadre for an action, as we find for example in "Une famille". The reference to the city here amounts to little more than a passing mention, and the narrative itself does not take place in the city at all. But like the river stories, it requires the reader to know that the characters are Parisian in order to comprehend fully the significance of their behaviour.

But what is striking about these stories as a group is the relative infrequency with which Maupassant refers to the external aspects of the city. While our investigation shows that about one hundred stories make direct reference to Paris, about two-thirds of these offer only the briefest mention of the exterior world of urban life, if indeed they mention it at all. The importance of the outdoors is very much reduced with them although as we have seen, not entirely lost. If Maupassant seeks a "link", then surely a simple examination of outdoor description will not provide us with all the answers to this important relationship.

But obviously descriptive passages in Maupassant's short stories are not limited to the exterior world, whether the natural settings of land and sea or the cityscapes of late nineteenth century France. If the external world of Maupassant is dual, the natural and the man-made, so too is the internal – the interior *décor* and man himself. From a descriptive point of view both the appearance of his characters and their habitat will occupy his attention in no small way. Both these subjects focus our eye on the small detail; they are restricted and restrictive in scope, not expansive as was the external world. They are inward rather than outward probings, and in that sense, internal in nature.

From relatively early publication dates we know that he does not limit his interests nor his descriptive powers to the outdoors. "Mademoiselle Fifi" proves that from the beginning of his career (it appeared in 1882 in his first published volume of short stories), he could with success confine an entire tale to an interior décor. Apart from the references to the frightful weather which confines the Prussian officers indoors, a significant detail in itself, and to the bell-tower which provides refuge for the murderess, our attention is focussed exclusively on the opulent interior of the captured *château*. The barbarian invaders while away the hours smashing the furniture and crystal, defacing the table-tops and shooting the eyes out of the portraits on the wall. The orgiastic dinner party takes place in this setting and the murder itself is facilitated by the objects on the table. There is no lack of description of this interior, and indeed, integrated as it is with characterization and intrigue it contributes much to the success of the story.

Nor is this the only piece in which the interior of a building performs an important function. The storage of the body in the bread-box, and the interior of the peasant's home are vital aspects of "Un réveillon" (one of the stories of "Mademoiselle Fifi"), and the layout of the home is one of the central facts necessary to understand "Le diable" (1886) or to appreciate the poor lover's frustration in "Le mal d'André" (1883). In "Mademoiselle Perle" (1886) the whole narrative takes place within the house, as we move with the hero from the dining-room to the billiard room and back. This house is a kind of island in the heart of Paris, with only minimal communication with the outside world. The wardrobe in the bedroom is the single most significant fact in "L'enfant", as is the window in the story to which this object provides a title. And certainly most of the action of such lengthy stories as "L'héritage" (1884) or "Monsieur Parent" (1886) is intensified and concentrated because it is confined to such a limited indoor stage. The mistress' Rouen apartment in "Hautot père et fils" (1889) Yvette's bedroom, the layout of the pension in "La patronne" (1884), the bedrom in "Le Horla" (1886), the dining-room in "Le champ d'oliviers" (1890), all vividly demonstrate that in-door surroundings are equally as important as outdoor in Maupassant and are as carefully combined with other elements to serve the greater purpose of the story as a whole. Indeed the interior and exterior can often be linked by means of an architectural feature, a window or a door. "La confession"[11] or "Le signe" (1886) show how important this factor can be, while such interior stories as "Le diable" (1886) find their only real link with the outside world in this same object.

But what about the description of these interiors? We have already seen in "Mademoiselle Fifi" (1882) that Maupassant can give his reader fairly detailed presentations. After introducing his characters he moves to the details of the room – the portraits, mirrors and tapestries on the wall apparently being what interests him most.

We become acquainted with the interior of the celebrated "Maison Tellier" almost at the outset of the story, pausing particularly to view the elegance of the "salon de Jupiter". Again the wall décor, this time Leda and the swan, is especially brought to our attention. But on returning to the house in the closing pages we can discover no further development of this, and the final scene contains virtually no description of the setting. "L'héritage" opens with a description of the labyrinthine "ministère de la Marine" and draws the reader particularly to the office which will appear again without description during the course of the narrative. At the beginning of the second chapter we are briefly introduced to Cachelin's apartment, with its location and general layout of rooms. As for its con-tents, Maupassant spends little time showing them to us, and objects

[11] Maupassant, "La confession", Le rosier de Madame Husson, Oeuvres complètes, p. 153. First published in Le Gil Blas (August 12, 1884).

appear only when required by the action of the story for purposes of elucidation. "Monsieur Parent" is similar to this in that when Parent returns with his son to the apartment which will be the scene of the family crisis, our eye is not permitted to wander about the rooms for one moment.

In direct contrast to these relatively long stories is the brief little item entitled "Un portrait" (1888). As this title would indicate, description is really the essential element of the piece, and although we are clearly in a salon, the visual element of the story is concentrated almost entirely on the woman's portrait, whose mysterious quality hypnotized the viewer. "La chambre 11" (1884), as the title would suggest, deals with an interior, confining our view to a hotel room, scene of certain scandalous escapades on the part of a seemingly respectable woman. And again we are drawn to the wall decoration – a grey paper and three military photographs which mutely testify to past activities. "Nos lettres" (1888) is also devoted to an interior, a kind of museum of a country house visited by the narrator. In his bedroom, formerly Aunt Rose's room, hangs a pastel portrait of her. The period furnishings and this portrait occupy the narrator's interest at great length. Combined with the sight, we notice the evocative power of the smell of the room, the smell of memories permanently embedded in the décor. And smells are frequently associated with interiors in Maupassant's presentation – the musty smell of the past in the antique piece from which the hair is extracted in "La chevelure" (1884), or the peasant kitchen in "Odyssée d'une fille" (1883), to mention only two examples.

Certainly one of the clearest illustrations of the power of interior descriptions in Maupassant's short stories is provided by "Hautot père et fils". After the accidental death of his father, Hautot fils travels hesitantly to Rouen, carrying out his parent's deathbed instructions, to break the news to his father's mistress. As he enters the apartment, this is what we see:

Il n'osait plus parler, les yeux fixés sur la table dressée au milieu de l'appartement, et portant trois couverts, dont un d'enfant. Il regardait la chaise tournée dos au feu, l'assiette, la serviette, les verres, la bouteille de vin rouge entamée et la bouteille de vin blanc intacte. C'était la place de son père, dos au feu! On l'attendait. C'était son pain qu'il voyait, qu'il reconnaissait près de la fourchette, car la croûte était enlevée à cause des mauvaises dents d'Hautot. Puis, levant les yeux, il aperçut, sur le mur, son portrait, la grande photographie faite à Paris l'année de l'Exposition, la même qui était clouée au-dessus du lit dans la chambre à coucher d'Ainville.[12]

_____

[12] Maupassant, "Hautot père et fils", *La main gauche, Oeuvres complètes*, p. 63. First published in *L'Écho de Paris* (January 5, 1889).

It would seem from this, and indeed from a multitude of other passages that we have so far mentioned that Maupassant had learned much from Flaubert. One might say that, in their context, these objects have a whole story to tell. Selective detailed description and precise notation of fact preserve a seeming objectivity, a common enough device of Maupassant. Indeed we are witnessing this scene through the eyes of a fictional character, and thus the creator is doubly concealed. But in this fact lies an essential difference between the junior and the senior artists. By viewing the scene exclusively through the eyes of César Hautot, we the readers are much more immediately concerned with the people involved and their reactions to the situation, than with the objects. Unlike Charles Bovary's celebrated cap or Salammbô's anklet, these things speak only subjectively to the personnages directly involved, and not objectively to the outsider. The significant detail conveys meaning directly to the characters, and only indirectly to us. We must proceed through *them* to the object. The presence of the photograph underlines the basically introverted nature of the description. It is as if the father were physically present at this scene, viewing the confrontation of the two strangers whose lives are linked through him alone. The description is thus not objective at all in the true sense. To the reader it is in itself meaningless without the reactions of the fictitious characters who view it. It is as if these objects had no existence at all except that conferred on them by Hautot and family. This is the same relationship which exists between Miss Harriet, the landscape, and the painting, of which more will be said in a later chapter.

The "real" world thus tends to be relegated in significance, through artistic presentation, to a secondary position. For if objects rely totally on personalities instead of the contrary, then they need not be introduced at all to establish character. The *rôle* of the *décor* becomes something quite distinct from Flaubert's concept. Perhaps "Le Horla" will serve to clarify this point further. As the tension increases, the world of the narrator narrows down to his own bedroom. He lies in wait for this "being" to make its presence felt, and we see the following:

En face de moi, mon lit, un vieux lit de chêne à colonnes; à droite, ma cheminée; à gauche, ma porte, fermée avec soin, après l'avoir laissée longtemps ouverte, afin de l'attirer; derrière moi, une très haute armoire à glace, qui me servait chaque jour pour me raser, pour m'habiller, et où j'avais coutume de me regarder, de la tête aux pieds, chaque fois que je passais devant.[13]

---

[13] Maupassant, "Le Horla", *Le Horla*, *Oeuvres complètes*, pp. 42–43. First published in *Le Gil Blas* (October 26, 1886).

What could appear to be more objective? And again the author conceals himself behind his protagonist. But like the carafe, the milk, and the turning pages of the book, these things, particularly the mirror, will take on new meanings for him, which we the spectators can only indirectly share. Again the objects are turned inwards. We do not interpret them as we do Félicité's parrot in "Un coeur simple". The narrator does this himself.

Setting is frequently reduced in importance in Maupassant's short stories, yielding to a single object set apart from its physical context, and dominating the lives of the people concerned. And in many cases of this type the object itself is the title of the story. A list of these would include some of the author's best known works – "Les bijoux" (1883), "La parure" (1884), "Les épingles" (1888), "Le gâteau" (1882), "Le masque" (1889), "Le parapluie" (1884), and "La ficelle" (1883), to mention only some of the most popular. In every one, it is the object which is to mould the lives of the people and can even decide their fate. Poor Maître Hauchecorne's whole existence is destroyed by that cursed piece of string which he innocently salvaged; the Loisel couple struggle to pay for the lost necklace; Monsieur Lantin only discovers his dead wife's infidelity through the presence of the jewels; and Monsieur Oreille's insecurity is intensified by that seemingly innocent umbrella. Much more than simply described, these objects take on a kind of life of their own, and speak by their very presence or absence (as is the case in "La parure") to their victims. They have far greater vitality than the famous "zaïmph" of Salammbô. And again the same contrast with Flaubert's technique is self-evident. Félicité's approach to life leads her inevitably and inexorably towards her parrot, whereas Maître Hauchecorne and the Loisels are destroyed by the seemingly inert thing which increasingly controls their lives. Félicité bestows life on her parrot, whereas Maupassant s people are affected by things which take on a kind of independent vitality because of the unique relationship between them and their possessors. It is the fact that they are the possessors of a kind of life which indicates that Maupassant's position is veering away from a narrow and conventional determinism. The movement is not outward, drawing our attention to the object that instigates the conflict, but rather inward to the person affected by that object. They speak not of the person but to the person. Reality itself turns inward. Victims as these people inevitably are, they all struggle with their situation. If Maupassant finds himself in a corner, he is not going to abandon life without a fight.

It would follow that he could create stories while dispensing almost totally with setting. This is certainly visible on the literal level in his courtroom narratives such as "Tribunaux rustiques" (1884), "Le cas de Madame Luneau" (1883), "Rosalie Prudent" (1886) or "Un cas de divorce" (1886). In all of these we have a method of presentation basically the same as that of some of the landscape. The courtroom testimony or the lawyer's summing up represent a kind of cadre in which the story unfolds. But only in the first of the stories mentioned is there any attention at all paid to description of this "real" setting. The narrative develops in a kind of physical void, and thus heightens the fictitious nature of the situation with which the plot is concerned. The lack of description diminishes the immediate veracity of the subsequent testimony and again turns it inward onto itself rather than outward towards the reader. The comedy or the pathos depends on the individual's interpretation of his own world, not on ours.

And these are by no means the only examples of tales which are devoid of "real" descriptive material. Parisian stories such as "Sauvée" (1885) and "La confidence" (1885) take place in an undescribed salon, "Les caresses" (1883) and "Mots d amour" (1882) are nothing more than an unintroduced exchange of letters with no reference at all to a physical context. But very often the framework or cadre technique functions as we have already described with regard to the courtroom scenes. A brief reference to an after dinner conversation, a social evening or a doctor s visit, for example, can precipitate a whole narrative. This technique is so common that precise illustrations of it are not really necessary and would only be redundant.

I have reserved for special attention one type of setting often used by Maupassant, the interior of a travel conveyance, since it demonstrates perhaps more clearly than any other the significance of the interior setting in conjunction with the exterior. Be it train, boat or coach, in every case the milieu in which the narrative is rooted is significantly walled off from the outside world. At its most complete it represents a kind of microcosm, a self-sufficient little unit, set apart for detailed study. From "Boule de Suif" (1880) to "L'inutile beauté" (1890), that is to say from the beginning to the end of Maupassant's publishing careeer, this environment is of great value to him.

At itsimplest, the travel interior provides still another type of framework or cadre into which the story can be placed, and thus a connective between the narrator's present and his past. Of such a type is of course "Miss Harriet" (1883), in which the storyteller is inspired to relate his curious experience to his fellow travellers as they pass through the area in which these events occurred. In the initial paragraphs of the piece we are given this setting in which the actual narration takes place. But of course the exterior setting is vividly set forth here, and represents a kind of point of departure for the intrigue itself. It is as if the little group in the break were witnessing a re-creation of a series of incidents through imagination and memory against a backdrop of exterior reality from which they are physically separated by their means of locomotion, and the reality which is visually present is not a part of their first-hand experience. There is a theatrical quality to the physical world in its function as a link between past and present.

Although the travelling conveyance is an integral part of the little piece entitled "Idylle" (1884), a similar effect is created in the story, this time sustained from beginning to end. The two people involved, seated in a railway carriage, are the principal focal point of the reader's interest, but at the same time we catch glimpses of the passing countryside, the beautiful sights and smells of the "côte d'azur". Again the interest is quite distinct from external realities, focussed as it is on the activities of the people themselves. Whatever one's opinion of this pathetically amusing incident of human animality, it is nevertheless meaningful that the real world is both absent and present at the same time. The descriptive passages, while dealing with the natural setting through which they pass, are separate and distinct from the action itself, thanks to the location of the fictional characters.

The same observations can of course be made with regard to the encounter with Francesca Rondoli on the train. Description again occupies our attention at some length, but description of what is viewed from the train window, separate and cut off from the setting in which a trio of characters is located. Of this, virtually nothing.

The train compartment is undoubtedly a useful device for Maupassant. It may appear only very briefly as it does in "Nos Anglais" (1885) or "Notes d'un voyageur" (1884), in both of which we are simply told that the papers we are about to read were found in a train compartment by the author. This time it is the train itself, undescribed as always, which serves as the link so often required in his short stories. In others the setting may be entirely or in part a train, but with little or no reference to the world outside. The crucial scene of "Ce cochon de Morin" (1882) for example, depends on the proximity of the young girl occasioned by the compartment. The same can also be said of "Un duel" (1883) or "Adieu" (1884) although the dramatic moment dealt with in each of these is quite different.

Train compartments are not the only travel settings used, of course. Maupassant's most celebrated work, "Boule de Suif" is concerned with a coach, and once the characters are seated in the conveyance, we have no further reference to the setting itself. Our curiosity is aroused simply by the juxtaposition of such an unlikely group of people, perhaps as Sullivan suggests, a little too carefully selected to give a cross-section of society. They are in an exceedingly confined space, seated in very strict order, under conditions of fear and tension. It is the fact that they are so confined that gives rise to the development of the narrative. Extracted from their respective physical and social environments and thrown briefly together by the need to escape from Prussian hands, they are thrown into an intensity of contact which is almost physical, and their undescribed surroundings are the major contributing factor to the story's intrigue, once the situation has been established.

This kind of setting then is an essential, as we can see, for the creation of certain situations in which the characters are removed from their own world. The travel cadre represents a technique by which the author separates certain phenomena from their environment in order to juxtapose them with specimens from other backgrounds and deal with the resultant conflict, or in other cases to consider them in isolation. The physical world often passes by the window, but in all cases it is clearly isolated from the narrative situation under examination. An excellent illustration of this may be found in the development of the marital conflict of the first chapter of "L'inutile beauté". As the elegant couple ride in the direction of the Bois de Boulogne, we catch glimpses of the Arc de Triomphe and the setting sun, of the flow of people and carriages, and generally of the activity perceivable outside. But our interest lies entirely with these two people and the reasons for their friction.

The travel setting is a rather special sort of "interior" setting for two rather obvious reasons which I have already suggested. In none of the stories and novels in which it is used is there a detailed presentation of the interior of the conveyance in question, so that our interest in that interior is exclusively directed towards the people of the narrative. It is thus the clearest manifestation of this general lack of concern which we have already seen in Maupassant for immediate physical reality in which one might call a photographic sense. Selection is very discriminating indeed. Simply compare the use of the train in Maupassant with Zola's presentation in *La bête humaine,* or Boule de Suif's coach journey with Emma Bovary's ride through Rouen with Léon. The purpose of selection is quite different here.

Secondly, the travel setting often, but not always, links the interior with the exterior as it passes by the vehicle, as indeed it does in both Flaubert and Zola. The inside setting which interests the reader seems quite stationary by comparison. In other words there is, as well as a bond between the two, a barrier which inhibits the intermingling of them. The settings are viewed and admired, but not contacted directly. The reaction of the character to external nature is an experience in which we the readers are concerned more with the mood and the dramatic tension than with the exterior objects which do admittedly contribute to them. Here again we might conclude that the rôle of the physical world has been shifted to some extent, since again external reality imposes itself on the characters in such a way that it is reduced in significance and only serves to intensify and clarify other aspects of the story. The movement is retractive, not expansive.

One must not forget, in dealing with the physical world of Maupassant, that for each individual in his stories, other individuals too are part of his reality. It therefore becomes important to glance briefly at how they reveal themselves, and how Maupassant chooses to present them. Here too there emerges a basic pattern and a curious development of technique. "Boule de Suif" offers an excellent starting point for the consideration of this factor.

The story is introduced by a rather lengthy and very effective description of the Prussian arrival in Rouen, and proceeds to the particular series of events which occupy the major portion of the narrative. Our first introduction to the occupants of the coach is the voices of three unidentified men who meet in front of the Hôtel de Normandie. It is not until the coach is well under way and until the dawn appears, that their shadowy forms are brought into clear focus. First, the three married couples are introduced, with fairly complete indications of their social backgrounds, and some slight indication of their physical appearance. Following this, there is reference to the nuns, then to Cornudet and his past, and finally to Boule de Suif herself. And it is only this last named who merits a detailed physical portrait.

Both "Mademoiselle Fifi" and "La maison Tellier" are begun in a similar fashion. There is at first an indication of the setting, and then the characters, one by one, are introduced. In the case of the former, we see the major first in a reclining position reading his mail, and then are given descriptions of him and his subordinates in some detail, terminating with the appearance of Mademoiselle Fifi. In the latter story we learn first of Madame's background, then we see her in some detail. After an introduction to their establishment, physical descriptions of the employees follow one after the other.

In all three of these relatively early pieces, Maupassant attaches a good deal of importance to the presentation of his personages before the story *per se* can be really launched. It is quite obvious that, in his emulation of his illustrious predecessors, the younger author is using a tried and true technique in order to set his story in motion. The characters are methodically catalogued, introduced one by one, before we can have any clear indication as to the nature of the story. Their physical appearance, whether presented in minute detail, or rapidly sketched in, is placed in a position of emphasis and would appear to vary in detail in direct proportion to his or her significance in the subsequent development.

Physical description as a means of introducing a character to the reader is frequently used by Maupassant. Tall gaunt Miss Harriet briefly appears before the narrator's eyes, and is associated in his mind with a herring. We are given a description of Francesca Rondoli's black hair and eyes, her somewhat vulgar style of dress, as two men return to their compartment after the stop at Maresilles. Renardet, the mayor, and central character of "La petite Roque (1885) is presented only in the most general terms which sketch in his robust physique, before Maupassant explores far more completely his temperament. In "Yvette" (1884) we have a curious complication. Firstly the two gentlemen are presented to us, with much more attention paid to their backgrounds than to their actual appearance, and then Saval, one of the two, broaches the topic of Yvette and her mother. When we finally do encounter these two beauties, there is a great deal of interest in their figures, their eyes, the mother's voice and the daughter's grace of movement. And in "L'inutile beauté" we find Maupassant presenting the countess in similar terms – her ivory oval face, jet black hair, her graceful figure – details which are repeated in a scene strongly reminiscent of a well-known Renoir portrait, when she appears at the opera in chapter three.

Physical description is indeed an element of which Maupassant makes good use. But it would be a misinterpretation of the facts to suggest that it is central to his establishment of character in every case. Again in "L'inutile beauté", we meet the husband of the aforementioned countess, admittedly less clearly developed than she, but nevertheless of some significance in the conflict. From the strictly physical point of view, one might almost say that he is invisible, since Maupassant wastes little time in describing him to the reader. Nor is this an isolated example. Nowhere do we find clearly outlined the appearance of Monsieur Parent in the story

of the same name, and, with the exception of the blond hair, little idea as to
the supposedly striking resemblance between little Georges and the lover
Limousin is offered. In "Le champ d'oliviers" we are given only the briefest
suggestion of the priest's well-developed physique and of his attire, and
only a general indication of the slovenly appearance of his son. It is even
possible to find cases in Maupassant's stories in which two characters
are described together, with little or no attempt to differentiate between
them on the physical level at least. The two lonely recruits of "Petit
soldat" (1885) could very well be only one person, and the Orgemol
brothers in "Les bécasses" (1885) appear as identical twins.

Out of this general review of descriptive material within the short
stories there emerges then a series of patterns which, when considered
in the broader context of all of Maupassant's prose work becomes helpful
in ascertaining his major artistic contribution.

The frequent landscape and seascape passages seem to share certain
general characteristics. Whether it be the Norman coast of "Miss Harriet", the Seine Valley of "Le Horla" or the city of Rouen as we find
it in "Un Normand" (1882) or the Mediterranean coast of "Les soeurs
Rondoli" we can discern an underlying, one might say almost abstract
pattern of strong horizontal and vertical sweeps. The movement here is
generally outward, reaching towards a horizon, towards an infinity which
is given depth by the sudden intervention of masts, rocks, steeples or
other striking verticals.

The means by which Maupassant integrates these passages into the
fabric of the story also has significance. The more elaborately detailed
descriptions come generally in one of two important locations. They may
occur in the introduction or conclusion, that is to say in the "cadre" such
as we find in "La peur", or "La légende du Mont Saint-Michel", and thus
attempt to link two distinct time sequences, the "real" one of the narrator
and the fictional one of the story itself, or indeed we may discover them
within the context of the narrative, where again they have a certain
linking function. In "Les soeurs Rondoli" description links the interiorized situation of the railway carriage with the outdoor world of the passing
Mediterranean coast. In "La petite Roque" it links the internal suffering
of the criminal with the deed itself. Generally speaking the descriptive
passage attempts to underline and give lasting value to a particular
moment in the narrative. Time again is intimately bound up with description and deserves careful consideration.

The interior descriptions too fall into a broad pattern. In his fidelity
to the Flaubertian concept, Maupassant too attaches much value to

the little significant detail – the photo in "Hautot père et fils", the pictures on the wall in "La chambre 11", the piece of string in "La ficelle". In each case the descriptive material is scrupulously pertinent to the characters and situation at hand. Indeed we see a tendency away from the materialistic, essentially visual rendition of real objects towards a more internalized vision in which these objects, like the jewels of "Les bijoux", the necklace of "La parure" or indeed the mysterious, invisible "Horla" become meaningful only through the internal life of the characters present, and not through some objective external communication between the described world and the reader. Here too we have a quest for a new dimension, a new interpretation of man's universe. The dominant object, the travel setting, the interior décor, the hallucination, the landscape in the short stories all point in the direction of a deepening interrogation of the meaning of existence itself.

Generally one can conclude then that the descriptive element in the short stories indicates a shift in emphasis, a change in perspective on the part of the artist. Techniques of the "realistic" tradition, impressionistic presentation, the little significant detail are maintained in Maupassant, but there is the suggestion of a new dimension not clearly discernable in the conventional interpretation of sense perceptions.

III

THE NOVELS

By reserving the novels for special consideration we can approach the general problem of chronology with a good deal more assurance than is possible with regard to the short stories.[1] Thanks both to publication dates and to references in Maupassant's correspondence, we can with some confidence view them, as both Sullivan and Vial do, as a progression, and by so doing arrive at some conclusion with regard to development of technique. One must constantly bear in mind the brevity of Guy de Maupassant's literary career, and therefore take care not to push such arguments to an absurd extreme.

It is no revelation to state that external décor, almost entirely rural in nature, is one of the foundation stones of the first novel, *Une vie*. The countryside in the rain passes before our eyes as the coach bearing Jeanne and her family rolls in the direction of "Les Peuples", centre of activity for almost the entire narrative. The first four chapters develop and present the character of the central figure in intimate relation with the setting of the family home on the Norman coast. In the first chapter she contemplates the moon from her window, in the second she lies in the grass viewing the beauties of a summer day. The intense degree of feeling linking Jeanne to her natural surroundings is clearly stated:

Elle demeurait souvent pendant des heures immobile, éloignée dans ses songeries; et son habitation des Peuples lui plaisait infiniment parce qu'elle prêtait un décor aux romans de son âme, lui rappelant et par les bois d'alentour, et par la lande déserte, et par le voisinage de la mer, les livres de Walter Scott qu'elle lisait depuis quelques mois.[2]

---

[1] As an introduction to the "Bibliographie générale" of his *Maupassant, journaliste et chroniqueur*, Gérard Delaisement reviews the various contributions towards the clarification of problems of chronology. See pp. 245–247 of that volume for precise information.

[2] Maupassant, *Une vie, Oeuvres complètes*, p. 33.

The Flaubertian point of view is never more clearly stated in Maupassant than at this point, and I will come back to this problem later. For the moment we should note only that external nature is closely linked to establishment of character as we have seen from certain of his short stories. The wedding trip to Corsica in chapter five again has a strong undercurrent of nature's beauties in the terrain, the sun, the sky and the sea. Petite-Mère's habitual walk, Jeanne's hysterical dash into the snow at the birth of Rosalie's child, the death of Julien all demonstrate the utility of the surroundings in the advancement of plot and the development of character, and here too the broad vertical and horizontal interplay, the cliffs of the Norman coast, the tall trees of the estate, the mountains of Corsica, and the omnipresent sea. Maupassant's "objective" technique clearly involves external nature in its overall plan. The closing description, with Jeanne now removed from her maritime panorama, destroyed and alone, follows the identical pattern:

Le soleil baissait vers l'horizon, inondant de clarté les plaines verdoyantes, tachées de place en place par l'or des colzas en fleur, et par le songe des coquelicots. Une quiétude infinie planait sur la terre tranquille où germaient les sèves. La carriole callait grand train, le paysan claquant de la langue pour exiter son cheval.

Et Jeanne regardait droit devant elle en l'air, dans le ciel que coupait, comme des fusées, le vol cintré des hirondelles. Et soudain une tiédeur douce, une chaleur de vie traversant ses robes, gagna ses jambes, pénétra sa chair; ...[3]

It is at this expansive moment that, overcome with emotion she seems to have discovered something and showers the baby on her knee with affection.

The significance of the interior description in *Une vie*, that is to say more precisely the interior of "Les Peuples" which we find fully described in the first chapter cannot be underestimated. The salon, the library, the corridors and staircases, and finally Jeanne's own room are presented in such a way as to give to the reader what amounts almost to a blueprint of the old house. Certain details are meant of course to be much more than simple descriptions. The furniture of the salon upholstered in tapestry illustrating La Fontaine's fables, the almost baroque voluptuousness of Jeanne's bed, the tapestry illustrations of the myth of Pyramis and Thisbe, the elegant clock with its ever-moving little enamelled bee, are all quite obviously (in the Flaubertian sense) little significant details. Jeanne, just out of the convent and full of romantic ideals in the best

---

[3] Maupassant, *Une vie*, p. 379.

Emma Bovary tradition admires these objects. They are undoubtedly
projections of what lies within her. In this, Maupassant's first novel, the
so-called objective technique offers very little originality in the hands of
the young author. The described objects are reflections of character,
comments on personality, a narrative technique by which individuals are
defined. The interiors of *Une vie* loom very large in character presentation
– the shrouded interior of the great *château* of the Vicomte de Briseville,
the many-windowed salon of the Fourville home, and of course the tragic
departure from "Les Peuples" itself – are all in keeping with the characters
and situations involved. Description of interior *décor* is clearly a function
of the development of the characterization and of the events of the whole
novel. They are a device by which the reader is constantly kept informed
without the author's direct intervention.

In direct parallel with the short stories, the novels also contain several
incidents in which the characters are aboard travel conveyances. In the
opening pages of *Une vie*, Jeanne returns to "Les Peuples" with her parents for the summer, and the setting permits not only a flashback technique in which we are provided with the essentials of the heroine's formative years, but also, as mentioned, a reference to the passing countryside
in the rain. Here is Jeanne on the threshold of life, on the threshold of
the novel. This is a moment to be cherished and remembered like the
subsequent description of the château; we have here a prefiguration of
her tragic life. The silence in the coach, the desolate view from the
window, the incessant and all-blanketing rain are precursors of the
emptiness, the slow erosion of life which the novel will trace. And like
this incident the honeymoon trip through the wild beauties of Corsica
in chapter five and the sailing excursion in chapter three make use of the
travel conveyance to link the reality of Jeanne's interior world with the
exterior world of nature. The breathtaking speed with which the view
of the countryside flashes by her train window as she hurries towards
Paris in quest of her son in chapter thirteen is a clear statement of
Jeanne's dependence on her surroundings, particularly if viewed in the
light of the journey of the opening pages. It is as if she were being carried
away into a new strange world which was not her own.

The presentation of character through description of physical appearance focusses our attention again on that all important first chapter.
As Jeanne packs a few last minute items she finds among them that
calendar to which she will cling in old age. It is only after her father
enters and we are given a rapid summary of his character and his method
of raising his daughter that we see Jeanne in detail.

Elle semblait un portrait de Véronèse avec ses cheveux d'un blond luisant qu'on aurait dit avoir déteint sur sa chair, une chair d'aristocrate à peine nuancée de rose, ombrée d'un léger duvet, d'une sorte de velours pâle qu'on apercevait un peu quand le soleil la caressait. Ses yeux étaient bleus, de ce bleu opaque qu'ont ceux des bons hommes en faïence de Hollande.

Elle avait, sur l'aile gauche de la narine, un petit grain de beauté, un autre à droite, sur le menton, où frisaient quelques poils si semblables à sa peau qu'on les distinguait à peine. Elle était grande, mûre de poitrine, ondoyante de la taille....[4]

What we have here, quite obviously, is a verbal portrait in the strictest sense. With the reference to Veronese, Maupassant leaves no doubt in our mind as to the effect he is seeking. Composed of colour, texture, light and shadow, it owes much to the graphic arts for its effect.

And it is indeed important that we have this image of the heroine before the narrative is really launched. It is as if Maupassant is attempting to fix something permanent, a solid foundation on which he can build his character. The initial appeal to the reader is without doubt visual. Even the relatively minor figures of the piece require this kind of presentation before they are woven into the fabric. The Abbé Picot is seen, heavy set, red, and rather sloppily dressed (as are so many of Maupassant's clerics), as he appears on the road. A brief portrait of Julien de Lamare accompanies his first appearance as Jeanne and her mother leave the church – long eyelashes, charming expression, bearded but prominent chin.

In the great tradition of Balzac and Flaubert there is quite evidently a studied correlation between physical appearance and character development in this method, as the details offered of Jeanne's future husband would indicate. Description is an essential of character presentation, and would seem to vary in detail in proportion to the personage's significance in the work. Only Jeanne and Julien produce complete and clear images. Of the others, only pertinent details – her mother's obesity and shortness of breath, her father's aristocratic demeanour. There is, as we have already witnessed in the short stories, a correlation between the physical aspects of reality and what cannot be perceived by the senses. *Une vie* is clearly within the Flaubertian tradition with little to differentiate it from works of his predecessors.

With *Bel-Ami*, Maupassant's second, and some maintain one of his most successful attempts at the novel, we enter quite a different world, but again one we have seen in his shorter writings as well – the city. In the first section of the novel, eight chapters in length, there are really only

[4]   Maupassant, *Une vie*, p. 3–4.

three significant manifestations of external Paris – the first encounter with Forestier on the boulevard, the much discussed conversation with Norbert de Varenne as he and Duroy return from the Walters' late at night, and the duelling chapter in which the coldness of the early morning adds substantially to the creation of the mood. The rest of the action takes place principally indoors – Les Folies Bergère, the Forestiers, Madame de Marelle's and the Walters' homes, in the offices of the newspaper, or in Duroy's miserable little room. But significantly the one chapter in which the setting is not Paris, that of Forestier's death, again substantiates what we have observed about Maupassant's treatment of the Midi in the short stories. He cannot seem to resist exercising his powers of observation when focussing his attention on this area of his experience, and the chapter is full of references to the beauties of the surroundings. It must be admitted of course that such lengthy passages as this chapter contains are not gratuitously included. As we shall see they contribute substantially to the development of the relationship between Madeleine and Georges.

In Part Two, nine chapters in length, we have a similar ratio of important references to the outdoor world. Again only one chapter is set clearly beyond the confines of the city, and it is introduced by the view from the train window. The Seine Valley at Rouen has also been seen in the short stories, but nowhere is presented with such loving care as at this point in the longer work. Returning to Paris in the second chapter, we find in the rest of the novel only three more important contacts with the external surroundings. Madeleine and Duroy ride to the Bois de Boulogne, and the procession of elegance we noted in *A cheval* is repeated in detail, including a reference to the Arc de Triomphe and the Champs-Élysées which has much in common with the parallel passage in "L'inutile beauté". A return to the Seine occurs in the seduction of Suzanne Walter, and the book ends outdoors with the apotheosis of Georges Duroy on the steps of the Madeleine.

The broad pattern which emerges from these two novels offers still another interesting comparison with the short stories. Not only does Maupassant return frequently to the same material, it would appear that he expands his techniques from the lesser form to suit the requirements of the greater. The type of immediate presentation achieved by the "cadre" is obviously unsuited to the novel because of its greater depth and complexity. We are not hearing about something that has happened, but witnessing a series of events as they happen. One should note in the case of *Une vie* and *Bel-Ami* a similarity of opening and closing. Both begin with the central figure observing what passes by, in the first case as Jeanne proceeds by coach from Rouen to "Les Peuples", in the second as Duroy strolls down the boulevard. In other words the reader is led into both narratives by the description of the passing scene. One thinks immediately of the famous river description at the beginning of *L'éducation sentimentale*. But it would seem to me that there is a basic distinction to be drawn between Flaubert's method and that of his follower. Whereas in the case of the senior author the river dominates the reader's attention first, and then the characters are painted in, in both the novels of Maupassant we are aware of observing external phenomena through the eyes of the principal character, whom we meet immediately. The function of description thus becomes less thematic and more direct, closer to the establishment of personality and less significant in itself through a subtle shift of point of view.

The conclusions of both these works also share a certain pattern in that the totally static image of Jeanne at her window, and George Du Val de Cantal on the steps of the church transfix the characters involved into immobile statues. Jeanne's life is now an eternal nothingness, Duval's an endless drive for power, a kind of abyss of ambition and deceit. There can be no further development, no modification, no resolution.

From dynamic introduction to static conclusion then, external description encloses the action of these novels as the cadre enclosed that of the short stories. Immediacy of effect would appear to be a characteristic of the Maupassantian approach. The aesthetic consequences arising from these observations will require much closer attention and deeper analysis.

Again in *Bel-Ami*, Maupassant goes to some length to present to his reader descriptions of the various interiors in which the action of the novel takes place. The Forestier apartment in the second chapter of Part One illustrates this very early in the book. The salon, to which the entire group withdraws for coffee and conversation in the tradition of Zola's *La curée*, is dominated by rubber plants and other exotic greenery, and furnished with a calculated view to casualness.

Madame de Marelle's rather slovenly salon with its four banal pictures, Duroy's iron bed and dirty walls, the Walters' elegant home, are all manifestations of this same technique, a correlation between habitat and inhabitant that is traceable, as Vial so rightly observes, through Zola and Flaubert back to Balzac. Again in this novel, one could not even suggest that Maupassant's originality might lie with his treatment of physical description.

The travel incident as a vehicle for descriptive material is of course present in *Bel-Ami*. Among all the little journeys the narrative takes around Paris, two extra-Parisian interludes stand out and deserve special mention. The first is of course in the carriage ride along the Mediterranean coast with Madeleine, Duroy and Forestier which precedes and indeed preechoes the latter s death. The other, opening Part Two is the wedding trip of Madeleine and Georges to Rouen, and again from the train we view in the typical fashion the passing scene – the Seine in sunshine covered with boats, the approach to Rouen, and from a carriage a panorama of the city. And here again characters are both distinct from and in sympathy with what they view. Within the confines of Paris the major sequence of this type is found in the subsequent chapter – Madeleine and Georges ride up the Champs-Élysées and through the Bois de Boulogne where again the exterior setting strikes for a moment a harmonious chord in the newly-weds.

Turning to the description of the characters themselves one can observe a similar correlation between interior and exterior as we saw in the case of *Une vie*. Much the same kind of observation can of course be made with regard to *Bel-Ami*. Georges Duroy, self-conscious from the very beginning, considers his own appearance as he walks down the street. This attitude leads logically to the portrait of him found very early in the first chapter. As suggested by the final comment of the photograph, this is unmistakably the basis on which his whole character will be presented.

Quoique habillé d'un complet de soixante francs, il gardait une certaine élégance tapageuse, un peu commune, réelle cependant. Grand, bien fait, blond, d'un blond châtain vaguement roussi, avec une moustache retroussée, qui semblait mousser sur son lèvre, des yeux bleus, clairs, troués d'une pupille toute petite, des cheveux frisés naturellement, séparés par une raie au milieu du crâne, il ressemblait bien au mauvais sujet des romans populaires.[5]

Words like *tapageuse* and *commune* are hardly accidental. Clearly our point of departure in dealing with this individual is the physical, the visible.

This novel is inhabited by a crowd of lesser figures, whose appearance is often enlightening in the analysis of this technique. Both Forestier and his wife Madeleine, he in this same first chapter, she in the second, are first viewed by Duroy, and the reader uses the hero's eyes, so central to his own appearance, to see them. Madeleine's blonde hair, her eyes, her figure, her dress attract Duroy's and therefore our attention. Her portrait is directly contrasted with that of Madame de Marelle who is viewed

[5] Maupassant, *Bel-Ami, Oeuvres complètes*, p. 3.

almost immediately afterward. One should also note that Madame Walter
is present at this first dinner party, but there is at this point only passing
reference to her aristocratic elegance. She does not figure significantly in
the life of the hero until much later and she is not really painted in detail
until the sixth chapter of the first part, at the point at which Duroy shows
some real interest in her. Suzanne Walter, the fourth woman in Georges'
life, does not appear before our eyes until the third chapter of Part Two,
and here especially the painter's method of presentation is much in evidence:

Il regardait la plus jeune des demoiselles Walter, et pensait: "Elle n'est pas
mal du tout, cette petite Suzanne, mais pas du tout." Elle avait l'air d'une frêle
poupée blonde, trop petite, mais fine, avec la taille mince, des hanches et de la
poitrine, une figure de miniature, des yeux d'émail d'un bleu gris dessinés au
pinceau, qui semblaient nuancés par un peintre minutieux et fantaisiste, de la
chair trop blanche, trop lisse, polie, unie, sans grain, sans teinte, et des cheveux
ébouriffés, frisés, une brousaille savante, légère, un nuage charmant, tout pareil
en effet à la chevelure des jolies pupées de luxe qu'on voit passer dans les bras
de gamines beaucoup moins hautes que leur joujou.[6]

And to make sure that this portrait is taken at full value, he makes
reference to a painter, this time to Watteau.[7] In the case of her mother,
he mentions a photograph he has seen in a shop window.[8]

One must conclude that all the characteristics of description found in
Une vie are still present, and at least superficially *Bel-Ami* offers little
evidence of a new direction. But the answer is in fact not quite that simple.

The overall concept of *Mont-Oriol* is double. Combined with the world
of Andermatt, Parisian high finance and commercial exploitation, is that
of Christiane, a world of love and childbearing. Sullivan may be correct
in considering this the weakest of Maupassant's novels,[9] but from the
standpoint of the function of external nature, it offers a curious variation.
Set in Auvergne, again remaining within the confines we established with
the short stories, its treatment of the rough terrain, broad vistas, lakes
and trees is at the heart of the development of both sub-plots. If the novel
has any unity it is to no small degree due to the method of presentation
of the landscapes and the means by which they are integrated into the
somewhat complex and confused action of the book.

The novel opens with a detailed description of the spa and the area –

---

[6] Maupassant, *Bel-Ami*, p. 363.
[7] Maupassant, *Bel-Ami*, p. 371.
[8] Maupassant, *Bel-Ami*, p. 370.
[9] Sullivan, *Maupassant the Novelist*, Part 2, Ch. 8, pp. 94–101.

valley, mountains, trees. Its position of prominence suggests not only theme and mood as did Flaubert's Seine but also fixes our attention on an actual location which will become an active player in the developing human drama. The central and vital element of this external setting is reserved until the second chapter – the blasting of the rock and the discovery of the spring in a location with an impressive view of the surrounding countryside. It is this event which sets off the whole series of financial moves resulting in the establishment of Mont-oriol and which at the same time will create and destroy the relationship between Paul and Christiane. Auvergne is the source of inspiration for Paul Brétigny and his instinctive love for it will modify and develop Christiane's whole view of life. A number of excursions follow, to the Lake of Tazenat and to a ruined castle, among others. The physical presence of this magnificent countryside, first viewed by the pair in Chapter Two, draws the couple together:

S'ils s'étaient aimés dans une ville, leur passion, sans doute, aurait été différente, plus prudente, plus sensuelle, moins aérienne et moins romanesque. Mais là, dans ce pays vert dont l'horizon élargissait les élans de l'âme, seuls, sans rien pour distraire, pour atténuer leur instinct d'amour éveillé, ils s'étaient élancés soudain dans une tendresse éperdument poétique, faite d'extase et de folie. Le paysage autour d'eux, le vent tiède, le bois, l'odeur savoureuse de cette campagne leur jouaient tout le long des jours et des nuits la musique de leur amour; ...[10]

The natural properties of the region are equally creative for the other aspect of this novel as well. After the discovery of the spring, much of Part One is devoted to this theme of commercial exploitation. As the scientific equivalent of Paul's view of nature we have, in the third chapter, the engineer's long and detailed explanation to Andermatt of the means of development of mineral water. The physical properties of the terrain are again to the fore, but this time viewed under the cold light of scientific fact.

The six chapters of Part Two are again dominated by the same external object – the mineral spring. But, since a year has passed, there is a very obvious difference. We now have a man-made establishment dominating the site and curiously the emphasis will now be on destruction rather than on construction. External nature takes on the aspect of the formal gardens, of an extinct volcano, and again of the ruins. We have returned to a setting whose charm has been mysteriously lost. Mont-Oriol is the

[10] Maupassant, *Mont-Oriol, Oeuvres complètes*, p. 191–92.

destroyer of love between Christiane and Paul just as it is the destroyer of its rival establishment. Paul will marry the Oriol sister for economic reasons. Geological science, economics and medicine, a trio of logic and reason, have together destroyed feeling.

External description is obviously then a vital force in the narrative art, inextricably woven into the web of a dual plot. But Mont-Oriol represents a slight deviation from this pattern in that we do not see the main characters, with the exception of the Oriol family, in their usual surroundings, that is to say, in their homes. Interior descriptions are for the most part of the health establishment. Figuring largely in the second part of the book with the construction of Mont-Oriol itself, they are contributory to the second of the two themes of the work, commercial exploitation. This is most vividly demonstrated of course by the exercise room with its complex machinery, described faithfully by the author in its every detail. Maupassant has been frequently attacked for the inclusion in this book of what is considered to be extraneous material, but if one considers this as an extension of the techniques which he has inherited from the masters of the past, it is at least understandable as a comment on Andermatt and his scheming financiers as well as on the unscrupulous practitioners of the art of medicine so much in evidence in the novel, and with which Maupassant was certainly intimately acquainted.

The rôle of the outdoor setting with regard to the Paul Brétigny–Christiane Andermatt relationship is enhanced by the travel device along the same lines as that of Madeleine and Georges in *Bel-Ami*. The emotive power of the passing scene is repeatedly stressed as Paul and Christiane ride through it seated side by side in a carriage.

We need not deal at great length with physical portrayal as interpreted in *Mont-Oriol* since this novel contributes little to the facts already established. But two points do deserve our attention. When we are first introduced to Christiane Andermatt, the usual descriptive passage ensues. What is really striking about this portrait is the attention drawn to the eyes. They are in fact the only feature presented with more than a passing mention, and are indeed dealt with at some length. And later on in the book, as the relationship between herself and Paul Brétigny becomes more firmly established, his eyes are revealed to have great power over her:

Il riait, en racontant cela, ouvrait ses grands yeux ronds, tantôt sur le bois et tantôt sur Christiane; et elle, surprise, étonnée, mais facile à impressionner, se sentait aussi dévorée, comme le bois, par ce regard avide et large.[11]

[11] Maupassant, *Mont-Oriol*, p. 101.

The eyes have always been a very necessary part of Maupassant's revelation of character and relationship. Madeleine's fascinated Georges
Duroy right from first encounter. And in this relationship they became
a central means of communication between the lovers.

This leads me directly to the second remark to be made in considering
Mont-Oriol. For we are given the portrait of Paul Brétigny through the
eyes of Christiane, as we saw so many people in *Bel-Ami* through Georges.
As the relationship develops, this portrait is modified. Madame Walter's
was brought into focus as she grew in importance, Jeanne de Lamare's
evolved as she aged from the Veronese beauty to a white-haired old lady,
but here for the first time it changes because of the attitude of the behol-
der. When Christiane first sees Paul, we read:

Elle le trouva laid. Il avait les cheveux noirs ras et droits, des yeux trop ronds,
d'une expression presque dure, la tête aussi toute ronde, très forte, une de ces
têtes qui font penser à des boulets de canon, des épaules d'hercule, l'air un peu
sauvage, lourd et brutal.[12]

It strikes one first of all that the emphasis here is on form as opposed to
texture, colour, light and shadow as we have seen elsewhere. It is the
shape most of all which is aesthetically displeasing to Christiane. But as
they become more intimately acquainted, she remarks:

Et puis sa tête avait quelque chose de brutal, d'inachevé, qui donnait à toute sa
personne un aspect un peu lourd au premier coup d'oeil. Mais lorsqu'on s'était
accoutumé à ses traits, on y trouvait du charme, un charme puissant et rude qui
devenait par moments très doux, selon les inflexions tendres de sa voix toujours
voilée.[13]

Could there be more to reality than its physical appearance is capable
of suggesting? The basic forms remain admittedly constant, but it would
appear that they may not be the solid foundation for character that they
have seemed.

Admittedly Paul Brétigny's treatment of Christiane might leave something to be desired, but in spite of the first impression, he has the capacity
to attract her inexplicably. Clearly there is evidence here that Maupassant
is modifying his techniques.

There can be no doubt that the natural setting is meaningful in *Pierre
et Jean*. The city of Le Havre, whose presence has already been noted in
the stories, was at the end of the last century as closely identified with
the sea as it is to this day. It is against this backdrop that Maupassant

[12] Maupassant, *Mont-Oriol*, p. 31.
[13] Maupassant, *Mont-Oriol*, p. 115.

works out his tense drama of parental identification. Right from the opening lines the sea, presented in great detail during the course of the novel, is paralleled with the introduction of the main characters, all out for a boating excursion and some fishing. Chapter Two returns us to the waterfront as Pierre wrestles with the suspicion that has been stirred in his mind by the news at the end of chapter one. And again in chapter four, in a contemplative mood, he is attracted to the sea. In Chapter Six all the major figures of the novel are brought to the coast for their second fishing excursion, set among the rocks and pools left by the ebbing tide at the base of the Norman cliff. The terrain is again familiar to the reader of Maupassant's short stories. Chapter Nine comes back to the sea, and in concluding the novel, Maupassant presents us with the vastness of its horizon as Pierre's ship disappears. The initial scene, in its point of view, has a great deal in common with the opening pages of *Mont-Oriol*. And in a way comparable to that considered in *Une vie* and in *Bel-Ami* the novel begins and ends outdoors. Again the protagonist is seemingly emprisoned for eternity by his environment. A picture painted in words is the last view we have of Pierre, and this time the central figure's presence is only suggested by the ship. It is as if he were swallowed up, finally and pitilessly. The cycle is completed from the scene of activity and conversation against a maritime background in which we look inward towards the shore, to the scene of vast emptiness, the limitless horizon of the concluding lines.

There emerges from this novel a very curious pattern of fluctuation from exterior to interior. With surprising regularity the action moves from one to the other, from confined space to infinity within a chapter or from chapter to chapter. The exterior world again in this work, certainly one of the author's most powerful, represents an essential tool of his art.

The other outstanding manifestation of the outside world in this the briefest of his novels is undoubtedly the fog. It too is an understandable and logically acceptable part of the physical setting. As Sullivan points out, there can be no misunderstanding about its close symbolic relationship to Pierre himself, but I feel that to explain it fully, its counterpart, the sea, must be carefully examined along with it. Both are limitless in dimensions, but the one is an everchanging infinity of clarity and expansiveness while the other is confused, static and retractive.

The fact then that external nature functions in a most profound way here is easily demonstrable. What we would seem to be witnessing in the novel of Maupassant would appear to be not a marked shift in the attention devoted to the exterior but an evolution with regard to its narrative significance, a change in the author's interpretation of his world.

Turning then to the indoor scenes we find that in the course of the narrative there are really only three interiors of any real importance, the Roland household, Madame Rosémilly's and Jean's apartments.

The latter half of the first chapter takes place in the dining room and salon of the Roland home. All we are told of the first room is that it is small, and on the main floor. Of the second, nothing but its location. Here upstairs, they receive Monsieur Lecanu the notary. We return to the same dining room at the beginning of the third chapter and again the scene is totally devoid of descriptive material. At the end of this chapter, the description of the dinner celebrating Jean's unexpected good fortune is concentrated on the table itself. Chapter Seven provides the first real evidence of description of an interior, but not the interior of the family residence. It is rather the much discussed apartment which Jean has been able to rent and which Pierre silently covets. Jean and his mother have spent much time and money furnishing it in a fashion suitable to the younger son's taste, of which Pierre quite obviously disapproves. The description is thus not simply a reflection of the taste and character of Jean and Madame Roland, but a concrete manifestation of Jean's material success, of Pierre's greater refinement of taste, and of his jealousy. And it is precisely in this environment that Pierre can no longer restrain himself. The crisis has been brought about by a number of factors, culminating with the visit to these new surroundings. As in "Hautot père et fils", the *décor* here is no longer a simple reflection, comment on, or projection of character, albeit this element is very much a part of the technique. Reality is now playing a subtler, deeper and indeed much more vital rôle. It would appear to be acquiring more life than in the author's earlier novels.

It is, significantly enough, in the subsequent chapter that we first visit the apartment of Madame Rosémilly. On entering her salon we are treated to a lengthy description of four engravings hanging on the walls. Their poetic banality, their "sensation de propreté et de rectitude", coupled with the bourgeois bad taste of the rest of the décor, is sufficient evidence both to Pierre and to the reader that any permanent relationship between Madame Rosémilly and himself is quite out of the question. Again the *décor* is imbued with a direct function in the advancement of plot, for it is not simply a reflection of the proprietress' taste, but a clear statement of her relationship with the two brothers.

This novel then represents a noticeable progression from its predecessors. As we saw only suggested by the circumstances surrounding the basic choice of milieu in *Mont-Oriol*, we see clearly proven here by the Roland home that the habitat-inhabitant interrelationship is no longer required by Maupassant to establish character. On the other hand, this kind of description, like its external counterpart, is becoming more exclusively selective and more deeply meaningful within the overall concept of the work.

Travel in the large sense is not a major device of *Pierre et Jean*, but the little family boat, the "Perle" serves to unite the participants in the drama as the novel opens, in much the same way as the coach in "Boule de Suif". All the major characters of the novel are closely confined in a limited space, and their relationships are quite clearly defined from the outset. However the "Perle" will assume deeper meaning in the fourth chapter when Pierre ventures out in her alone. She strikes out as if:

... animé d'une vie propre, de la vie des barques, poussée par une force mystérieuse cachée en elle.[14]

The whole of the setting can by this means take on an independence culminating in the enveloping fog. In its capacity for action it too speaks to Pierre with its silence. The same shift in emphasis we have already observed is operative here as well.

The depiction of character in *Pierre et Jean* is, as one might expect, much less dependent on the descriptive element than heretofore observed. We have seen that the major characters of the novel are gathered together in the opening chapter in a fashion common in Maupassant.

But just what do we see of them? Pierre is dark and clean shaven, Jean blond and bearded. And their rowing prowess is a direct reference to the rivalry up to now only latent in their relationship. Something of their past, their education and profession is rapidly sketched in. Madame Rosémilly is blond. Madame Roland is putting on weight since the family came to Le Havre, and we are told something of her romantic, Emma Bovary-type temperament.[15]

If these are the only ascertainable facts then the physical appearance of his characters cannot be a major concern of Maupassant here. Only those details which contribute to the explanation of the human, interior relationships in the novel are deemed noteworthy.

[14] Maupassant, *Pierre et Jean, Oeuvres complètes*, p. 86.
[15] Maupassant, *Pierre et Jean*, pp. 4–16.

But, curiously enough, physical appearance is in reality the keystone of the book. It is Pierre's friend the waitress who first suggests the possibility of his brother's illegitimacy, and from that point on the portrait of the deceased Léon Maréchal dominates Pierre's quest. He even goes so far as to study his brother's face in repose in order to try to decipher the truth, but again we the readers see only his blond hair and beard. It is very late in the book that the vital piece of evidence makes its appearance, and we are given only the briefest account of the miniature portrait from a visual point of view. Pierre remarks on its resemblance to his brother, but there is no clearly established evidence for this within the text itself. Maréchal has, we are told, the same forehead and the same beard, and nothing further is filled in. Just how they are alike we are not told. The colour of the hair, remembered earlier by Pierre, becomes the only really concrete link between his brother and the deceased as far as the reader is concerned.

The descriptive occupies a new and deeper rôle in this novel. Appearance speaks to Pierre, but does not reveal itself to the reader for more than a fleeting moment. The visual has no meaning for Maupassant in itself, but integrated into the psychological structure of the work, its muted presence speaks with eloquence. And it has become so completely a part of the fictional universe that we lose sight of it. We are concerned not with the portrait, but with the reactions of Pierre, of his mother, and to a lesser degree of his father, to the object in question. This is not a Flaubertian symbol, a little significant detail, but an object which, exterior to all the people directly involved in the situation, is meaningful to everyone. Like the apartment of Hautot père's mistress, it requires interpretation within the work and by those involved in order to be developed. It contains within its frame a whole tale of illegitimacy and marital infidelity, of feminine longings and love. Maréchal's physiognomy *per se* is meaningless.

What we would appear to be witnessing is not really a marked change of direction in the novel, but rather a gradual evolution with regard to Maupassant's position in relation to the physical world and his interpretation of it.

This shift is nowhere more obvious than in those last two, much discussed novels, *Fort comme la mort*, and *Notre coeur*. Both of these works take place for the most part within the confines of Paris, and the material used in presenting the outside world must vary accordingly.

The first part of the earlier of these two contains only very few scenes in which the world outdoors looms large. In the third chapter Bertin and young Annette walk in the Parc Monceau after the ride through the Bois de Boulogne (and again the author makes use of similar descriptive material). The other venture into what might be called the outside world of Paris society, that of the painting exposition, offers us virtually no description.

But a most interesting revelation of the outdoors does occur in the only non-Parisian interlude of the novel, the first chapter of the second part. Again we return to the green of the Norman landscape. In the second chapter we accompany the mother-daughter-lover trio on a shopping trip through the crowded Paris streets, and in the fourth chapter we are back to the Parc Monceau for what might be considered the most complete descriptive passage in the novel. And in the final chapter Bertin's accident, which we do not witness, takes place in a city street.

Briefly then, we see again a kind of overall pattern emerging, an alternation between indoors and outdoors, between seclusion and society, between Paris and the countryside which is located at the exact centre of the work. Once more we see that author using elements of description which he has elsewhere utilized to the fullest extent.

But *Fort comme la mort* is more an indoor novel. It opens with a fairly detailed description of Olivier Bertin's studio as he searches for a subject for a new painting, and this, the second paragraph of the novel is of great value both in the evolution of the artist's technique, and within the framework of the novel itself. Lengthy as it is, it must be quoted in its entirety.

Mais à peine entrée dans la haute pièce sévère et drapée, la clarté joyeuse du ciel s'atténuait, devenait douce, s'endormait sur les étoffes, allait mourir dans les portières, éclairait à peine les coins sombres oú, seuls, les cadres d'or s'allumaient comme des feux. La paix et le sommeil semblaient emprisonnés là-dedans, la paix des maisons d'artistes où l'âme humaine a travaillé. En ces murs que la pensée habite, où la pensée s'agite, s'épuise en des efforts violents, il semble que tout soit las, accablé, dès qu'elle s'apaise. Tout semble mort après ces crises de vie; et tout repose, les meubles, les étoffes, les grands personnages inachevés sur les toiles, comme si le logis entier avait souffert de la fatigue du maître, avait peiné avec lui, prenant part, tous les jours, à sa lutte recommencée. Une vague odeur engourdissante de peinture, de térébenthine et de tabac flottait, captée par les tapis et les sièges; et aucun bruit ne troublait le lourd silence que les cris vifs et courts des hirondelles qui passaient sur le châssis ouvert, et la longue rumeur confuse de Paris entendue par dessus les toits.[16]

We have come a long way here from the description of "Les Peuples". This is indeed no architect's plan, no photograph. It is rather a kind of

[16]   Maupassant, *Fort comme la mort, Oeuvres complètes*, pp. 1–2.

painting which, through the interplay of light and shadow on form, stresses the basic shape of the frames and canvasses, while at the same time it penetrates to a deeper level of observation. As many critics have commented, this is the novel of old age, and the description here is a comment on further development. The room is given a life, is identified with the thoughts it has witnessed. Like Bertin it is tired, it is almost dead, its contents are incomplete. It is penetrated with the smells that remain from past activity and stands now as a kind of vacuum, a shell of its former self. One can with justice view this as a reflection of character, just as were Jeanne's tapestries. But in the earlier piece the effect was entirely geared to this and to nothing else. Here the concrete speaks to us not only of Bertin's state of mind now, at the opening of the book, but of all further developments in his life until his final demise. It is a projection in the same sense as the incessant rain would seem to be in the opening paragraphs of *Une vie*. It is also, and more importantly, in ceaseless and immediate communication with its occupant. It tells us not of a potential, nor is it an exteriorized dream, but stands as a three dimensional witness not simply to what has happened or to what might or will take place, but to what *is* occurring at that moment. For Jeanne, as we have observed, Maupassant remains objective. Here he is much less faithful to his master's tenet. We are not dealing here with description, but with analysis. The passage is a kind of summing-up of the action of the book, but not simply a reflection of a state of mind. It is not just a vague prefiguration nor a projection, but concrete evidence of what is already an accomplished fact. The room is only alive insofar as Bertin himself is alive. Reality is clearly no longer exterior to the characters, but is intimately and frankly bound up with them in a kind of organic unit.

Our first introduction to Anne de Guilleroy's home obviously mentions its opulence, but more significantly deals with wall-hangings in the salon in the style of Watteau. Although brief, this description again substantiates our argument. Unlike Jeanne's tapestries, we do not see these except in the most general terms. What is more in evidence here is their meaning as if they were "faites, dessinées et exécutées par des ouvriers rêvassant d'amour". The significance here cannot be measured in terms of creation of character or plot, but rather in terms of human relationships, in terms of Bertin and his mistress. The details are meaningless, but deeper values of interpretation, take precedence over physical presence. Of course the central piece of interior description is without doubt that of the portrait of Anne de Guilleroy found on p. 71 of the Conard edition of the novel.

It seems to give life to the room, and is visual evidence of the novel's
central problem. Since it is perhaps the most completely developed image
of a type absolutely vital to the appreciation of Maupassant, I have
chosen to reserve any further comment on it until I come to deal more
specifically with certain precise images, and its analysis will, I feel, be
more relevant in that context.

Maupassant's favourite Parisian promenade, up the Champs-Élysées,
past the Arc de Triomphe, and thence to the Bois de Boulogne occurs
again in the third chapter of *Fort comme la mort*. Once more we witness
the endless stream of elegant coaches, but the reactions of the three
people, Olivier Bertin, Anne de Guilleroy and her daughter are significantly different from those of Georges and Madeleine Duroy, a difference
not entirely attributable to their difference of social status. Two of the
most celebrated beauties of Paris society are seen among the crowd,
Madame Mandelière and the comtesse de Lochrist, and the conversation
runs to a discussion of beauty and age. The scene is clearly not a projection of interior psychology into concrete objectivity, but a living entity
which spurs the characters on to deal with the problem which is central
to their own relationships.

With regard to descriptive passages dealing with the appearance of the
characters *Fort comme la mort* differs from *Pierre et Jean*. We are given
quite detailed physical descriptions of the protagonists. But it should not
for this reason be viewed as a regression towards an earlier method. The
novel moves from the opening description of Bertin's studio to a discussion of his artistic career. Only then do we begin to see what Olivier really
looks like. But the circumstances which give rise to this description are
very enlightening indeed. Raising a drapery, he looks at himself in a full-
length mirror, used in the studio to verify certain artistic problems of
pose and perspective.

The resultant description is thus externalized and equated with a product of his artistic endeavours. Age is beginning to take its toll on his
handsome appearance, a transformation of which he is only too aware.
His professional perception leads him to scrutinize the physique, the
forms and colours, black, white and grey, with only a touch of brown,
which comprise his portrait. For this physical description is doubtless
a kind of instantaneous self-portrait. The mirror has already been a
useful device in *Bel-Ami*, as we shall shortly see, but its relationship to
the work as a whole has been much more carefully calculated here. For
the artist, the sense of sight is a prime essential, and the presentation here
is as much an analysis of Bertin's perceptiveness as it is a verbal painting.

Description is thus very curiously linked with psychology and again has this double function of speaking of and to the character.

It follows then that the portrait will be a major device in this novel. Anne de Guilleroy enters immediately following this scene, and we have a description which stresses her slightly fading beauty. But significantly her head appears in the mirror before we see her in detail. She too is linked up with the art form. It is understandable, given the context of the novel, that physical appearance be stressed. During the dinner conversation of the second chapter we have sketches of la Duchesse de Mortemain, and of Musadieu, for example, as we had of Monsieur de Guilleroy in the first:

C'était un homme de petite taille, sans moustaches, aux joues creuses, ombrées sous la peau, par la barbe rasée.
Il avait un peu l'air d'un prêtre ou d'un acteur, les cheveux longs rejetés en arrière, des manières polies, et autour de la bouche deux grands plis circulaires descendant des joues au menton et qu'on eût dit creusés par l'habitude de parler en public.[17]

This is the description of an artist in which the interest lies predominantly with form. And these forms tell the observer not only of the man's interior, but also something about his background, his interests, his way of life. Maupassant has maintained his painter's presentation, but stripped it to the essentials in which form seems to take precedence over colour, a trend already discernable in *Mont-Oriol*, and substantiated by the presentations in this novel of the duchess and of Musadieu. Indeed the latter is seen at one point as a kind of silhouette.[18]

But these descriptions, significant as they may be, cannot be said to represent the essentials of the narrative. Frankly the product of artistic selection, they do however, underline the broader function reality has to perform. And it is precisely this more probing rôle that makes *Fort comme la mort* so strikingly similar to its predecessor. It is without question the portrait of Anne de Guilleroy, painted many years earlier that contains within it the seeds of destruction of the central figure. Physical description, in the form of its appearance, or more precisely its resemblance, is the cornerstone on which the fiction is erected.

It is unhappy physical duplication of Anne de Guilleroy in her daughter, or rather the duplication of the mother's portrait which will annihilate Olivier Bertin. As in *Pierre et Jean* a physical object, the painting on

[17]   Maupassant, *Fort comme la mort*, p. 22.
[18]   Maupassant, *Fort comme la mort*, p. 72.

which a longstanding love relationship is established, contains a depth of psychological impact bearing on the lives of all the participants in this drama. We share in its creation, we are aware of its power as it dominates Madame de Guilleroy's salon, but, significantly enough, we do not actually see the finished product. We see only the mother and daughter, the so-to-speak raw material of the artistic product. The passage of time has put a gulf between this reality and its artistic interpretation with regard to both of these women. For Anne there is the problem of physical deterioration as there is for Olivier. In her daughter it is the interior essence of the youthful temperament which creates the barrier for Bertin. This factor, like all the others, has a life of its own in which it is capable of change and modification. Bertin's ideal, once attained, cannot be sustained, but remains to haunt him the rest of his days.

Notre coeur is directly comparable with *Fort comme la mort* and demonstrates a strikingly similar pattern. Just as Part Two of the former opens with the Norman interlude, so Part Two of this three part work opens with the excursion to Mont Saint-Michel. Up until this point the action had been confined almost entirely indoors, to Madame de Burne's salon. And again this non-Parisian interlude contains a turning point, a crisis in the affair which occupies the central stage, the affair between Mariolle and Michèle de Burne. This external-internal interplay is sustained in this part by Mariolle's cooling off.

Part Three again returns us outside Paris, this time to Fontainebleau, and again nature plays its *rôle* in Mariolle's evolution and the problems he faces in his emotional ties with Madame de Burne.

A similar pattern becomes evident here of alternation between the indoors and the outdoors, closely linked with the total concept of the work, and binding it together into a unified whole. Indoor description is very much in evidence in the novel and deserves some scrutiny at this point.

The presentation of Michèle de Burne's apartment contained in the first chapter of *Notre coeur* is much too lengthy to quote here. In a fashion surprisingly similar to that of "Les Peuples", Maupassant leads us from room to room, to view the contents as they pass. The layout of the apartment is suggested, the number of rooms, and the view from the windows of each – the street, the garden, etc. It is clearly the creation of Madame de Burne herself, and is in this sense an objective correlative of her personal taste. But again, the similarity with *Une vie* is only superficial. The presentation of the setting in this novel is strictly impersonal in the sense that its inhabitant is nowhere to be seen, and the rooms are empty. By extracting her from them, Maupassant gives to the passage a value which, unlike the description in the first novel has an abstract quality. Full of works of art, of rare objects of exquisite taste, chosen, as is told to us, partly through her instinctive good taste, and partly on the advice of her artist friends, this apartment too takes on a kind of independent existence. It is in itself a work of art, and the layout becomes thus a description of its physical, one might even say sculptural contours. In its independence, it appears in the most general terms. All reference to precise details of the furnishings is carefully avoided. None of these priceless objects is isolated, set apart, or revealed in specific, concrete terms. It is the apartment as a whole, as an organic unit, which is significant, and which is imbued with a kind of life. An apartment has the ability to be congenial, to attract or repel, just as people do. Its elegance is Michèle de Burne's elegance, its life is her life, its coldness is her coldness. Its self-sufficiency is nowhere more evident than in the much discussed visit by Prédolé, the renowned sculptor. He is captivated by it but totally oblivious to Madame de Burne. Her domicile has become her rival. Significantly, she is successful with her admirers as much because of the charms of her abode as because of her personal appeal. Men constantly return because the *décor* welcomes them, in its impersonal way, as much as she does herself. And at the centre of it all sits Michèle de Burne, surrounded by her Persian hangings and studying herself in her three-panelled mirror. Description again takes on an added dimension. It is now not only a means of maintaining objectivity while exploring a character, but also a manifestation of that unseen world. What we have seen happening here is the gradual evolution of Maupassant from a derivative, objective novelist, to a much more original position in which the traditional techniques of that objectivity are put to a new, deeper and more probing test. Reality is not a kind of constant, a means by which human behaviour can be exteriorized and transfixed for posterity, but is as much a living thing, as capable of modification, even of life or death as the humans who inhabit it. Michèle de Burne's apartment and Olivier Bertin's studio constitute much more than objectifications of their owner's make-up. They are active participants in their lives, endowed with a strength, a life. What they say is directed at least as much to the characters in the book as to the reader. Whereas "Les Peuples" told us *about* Jeanne, these rooms speak not only about their inhabitants, but much more distinctly *to* them and to their associates.

In the travel context as well this living aspect of the countryside is stressed, as Mariolle travels by train towards Avranches and his rendez-

vous with Michèle. The relationship with the world is not simply a
vicarious experience. It is a *living* relationship, vital and meaningful.

On touchait à la fin de juillet[c'était la saison vigoureuse où cette terre, nourrice
puissante, fait épanouir sa sève et sa vie.[19]

Michèle de Burne's reluctant cab-ride to Auteuil makes no reference of
any kind to the world beyond her window. Isolated as she is, the scene is
a kind of self-analysis rendered possible by the very setting. But what
about the people of the novel? Here too the visual element is dominant.

André Mariolle's description does not appear to introduce the first
incident of *Notre coeur*, but rather, concludes it.

De taille plutôt grande, portant la barbe noire courte sur les joues et finement
allongée en pointe sur le menton, des cheveux un peu grisonnants mais joliment
crépus, il regardait bien en face, avec des yeux bruns, clairs, vifs, méfiants et
un peu durs.[20]

Again the same interest in form is visible, combined with an attention
to the eyes of the subject which we have already noticed. But the paragraph is contained in a lengthier passage dealing first of all with his
background – social position, tastes, interests, then his appearance, and
it ends with reference to more hidden values – his judgement and his
intelligence. Maupassant has always concerned himself with these factors
to a greater or a lesser degree, but it is evident here that the unseen elements take precedence over the physical appearance, and the two factors
are bound together by the eyes, which terminate the physical description.
The progression from the earlier works is clear. The identical technique
insofar as description is concerned can be noticed in the introduction of
the sculptor Prédolé, who it must be remembered, is not a central figure
of the plot of the novel.

Il parut enfin. On fut surpris. C'était un gros homme d'un âge indéterminable,
avec des épaules de paysan, une forte tête aux traits accentués, couverte de
cheveux et de barbe grisâtres, un nez puissant, des lèvres charnues, l'air timide
et embarrassé. Il portait ses bras un peu loin du corps, avec une sorte de gauche-
rie, attribuable sans doute aux énormes mains qui sortaient des manches. Elles
étaient larges, épaisses avec des doigts velus et musculeux, des mains d'hercule
ou de boucher; et elles semblaient maladroites, lentes, gênées d'être là, impos-
sibles à cacher.
  Mais la figure était éclairée par des yeux limpides, gris et perçants, d'une
vivacité extraordinaire. Eux seuls semblaient vivre en cet homme pesant. Ils

[19] Maupassant, *Notre coeur, Oeuvres complètes*, p. 73.
[20] Maupassant, *Notre coeur*, pp. 4–5.

regardaient, scrutaient, fouillaient, jetaient partout leur éclair aigu rapide et mobile et on sentait qu'une vive et grande intelligence animait ce regard curieux.[21]

Notice the same progression of interest. The general physical description, in harmony with the artist's mode of expression, is essentially sculptural, proceeding as it does from weight and form and reflecting both is peasant origins and his profession. It concludes with the eyes, thus linking it with the interior life of the mind. Again the exterior is only a function of the interior being, and the hands and eyes speak with great eloquence. The description is indeed stylized to arouse the reader's attention to Prédolé's deeper values. Although the passage introducing this relatively minor character is briefer than that referring to Mariolle, the purely descriptive aspect is much more detailed than in the case of the hero. One cannot say that description varies in proportion to the importance of the character presented, but rather in proportion to the depth of that character in the mind of the author. Sullivan shows very convincingly Maupassant's relationships to Lamarthe the successful novelist, Prédolé the sculptor and Mariolle the dilettante, three distinct artistic types. If Prédolé is his unrealized ideal, as Sullivan suggests, then the apparently undue attention paid to him here is easily justifiable in personal terms, and demonstrates conclusively that while maintaining the techniques of objectivity, Maupassant quite consciously displaces the emphasis in order to modify its artistic function. The author lets Gaston de Lamarthe define the aesthetic problem:

Avec ces deux sens très simples, une *vision* nette des *formes* et une *intuition* instinctive des *dessous*, il donnait à ses livres, où n'apparaissaient aucune des intentions *ordinaires* des écrivains psychologues, mais qui *avaient l'air* de morceaux d'existence humaine arrachés à la réalité, la couleur, le ton, l'aspect, le mouvement de la vie même.[22] [Italics mine]

If, as Sullivan does, we take Lamarthe as a partially objectivized version of Maupassant himself, the descriptive passages and their functions become clear. Not a realist, like Flaubert he wishes only to convey a feeling of reality. Rooted in the physical, his art tries to leap the bounds, not into Flaubert's pure style, but into a psychological reality which will have genuine life.

However it is Michèle de Burne who best illustrates the purpose of physical description in the novel. She is first seen through Mariolle's

---

[21] Maupassant, *Notre coeur*, pp. 209–10.
[22] Maupassant, *Notre coeur*, pp. 17–18.

eyes, bathed in the glow of a nearby lamp. Briefly, the same elements are present – face, hair, contour of mouth and cheeks, with the eyes and their enigmatic expression as the culminating point. Many of the same details reappear in Mariolle's eyes shortly thereafter, with the addition of the velvety texture of her skin. Her profile draws his attention a little later and we have reference to her figure.

One cannot doubt that he is captivated by her physical beauty. If Prédolé is a kind of ideal artist, I think it is safe to say that Michèle de Burne represents a very closely related ideal, the ideal artistic product. And she is acutely conscious of her physical charms.

As the portrait dominated *Fort comme la mort*, so Michèle de Burne's beauty controls the development of *Notre coeur*, and again the descriptive element does much more than convince the reader of the physical contours of the work. It is the vital key to the interior, the psychological for which the author has been so frequently criticized.

By their very nature the unfinished novels can furnish us only with a minimal amount of material which will substantiate an argument. Obviously Maupassant selects again well known settings for his writings, the Riviera in "L'âme étrangère", Normandy in "L'angélus", and one can only suppose that the descriptive material they would have contained would share something with that which we have already observed.

But there is of course a third genre which Maupassant explored and which must be reviewed before any real systemization of material can be seriously attempted.

IV

THE TRAVEL BOOKS

This third major grouping of Maupassant's published material, by its very nature furnishes us with an abundance of descriptive material. The world of sights, of smells, of sounds, occupies the writer's attention at considerable length here, and should therefore be reviewed with some care. Unlike the fictional writings, these works more clearly represent first-hand experience on Maupassant's part and can therefore be taken as more immediate revelations of the author's personal preoccupations. Yet one must constantly bear in mind that these three volumes are, after all, published works, to some extent re-workings of newspaper articles, and therefore their immediacy of impact is quite possibly tempered by more artistic, that is to say more "objective" criteria on Maupassant's part, not to mention the more practical modifications that publishing can make necessary.

We will not look at them in their order of publication, since an attempt to establish any dynamic, that is to say evolutionary interpretation of their importance is futile. Parts of all three were published separately at various times, thus rendering chronological considerations rather open to conjecture. It is obviously more useful to try to establish just what captivates Maupassant's eye and to see if there is any possible means by which to catalogue the essentially descriptive passages.

The Riviera, Italy, North Africa, these are the places to which the author travelled, and which he records for us in the three volumes. Landscapes, seascapes, cityscapes abound in the works. As substantiated in the fiction we have reviewed in the last two chapters, here too Maupassant is strongly attracted by the panoramic view, in which a sense of vastness, of the enormity of man's world, is strongly evoked. Such passages abound of course in *Sur l'eau*, in which we are treated to detailed studies of the Mediterranean coast as he sails by. For example:

La chaîne des monts correctement et nettement dessinée se découpe au matin sur le ciel bleu, d'un bleu idéal de plage méridionale. Mais le soir, les flancs boisés des côtes s'assombrissent et plaquent une tache noire sur un ciel de feu, sur un ciel invraisemblablement dramatique et rouge. Je n'ai jamais vu nulle part ces couchers de soleil de féerie, ces incendies de l'horizon tout entier, ces explosions de nuages, cette mise en scène habile et superbe, ce renouvellement quotidien d'effets excessifs et magnifiques qui forcent l'admiration et feraient un peu sourire s'ils étaient peints par des hommes.[1]

One type of pattern already begins to emerge. We have witnessed descriptions of similar geographic settings both in the novels *(Bel-Ami)* and in the short stories ("Rose"). But of course *Sur l'eau* deals exclusively with this region, and much variety in its presentation can be discovered.

La longue côte rouge tombe dans l'eau bleue qu'elle fait paraître violette. Elle est bizarre, hérissée, jolie, avec des pointes, des golfes innombrables, des rochers capricieux et coquets, mille fantaisies de montagne admirée. Sur ses flancs, les forêts de sapins montent jusqu'aux cimes de granit qui ressemblent à des châteaux, à des villes, à des armées de pierres courant l'une après l'autre. Et la mer est si limpide à son pied, on distingue par places les fonds de sable et les fonds d'herbes.[2]

The mountainous landscape so vivid in the mind of anyone familiar with the Riviera is presented by Maupassant with great vividness:

Maintenant toute la chaîne des Alpes apparaît, vague, monstrueuse, qui menace la mer, vague de granit couronnée de neige dont tous les sommets pointus semblent des jaillissements d'écume immobile et figée. Et le soleil se lève derrière ces glaces, sur qui sa lumière tombe en coulée d'argent.[3]

Studies in form and colour, these panoramic views of the Provençal coast let nothing escape the keen eye of the observer. The coastal cities too are conjured up by Maupassant, the verbal painter. This is what we see of Antibes:

Devant moi, Antibes apparaissait vaguement dans l'ombre éclaircie, avec ses deux tours debout sur la ville bâtie en cône et qu'enferment encore les vieux murs de Vauban.[4]

Saint-Tropez too is brought into view with the same enormous sweep:

Saint-Tropez, à l'entrée de l'admirable golfe nommé jadis golfe de Grimaud, est la capitale de ce petit royaume sarrasin dont presque tous les villages, bâtis au sommet de pics qui les mettaient à l'abri des attaques, sont encore pleins

---

[1] Maupassant, *Sur l'eau, Oeuvres complètes*, p. 11.
[2] *Sur l'eau*, p. 62.
[3] *Sur l'eau*, p. 10.
[4] *Sur l'eau*, p. 6.

de maisons mauresques avec leurs arcades, leurs étroites fenêtres et leurs cours
intérieures où ont poussé de hauts palmiers qui dépassent à présent les toits.[5]

All these passages would seem to suggest a taste on the part of the author
for the all-embracive, the broad evocative vision in which the general
would seem to take precedence over the particular. Such panoramas are
present, as we have noted, in Maupassant's fictional writings as well,
and indeed, in the frame of reference of this particular chapter are by no
means limited to *Sur l'eau*.

Au soleil as any reader of Maupassant will know, deals rather specifically with Algeria, and while the descriptive details will of necessity vary
considerably from the mountainous coastline of south-eastern France,
the overall patterns remain surprisingly similar. For example, this brief
description of the Atlas Mountains:

Quand on regarde l'Atlas, de l'immense plaine de la Mitidja, on aperçoit une
coupure gigantesque qui fend la montagne dans la direction du sud. C'est
comme si un coup de hache l'eût ouverte. Cette trouée s'appelle la gorge de la
Chiffa. C'est par là . . .[6]

The sea has of course been replaced by the plain, but the mountainous
backdrop which limits it gives to the scene the same basic skeletal
structure as heretofore observed. The same feeling of vastness, same
enormity, the same perspective and depth of vision characterize a whole
series of studies of the Algerian landscape.

Ces plaines d'Afrique sont surprenantes.
   Elles paraissent nues et plates comme un parquet, et elles sont, au contraire,
sans cesse traversées d'ondulations, comme une mer après la tempête, qui,
de loin, semble toute calme parce que la surface est lisse, mais que remuent
de longs soulèvements tranquilles. Les pentes de ces vagues de terre sont
insensibles; jamais on ne perd de vue les montagnes de l'horizon, mais dans
l'ondulation parallèle, à deux kilomètres de vous, une armée pourrait se cacher
et vous ne la verriez point.[7]

We can even find in this work a passage which deals with that moment
in time which so fascinates Maupassant – the sunset. And here again
a striking study in colour, painted in vast splashes on a limitless horizon
is the dominant characteristic of the paragraph:

Le soleil, près de disparaître, se teintait de rouge, au milieu d'un ciel orange.
Et partout, du nord au midi, de l'est à l'ouest, les files de montagnes dressées

[5] *Sur l'eau*, pp. 117–18.
[6] Maupassant, *Au soleil, Oeuvres complètes*, p. 56.
[7] *Au soleil*, pp. 84–85.

sous mes yeux jusqu'aux extrêmes limites du regard étaient roses, d'un rose extravagant comme les plumes de flamants. On eût dit une féerique apothéose d'opéra d'une surprenante et invraisemblable couleur, quelque chose de factice, de forcé et contre nature, et de singulièrement admirable cependant.[8]

La vie errante too contains passages which are structurally parallel. In the early chapters of this work we return to the "côte d'azur" and find passages almost identical to those of *Sur l'eau*. For example:

Ici, la terre est tellement captivante, qu'elle fait presque oublier la mer. La ville est abritée par l'angle creux des deux montagnes. Un vallon les sépare qui va vers Gênes. Sur ces deux côtes, d'innombrables petits chemins entre deux murs de pierres, hauts d'un mètre environ, se croisent, montent et descendent, vont et viennent, étroits, pierreux, en ravins et en escaliers, et séparent d'innombrables champs ou plutôt des jardins d'oliviers et de figuiers qu'enguirlandent des pampres rouges. A travers les feuillages brulés des vignes grimpées dans les arbres, on aperçoit à perte de vue la mer bleue, des caps rouges, des villages blancs, des bois de sapins sur les pentes, et les grands sommets de granit gris. Devant les maisons, recontrées de place en place, les femmes font de la dentelle.[9]

It would be very dangerous indeed to presume that all the sea- and landscapes of Maupassant followed the identical pattern. But the striking parallels in perspective, point of view and method of presentation of these passages, combined with certain trends already mentioned in the novels and short stories is rather convincing evidence of Maupassant's own tastes and preferences with regard to the world he observes. But he is a complex and sensitive individual, capable of great variety and surprising imaginative power. There is another type of descriptive passage which is, I think, still more revealing of his capacity to observe and evoke.

The horizons viewed so far have been panoramic, but constantly limited by immense, mountainous and impenetrable backdrops, and revealing a foreground dominated by the horizontal. Maupassant's visual depth leads him as well to view the scene which is vast, uninterrupted and seemingly endless. Again both sea- and landscapes bear witness to this fascination with the horizon.

The sea, with its all-pervasive horizontality, its view of the infinite, is of course the backdrop for much of *Sur l'eau*, as the title would suggest. It somehow provides Maupassant both with an internal peace and the suggestion of something beyond which is disquieting.

---

[8] *Au soleil*, p. 84.
[9] Maupassant, *La vie errante, Oeuvres complètes*, pp. 45–47.

Je me lève et monte sur le pont. Il es trois heures du matin; la mer est plate, le ciel infini ressemble à une immense voûte d'ombre ensemencée de graines de feu. Une brise très légère souffle de terre.[10]

Surprisingly perhaps, it is in *Au soleil* that the author evokes this series of associations perhaps most succinctly. Crossing the Mediterranean, he presents a scene reminiscent of "La peur":

Puis on remonte sur le pont. Rien que la mer, la mer calme, sans un frisson, et dorée par la lune. Le lourd bateau paraît glisser dessus, laissant derrière lui un long sillage bouillonnant, où l'eau battue semble du feu liquide.

Le ciel s'étale sur nos têtes, d'un noir bleuâtre, ensemencé d'astres que voile par instants l'énorme panache de fumée vomie par la cheminée; et le petit fanal en haut du mât a l'air d'une grosse étoile se promenant parmi les autres. On n'entend rien que le ronflement de l'hélice dans les profondeurs du navire. Qu'elles sont charmantes, les heures tranquilles du soir sur le pont d'un bâtiment qui fuit![11]

The sea is a great consolation to Maupassant, a source of peace, a means of isolation from the pressures of the popular and successful artist's life, and of course a means of flight – a flight which Pierre takes advantage of *(Pierre et Jean)* and which is denied to Jeanne *(Une vie)*.

And the theme of flight can also carry with it that fear of the unknown which we have already noted in Maupassant's view of the world. This is clearly expressed in a passage drawn from *Sur l'eau.*

Nous voilà glissant sur l'onde, vers la pleine mer. La côte disparaît; on ne voit plus rien autour de nous que du noir. C'est là une sensation, une émotion troublante et délicieuse: s'enfoncer dans cette nuit vide, dans ce silence, sur cette eau, loin de tout. Il semble qu'on quitte le monde, qu'on ne doit plus jamais arriver nulle part, qu'il n'y aura plus de rivage, qu'il n'y aura pas de jour ....[12]

But of course the sea is not always liquid. In the sand of Algeria it again dominates. The archetypal associations of the sea with totality, chaos, the infinite, and indeed with death are easily transferable to the desert. There can be no doubt of this parallelism in Maupassant's mind:

Le lendemain on traversa les dunes. On eût dit l'Océan devenu poussière au milieu d'un ouragan; une tempête silencieuse de vagues énormes, immobiles, en sable jaune. Elles sont hautes comme des collines, ces cagues, inégales, différentes, soulevées tout à fait comme des flots déchaînés, mais plus grandes encore et striées comme de la moire. Sur cette mer furieuse, muette et sans mouvement, le dévorant soleil du sud verse sa flamme implacable et directe.[13]

[10] *Sur l'eau,* p. 60.
[11] *Au soleil,* pp. 11–12.
[12] *Sur l'eau,* pp. 60–61.
[13] *Au soleil,* p. 124.

And like the sea, the desert has associations with the world of dreams, the world of the beyond. The panoramic, the all-embracive view of the world reaches a kind of apogee in these perceptions of infinity. It would appear that such views, by their very unity and lack of limitation, have a peculiar fascination for Maupassant, a fascination which is based on an extremely fragile communication. Herein lies a kind of absolute, an absolute which, as he suggests in the last line of the following quotation is too easily destroyed:

Elle est monotone, toujours pareille, toujours calcinée et morte, cette terre; et, là, pourtant, on ne désire rien, on n'aspire à rien. Ce paysage calme, ruisselant de lumière et désolé, suffit à l'oeil, suffit à la pensée, satisfait les sens et le rêve, parce qu'il est complet, *absolu*, et qu'on ne pourrait le concevoir autrement. La rare verdure même y choque comme une chose fausse, blessante et dure.[14]

Gone are nature's barriers, the striking mountain verticals which deny that total view. The horizon is uninterrupted and life appears complete. But this is, as one must bear in mind with the sea as well, a viciously hostile environment, an environment in which man cannot survive for long. Man's world, the world of society and civilization has quite different proportions. Maupassant's all-pervasive eye takes note of this world as well as that of nature.

Illustrations of this fact have already been seen in the passages which deal with the Mediterranean coast. Towns and cities caught between mountain and sea are frequent splashes of form and colour which stand out vividly against the natural backdrop. We see them from a kind of bird's eye point of view, a perspective in which their overall impact takes precedence over particular details. And such tendencies are by no means exceptional. In the course of his Sicilian travels, described in considerable detail in *La vie errante* he includes the following broad vista of Palermo:

La forme de Palerme est très particulière. La ville, couchée au milieu d'un vaste cirque de montagnes nues, d'un gris bleu nuancé parfois de rouge, est divisée en quatre parties par deux grandes rues droites qui se coupent en croix au milieu. De ce carrefour, on aperçoit, par trois côtés, la montagne, là-bas, au bout de ces immenses corridors de maisons, et, par le quatrième, on voit la mer, une tache bleue, d'un bleu cru, qui semble tout près, comme si la ville était tombée dedans![15]

Here again the dominant pattern emerges. Maupassant's attention is drawn to the broad, to the general view of a kind of totality which is

[14] *Au soleil*, pp. 85–86.
[15] *La vie errante*, pp. 59–60.

held together by an underlying visual structure. This is not a fleeting impression of the external world, but a presentation of it which contains within it some intrinsic organization, a kind of organic unity in which the component parts are carefully, and one might say aesthetically fitted together. One of the most striking cityscapes in Maupassant is also to be found in *La vie errante*, in a rather lengthy passage which again is devoted to the general pattern formed by the component units. The visual effect of the panoramic view of Tunis is indeed most vivid:

Pour en bien découvrir l'ensemble, il faut monter sur une colline voisine. Les Arabes comparent Tunis à un burnous étendu; et cette comparaison est juste. La ville s'étale dans la plaine, soulevée légèrement par les ondulations de la terre, qui font saillir par places les bords de cette grande tache de maisons pâles d'où surgissent les dômes des mosquées et les clochers des minarets. A peine distingue-t-on, à peine imagine-t-on que ce sont là des maisons, tant cette tache blanche est compacte, continue et rampante. Autour d'elle, trois lacs qui, sous le dur soleil d'Orient, brillent comme des plaines d'acier. Au nord, au loin, la Sebkraer-Bouan; à l'ouest, la Sebkra-Seldjoum, apercue pardessus la ville; au sud, le grand lac Bahira ou lac de Tunis; puis, en remontant vers le nord, la mer, le golfe profond, pareil lui-même à un lac dans son cadre éloigné de montagnes.[16]

There is in the Maupassantian description, of sea, sand or indeed of the urban complex, a structural kind of symmetry. Here we have a city which is evoked as a central series of pale undulations, bordered on all four sides by glimpses of water to which the almost omnipresent mountains form a dramatic backdrop. It suggest that Maupassant's view of the outdoor world is hardly what one might call in the strictest sense realistic. Combined with this striking penchant for the panoramic, there would appear to be an almost innate concern with the essential organization of material which will at the same time heighten its visual impact and provide some kind of aesthetic harmony, providing in this way a more satisfying aesthetic experience. The deeper consequences of these patterns must be viewed in the broader context of Maupassant's works, and must therefore be reserved for later study.

As with both the short story and the novel, so too the three travel books provide us with descriptive material of a more inward looking nature, although, given the basic orientation of these volumes, examples of this type are understandably much less frequent. Buildings range in significance from the celebrated cathedral of Pisa to the Arab tents of *Au soleil*. In the former case, Maupassant seeks to convey the overall

[16] *La vie errante*, pp. 146–47.

impact of the building by a concentration on its proportions, its lines and forms, that is to say, its visible structure:

Mais on demeure tellement surpris et captivé par les irréprochables proportions, par le charme intraduisible des lignes, des formes et de la façade décorée, en bas, de pilastres reliés par des arcades, en haut, de quatre galeries de colonnettes plus petites d'étage en étage, que la séduction de ce monument reste en nous comme celle d'un poème admirable, comme une émotion trouvée.[17]

In the latter, the author again seeks to conjure up the total image of the tents as succinctly as possible:

On s'imagine généralement que les tentes arabes sont blanches, éclatantes au soleil. Elles sont au contraire d'un brun sale, rayé de jaune. Leur tissu très épais, en poil de chameau et de chèvre, semble grossier. La tente est fort basse (on s'y tient tout juste debout) et très étendue. Des piquets la supportent d'une façon assez irrégulière, et tous les bords sont relevés ce qui permet à l'air de circuler librement dessous.[18]

In these books we enter only a few buildings with Maupassant. Such incidents can be painted in a few simple lines to describe, for example, an Arab establishment in Algiers:

Les murs sont blancs, les tapis, par terre, sont rouges; les hommes sont blancs, ou rouges ou bleus avec d'autres couleurs encore, suivant la fantaisie de leurs vêtements d'apparat, mais tous sont largement drapés, d'allure fière; et ils reçoivent sur la tête et les épaules la lumière douce tombant des lustres.[19]

Here again it is quite obvious that it is the total effect, the real atmosphere which Maupassant seeks to capture.
On the other hand interiors can be the subject of much more elaborate study in which the effect is carefully calculated. During the Tunisian trip, Maupassant views with great delight the mosque of Djama-Kebir and finds in its interior the subject matter for a most detailed study:

Devant nous apparaît un temple démesuré, qui a l'air d'une forêt sacrée, car cent quatre-vingts colonnes d'onyx, de porphyre et de marbre supportent les voûtes de dix-sept nefs correspondant aux dix-sept portes.
    Le regard s'arrête, se perd dans cet emmêlement profond de minces piliers ronds d'une élégance irréprochable, dont toutes les nuances se mêlent et s'harmonisent, et dont les chapiteaux byzantins, de l'école africaine et de l'école orientale, sont d'un travail rare et d'une diversité infinie. Quelques-uns

[17] *La vie errante*, p. 17.
[18] *Au soleil*, p. 88.
[19] *Au soleil*, pp. 53–54.

m'ont paru d'une beauté parfaite. Le plus original peut-être représente un palmier tordu par le vent.

A mesure que j'avance en cette demeure divine, toutes les colonnes semblent se déplacer, tourner autour de moi et former des figures variées d'une régularité changeante.[20]

A detailed description, without doubt, but one in which again it is the total effect which has immediate impact as we see from the opening lines. The accumulation of carefully noted details comes after the initial impact and not before – a fact which will be most significant in an analysis of Maupassant's creative imagination.

Man's world, the world of things, be they natural or man-made, would not be complete of course without man himself. Just as Maupassant's world is inhabited by people whose description he reveals so skillfully to his reader, so these travel books are full of Frenchmen, Arabs, Jews, Italians and numerous other lesser groups. And I intentionally use the word *groups*. For individuals rarely stand out visually in these volumes and hardly ever dominate the narrative. Again it would appear that he is attracted by a more general view, in an attempt to communicate the atmosphere which he had experienced himself. In this regard, two important passages stand out from all the rest. The first of these deals extensively with the Jewesses of Tunis. Women, one must note, have a particular and well-documented interest for Maupassant. His reputation in this regard is still very much alive.

Leur teint pâle, un peu maladif, d'une délicatesse lumineuse, leurs traits fins, ces traits si doux d'une race ancienne et fatiguée, dont le sang jamais ne fut rajeuni, leurs yeux sombres sous les fronts clairs, qu'écrase la masse noire, épaisse, pesante, des cheveux ébouriffés, et leur allure souple quand elles courent d'une porte à l'autre, emplissent le quartier juif de Tunis d'une longue vision de petites Salomés troublantes.

Puis elles songent à l'époux. Alors commence l'inconcevable gavage qui fera d'elles des monstres. Immobiles maintenant, après avoir pris chaque matin la boulette d'herbes apéritives qui surexcitent l'estomac, elles passent les journées entières à manger des pâtes épaisses qui les enflent incroyablement. Les seins se gonflent, les ventres ballonnent, les croupes s'arrondissent, les cuisses s'écartent, séparées par la bouffissure; les poignets et les chevilles disparaissent sous une lourde colée de chair. Et les amateurs accourent, les jugent, les comparent, les admirent comme dans un concours d'animaux gras. Voilà comme elles sont belles, désirables, charmantes, les énormes filles à marier![21]

[20] *La vie errante*, pp. 216–17.
[21] *La vie errante*, pp. 151–52.

It is perhaps significant to note that the entire passage is constructed in the plural. At any rate there can be no questioning of the fact that the trend is again towards the broad and the general – a stylization which suggests a kind of systemization, that is to say a pattern which is at least valid in this context.

The second passage which comes to mind can be found in *Sur l'eau* in which Maupassant deals descriptively, that is to say visually, with the entire human race:

Mais aujourd'hui, ô Apollon, regardons la race humaine s'agiter dans les fêtes! Les enfants ventrus dès le berceau, déformés par l'étude précoce, abrutis par le collège qui leur use le corps à quinze ans en courbaturant leur esprit avant qu'il soit nubile, arrivant à l'adolescence, avec des membres mal poussés, mal attachés, dont les proportions normales ne sont jamais conservées.

Et contemplons la rue, les gens qui trottent avec leurs vêtements sales! Quant au paysan! Seigneur Dieu! Allons voir le paysan dans les champs, l'homme souche, noué, long comme une perche, toujours tors, courbé, plus affreux que les types barbares qu'on voit aux musées d'anthropologie.

Et rappelons-nous combien les nègres sont beaux de forme, sinon de face, ces hommes des bronze, grands et souples, combien les arabes sont élégants de tournure et de figure![22]

This is a kind of visual panorama very much in keeping with what we witnessed in the other passages. Here as well there is a broad pattern, a kind of skeletal framework, that is to say an essential form by which man's world can be evoked imaginatively. Mankind's infinite variety is suggested by the multiplicity of shapes in which he appears.

Maupassant the "naturalist", or indeed the "realist" becomes thus a very stylized writer indeed, in which artistic deformations of perceived phenomena would appear to fall into some kind of overall pattern. Such aesthetic preoccupations on his part are by no means the reader's fancy, for he himself talks about the aesthetic impact of the visual on two very significant occasions, both of which are to be found in *La vie errante*. And it is here, in a deeply artistic experience, that man attempts to go beyond the visible contours of a perceived reality:

Et on songe, en l'admirant, au bélier de bronze de Syracuse, le plus beau morceau du musée de Palerme, qui, lui aussi, semble contenir toute l'animalité du monde. La bête puissante est couchée, le corps sur ses pattes et la tête tournée à gauche. Et cette tête d'animal semble une tête de dieu, de dieu bestial, impur et superbe. Le front est large et frisé, les yeux écartés, le nez en bosse, long, fort et ras, d'une prodigieuse expression brutale. Les cornes, rejetées en arrière

[22] *Sur l'eau*, p. 105.

tombent, s'enroulent et se recourbent, écartant leurs pointes aiguës sous les oreilles minces qui ressemblent elles-mêmes à deux cornes. Et le regard de la bête vous pénêtre, stupide, inquiétant et dur. On sent le fauve en approchant de ce bronze.[23]

What Maupassant sees in this statue is a structural harmony, a formal unity which suggests by its very animality something greater than itself. Man's world is a series of component parts, but in that moment of synthesis, of artistic harmony, it must become greater than the sum of those parts. It is at that moment that the limitlessness of sand and sky, that "absolu" which Maupassant experiences in the desert scene, is opened up in all its fullness. It is an intense visual experience, and I cannot overstress the word *visual:*

Une oeuvre d'art n'est supérieure que si elle est, en même temps, un symbole et l'expression exacte d'une réalité.

Devant la tête de la Joconde, on se sent obsédé par on ne sait quelle tentation d'amour énervant et mystique. Il existe aussi des femmes vivantes dont les yeux nous donnent ce rêve d'irréalisable et mystérieuse tendresse. On cherche en elles autre chose derrière ce qui est, parce qu'elles paraissent contenir et exprimer un peu de l'insaisissable idéal. Nous le poursuivons sans jamais l'atteindre, derrière toutes les surprises de la beauté qui semble contenir de la pensée, dans l'infini du regard, qui n'est qu'une nuance de l'iris, dans le charme du sourire venu d'un pli de la lèvre et d'un éclair d'émail, dans la grâce du mouvement né du hasard et de l'harmonie des formes.

Ainsi les poètes, impuissants décrocheurs d'étoiles, ont toujours été tourmentés par la soif de l'amour mystique.[24]

The symbolic and the literal, the factual and the intuitive, the documented and the imagined – herein lies the dichotomy of Maupassant's world which he struggles endlessly to reconcile. This is the source of tragedy; this is also the source of the energy which never ceases to drive him on in the search. We must now attempt, with the facts available to this point, to discover the nature of that quest.

[23] *La vie errante*, p. 126.
[24] *La vie errante*, pp. 121–22.

V

THE OUTWARD PROBE

From all the examination of the presence of description in the works of Guy de Maupassant which we have examined up to this point there emerges one dominating problem, a problem by no means unique to him, but one which he wrestles with in a special way, suited to this own tastes, his own philosophical and aesthetic formation. This is of course the old question of the relationship between man as a thinking being and the physical world in which he lives. A distinction basic to Schopenhauer between the external world of objective reality and the internal world of the individual is present in Maupassant's mind throughout his creative period. He states it himself on several occasions, ad most unequivocally in *Sur l'eau:*

Consolez-vous, dit-on, dans l'amour de la science et des arts.
   Mais on ne voit donc pas que nous sommes toujours emprisonnés en nous-mêmes, sans parvenir à sortir de nous, condamnés à traîner le boulet de notre rêve sans essor![1]

It is in the final analysis a problem of communication. What relationship can exist between man, the slave of the Schopenhauerian will, and the world in which he finds himself. The intensely tragic and pessimistic feeling of individual solitude can however, according to Schopenhauer, be momentarily lifted by chance circumstance or by a kind of interior harmony which will alleviate the power of the will and permit the individual to find repose.

   There is in Maupassant's fiction a significant number of themes and images which, when viewed systematically, offer some suggestion of how this dilemma is approached by him. Since the tragic situation is one which is by nature intensely personal, the images and themes involved represent quests on the part of the individual to discover himself.

[1]   Maupassant, *Sur l'eau, Oeuvres complètes,* p. 42.

Following the pattern already established in this study of distinguishing between the exterior physical world and its indoor counterpart, let us attack the problem by looking first at how Maupassant describes the countryside. As a wedding party returns on foot to the farm after the ceremony, the author offers us a glimpse of the rich Norman landscape:

La grande ferme paraissait attendre là-bas, au bout de la voûte de pommiers. Une sorte de fumée sortait de la porte et des fenêtres ouvertes, et une odeur épaisse de mangeaille s'exhalait du vaste bâtiment, de toutes ses ouvertures, des murs eux-mêmes.[2]

Incidental to the main interest of this tale, which deals more specifically with the wedding feast and an amusing prank played on the young couple during the night, this relatively brief descriptive passage is however indicative of Maupassant's technique. The interest has been almost entirely devoted to colour, contrasting the natural surroundings with the brilliant dress of the members of the procession, and with the mention of the farm in the passage cited, moves on to the sense of smell. Maupassant is giving to his reader an immediate impression of the world in its brief and fleeting moment, albeit a certain permanency is suggested by certain structural references in the first sentence.

The colour contrast with the much longer description of a winter scene which appears in "Conte de Noël" (1882) is quite striking. Form here is reduced to the square shape of the farmyards and the thin wisps of smoke rising from the chimneys. Everything is rendered motionless, as if the snowfall has killed activity and we have this time an impression of whiteness and death in a vastness punctuated here and there by hedges, trees and buildings.

"Le Père Judas" (1883), introduced as it is by a descriptive passage, demonstrates similar tendencies. The circle of trees is the only form specifically mentioned, and the dominant impression is one of immensity and desolation, interrupted only by a single house. But these are all relatively short passages. A clearer illustration of this method can be seen in "Clair de lune"[3], in a series of related paragraphs as the Abbé Marignan ponders about God's creation. He first views his immediate surroundings:

Dans son petit jardin, tout baigné de douce lumière, ses arbres fruitiers, rangés en ligne, dessinaient en ombre sur l'allée leurs grêles membres de bois à peine

[2] Maupassant, "Farce normande", Contes de la bécasse, Oeuvres complètes, p.89. First published in Le Gil Blas (August 8, 1882).
[3] Maupassant, "Clair de lune", Clair de lune, Oeuvres complètes, p. 1. First published in Le Gil Blas (October 19, 1882).

vêtus de verdure; tandis que le chèvrefeuille géant grimpé sur le mur de sa maison, exhalait des souffles délicieux et comme sucrés, faisait flotter dans le soir tiède et clair une espèce d'âme parfumée.[4]

The description expands as the priest moves farther out in the night, and we begin to see the entire plain inundated in "cette lueur caressante". The music of nature, the short metallic note of the toad and the distant nightingale combine in a dreamy harmony. It is a music made for love, for seduction.

Gradually the vision expands. Over the curves of the river and the long line of poplars rises a fine white vapour which blurs outlines slightly as the moon's white rays filter through.

There can be no doubt that we have here an impressionistic presentation, bathed as the landscape is in the romantic glow of the moon. It is this play of light that takes precedence over the serpentine forms of the river and the striking verticals of the trees. Combined with this, the chorus of wild life, the pleasant odours of plant life, render the whole scene immensely appealing to the senses. Like previous illustrations, these passages show an all-encompassing vastness, a kind of panoramic propensity on the part of Maupassant. It is the capturing of a fleeting moment in which all elements blend in a full rich chord.

Like the Abbé Marignon, Jeanne de Lamare too views the countryside in the light of the moon. From her window she looks down on the lawn, the night of her arrival at "Les Peuples":

C'était d'abord, en face d'elle, un large gazon jaune comme du beurre sous la lumière nocturne. Deux arbres géants se dressait aux pointes devant le château, un platane au nord, un tilleul au sud.

Tout au bout de la grande étendue d'herbe un petit bois en bosquet terminait ce domaine garanti des ouragans du large par cinq rangs d'ormes antiques, tordus, rasés, rongés, taillés en pente comme un toit par le vent de mer toujours déchaîné.

Cette espèce de parc était borné à droite et à gauche par deux longues avenues de peupliers démesurés, appelés *peuples* en Normandie, qui séparaient la résidence des maîtres des deux fermes y attenantes, ...[5]

The passage opens with a definition of the light under which the scene is viewed, and again an impression of limitlessness is conveyed. Form here is a meaningful part of the description. Indeed, after the initial attack, the entire view is conjured up from this standpoint – the shape and arrangement of the trees, their position and size, as if they were the frame

---

[4] "Clair de lune", pp. 8–9.
[5] Maupassant, *Une vie*, pp. 17–18.

in which the scene is contained. Although immensity is a factor, it is clearly not the vastness of infinity. There are vertical barriers in every direction, elements which have not been absent from most of the other passages reviewed. If infinity is suggested there are commonly attempts to limit it, to grasp it.

Chapter Five of this same novel offers a variety of illustrations of landscape description as Jeanne and Julien travel in Corsica, of which the following is perhaps one of the most effective:

Le pays inculte semblait tout nu, les flancs des côtes étaient couverts de hautes herbes, jaunes en cette saison brûlante ...

Le mordant parfum des plantes aromatiques dont l'île est couverte semblait épaissir l'air; et la route allait s'élevant lentement au milieu des longs replis des monts.

Les sommets de granit rose ou bleu donnaient au vaste paysage des tons de féerie; et, sur les pentes plus basses, des forêts de châtaigniers immenses avaient l'air de buissons verts tant les vagues de la terre soulevée sont géantes en ce pays.[6]

Each paragraph of this passage is introduced by a reference either to colour or smell. It would appear that Maupassant is inclined towards impressionistic presentation, although particularly the first of these two references to *Une vie* gives cause for some reservation. Colour usually but not always controls and determines form, but basic shapes are not lost in the interplay of light and shadow. This interest in form is perhaps nowhere more obvious than in another evocation of the Corsican terrain found in the same chapter.

Ils partirent au soleil levant en bientôt ils s'arrêtèrent en face d'une forêt, d'une vraie forêt de granit pourpré. C'étaient des pics, des colonnes, des clochetons, des figures surprenantes modelées par le temps, le vent rongeur et la brume de mer.

Hauts jusqu'à trois cents mètres, minces, ronds, tortus, crochus, difformes, imprévus, fantastiques, ces surprenants rochers semblaient des arbres, des plantes, des bêtes, des monuments, des hommes, des moines en robe, des diables cornus, des oiseaux démesurés, tout un peuple monstrueux, une ménagerie de cauchemar pétrifiée par le vouloir de quelque Dieu extravagant.[7]

All these passages, from their dates of publication, are from the early years of his career, and are by no means conclusive evidence in themselves. But they do have a number of things in common. Colour, smell, sound, these three elements rank very high in them all. From, although

[6]   *Une vie*, pp. 101–02.
[7]   *Une vie*, p. 105.

not absent from most, thanks perhaps to Flaubert, tends to play a lesser although highly imaginative rôle nevertheless. Many other descriptive passages may be added to this list. "L'aveu" published in 1884 opens with the noon sun pouring down on trees, buildings and the ripening fields of wheat. "Le, vieux" (1884) is introduced with the autumn sun over the dampness of the earth. And in neither of them is there any real indication of form as a major descriptive factor. The opening of Chapter Two of "Yvette" also is indicative of these same propensities – the mass of trees, the calm evening, the fresh smell of the river, the setting sun, and again no specific reference to shape.

But Maupassant's landscapes are not perennially bathed in moonlight or sunshine. The method of opening a story by a descriptive passage, such a common device in the art of prose fiction, is well handled in "Le Père Amable (1886). Here we have a wet grey sky like a weight hanging over the endless brown plain. This is followed by the introduction of the smell of autumn, a sad smell of bare wet earth, decaying leaves and dead grass. In the heavy stagnant evening air the peasants continue their labour, and behind the naked trees we catch sight of the thatched roofs of their cottages.

The passage presents still further evidence of the use of impressionistic techniques of light and smell. The time of day is precisely mentioned, and we have an exact but rapidly disappearing moment in which form again is reduced to a minimum. Clearly introductory descriptive passages such as this are intended as more than the simple establishment of setting. The lighting, intense or subdued, the smells, pleasant or otherwise, are contributory to the general mood which the particular tale requires. In "Clair de lune", which has provided us with a very convincing illustration, the description has been seen to be much more than a simple décor. It speaks directly to father Marignan. Although the presentation is impressionistic, a new note is struck in the closing lines. Inspired by Biblical passages, he equates the setting with a temple in which he is a trespasser. The whole of the description thus takes on a new form, that of a construction which is not a backdrop, but a container for the action of the story, slight as it is. For the most part descriptive passages seem to lie entirely within the accepted concepts of nineteenth century fiction, lending as they do a basic element of truth to the development which follows or precedes.

And the novels furnish a multitude of examples. In *Mont-Oriol* the panoramic view of Auvergne, the high hills and vast plain stretching right to the horizon, dotted with towns and villages, the whole bathed in brilliant sunshine, would seem to suggest the same conclusions, a study in colour and light. And yet an original note is struck in the latter half of this same passage:

... Et sous la brume transparente, si fine, qui flottait sur cette vaste étendue de pays, on distinguait des villes, des villages, des bois, les grands carrés verts des herbages, des usines aux longues cheminées rouges et des clochers noirs et pointus avec les laves des anciens volcans.

"Retourne-toi", dit son frère. Elle se retourna. Et derrière elle, elle vit la montagne, l'énorme montagne bosselée de cratères. C'était d'abord le fond d'Enval, une large vague de verdure où on distinguait à peine l'entaille cachée des gorges. Le flot d'arbres escaladait la pente rapide jusqu'à la première crête qui empêchait de voir celles du dessus. Mais comme on se trouvait tout juste sur la ligne de séparation des plaines et de la montagne, celle-ci s'étendait à gauche, vers Clermont-Ferrand, et s'éloignant, déroulait sur le ciel bleu d'étranges sommets tronqués, pareils à des pustules monstrueuses: les volcans éteints, les volcans morts. Et là-bas, tout là-bas, entre deux cimes, on en apercevait une autre, plus haute, plus lointaine encore, ronde et majestueuse, et portant à son faîte quelque chose de bizarre qui ressemblait à une ruine.[8]

Form is emphasized throughout this latter half of the passage in question, and colours as well as other more fleeting attributes of the countryside are being relegated to a secondary position. It is important to note that those objects which are described in terms of their shape are precisely those which will come to have great depth of meaning for Christiane. As with the illustration taken from *Une vie*, this scene is viewed by the heroine of the novel. And in this case it stands as a prelude to the most important descriptive passage of the book – the dynamiting of Oriol's rock which will lead to all the economic and business development of *Mont-Oriol*. One must agree with Sullivan's view of this vital scene as a kind of pre-echo, a symbol of Christiane's awakening in response to Paul Brétigny. The incident with the dog is incidentally a nice little Flaubertian touch.

In describing this rock, Maupassant defines its shape for his reader:

Sous leurs pieds, la côte rapide descendait jusqu'à la route de Riom, ombragée par les saules abritant sa mince rivière; et au milieu d'une vigne au bord de ce ruisseau, s'élevait une roche pointue que deux hommes agenouillés à son pied semblaient prier. C'était le morne.[9]

The attention paid to form in the major descriptive passages of this novel is quite striking. The Lake of Tazenat for example is presented as a kind of deep, funnel-shaped crater with a shining metal-like bottom, formed

[8]   Maupassant, *Mont-Oriol*, p. 34.
[9]   *Mont-Oriol*, pp. 35–36.

by the unruffled water. Maupassant goes on to state that this geographical formation is a kind of container for the passion, the emotion of Christiane and Paul, and its water is as one might presume a mirror of love. The episode is without doubt a high point in the relationship between these two people. This décor is consciously contrasted with that other strikingly descriptive scene, the excursion to the extinct volcano in Chapter Three of the second part. Again the description is of a hole, a crater, this time dry, dead, sterile. It is here that Christiane's brother Gontran, influenced by the financial manipulations of her husband, declares himself for Louise Oriol, and thus opens the way for Paul to betray his mistress. One might compare these passages with the more impressionistic treatment of the same type of terrain which we find in "Mes 25 jours" (1885).

There is then a very deep relationship between these scenes and the people who inhabit them. They do more than set a backdrop or mood for narrative, or even project an individual's interior longings, directly linked as they are with the human relationships the novel sets out to treat. Both characters and plots become very closely identified with externals.

This goes a long way towards explaining why the formal or structural aspects of the scene become so much more important. It is precisely through this use of form that identity takes place. Restricting ourselves to landscape description for the moment, we can see the same pheno-menon in the twisted tree trunks in the forest of Fontainebleau that are so meaningful to Mariolle. The domed trees, like leafy monuments in the Parc Monceau provide the setting for one of the most poetic chapters of *Fort comme la mort*. Nor is this type of descriptive technique reserved exclusively for the novel. The famous "futaie" scene of the vicious murder of the little Roque girl is first seen as a kind of vault supported by the columns of the tree trunks. A vaulted tunnel of sycomores leads to the narrator's house in "Qui sait?" (1890). The pink walls of the little house in "Le champ d'oliviers" are suddenly illuminated at the end of the story, "bas et carré" as the neighbours rush to view the tragic scene. What lacked form because of the darkness of the night becomes clearly, if fleetingly outlined before the story ends.

The change in emphasis in descriptive material relating to scenes in nature becomes all the more striking if we pause to examine a number of passages in which Maupassant deals with the same scene. The valley of the Seine near Rouen is one subject to which he returns on several occasions, and the change in approach is so clearly demonstrated by these that I feel I must quote extensively from them in order to substantiate clearly my argument.

A brief little story published in 1882 entitled "Un Normand" furnishes us with a very detailed and vivid rendition:

C'est là un des horizons les plus magnifiques qui soient au monde. Derrière nous, Rouen, la ville aux églises, aux clochers gothiques, travaillés comme des bibelots d'ivoire; en face Saint-Sever, le faubourg aux manufactures, qui dresse ses mille cheminées fumantes sur le grand ciel vis-à-vis les mille clochetons sacrés de la vieille cité.

Ici la flèche de la cathédrale, le plus haut sommet des monuments humains; et là-bas, la "Pompe à feu" de la "Foudre", sa rivale presque aussi démesurée, et qui passe d'un mètre la plus géante des pyramides d'Egypte.

Devant nous la Seine se déroulait, ondulante, semée d'îles, bordée à droite de blanches falaises que couronnait une forêt, à gauche de prairies immenses qu'une autre forêt limitait, là-bas, tout là-bas.[10]

We have here a sort of "vue d'ensemble" almost devoid of colour. While there is a dominant interplay between the horizontal infinity of the view and the verticality of steeples and chimneys, nonetheless the actual forms are not specifically described. The passage must be considered as a suggestion of the general layout, essentially a two-dimensional vision, carefully organized and presented.

In "Le garde" (1884) we have a similar although much briefer depiction of the same scene, with the same concern for the general composition of the view and with even less reference to specifics of colour and shape. The description here is quite exterior to the main interest of the story and serves only as a setting for the introduction. Both these passages give the impression of general form without dealing with it in any genuine detail.

Every reader of Maupassant is familiar with what is perhaps the most striking evocation of this same site, the description found in the first chapter of Part Two of *Bel-Ami*. It will be remembered that at this point in the novel, Georges Duroy has just married Madeleine Forestier, and their wedding trip takes them to Georges' Norman home. As they ride out of Rouen up the escarpment, in the direction of his village of Cantal, they pause to view the scene below:

On dominait l'immense vallée, longue et large que le fleuve clair parcourait d'un bout à l'autre, avec de grandes ondulations. On le voyait venir de là-bas, taché par des îles nombreuses et décrivant une courbe avant de traverser Rouen. Puis la ville apparaissait sur la rive droite, un peu noyée dans la brume matinale, avec des éclats de soleil sur ses toits, et ses mille clochers légers, pointus ou

[10] Maupassant, "Un Normand", *Contes de la bécasse, Oeuvres complètes*, pp. 143–44. First published in *Le Gil Blas* (October 10, 1882).

trapus, frêles et travaillés comme des bijoux géants, ses tours carrées ou rondes coiffées de couronnes héraldiques, ses beffrois, ses clochetons, tout le peuple gothique des sommets d'églises que dominait la flèche aiguë de la cathédrale, surprenante aiguille de bronze, laide, étrange et démesurée, la plus haute qui soit au monde.

Mais en face, de l'autre côté du fleuve, s'élevaient, rondes et renflées à leur faîte, les minces cheminées d'usines du vaste faubourg de Saint-Sever.

Plus nombreuses que leurs frères les clochers, elles dressaient jusque dans la campagne lointaine leurs longues colonnes de briques et soufflaient dans le ciel bleu leur haleine noire de charbon.

Et la plus élevée de toutes, aussi haute que la pyramide de Chéops, le second des sommets dus au travail humain, presque l'égal de sa fière commère la flèche de la cathédrale, la grande pompe à feu de la foudre semblait la reine du peuple travailleur et fumant des usines comme sa voisine était la reine de la foule pointue des monuments sacrés.[11]

The passage obviously shares much with its predecessors, the vastness of the horizon and the striking verticality of the steeples and chimneys, the comparison with the pyramid of Cheops, the undulations of the river. But the geometry of it is much more precise – the curves of the river, the square and round belfreys, the needle-like steeple of the cathedral, the round and slender chimneys of the factories are details absent from the other passages mentioned. The impression is made much more precise, exact and concrete, and has a three-dimensional, sculptural quality previously lacking. And like the Auvergne of Christiane Andermatt this scene is by no means an incidental description of décor, but has a deeper value with reference to the two viewers. This, after all, is the home of Georges Duroy, ambitious, self-made, and a Norman through and through. Madeleine, the Parisian, reacts with a noticeable uneasiness to the whole environment. Unused to vastness such as this, unable to communicate with his peasant parents and disturbed by the forest of Roumare, she is the one who expresses the desire to leave and return to Paris. The physical world is thus not just an explanation of character, but again an active participant in the relationship between two human beings. What it says to the one is a clear suggestion of future complications in the marital relationship at the same time as it demonstrates in concrete terms the husband's innate desire to encompass all that he can grasp. She, the product of urban life is by nature introverted, while he, raised in this broad expanse is unusually outgoing. The "real" world then assumes a very complex rôle indeed. Not only does it in true naturalistic practice serve to explain much of the interior complexity of its in-

---

[11] Maupassant, *Bel-Ami*, pp. 321–22.

habitants, but it also contributes actively to a relationship between individuals. The visible and tangible world in Maupassant acquires the capacity to participate in narrative development. It is present in the fabric of the story not simply as comment on, but comment to the characters. There is a kind of communication, an identity between these seemingly isolated and fragmented parts of life, and we have seen that in *Mont-Oriol*, form is the basic mode of contact. Luplau–Janssen makes a very valid point with regard to this description when he remarks:

La vue de Canteleu est – pour ainsi dire – encadrée, elle est limitée à gauche et à droite et l'angle de la vue n'est pas grand, en d'autres termes la vue de Canteleu est un vrai sujet de peinture, pendant que la vue de Bon-Secours est plutôt un panorame, très beau, il faut l'avouer, mais il ne possède pas l'unité nécessaire pour être représenté soit en mots, soit en couleurs sur une toile. Comme Maupassant est un artiste, il a choisi la vue de Canteleu, ce qui nous est bien intelligible.[12]

What he is saying in essence is that Maupassant, as he did with Jeanne's view from the window, is imposing a frame on his scene. There is a need to limit, to give form to what could have been limitless.

It would be somewhat unfair to juxtapose the lengthy description of a critical chapter of a novel with the brevity of the short story if it did not reveal how Maupassant goes about giving deeper values to the same scene. But we can also substantiate this tendency towards form by presenting still another version, this time drawn from the "minor" genre. It is found close to the beginning of "Le Horla".

A gauche, là-bas, Rouen, la vaste ville aux toits bleus, sous le peuple pointu des clochers gothiques. Ils sont innombrables, frêles ou larges, dominés par la flèche de fonte de la cathédrale et pleins de cloches qui sonnent dans l'air bleu . . .[13]

Impressionistic, yes, particularly with the addition of the ringing bells which follows in the next few lines, but more than that. Brief as this description is, and for that reason perhaps more valid as a comparison with the first two, it again deals in tangible and concrete terms more like those of *Bel-Ami*. The Seine, seen in the paragraph preceding the quotation is "grande et large", the steeples are pointed, the cathedral spire is "une flèche de fonte" and not merely "une flèche". This is the scene from the narrator's garden, the décor in which the haunting manifestation

[12] C. Luplau-Janssen, *Le décor chez Guy de Maupassant*, p. 56.
[13] Maupassant, "Le Horla", *Le Horla, Oeuvres complètes*, p. 4.

called Le Horla will first make its presence felt. The pleasure of these opening lines will soon be converted into mental torture.

There is another and perhaps more revealing aspect of the outdoor world which is perhaps more important than the landscape. The sea, so commonly seen in Maupassant's work, is absolutely central to our problem and must be dealt with in some detail. Again we can offer only what may be considered representative examples of this expression of the external world.

With a few exceptions the sea for Maupassant means of course the English Channel and the Norman coast, or the Mediterranean. Often one of his short stories will be launched with a careful description of it, like with the opening lines of "La peur":[14]

On remonta sur le pont après dîner. Devant nous, la Méditerranée n'avait pas un frisson sur toute sa surface qu'une grande lune calme moirait. Le vaste bateau glissait, jetant sur le ciel, qui semblait ensemencé d'étoiles, un gros serpent de fumée noire; et derrière nous, l'eau toute blanche, agitée par le passage rapide du lourd bâtiment, battue par l'hélice, moussait, semblait se tordre, remuait tant de clartés qu'on eût dit de la lumière de lune bouillonant.[15]

What captivates Maupassant's eye and his pen here is the play of the moonlight on the water, a phenomenon dear to the heart of every impressionist. Words like "un frisson", "glissait", "moirait" are all contributory to the establishment of an atmosphere suited to the development of itself. But neither of the two incidents inspired by this setting is directly related to the sea. The passage would thus appear to be only an introduction, significant solely on its face value, and has no narrative use other than to set a mood and to link together two experiences in a process already discussed in some detail.

Remaining for the moment in the same story, we find another description which, while an obvious parallel with the introductory paragraph, clearly illustrates a change in the method of presentation. The North African desert, which Maupassant himself viewed personally on more than one occasion, is frequently equated with the ocean, as it is here:

Je traversais les grandes dunes au sud de Ouargla. C'est là un des plus étranges pays du monde. Vous connaissez le sable uni, le sable droit des interminables plages de l'Océan. Eh bien! figurez-vous l'Océan lui-même devenu sable au milieu d'un ouragan; imaginez une tempête silencieuse de vagues immobiles en

[14] Maupassant, "La peur", *Contes de la bécasse*, *Oeuvres complètes*. First published in *Le Gaulois* (October 23, 1882).
[15] "La peur", p. 73.

poussière jaune. Elles sont hautes comme des montagnes, ces vagues inégales, différentes, soulevées tout à fait comme des flots déchaînés, mais plus grandes encore, et striées comme de la moire. Sur cette mer furieuse, muette et sans mouvement, le dévorant soleil du sud verse sa flamme implacable et directe. Il faut gravir ces lames de cendre d'or, redescendre, gravir encore, gravir sans cesse, sans repos et sans ombre. Les chevaux râlent, enfoncent jusqu'aux surprenantes collines.[16]

The desert, seen as a transfixed ocean, is dealt with, not with nouns and verbs conveying motion, but with adjectives and past participles suggesting permanence – "uni", "droit", "immobiles", "striées". The play of light, that is to say the burning southern sun, is quite secondary. Colour and movement only enter the scene late in the description. It is the fundamental form that is of interest initially. Significantly enough this passage is drawn not from the introductory cadre but from the body of the story itself, from the first of the two illustrations of fear which form the narrative. And it is within this context that basic human emotion manifests itself as a response to this environment and its mysterious drums. The structural nature of the setting is stressed at this point:

... et je sentais se glisser dans mes os la peur. la vraie peur, la hideuse peur, en face de ce cadavre aimé, dans ce *trou* incendié par le soleil entre quatre *monts* de sable ... [italics mine].[17]

The impressionistic approach may be found on numerous occasions in the introductory passage of a short story, always performing the same function of creating a general atmosphere, providing a backdrop for the intrigue, and linking it with the narrator's reality. Of such a type is the description of the coast at Cannes in "Première neige" (1883). We see the sweep of the wide gulf and of the mountains behind the city, with a multitude of white villas sleeping in the sun. From a distance they seem to cover the mountains from top to bottom with little white dots like snowflakes in the dark green vegetation. Through initial description Maupassant has here linked up three experiences – his own, and Normandy and Provence, in which the story will be set.

This method is not always confined to the idyllic calm of the Mediterranean. The description of the sea off the coast at Yport in a winter gale is filled with movement and constructed on a series of verbs and restless adjectives combined with present participles:

[16]   "La peur", pp. 76–77.
[17]   "La peur", p. 78.

La mer démontée mugissait et secouait la côte, précipitant sur le rivage des vagues énormes, lentes et baveuses, qui s'écroulaient avec des détonations d'artillerie. Elles s'en venaient tout doucement, l'une après l'autre, hautes comme des montagnes, éparpillant dans l'air, sous les rafales, l'écume blanche de leurs têtes ainsi qu'une sueur de monstres.[18]

Motion and its counterpart, immobility, are of course inseparable characteristics of the sea, wild as in this introduction to a tale of incredible violence brought on by alcoholic stimulation, or subdued as in the opening lines of "L'épingle" (1885). The seascape is found not only in introductory passages, but also worked right into the text itself, as we find in the second chapter of "Les soeurs Rondoli" (1884). As the train progresses along the coast from Marseilles towards Italy, Maupassant stops for a moment to view the passing scene. The coast is bathed by the immobile water, and the heavy sun spreads fire over the mountains, the sandy coast, on the hard blue of the sea. Meanwhile the train continues its progress along the steep walls of the rough coast and a faint salt smell mingles with the heavy scent of the flowers.

Coming as this passage does, immediately after several paragraphs dealing more precisely with the flowers of the area and their odour which permeates the atmosphere, the more concrete aspects of the scene are stressed. The sun is "pesant", its light a "nappe de feu", the sea is of a "bleu dur et figé", the coastline is a series of straight walls. Then, in the final paragraph we return to the earlier olfactory theme.

There is much in common between this passage and the one dealing with the desert in "La peur",[19] for in both the natural setting is motionless, transfixed, almost petrified. Motion in both is introduced by an exterior element, a means of locomotion – animals in the first case, a train here. Both passages are integral parts of their respective narratives, and communicate to the characters a basic human emotion, a deep-seated feeling. Significantly enough, Paul, who is unaware of the passing view, does not become so inextricably involved with Francesca Rondoli as does the narrator.

The identical relationship between character and setting is discernable in the description of Etretat which opens the narrative of "Adieu". The horseshoe-shaped beach, framed by the white rocks, limits the view of the sea, imposes a frame, as it were, on a brightly coloured painting. It is in this setting that the affair between man and woman begins. Emotion is

---

[18] Maupassant, "L'ivrogne", *Contes du jour et de la nuit, Oeuvres complètes*, p. 126. First published in *Le Gaulois* (April 20, 1884).
[19] See note 14.

again connected with the seascape. And it is again more than a vague longing. There is always precision in the relationship.

"Miss Harriet", a story concerned almost uniquely with the character of that most unusual English tourist, offers a striking illustration of the use of description in the short story. Although the passage is lengthy, it deserves some attention, and must therefore be quoted in full. After viewing the artist's canvas, a seascape in the setting sun, Harriet accompanies him to the shore to view the real thing:

... Nous allions maintenant au bord de l'abîme, au-dessus de la vaste mer qui roulait, à cent mètres sous nous, ses petits flots. Et nous buvions, la bouche ouverte et la poitrine dilatée, ce souffle frais qui avait passé l'Océan et qui nous glissait sur la peau, lent et salé par le long baiser des vagues.

Serrée dans son châle à carreaux, l'air inspiré, les dents au vent, l'Anglaise regardait l'énorme soleil s'abaisser vers la mer. Devant nous, là-bas, là-bas, à la limite de la vue, un trois mâts couvert de voiles dessinait sa silhouette sur le ciel enflammé, et un vapeur, plus proche, passait en déroulant sa fumée qui laissait derrière lui un nuage sans fin traversant tout l'horizon.

Le globe rouge descendait toujours, lentement. Et bientôt il toucha l'eau, juste derrière le navire immobile qui apparut, comme dans un cadre de fer, au milieu de l'astre éclatant. Il s'enfonçait peu à peu, dévoré par l'Océan. On le voyait plonger, diminuer, disparaître. C'était fini. Seul le petit bâtiment montrait toujours son profil découpé sur le fond d'or du ciel lointain.

Miss Harriet contemplait d'un regard passionné la fin flamboyante du jour. Et elle avait, certes, une envie immodérée d'étreindre le ciel, la mer, l'horizon.[20]

It would be foolish to suggest that this passage is not a brilliant piece of impressionistic description. But it has very clearly an organized and indeed a poetic quality that set it apart from what can strictly be called realism.

One must bear in mind that this story, from its publication date, is a rather early one, and it is, perhaps surprisingly, one of a number of pieces of Maupassant in which a genuine feeling of sympathy overcomes the generally accepted view of him as a monster of objectivity. The narrator can see how Miss Harriet, in her insatiable quest for love, wants to answer the call of infinity, and there is in this passage a three-part silent conversation. In spite of the impressionism, the description is to some extent indicative of Maupassant's new direction, since the story does in effect remove reality one step. This same scene is also treated in a painting, and the comparison between it and reality, the one permanent, the other fleeting and evanescent, is hardly accidental. The second-last paragraph

[20] Maupassant, "Miss Harriet", *Miss Harriet, Oeuvres complètes*, pp. 17–18. First published in *Le Gaulois* under the title "Miss Hastings" (July 9, 1883).

quoted draws the reader's attention directly to this parallelism. A vista dominated by colour and light, containing a certain structural reference to the shape of the sun, and to the silhouette of the ship framed in the fiery light, it is in a sense reminiscent of Flaubert's treatment of the city of Carthage in *Salammbô*. A derivative method, no doubt, but one on which the author will build.

The presence of the outdoors forms a very complex pattern in this most interesting short story. On the primary level we have the cadre scene which inspires the narrator to relate his tale. Beneath this we have the past reality viewed in the above passage, and the artistic interpretation of it on the painter's canvas. And there is in this piece a constant search for identity from beginning to end, a search that ends only in death.

The triangular shape of the sea, limited by the contours of the hills from which it is viewed, emphasizes the structure of the setting in "Le saut du berger".[21] This is the site of the violent death of Julien de Lamare and his mistress in *Une vie*. Shapes are thus discernable even in the earliest Maupassant. Unlike the passage from "Miss Harriet" this site is related principally not to character, but more directly to situation and conflict. The Druidic monuments by the rock-studded sea in the introductory passage of "Le baptême", and the mountain crests of Corsica rising from the sea in "Le bonheur" are symbolic premonitions of the subsequent action in which form is the essential quality. That physical reality has an underlying structure which is vital for Maupassant, there can be no doubt. The views of the sea contain the same elements far too frequently to be considered accidental.

"Madame Parisse" opens with a seascape that reminds us distinctly of the Etretat of "Le modèle" because of its form. The city is first of all enclosed in walls, and jutting out into the immense gulf of Nice. Surrounded by water, it breaks the waves at its feet. Above, the houses climb one on the other, culminating in two high towers which appear like the two horns of an ancient helmet. Behind is the milky white wall of the Alps, barring the horizon, against which they are etched.

As with his description of Etretat, a crescent-shaped town contained in white cliffs with clearly defined projection into the sea at the two extremities of that crescent, Maupassant is here trying to give symmetrical order to reality by imposing formal limits on it. In both passages, the

[21] Maupassant, "Le saut du berger", *Oeuvres postumes* I, *Oeuvres complètes*, p. 31. First published in *Le Gil Blas* (March 9, 1882).

scene of infinity, the sea, becomes secondary to the shore which contains
it – a series of towers, cliffs and walls, natural and man-made. And like
all the descriptions in which form is emphasized, this one is related to
the narrative not through one character, but through a relationship, a
communication between characters. Form tries to break the barrier of
solitude and find identity.

The extent to which the containment of infinity matters to Maupassant
is perhaps nowhere more evident than in "L'épave", which takes place
on the low-lying Atlantic coast of France near La Rochelle. On the île
de Ré the narrator becomes almost unable to grasp the limitless expanse
of sand and sea. Reality assumes fantastic, gigantic proportions because
it cannot be contained.

J'allais vite sur cette plaine jaune, élastique comme de la chair et qui semblait
suer sous mon pied. La mer, tout à l'heure, était là; maintenant, je l'apercevais
au loin, se sauvant à perte de vue, et je ne distinguais plus la ligne qui séparait
le sable de l'Océan. Je croyais assister à une féerie gigantesque et surnaturelle.
L'Atlantique était devant moi tout à l'heure, puis il avait disparu dans la
grève, comme font les décors dans les trappes, et je marchais à présent au
milieu d'un désert.[22]

Again with the evocations of the sea in his short stories, we see two
trends in Maupassant's descriptive technique. The fundamentally impressionistic type which provides useful background material and establishes both setting and mood, and which can be directly related to the
presentation of character, as we saw with "Miss Harriet", or a more
permanent, structural type of description with an increasingly important,
more penetrating purpose, connected as it usually is to the human relationships developed in the narrative.

Of course the sea is often present in his novels too, and nowhere more
significantly than in *Une vie*. In this, the least original although by no
means the weakest of his longer works, the sea is directly related to the
heroine. Its broad limitless expanse is in parallel with the young girl's
romantic Bovary-like longings:

Une mollesse parfois la faisait s'étendre sur l'herbe drue d'une pente; et parfois,
lorsqu'elle apercevait tout à coup au détour du val, dans un entonnoir de gazon,
un triangle de mer bleu étincelante au soleil avec une voile à l'horizon, il lui
veinait des joies désordonnées comme à l'approche mystérieuse de bonheurs
planant sur elle.[23]

[22] Maupassant, "L'épave", *La petite Roque, Oeuvres complètes*, p. 78. First published
in *Le Gaulois* (January 1, 1886).
[23] Maupassant, *Une vie*, pp. 27–28.

And its absence at the end of the book is part and parcel of her failure in life to achieve these goals:

Ce qui lui manquait si fort, c'était la mer, sa grande voisine depuis vingt-cinq ans, la mer avec son air salé, ses colères, sa voix grondeuse, ses souffles puissants, la mer que chaque matin elle voyait de sa fenêtre des Peuples, qu'elle respirait jour et nuit, qu'elle sentait près d'elle, qu'elle s'était mise à aimer comme une personne sans s'en douter.[24]

The dialogue has been cut off.

And, as in other cases, Maupassant imposes limits on this view of the infinite – the triangular contours formed by the coast, or the frame of the window from which she day dreams. The first descriptive passage in the novel dealing with the sea also establishes a frame of cliffs on the one side.

The imposing of form would appear to be characteristic of the technique of *Une vie* and certainly the sea, as a descriptive theme in the novel, illustrates this. One further passage should prove the point conclusively.

... Vers l'horizon, le ciel se baissant se mêlait à l'océan. Vers la terre, la haute falaise droite faisait une grande ombre à son pied et des pentes de gazon pleines de soleil l'échancraient par endroits. Là-bas, en arrière, des voiles brunes sortaient de la jetée blanche de Fécamp et là-bas, en avant, une roche d'une forme étrange, arrondie et percée à jour, avait à peu près la figure d'un éléphant énorme enfonçant sa trompe dans le flots. ...[25]

The delineation of forms is directly concerned with the search for truth, for the essentials of man's world. At this point she admires three beauties of nature – light, space, and water. These are curiously enough three basic elements of the impressionist's interest, but coming as they do after the above passage, they become much less fleeting, and acquire a permanence which often escaped the impressionist's brush.

The connection between the sea and emotion is also clearly indicated in *Une vie*, in a passage of such a blatantly sexual nature that no explanation is really required.

Le soleil, plus bas, semblait saigner; et une large traînée lumineuse, une route éblouissante courait sur l'eau depuis la limite de l'océan jusqu'au sillage de la barque.

Les derniers souffles de vent tombèrent; toute ride s'aplanit; et la voile immobile était rouge. Une accalmie illimitée semblait engourdir l'espace, faire le silence autour de cette rencontre d'éléments; tandis que, cambrant sous le ciel son ventre luisant et liquide, la mer, fiancée monstrueuse, attendait l'amant

---

[24] *Une vie*, pp. 342–43.
[25] *Une vie*, p. 45.

de feu qui descendait vers elle. Il précipitait sa chute, empourpré comme par le désir de leur empressement. Il la joignit; et, peu à peu, elle le dévora.[26]

Is this not a more youthful version of Miss Harriet's vision?

This one novel thus contains all the elements related to the sea that we have observed dispersed among the short stories. But it is of course only one of a number of aspects of the physical world used by the author in this first novel. Jeanne undoubtedly indentifies with the see, but similar relationships occur between herself and other presences – the château, its interior and its grounds, for instance. The sea is simply a means by which Maupassant preserves his Flaubertian objectivity all the while delving to the innermost reaches of Jeanne's mind. And one must remember that this is the novel of *a* life as the title says. The interest lies with Jeanne herself, and the relationships established during the course of her life are not important outside that very limited context. We are watching one person for several hundred pages. Maupassant will make use of all the descriptive factors at his disposal in order to illustrate this life. He will show little real favouritism for that aspect which will so clearly character-ize his later work. Form in *Une vie* is important, but colour, smell, all the sense perceptions are equally so. Form is present in *Une vie* but not dominant.

The sea appears on only one occasion in *Bel-Ami*. In the final chapter of the first part, Georges Duroy, at the request of Madeleine Forestier, travels from Paris to Cannes to visit her dying husband. In the sick room the wife draws the attention of the newly arrived visitor to the magnificent view from the window:

En face d'eux, la côte semée de villas descendait jusqu'à la ville qui était couchée le long du rivage en demi-cercle, avec sa tête à droite vers la jetée qui dominait la vieille cité surmontée d'un vieux beffroi, et ses pieds à gauche à la pointe de la Croisette, en face des îles de Lérins. Elles avaient l'air, ces îles, de deux taches vertes, dans l'eau toute bleue. On eût dit qu'elles flottaient comme deux feuilles immenses, tant elles semblaient plates de là-haut.

Et tout au loin, fermant l'horizon de l'autre côté du golfe, au-dessus de la jetée et du beffroi, une longue suite de montagnes bleuâtres dessinaient sur un ciel éclatant une ligne bizarre et charmante de sommets tantôt arrondis, tantôt crochus, tantôt pointus, et qui finissaient par un grand mont en pyramide plongeant son pied dans la pleine mer.[27]

The use of form in the description should be perfectly obvious, but its function in the novel suggests something not clearly defined in *Une vie*. External nature, the Mediterranean coast, dominates this chapter, and

[26] *Une vie*, p. 54.
[27] Maupassant, *Bel-Ami*, p. 261.

is not connected simply with the state of mind of one of the three characters. For this is a novel of a society as well as of an individual. All three
persons are bound up in an interrelationship whose results are yet to be
seen. Forestier's death, symbolized by the blood-red sunset, is only one
small part of the identification. Duroy is torn between his ambition-
inspired attraction to Madeleine and his sympathy (for he is capable of
tenderness on occasion) for the dying Forestier. He spends long hours at
the window trying to decipher the complexities of life. Madeleine is as
enigmatic as the sea. Faithful to the principles of objectivity, Maupassant
is beginning to endow the physical world with a capacity for participation
in character and plot, in fact, in all the essentials of the narrative technique
which will gradually cause him to remould his concept of the novel. The
external world is no longer a simple reflection of or comment on character, and Flaubertian objectivity cannot, as the latter so tragically proved
himself, decipher the enigma of identity.

The new trend in Maupassant becomes much more clearly defined in
Pierre et Jean with respect to the sea, since its presence is felt throughout
the narrative. On first consideration, it might be thought that its obvious
equation with Pierre suggests the same basic function for it as we have
witnessed in *Une vie*. But it is in fact much more subtle. We have already
seen that there is in the work a kind of alternation between exterior and
interior from chapter to chapter. It is the sea that is the setting for the
majority of situations that involve the exterior physical world. In the first
chapter it is first described as flat, and "tendue comme une étoffe bleue,
immense, luisante, . . .". Very soon however, clear cut limits are imposed
on it as we view the contours of the coastline. The Seine, separating Upper
and Lower Normandy also divides the gentle sloping coast of the former
from the steep cliffs that form a white wall as far as Dunkirk. This is
Pierre's father's description. He is of course identified with this environment because of his enthusiasm for fishing and for things nautical in
general. Madame Roland finds both physical and mental comfort in the
gentle motion of the water, and again we see a kind of Bovary-like quality
in the feminine make-up. Pierre too is involved in the sea, in a much more
complex way than his parents. This becomes obvious in the second
chapter, in which Pierre studies the play of the lighthouse beams over its
broad expanse. In darkness, the water becomes a kind of undefined limitlessness, and the lights, even that enormous beam, the moon, which emerges at the end of the paragraph, are only guides directing a safe passage
through it. Pierre's momentary happiness on board the "Perle" is interrupted by the sea's assumption of an undefinable infinity thanks to the fog

which forces him to return to port. The fog shrouds the sea and the incessant fog horns assume super-human proportions to Pierre. We discover
the identical reaction to formlessness that we already witnessed in
"L'épave":

> ... Et soudain, comme si elle l'eût entendu, comme si elle l'eût compris et lui
> eût répondu, la sirène de la jetée hurla tout près de lui. Sa clameur de monstre
> surnaturel, plus retentissante que le tonnerre, rugissement sauvage et formi-
> dable fait pour dominer les voix du vent et des vagues, se répandit dans les
> ténèbres sur la mer invisible ensevelie sous les brouillards.[28]

In Pierre's case, the rôle of the sea as an objective correlative is related not
to a vague emotional longing but to a very precise situation involving a
number of other personages in the novel. It is his task to decide upon a
course of action. Related in its clarity to his father's superficiality, in its
mystery to his mother's longing, and in its infinity to his own quest for
the truth, it is also symbolic of his brother's true identity. It thus becomes
a comment on the entire dramatic situation of the book, and assumes far
broader and deeper proportions than heretofore witnessed in Maupassant.
Its mystery is the mystery of a family, of a son's legitimacy, of a mother's
fidelity, of another son's quest. The sea is inextricably interwoven with the
thread of plot, the presentation of character and the structure of the
book. For in Pierre's eyes, the sea has sharp, well-defined contours in the
last chapter:

> Il n'y avait aucun souffle d'air; c'était un de ces jours secs et calmes d'automne,
> où la mer polie semble froide et dure comme de l'acier.[29]

It is not the sea that is vague in the closing lines of the book, but the
ship that carries Madame Roland's son out of her life. And it is not from
Pierre's perspective, but rather from his mother's that a mist remains.
Identity with exterior reality is not now a question of character, but of the
work as a whole.

Robert Niess's[30] criticism of the interpretation that Edward Sullivan[31]

---

[28] Maupassant, *Pierre et Jean*, pp. 103–04.
[29] *Pierre et Jean*, p. 237.
[30] Robert J. Niess, *"Pierre et Jean:* Some Symbols". Sullivan, in his *Maupassant the
Novelist*, sees the fog as the central symbol of *Pierre et Jean* and, tracing its use through
the novel, concludes that Pierre never completely clarifies the problem of his brother's
identity and his mother's reputation. Niess sees other symbols, namely those of light,
as a counterbalance to Sullivan's fog, and maintains that Pierre is certain of the truth.
The closing lines of the novel, for Niess, suggest that the protagonist is attempting to
eradicate that truth from his mind.
[31] Sullivan, *Maupassant the Novelist*.

gives to the closing lines of this novel is in my view quite valid, although his analysis of the novel as a pattern between darkness and light would to me be more meaningful as an interplay between form and formlessness, between precision and vagueness in which light and shadow function as major contributors. For after all, the "bec de gaz" which introduces the episode involving old Marowsko the druggist is only the means by which we can see his beak-like nose and diminutive form.[32]

As in the case of the landscape, there is one seascape that returns on several occasions to Maupassant's pen – the picture of Mont Saint-Michel, and the modifications of its presentation which take place are just as significant as those surrounding the Seine valley. His earliest detailed reference to the famous monument occurs in "La légende du Mont Saint-Michel" as an introduction to the legend itself. The narrator views it, and it serves the predictable purpose of linking his reality to the fictitious one of the legend.

Je l'avais vu d'abord de Cancale, ce château de fées planté dans la mer. Je l'avais vu confusément, ombre grise dressée sur le ciel brumeux.

Je le revis d'Avranches, au soleil couchant. L'immensité des sables était rouge, l'horizon était rouge; seule, l'abbaye escarpée, poussée là-bas, loin de la terre, comme un manoir fantastique, stupéfiante comme un palais de rêve, invraisemblablement étrange et belle, restait presque noire dans les pourpres du jour mourant.[33]

It is still another study in colour, in black and red, in which outlines are intentionally blurred by the first paragraph. The strangeness, and the mystery of the edifice take precedence over its size and shape. Only one vague suggestion of form is made besides that to the vast expanse of the bay in which it is situated – it is a silhouette against the red sky.

The same scene is presented in "Le Horla", published some four years later:

Quelle vision, quand on arrive, comme moi, à Avranches, vers la fin du jour! La ville est sur une colline; et on me conduisait dans le jardin public, au bout de la cité. Je poussai un cri d'étonnement. Une baie démesurée s'étendait devant moi, à perte de vue, entre deux côtes écartées se perdant au loin dans les brumes; et au milieu de cette immense baie jaune, sous un ciel d'or et de clarté, s'élevait sombre et pointu un mont étrange, au milieu des sables. Le soleil venait de disparaître, et sur l'horizon encore flamboyant se dessinait le profil de ce fantastique rocher qui porte sur son sommet un fantastique monument.[34]

---

[32] Maupassant, *Pierre et Jean*, p. 48.
[33] Maupassant, "La légende du Mont Saint-Michel", *Clair de lune*, p. 103. First published in *Le Gil Blas* (December 19, 1882).
[34] Maupassant, "Le Horla", *Le Horla, Oeuvres complètes*, pp. 10–11.

This is the identical scene, viewed at the same time of day from the same vantage point! But in contrast, the colours are much subdued, the vantage point itself is more clearly defined, and the object in question becomes much more distinctly visible in contour and much less a study in contrasting hues. We even see the symmetrical shape of the bay, limited by the shoreline on either side. There is in other words a greater balance between colour and form.

The longest and most detailed treatment of Mont Saint-Michel occurs of course in *Notre coeur*. The site itself from which it is viewed is of necessity rendered with precision since the "jardin public" of Avranches is the location for a pre-arranged rendez-vous between Mariolle and Michèle de Burne. But it is the description of the view which is of such great significance:

Du pied de la côte sur laquelle il était debout parait une inimaginable plaine de sable qui se mêlait au loin avec la mer et le firmament. Une rivière y promenait son cours, et sous l'azur flambant de soleil, des mares d'eau la tachetaient de plaques lumineuses qui semblaient des trous ouverts sur un autre ciel intérieur.

Au milieu de ce désert jaune, encore trempé par la marée en fuite surgissait, à douze ou quinze kilomètres du rivage, un monumental profil de rocher pointu, fantastique pyramide coiffée d'une cathédrale.

Elle n'avait pour voisin dans ces dunes immenses, qu'un écueil à sec, en dos rond, accroupi sur les vases mouvantes: Tombelaine.

Plus loin dans la ligne bleuâtre des flots aperçus, d'autres roches noyées montraient leurs crêtes brunes; et l'oeil, continuant le tour de l'horizon vers la droite, découvrait à côté de cette solitude sablonneuse la vaste étendue verte du pays normand, si couvert d'arbres qu'il avait l'air d'un bois illimité. C'était toute la nature s'offrant d'un seul coup, en un seul lieu, dans sa grandeur et dans sa grâce; et le regard allait de cette vision de forêts à cette apparition du mont de granit, solitaire habitant des sables, qui dressait sur la grève démesurée son étrange figure gothique.[35]

One suspects that all three passages are reworkings of a single experience. And all three of them continue with the description as the narrator or central character draws nearer the building the following morning shortly after sunrise. The evolution into a more symmetrically balanced form that more and more distinctly defines the third dimension is more meaningful with these passages if they are taken within their respective contexts. As we mentioned, the first description appears as nothing more than a décor, establishing atmosphere for a bit of local folk-lore. In "Le Horla" the visit to this tourist's Mecca represents a temporary cure for the narra-

---

[35] Maupassant, *Notre coeur*, pp. 75–76.

tor, a relief from the omnipresent Horla. The description thus takes on a deeper interior value and is not included in the story as a simple piece of local colour. The "bloc de pierres" as he calls it in a subsequent paragraph furnishes a rich and rewarding experience, if not a lasting one, for the writer of the diary.

Chapter One of the second part of *Notre coeur* is the climax of the long introduction of the first section. This will be the site of Michèle de Brune's conquest by Mariolle, and its location is unquestionably contributory to the advancement of this relationship. The audacious walk on the dizzy parapet and the subsequent seduction scene are a summit, a "trou ouvert sur un autre ciel intérieur" as Maupassant puts it. This is the fulcrum on which the novel swings. The pointed form of Mont Saint-Michel is thus in a sense, standing as it does at the turning point in the action, a symbol of the form of Mariolle's relationship with Michèle as well as of the structure of the novel itself.

As one can see, form increases its domination in direct proportion to the degree of importance of the subject involved. While these passages are not simple seascapes, the infinity of the sea is present in the scene and the contours of its confines become more sharply focussed with each elaboration. Again one must conclude that identity between the interior world of personality and conflict becomes linked with the external physical world basically through the interest in the forms of that external world.

The travel literature in Maupassant's works offer numerous examples of the seascape and landscape which will substantiate the arguments presented here. The most striking and perhaps the longest descriptive passage occurs in the first of these three, *Au soleil*, in the section entitled "Le Zar'ez". This lake of cristalline salt, like a vast sea appears gleaming under the intense African sun like a "miroir démesuré", "une plaque d'acier". The passage goes on to deal with the intense yellow of the surrounding hills and the whole thing takes on such an appearance of water, with reeds interrupting the smooth polished surface that it becomes a kind of supernatural phenomenon. The brilliance, the heat, these fleeting elements become eventually a question of distortion of form, by which the author accounts for the unreal nature of the terrain:

Tant que nous avions dominé le Zar'ez, nous avions gardé la perception nette des distances et des formes; dès que nous fûmes dessus, toute certitude de la vue disparut; nous nous trouvions enveloppés dans les fantasmagories du mirage.[36]

[36] Maupassant, *Au soleil, Oeuvres complètes*, pp. 113–14.

As the party advances across this most hostile terrain, enormous rocks appear in what seemed to be a flat surface, and then suddenly disappear. The reeds are really dried grass and even the seemingly sharp line of the horizon fluctuates in the distance. It is a world of disintegrating forms.

A more specifically maritime description occurs in the opening chapter of *Sur l'eau*, as one might expect from the title. Dealing with the contours of the Mediterranean coast, Maupassant evokes before our eyes the town of Antibes in a passage very reminiscent of "Madame Parisse". Here it is built in a cone shape, and the whole chain of mountains is etched first against a brilliant blue sky, and then against the blood red of the sunset. Form is as much an essential of the entire vision as are light and shadow and colour. The approaching storm is announced by a blue-black line visible on the horizon, and the dangers of a rock near the Île Saint-Honorat are conjured up by its jagged form, "hérissé comme un porc-épic".

The travel books, by their very nature offer a great deal of descriptive material dealing with the exterior physical world on land and sea, the Riviera, North Africa and Italy. But what interests the reader more than the description is the portrait of Maupassant the artist that emerges from the three volumes. Brilliantly coloured as the scenes are, full of the sights and smells of reality, there runs as an undercurrent to them all a concern with form which should not be underestimated. From the Eiffel Tower in *La vie errante*, that "haute et maigre pyramide d'échelles de fer, squelette disgracieux et géant, dont la base semble faite pour porter un formidable monument de Cyclops et qui avorte en un ridicule et mince profil de cheminée d'usine" to the mountain wall of the Mediterranean coast and the broad expanse of the Sahara, form consistently underlies the broad splashes of colour. External reality here serves a very complex and subtle purpose of both reflecting Maupassant and speaking to him in the most eloquent of fashions. It is clearly both his taste and his source of inspiration, his solace and his thirst for knowledge. These three books are more dialogues than monologues.

One might mention also the cityscape as a part of this general presentation of the outdoor world, but its appearance in his prose does not offer sufficient material for detailed separate analysis. The one recurrent urban scene which most clearly substantiates our general point of view is the striking description of the Arc de Triomphe standing at the end of the Champs-Élysées to which we have already made repeated reference. On the many occasions on which it does appear, in both novels and stories, it is presented under remarkably similar conditions. It is as if Maupassant had viewed this most celebrated of Parisian sights on but one occasion and reworked the same impression to fit the work at hand – a technique not unusual in his production as we have already witnessed in examining his use of Mont Saint-Michel.

The first of these occurs in a brief piece first published in May 1884 and entitled "Promenade". The lonely protagonist, Monsieur Leras, an aging office clerk whose life is predictably devoid of meaning, ventures out on the Champs-Élysées on a summer evening. The sun setting behind the famous monument is a kind of pre-echo of his ultimate demise, his suicide, and as will other descriptive passages, concerns itself to some extent with both colour and form:

Le ciel entier flambait; et l'arc de triomphe découpait sa masse noire sur le fond éclatant de l'horizon, comme un géant debout dans un incendie.[37]

The similarity to the method of presentation found in *Bel-Ami* is certainly no accident. But despite the identical simile the emphasis is much more clearly placed on form in the novel, while colour does not warrant mentioning.

It should be noted that the aforementioned presentation of colour mentions specifically only the black while suggesting the red through the verb *flambait*, the noun *incendie*, and the adjective *éclatant*.

Quite the opposite with regard to colour may be noted in the second of these passages, found in "L'inconnue", first published in January 1885. The dominant colours here are red and gold – "poussière d'or", "clarté rouge" are specifically mentioned. Dealing as this second story does with a theme involving physical passion, it would seem that Maupassant modifies his description to suit the subject with some real concern for detail.

But in neither of the passages referred to does he deal to any large extent with form. The simile of the standing giant in the first mentioned passage must be interpreted as a reference to the two-legged appearance of the structure. It suggests without specifying, or in other words conveys an impression only. The other passage simply mentioned that the arch "se dessinait sur le rideau de fer du ciel".

Early in the opening chapter of "L'inutile beauté", the last of Maupassant's *nouvelles*, the count and countess de Mascaret proceed up the Champs-Élysées in their elegant victoria towards the Place de l'Étoile.

---

[37] Maupassant, "Promenade", *Yvette, Oeuvres complètes*, p. 205. First published in *Le Gil Blas* (May 27, 1884).

Standing at the end is of course the famous monument bathed in the same light:

... L'immense monument au bout de la longue avenue, ouvrait dans un ciel rouge son arche colossale. Le soleil semblait descendre sur lui en semant par l'horizon une poussière de feu.[38]

As brief as the other passages, this last one clearly differs from its predecessors in the emphasis placed on shape. The image takes on a much more architectural aspect as we clearly perceive its arched form silhouetted against the red sky. Colour and form combine in a very brief but effective little painting. The story from which this excerpt is drawn is a much more completely developed narrative than were the other two, and it is therefore not surprising that the descriptive element is more carefully and completely worked out. Coming in the opening lines of the piece, it has significance beyond mere local colour, a fact which requires no explanation when accepted with full knowledge of the totality of the work. Since this is a more complex human study than either "L'inconnue" or "Promenade", the greater attention paid to form is thus in keeping with the general tendencies already observed.

The brevity of these excerpts dealing with urban description if they were taken as isolated examples of this development and trend in Maupassant might not prove particularly enlightening or convincing, but it would I think be redundant to deal more exhaustively with a descriptive element which as I have stated is not common in Maupassant's work.

What emerges as a general characteristic of Maupassant's descriptive interest in dealing with the external world is then multiple. First of all, as we have noted, there would appear to be a very limited amount of material, within which we can discover a movement in the direction of a greater concern with form as Maupassant works out his artistic method. Combined with this of course is the progression towards a deeper psychological interest, which his novels demonstrate most convincingly, and which his late short stories as well reveal. It is this change which leads him to attach greater value to his descriptions. Or more accurately, it is by means of this change in the nature of his vision that the deeper level is sought. Both the works as complete entities and the characters in thema tend to become more clearly identified with the description. And again in every case the description leads the eye of the reader towards the infinity of sea and sky. The movement in every one is clearly expansive, outward-

---

[38] Maupassant, "L'inutile beauté", *L'inutile beauté, Oeuvres complètes*, p. 5. First published in *L'Écho de Paris* (April 2 and 7, 1890).

looking, one might even say in some cases cosmic in perspective. External description is a vital link, the identification between man and man, between man and his world. The increasing emphasis on form witnessed here is a key to this identity. In every view of the infinite – desert scene, seascape, landscape, cityscape, the essential plane of the horizon is broken by vertical strokes – chimneys and spires, reeds, masts of ships, the Arc de Triomphe itself. In all these descriptions there is a curious interplay of form which suggests a kind of skeletal abstract pattern. These vertical interruptions serve as links between the finite of man's earthly existence and the inexplicable infinity beyond, offering as they do the suggestion of a third dimension to an otherwise flat panorama. But at the same time they interrupt, break the unity and thus the communication and the identity which is sought. The limitless is in some way limited, the identity is rendered imperfect, incomplete, all the while it tempts with its vision of the cosmic. The expansive motion towards a union through form, through the endlessness of infinity is regretfully contained. The frame is visible and the oneness is only fragmentary. If Maupassant contains within him the seeds of a kind of controlled mysticism, then the struggle to break through to the infinite becomes increasingly his central purpose. The movement outward seems to lead inevitably to deception, even to death. There must be another route to explore.

VI

THE INNER SEARCH

A shift of emphasis in descriptive function from objective manifestation of character and plot to an integrated, active and vital force in the totality of the work is a fact already substantiated in Maupassant. The technical analysis of this gradual modification can best be illustrated by dealing in detail with those parts of the description which can be deemed most significant, that is to say, those to which Maupassant most often devotes his attention, and those to which he returns with regularity. And again we find recurring in such passages with surprising frequency certain themes and images whose constancy cannot be written off as accidents of pure chance. From careful study of their use, an indication of the direction in which the author was moving will manifest itself still more clearly, and will, it is hoped, help to explain Maupassant's work as a unit in which each component builds to some extent on its predecessors.

One of the most striking elements which regularly recurs in descriptive passages is that of the window. We have noted elsewhere how the passing scene, viewed from a moving conveyance is linked to the action of the narrative by the window and is at the same time separated from it by this same object. It can be suggested that the travel conveyance provides an ideal milieu for the development of human relationships since it isolates the characters from the outside world and permits concentration of the reader's attention on the persons themselves.

Indeed the three travel books can be seen as manifestations of this process which are very revealing about the author himself. Maupassant is perhaps more clearly present here than in his correspondence. A correspondence which unlike Flaubert's is both very incomplete and rather unsatisfying.

As we have seen in "Les soeurs Rondoli" or "Idylle" for example, the exterior world frequently interrupts this isolation by means of the window, communicating with the passing scene. The window is thus a physical link between these two worlds, and as such can assume important proportions in certain of Maupassant's works. The brief introductory piece which opens the volume entitled *Contes de la bécasse* affords us an excellent example of the vitality the window can have. The old Baron des Ravots, confined by paralysis to his chair for the last five or six years is no longer able to participate actively in his favourite sport, hunting. But he can still shoot pigeons from the open window or door, and is thus not totally cut off from the life he knew. The window or doorway operate in an influential fashion in his day to day existence since they represent the only possible bond between his present incapacity and the outdoor life which he adored as a much younger man. But ironically enough they also represent the narrow confines into which his life has now been compressed. They are indeed as much prison bars as they are gateways, for he cannot pass beyond them out into the countryside he adores. And thus his other favourite activity is understood. Inviting his friends to his estate for the hunting season, he spends his evenings listening to the stories they relate. The window here is both bond and barrier.

A curious interplay between exterior and interior is found in the short story "La Reine Hortense" (1883), although the image of the window, significantly enough, is referred to only obliquely, with the sun shining on the central figure as she lies on her deathbed. There is in the story a kind of contrapuntal interplay between the external world of the animals of her life and the children playing, and the imaginary world of the old woman as she awaits death. No communication really takes place between these two worlds and as a consequence the window stands unnoticed in the narrative. Finally the dog, chased by the little boy, rushes into the death chamber at the crucial moment, and Hortense's brother-in-law Colombel makes use of the window to break the news to the other members of the family. The barrier is broken by her death, and communication is restored.

That the window is an important image in Maupassant's short stories cannot be denied. The object itself furnishes the title of a tale published in the same year as "La Reine Hortense". Admittedly this story of love is different in tone, and the window is the focal point of a rather tongue-in-cheek dénouement involving a mistaken identity. Being put to the test by his beloved, the lover mistakes the mistress for the servant girl as he perceives only a portion of her anatomy through a window, and is caught in a compromising action. But nevertheless the window again serves a very similar function. Again it is a question of communication between the inside and the outside, between two individuals this time. And again that communication, while not completely interrupted as it was in "La Reine

Hortense", is only fragmentary. The physical contours, position and size of the object limit the lover's view of the situation, and in a certain sense, distort it. It is precisely this duality which catches him up. It is as if the window itself were an active figure in the critical moment, a kind of unfaithful go-between in the relation between the sexes.

The window can also have in Maupassant a tragic connotation in the construction of a narrative. Such a type, and perhaps the most striking example of it, may be studies in "Le modèle", again published in 1883. Like "La fenêtre" this story too deals with the relationship between the sexes. But here it becomes an instrument of suicide, a suicide which fails admittedly, but which permanently cripples the girl and ties her like a dead weight to the lover. Again it offers a communication, in this case a drastic solution to an ostensibly impossible situation, and again it deceives. The attempt to break the barrier to communication, to human relationships, terminates in a tragedy perhaps more heart-breaking than the situation it attempted to remedy. The narrator's reaction to this window has some pertinence here:

Je n'oublierai jamais l'effet que me fit cette fenêtre ouverte, après l'avoir vu traverser par ce corps qui tombait; elle me parut en une seconde grande comme le ciel et vide comme l'espace. Et je reculai instinctivement, n'osant pas regarder, comme si j'allais tomber moi-même.[1]

At the crucial moment, the narrator shrinks from the window, the gateway to infinity, for its invitation is the invitation of the unknown, and in that sense, a deception. The dual rôle is again played.

This is not the only situation in Maupassant in which suicide is related to the window. Yvette chooses another and indeed much more romantic means of self-destruction, but here too the communication with the outside world, seemingly cut off for her by the ether, is provided by the open window and the extending balcony. Isolation and communication are again essential to the development of the tension, and are again provided in no small part by the presence of a window.

Up to this point we have examined stories demonstrating the techniques of incorporating this aspect of reality in which, for the most part, the window whether briefly mentioned or a fully developed image remains largely exterior to the person or persons involved. In these stories it is really nothing more than one example of the technique of objectivity so dear to a number of nineteenth century novelists. For all its vitality, its originality is only slight.

[1] Maupassant, "Le modèle", *Le rosier de Madame Husson, Oeuvres complètes*, pp. 83–84. First published in *Le Gaulois* (December 17, 1883).

"Le signe" (1886), an amusing but hardly significant little piece confers on the window an important value. The woman's experiment with love on a professional basis is inspired by what she observes in the street below her apartment, and the compromising situation that develops from this arises completely from the window – temptation, communication, deception – all the necessary threads are present to weave a highly entertaining little study. But even here, it is the psychological impact of the situation which interests the reader more than the plot. And one can see the tendency already witnessed elsewhere of reducing the immediate value of physical reality by tying it up intimately not just with character but with plot, structure, dramatic situation. Its function will deepen and shift somewhat in position as the author perfects his own narrative method, until, along with a number of other recurring concepts, the window will illustrate unequivocally the new point of view of Maupassant with regard to fictional aims.

In "Yvette" we find already, particularly in this last scene, a deeper concern with the workings of the human mind than was generally visible in the earliest period, but with direct reference to the window, two of the clearest of its exploitations are found in "La petite Roque" and "Le Horla".

"La petite Roque" (1885), which precedes "Le signe" chronologically, at least according to date of publication, is both by the nature of the subject and the extent to which it is developed, a more valid piece of material for our analysis.

Seated in an armchair late one evening, Renardet notices a slight trembling of the curtains at the window. He momentarily overcomes his fear and draws them back:

Il ne vit rien d'abord que les vitres noires, noires comme des plaques d'encre luisante. La nuit, la grande nuit impénétrable s'étendait par derrière jusqu'à l'invisible horizon. Il restait debout en face de cette ombre illimitée; et tout à coup il y aperçut une lueur, une lueur mouvante, qui semblait éloignée.[2]

What he eventually perceives is the naked and bleeding body of his little victim. There could not be a clearer demonstration of the function of the window in Maupassant. Attracting Renardet towards the exterior, towards the limitless bounds of the black night, its inky black panes are a barrier as strong as a stone wall. Both limiting and limitless, it produces a hallucination in Renardet's mind which will lead finally to his own

---

[2] Maupassant, "La petite Roque", *La petite Roque, Oeuvres complètes*, p. 52. First published in *Le Gil Blas* (December 18 and 23, 1885).

destruction. It is, throughout the scene, his silent interlocutor, actively beckoning him:

S'étant relevé, il but un verre d'eau, puis s'assit. Il songeait: "Que vais-je faire, si cela recommence?" Et cela recommencerait, il le sentait, il en était sûr. Déjà la fenêtre sollicitait son regard, l'appelait, l'attirait.[3]

The window is thus not the mere externalization of a personality. We have moved rather far from the so-called realistic method. The disillusionment with reality, the cyclic infinity of *Bouvard et Pécuchet* has gone one further step, bound up with all aspects of the narrative. For this is a crucial point in the story. The window on the world is also the window on the crime, the window on the criminal and the window through which the reader perceives the truth in concrete terms. Or in other words, physical objects are assuming new proportions more intimately linked with all aspects of living.

But no examination of the communication between the external and internal worlds in Maupassant would be complete without some mention of "Le Horla". On the superficial level this intercommunication is simply the penetration of the invisible creature from the exterior world into the hero's home and mind. As the tension mounts however we realize that the penetration goes much deeper than that, and will end up only with Le Horla's seizure of the narrator's entire being. Windows and doors necessarily loom large in the narrative, particularly in the final entries in the diary. A fortified door and window are installed in his room to trap the creature. By the destruction of the building, the Horla will also, it is hoped, vanish. The similarities of technique and function with what has already been traced need no further explanation and should be self-evident.

The novels too contain a number of interesting references to the window. *Une vie* opens and closes with the heroine dreaming in front of one. Jeanne even turns to it instinctively at the death of her mother. Georges Duroy's miserable lodgings contain a window with a monotonously depressing view of Paris. This is the site of much of the protagonist's contemplation. The view of the Mediterranean at the death of Forestier is also largely seen through a window.

These earlier novels offer in this respect little more than still another illustration of the Bovary problem of frustration and confinement. Soaring imagination is hemmed in on every side by walls, windows, bounds, limitations. But romantic aspirations in Maupassant eventually give way

---

[3] "La petite Roque", p. 52.

to a more modern psychological problem – the attempt to seize, to grasp, to understand reality not just rationally – tragedy enough for Flaubert's late creations – but on every level of the senses, by every possible means at human disposal.

This expansive movement, this quest for the union of the universe, this latent mysticism is indeed only latent in the very presence of the window-image or other connected ones. The window imposes, after all, a frame, a limit, that is to say a form on infinity, and while suggesting it, at the same time it denies it. Characters are prevented from ultimate communication with infinity, perhaps in the form of ultimate destruction as "Le modèle" seems to suggest, by the imposing of form. It is again the concern with form and its increased use in Maupassant's art which most clearly suggests the nature of his method and the direction in which he is headed. It will be his chosen route out of the Flaubertian *cul-de-sac*. The escape into aesthetics has become an involvement of aesthetics.

An extension of the window image is undoubtedly that of the conservatory. In it we have an internalization, an artificially re-created external world. Its implications in *Bel-Ami*, in the new residence of the Walters and the setting in which the valuable painting of Christ is exhibited are indeed as complex as they are in Zola's *La curée*. The artificiality of the whole scene is what strikes the reader immediately. The two worlds clash here in an impossible man-made situation which, as we shall see later evokes a scathing view of the protagonist's make-up.

The extent to which a seemingly external object can lose its objectivity and become actively and vitally involved in human relationships can also be illustrated by the theme of the conservatory as it is presented in "Un cas de divorce", a very curious little work published in 1890. In the excerpts from his diary read into the court record, the husband evokes a picture of an entire world contained within the confines of his green-house:

J'ai des serres où personne ne pénètre que moi et celui qui en prend soin.

J'entre là comme on se glisse en un lieu de plaisir secret. Dans la haute galerie de verre je passe d'abord entre deux foules de corolles fermées, entr'ou-vertes ou épanouies qui vont en pente de la terre au toit . . .[4]

The narrator has created for himself an artificial world on his own terms. The reality it represents to him is a totally invented, indeed hallucinatory one with no relationship to the so-called norm. The interplay between the

[4] Maupassant, "Un cas de divorce", *L'inutile beauté, Oeuvres complètes*, p. 226. First published in *Le Gil Blas* (August 31, 1886).

internal and external worlds is confined between glass walls, whose presence is responsible for both the view of life and its deceptive artificiality. Isolation, even in glass walls is no authentic solution.

Still another recurrent theme in the author's description is that of the mirror, closely related for obvious reasons to that of the window, but much more fully developed in the course of Maupassant's works. A rather significant number of short stories deal directly with the mirror and deserve our attention.

A brief work entitled "Adieu" provides us I think with quite a suitable illustration of the mirror as an image in Maupassant from which we can proceed to more complex connotations. A sudden unexpected encounter with a woman whose relationship with the narrator was on a most intimate basis twelve years ago leads him to a close scrutiny of the ravage of time. The story ends with his consulting his mirror, which informs him in the clearest terms that he is now old. How meaningful is the last utterance of the story, the simple word "Adieu".

We have here a straightforward example of the kind of dialogue Maupassant sets up between man and his environment. The mirror finds itself in frequent use when he wishes to deal directly with the intensely human problem of the passage of time. Another similar story, "Fini", is constructed between two references to this same image. Consulting his mirror upon dressing, the comte de Lormerin concludes happily that although grey, he is still handsome, and still very much alive. But an unexpected letter and an ensuing visit to one of his old loves of many years past shatters forever the illusion. He remembers her as her daughter now appears. The final consultation in the mirror casts the fearful shadow of age:

Mais comme il passait, une bougie à la main, devant sa glace, devant sa grande glace où il s'était contemplé et admiré avant de partir, il aperçut dedans un homme mûr à cheveux gris; et soudain, il se rappela ce qu'il était autrefois, au temps de la petite Lise; il se revit, charmant et jeune, tel qu'il avait été aimé. Alors, approchant la lumière, il se regarda de près, inspectant les rides, constatant ces affreux ravages qu'il n'avait encore jamais aperçus.

Et il s'assit, accablé, en face de lui-même, en face de sa lamentable image, en murmurant: "Fini Lormerin".[5]

Before moving to *Bel-Ami* the novel which must rise immediately to mind, let us briefly look at some other stories which deal with the mirror and age. In "Duchoux" (1887) the baron de Mordiane, travelling to Marseilles

---

[5]   Maupassant, "Fini", *Oeuvres postumes* I, *Oeuvres complètes*, p. 242. First published in *Le Gaulois* (July 27, 1885).

to locate his illegitimate son makes the same discovery as he rises from his pullman berth and views himself in the harsh morning light. Madame Hermet's constant concern with the preservation of her beauty is just cause for frequent consultations in a mirror. But when her beloved son falls mortally ill with that most disfiguring of diseases, smallpox, it is this same concern which bars her from even setting eyes on him through a window. The narcissus complex has become in this story much more than the harsh revelation of fact; it is the governor of human relationships. It is as if the maternal instinct were snuffed out, obliterated. The mirror is not simply reflecting, but controlling the situation. She is committed to an institution, a prisoner of her image.

But fear can take other forms than fear of vanishing beauty. Fear of death is of course best demonstrated in this context by that chapter of *Bel-Ami* first published separately and with only slight modification under the title "Un lâche" in the *Gaulois* of February 5, 1884. The unnamed protagonist, who will become Georges Duroy, is drawn towards the mirror in his room as he suffers the mental torture of the next morning's trial:

Et un singulier besoin le prit tout à coup de se relever pour se regarder dans la glace. Il ralluma sa bougie. Quand il aperçut son visage reflété dans le verre poli, il se reconnut à peine, et il lui sembla qu'il ne s'était jamais vu. Ses yeux lui parurent énormes; et il était pâle, certes, et il était pâle, très pâle.[6]

What we have here is of course a kind of exteriorization of the self, a "dédoublement du moi". By means of it the character is capable of coming to grips to some extent with the implications of a situation.

Yvette too undergoes a very similar experience. As she wrestles with the problem of her own life and that of her mother, she too is drawn to the looking-glass:

Elle contemplait attentivement son visage, comme si elle ne l'avait jamais aperçu, examinant surtout ses yeux, découvrant mille choses en elle, un caractère secret de sa physionomie qu'elle ne connaissait pas, s'étonnant de se voir comme si elle avait en face d'elle une personne étrangère, une nouvelle amie.

Elle se disait: "C'est moi, c'est moi que voilà dans cette glace. Comme c'est étrange de se regarder soi-même. Tous les autres sauraient comment nous sommes, et nous ne le saurions point, nous.[7]

Again we find the mirror objectively observing, and communicating its information with the person. But this last example demonstrates how

[6]   Maupassant, "Un lâche", *Contes du jour et de la unit, Oeuvres complètes*, pp. 113–14.
[7]   Maupassant, "Yvette", *Yvette, Oeuvres complètes*, pp. 115–16. First published in *Le Figaro* (August 29–September 8, 1884).

much more probing this theme can become than a simple expression of physical appearance. Yvette is seeking, and indeed seems to be discovering a deeper truth. The operative verb here is not *voir* but *savoir*. She is in search of her own significance, her own value, that is to say her own psychological identity. And one might conclude at this point that Maupassant holds that the only truth available to us is transmitted to us objectively through this external aspect, tangible, visible contours. In order to know herself, Yvette must see herself. But does she arrive at a final decision as a result of self-knowledge or on the basis of conscious self-deception?

Is the mirror a kind of oracle of truth, the revealer of identity which it seems to be here? One must not forget that what one sees in the glass is a reflection, an image, that is to say, an illusion in itself.

Maupassant sows the seeds of doubt in this regard in "Rencontre". The problem of marital infidelity first presents itself to the husband through the reflection in a mirror:

Par derrière, une grande tache claire donnait la sensation d'un lac vu par une haute fenêtre. C'était la glace, immense, discrète, habillée de draperies sombres qu'on laissait tomber quelquefois, qu'on avait souvent relevées; et la glace semblait regarder la couche, sa complice. On eût dit qu'elle avait des souvenirs, des regrets, comme ces châteaux que hantent les spectres des morts, et qu'on allait voir passer sur sa face unie et vide ces formes charmantes qu'ont les hanches nues des femmes, et les gestes doux des bras quand ils enlacent.[8]

This is the object which conveys to the husband the image of his wife locked in another's embrace. Even its description contains a certain element of conjecture, conveyed by verbal expressions such as *donnait la sensation, semblait, on eût dit.* And the story ends on such an enigmatic note that one is sorely tempted to doubt the accuracy of the original description.

Still another story makes this point. Mourning the loss of his beloved wife, a widower seeks her image in the mirror which so often reflected it:

J'étais là debout, frémissant, les yeux fixés sur le verre, sur le verre plat, profond, vide, mais qui l'avait contenue toute entière, possédée autant que moi, autant que mon regard passionné. Il me sembla que j'aimais cette glace, – je la touchai, – elle était froide! Oh! le souvenir! miroir douloureux, miroir brûlant, miroir vivant, miroir horrible, qui fait souffrir toutes les tortures! Heureux les hommes dont le coeur, comme une glace où glissent et s'effacent les reflets, oublie tout

---

[8]   Maupassant, "Rencontre", *Les soeurs Rondoli, Oeuvres complètes*, pp. 211–12. First published in *Le Gil Blas* (March 11, 1884).

ce qu'il a contenu, tout ce qui a passé devant lui, tout ce qui s'est contemplé, miré, dans son affection, dans son amour! Comme je souffre.[9]

In reality the mirror too is only a sham, a smooth piece of cold glass, whose message is ephemeral, which can, in the final analysis convey very little, if anything. It too is a distorter of truth.

This is made all the more evident by "Le Horla". The reader is necessarily dubious of the existence of the invisible creature other than in the mind of the narrator himself, and when the mirror seemingly substantiates its presence in the room, we are convinced that the entire physical world, with the mirror as its seemingly objective spokesman, is treasonous.

Je me dressai, les mains tendues, en me tournant si vite que je faillis tomber. Eh bien? ... on y voyait comme en plein jour, et je ne me vis pas dans ma glace! ... Elle était vide, claire, profonde, pleine de lumière! Mon image n'était pas dedans... et j'étais en face, moi! Je voyais le grand verre limpide du haut en bas. Et je regardais cela avec des yeux affolés; et je n'osais plus avancer, je n'osais plus faire un mouvement, sentant bien pourtant qu'il était là, mais qu'il m'échapperait encore, lui dont le corps imperceptible avait dévoré mon reflet.[10]

Like Madame Hermet, the narrator here has become a victim, a victim as much of his mirror as of his invisible creature. The identity he seeks, the same one that Yvette apparently recoiled from, has been lost to him. The distortion has become too great.

As with other images, that of the mirror cannot be fully developed with regard to Maupassant without careful consideration of the novels. To deal in detail with every isolated reference to the mirror in all six novels would be a thankless task, since, in a large number of cases the points they would illustrate would only serve as further evidence of what we have already shown.

Bel-Ami certainly deserves our careful scrutiny, since, as Sullivan so rightly observes:

The main theme and purpose of the novel are emphasized and made clear by the recurrence of an image – not a figure of speech, but an actual reflection in a mirror, used as a conscious artistic device. Nor is this Stendhal's mirror which is carried along a road reflecting life; it is a reflection within the reflection of life that the novel is supposed to be.[11]

[9]   Maupassant, "La morte", *La main gauche, Oeuvres complètes*, p. 224. First published in *Le Gil Blas* (May 31, 1887).
[10] Maupassant, "Le Horla", *Le Horla, Oeuvres complètes*, p. 43.
[11] Sullivan, *Maupassant the Novelist*, p. 86.

The first incidence of the mirror image is exactly that – an opportunity for Duroy to examine himself, to admire himself on the landing of the stairs in his elegant attire. Narcissism is again an essential aspect of narrative development, as we have already seen, and clearly marks Duroy's meteoric and unscrupulous rise in Parisian society. The progression is noteworthy. As he enters the building in which the Forestier apartment is located, he meets a gentleman on the first landing who turns out to be his own reflection in a full-length mirror. The exteriorization, the *dédoublement*, is thus convincingly established. At this juncture Duroy's sole concern is, as we have said, with his appearance. But the mirror on the second landing affords an opportunity for further exploration:

En arrivant au second étage, il aperçut une autre glace et il ralentit sa marche pour se regarder passer. Sa tournure lui parut vraiment élégante. Il marchait bien. Et une confiance immodérée en lui-même emplit son âme. Certes, il réussirait avec cette figure-là et son désir d'arriver, et la résolution qu'il se connaissait et l'indépendance de son esprit.[12]

The physical appearance serves as a buttress for the protagonist's ambition. The truth of the appearance gives him overwhelming self-confidence. During the course of the narrative Duroy will return to this scene on two significant occasions. By Chapter Two of the second part of the novel, he has married Madeleine Forestier and thus replaced her deceased first husband not only professionally but maritally as well. His complacency as he views himself in these same mirrors is thus doubly explainable. The incident marks the opening of phase two of Duroy's ascension. The third and last contact with these same mirrors follows immediately the acceptance of Madeleine's rather compromising (for Duroy at least) inheritance. Illuminated by the dim glow of a match, both he and Madeleine appear briefly, like phantoms, in the mirror. It is Duroy who studies them, and concludes triumphantly: "Voilà des millionnaires qui passent."

From the material point of view, he is already at the summit. Further conquest, even although they will bring considerable remuneration, will be in the social order of things. Maupassant has no further need for these mirrors in the novel, and will devise other means of portraying his hero.

However, these three incidents, meaningful as they are, are by no means the only important uses of the mirror in this work. The first open testimony of affection between Duroy and Madame de Marelle is associated as well with the mirror. Adjusting his tie in the glass as he waits for her to appear, he first spies her as a reflection in the glass:

[12] Maupassant, *Bel-Ami*, p. 30.

Il fit semblant de ne l'avoir point vue, et ils se considérèrent quelques secondes, au fond du miroir, s'observant, s'épiant, avant de se trouver face à face.[13]

If Duroy is truly capable of love, there can be no doubt that the object of his affection is Madame de Marelle. She is the only one of his conquests who brings him no clear advancement, material or social. In spite of interruptions, this affair remains very much alive right to the end of the book, with the suggestion on the last page that it will continue to prosper in the future in spite of Georges' marriage to Suzanne Walter. The presence of this mirror in the initial scene assumes then rather more than its surface value. For Duroy here is frankly out to conquer her, and attacks the problem calculating each move with precision. The mirror thus, while communicating their mutual glances, sets up a deception, a barrier, a distortion which is borne out by further developments. She is a persistent and unreal presence in his mind. For Duroy, whose capacity for human feelings is certainly limited, the relationship with Madame de Marelle is one which he can seemingly pick up or drop without compunction. He presents to her a sham love, an illusion of love which is in reality only a form of self-gratification. He remains in truth as smooth, as hard, and as invisible to her as is the surface of a mirror.

The mirror can deceive Duroy too. Invited to the Walter's, he is confused at first, out of his element, and loses his sense of direction because he first sees the guests as a reflection in a mirror and turns in the wrong direction. The chapter dealing with the preparation for the duel again associates the mirror image with Duroy as we have seen, and again is a source of distortion, of deception for him.

This association of image with character runs as a kind of *leitmotif* throughout the novel. The one image, which we saw used in the short stories for varied but interrelated purposes, can in the novel have numerous ramifications and thus assume great depth of meaning. The completion of this theme is contained in the conservatory scene already referred to, and which I intend to return to in greater detail when I come to deal with the third aspect of the internal image of identity, the picture.

Remaining for the moment with the mirror, we find manifestations of it in the last two novels which, like those of *Bel-Ami* are worthy of close consideration. In the opening chapter of *Fort comme la mort* the mutual exchange of glances between Anne de Guilleroy and her lover Olivier Bertin occurs under circumstances almost identical to those surrounding Georges Duroy and Madame de Marelle. She interrupts him looking at

[13]   *Bel-Ami*, pp. 131–32.

himself in the glass. Like those other Maupassant creations, Bertin and Madame de Guilleroy are both falling victim to the inexorable passage of time, and the mirror is of great importance to the pair. As her beauty wanes, particularly after the crisis of her mother's death, she is never without a hand mirror, which she consults with regularity. The presence of a mirror at their initial meeting in the novel is thus symbolic of the deterioration of their physical bodies and also of the bond between them. By self-delusion or by skillful application of make-up, they carry on their relationship, supported all the while by the distortions of their reflected images.

But by far the most fully developed mirror image in Maupassant's work is to be found in his final novel, *Notre coeur*. A lengthy description of Michèle de Burne's boudoir opens the second chapter, and occupying the place of honour in it, is a most elaborate glass:

> ... Puis tenant un mur entier, une glace immense s'ouvrait comme un horizon clair. Elle était formée de trois panneaux dont les deux côtés latéraux, articulés sur des charnières, permettait à la jeune femme de se voir en même temps de face, de profil et de dos, de s'enfermer dans son image.[14]

This, the novel of the modern woman, gives to Michèle de Burne a place of primacy. The mirror lends to this woman's appearance a type of independent existence, as if she were a kind of statue. And I say statue in preference to portrait or painting because, thanks to the nature of the mirror presented here, the description is intentionally three-dimensional. This kind of external presentation is carefully worked out in the first chapter, since we first espy her under the controlled, artificial light of a lamp, and it is her physical contours, her beauty, which immediately captivate Mariolle.

And even her bath has a mirror of Venetian glass placed in a strategic position. As Maupassant puts it, the mirror "abritait, enfermait et réflétait" the bath tub and the bather.

This image of the mirror is fully developed since it represents, one might rather say embodies, the character of the heroine. As we have seen it used before, here too it has become an instrument of self-analysis. If she more than any other feminine creation of Maupassant incorporates his Schopenhauerian disdain for the weaker sex, then it is I think safe to say that the mirror here has reached its full flower in his artistic method. For her image, which attracts Mariolle in the first place, is the greatest of deceptions. Full of beauty, magnetically attractive, she proves to be incapable

---

[14] Maupassant, *Notre coeur*, p. 37.

of that warmth of human communication which Mariolle desires. She is as cold and impenetrable as her three-panelled mirror, as was Georges Duroy before her. Mariolle is so much a victim of this consciously constructed image that when he does find sincerity in the person of Elizabeth, he cannot escape its influence. It is Michèle de Burne, an artificially created image, an aesthetic form, who emerges victorious. Mariolle's return at the end of the novel is a kind of self-delusion, yes, but a self-delusion which must be considered and weighed carefully. Within it lies the key to Maupassant's view of the world and the human condition, as we shall shortly see.

Pourtant, il était résigné à tout souffrir plutôt que la perdre encore, résigné à cet éternel désir devenu dans ses veines une sorte d'appétit féroce jamais rassasié et qui brûlait sa chair.[15]

By closing his eyes he would, in the confusion of "celle qu'il aimait" and "celle qui l'aimait" possess them both. In other words he will be able to escape the distortions of visual reality, of the image and its contours, and possess within himself an ideal. It is the introversion of that all-powerful sense of sight. The mirror, both communication and barrier, can thus and only thus be broken. Rather than the intensely pessimistic interpretation usually given to this novel, and particularly to its closing lines, it is my contention that a new direction towards greater interiorization is in the process of discovery. And the mirror is a key to Maupassant for this very reason. While imposing an ostensibly insuperable barrier on the human mind, it in fact will come to release it into a new internal dimension. And he makes this point very clearly himself in describing the sea-bottom in "Un soir":

Je me penchai de nouveau et j'aperçus le fond de la mer. A quelques pieds sous le bateau il se déroulait lentement, à mesure que nous passions, l'étrange pays de l'eau, de l'eau qui vivifie, comme l'air du ciel, des plantes et des bêtes. Le brasier enfonçant jusqu'aux rochers sa vive lumière nous glissions sur des forêts surprenantes d'herbes rousses, roses, vertes, jaunes. Entre elles et nous une glace admirablement transparente, une glace liquide, presque invisible, les rendait féeriques, les reculait dans un rêve, dans le rêve qu'éveillent les océans profonds. Cette onde claire si limpide qu'on ne distinguait point, qu'on devinait plutôt, mettait entre ces étranges végétations et nous quelque chose de troublant comme le doute de la réalité, les faisait mystérieuses comme les paysages des songes.[16]

[15] *Notre coeur*, pp. 292–93.
[16] Maupassant, "Un soir", *La main gauche*, *Oeuvres complètes*, p. 131. First published in *L'Illustration* (January 19 and 26, 1889).

The window and the mirror thus become instruments through which an individual may set out on his quest for a deeper meaning in life beyond that of tangible reality, the quest for an infinity returns, but not the infinity of the external world.

If the means we describe have some validity, then there is another recurrent image which assumes a great significance in Maupassant's technique, namely, the picture, including of course the portrait, perhaps its most meaningful manifestation.

When dealing generally with the problem of interior décor, we mentioned how much Maupassant owes to his predecessors in the field of the novel. And pictures on the walls form a necessary and very useful function in this descriptive technique. But that Maupassant shows a predilection for them is a fact that we have already established, and which should be obvious to any serious student of his work. From the pictures of military officers hanging in "La chambre 11", scene of the clandestine activities of a seemingly respectable bourgeoise to the seascapes in Madame Rosémilly's apartment, they are drawn to our attention every time Maupassant gives us something more than a passing reference to the furnishings of a room. And their purpose is perfectly obviously that which Balzac, Flaubert and Zola as well have exploited in dealing with descriptive material. But here again he goes further.

We have seen elsewhere that such an object can assume a rôle much greater than the simple character revelation it traditionally achieves. I refer here to the scene in "Hautot père et fils" (already dealt with in Chapter Two). Madame Rosémilly's taste in art in *Pierre et Jean* also is a commentary, not only on her character, but also on the relationship with the brothers. These inanimate objects thus convey a message both to the characters and to the readers.

That the picture and more precisely the painting have the capacity for communication is an essential factor in the structure of "Miss Harriet". The taciturn gaunt English old maid appears and disappears silently and mysteriously in the opening pages of the story until she casts her eye on the most recent product of the painter-narrator:

Miss Harriet rentrait et elle passait derrière moi juste au moment où, tenant ma toile à bout de bras, je la montrais à l'aubergiste. La démoniaque ne put pas ne pas la voir, car j'avais soin de présenter la chose de telle sorte qu'elle n'échappât point à son oeil. Elle s'arrêta net, saisie, stupéfaite. C'était sa roche, paraît-il, celle où grimpait pour rêver à son aise.

Elle murmura un "Aoh!" britannique si accentué et si flatteur, que je me tournai vers elle en souriant; et je lui dis:

"C'est ma dernière étude, Mademoiselle."

Elle murmura, extasiée, comique et attendrissante: "Oh! Monsieur, vô comprené le nature d'une façon palpitante!"[17]

In this most romantic of seacoast settings, the sharing of nature's beauties between these two sensitive souls stems initially from a two-dimensional interpretation of it by the painter. What establishes the rapport then is not the visible world, but its man-made reflection. Communication, identification springs from an imaginative and successful distortion and not from the scene itself.

The study entitled, significantly enough "Un portrait" is a curious elaboration of this same point. The narrator makes the acquaintance of a man for whom he feels a spontaneous, unexplainable bond of friendship. After only the briefest of times, he considers him as he might his oldest of friends. Invited to lunch at his new friend's home, he studies the portrait of a woman hanging on the wall. There follows a rather lengthy description of the painting which is seemingly endowed with a living force:

Elle était tellement seule, et chez elle, qu'elle faisait le vide en tout ce grand appartement, le vide absolu. Elle l'habitait, l'emplissait, l'animait seule; il y pouvait entrer beaucoup de monde, et tout ce monde pouvait parler, rire, même chanter; elle y serait toujours seule, avec un sourire solitaire, et seule, elle le rendrait vivant, de son regard de portrait.[18]

This expression in the eyes leads the viewer to quote Baudelaire:

Et tes yeux attirants comme ceux d'un portrait

and again an externalized description, interpreted as it is in a work of art, assumes life-like vitality. The eyes hide within them the secret of what is and what is not; the reflected object or person has a depth of meaning which can be perceived, unlike the opaqueness of the living world. It is this portrait which explains to the narrator the charm of his host. Communication is established between two living persons by means of the vision of the artist whose subject is long since dead. Again the question of the true value of the perceptible is put to the test. The intangible, the ethereal is explained by a visual aesthetic experience.

Maupassant's first novel, by its very title has a dominant theme the passage of time. If one of the functions of art is to render the fleeting

---

[17] Maupassant, "Miss Harriet", *Miss Harriet, Oeuvres complètes*, p. 16.
[18] Maupassant, "Un portrait", *L'inutile beauté, Oeuvres complétes*, p. 185. First published in *Le Gaulois* (October 29, 1888).

permament, to transfix the ephemeral, then the Veronese portrait of the first chapter would appear as an attemt to arrest time, to prevent the destruction of Jeanne's beauty and her life. This attempt is all the more convincing if one stops to analyse the method of presentation of this portrait, already quoted on p. 38.

The opening paragraph deals principally with textures, but ends on an emphatic note by describing her eyes in terms of a durable material. The author then moves to outline the forms of his subject – *petite, grande, ondoyante* and ends by endowing his work of art with a voice and movement.

Right from the beginning the reader must *see* the heroine before he can begin to understand her. And yet this portrait will not last. Its deterioration is really the central problem of the novel, a problem which involves not only Jeanne's physical appearance, but indeed every aspect of her make-up. The tragedy of this deterioration is rendered all the more poignant because of this visual, aesthetic point of departure. The picture fades as the novel progresses, and Maupassant makes only brief references to Jeanne's changing appearance in the rest of the narrative. Interesting as this method of presentation is, it ultimately constitutes just another example of the so-called objective technique. The portrait is clearly only external, a comment on character and not to it. But the very nature of the image makes it important in attempting to show a continuity in Maupassant's aesthetic approach.

The mirror images so carefully developed in *Bel-Ami* find their logical conclusion in the portrait of Christ which the Walters so ostentatiously display in celebrating the acquisition of their new home. It is set in the conservatory in a framework of tropical, that is to say artificial greenery and is unequivocally connected with Duroy as intimately as were the mirrors. Christ, walking on the waters, gained an imposing appearance in such a setting, and seemed like "un trou noir sur un lointain fantastique et saisissant". The dramatic light projected on the figure, and all else save the stars relegated to a semi-darkness, gives to the painting an illusory quality which is emotionally very effective indeed.

C'était bien là l'oeuvre puissante et inattendue d'un maître, une de ces oeuvres qui bouleversent la pensée et vous laissent du rêve pour des années.[19]

The effectiveness of the piece rests clearly with its dramatic use of light, and not with its fidelity to its subject matter. For after all the very nature of the subject itself is discordant with the tenets of realistic teachings.

[19]   Maupassant, *Bel-Ami*, p. 490.

The portrait is tied to Georges Duroy by the remarks of young Suzanne Walter, who, incidentally was herself first presented to the reader in terms of a miniature.

Suzanne s'écria: – Mais il vous ressemble, Bel-Ami. Je suis sûre qu'il vous ressemble. Si vous aviez des favoris, ou bien s'il s'était rasé, vous seriez tout pareils tous les deux. Oh! mais c'est frappant.[20]

Duroy is subsequently forced to stand beside the work of art in order for all to make the comparison. The point is clear. Duroy is as much a deceiver as is this unreal painting in its hot-house setting. And in his own frame of reference he is as effective a distorter of truth as was Jesus Christ himself. The bitter irony of Walter's remark which precedes this incident is inescapable:

Figurez-vous, dit-il en riant, que j'ai trouvé ma femme à genoux devant ce tableau comme dans une chapelle. Elle faisait là ses dévotions. Ce que j'ai ri![21]

This Jew turned Christian is totally insensitive to the feelings of his wife, but one must remember too that he is completely oblivious to the recently ended intimate relationship between Madame Walter and Bel-Ami. She stands in breathless admiration of the handsome figure in the painting clearly because it is so striking a likeness of her lover who compromised and then abandoned her.

The portrait becomes then a complex visual image, a reflection of Duroy, and brings into clear focus the true value of the incidents on the staircase. We said in discussing them that they were the means by which Bel-Ami objectivized his situation and formed a picture of it in his mind. But in the light of the portrait which concludes the chain the illusory aspect of it all comes quite clear. The last of the three mirror incidents occurred in a light remarkably similar to that of the painting, and I am convinced of Maupassant's intention to link them all together. Thus not only is Duroy deceiving all the other people in the book, but he is himself deceived by his own appearance. The entire novel is a series of visual tricks culminating on the steps of the Madeleine with his apotheosis. The sham is revealed to the reader by the same images which serve to deceive all the characters of the book. The visual image in *Bel-Ami* is a complex construction which serves to convey both illusion and truth, communication and barriers, identification and annihilation. It is the bitter irony of the novel

[20]   *Bel-Ami*, p. 508.
[21]   *Bel-Ami*, p. 507.

and the source of its success that Duroy is successful because there are distortions of truth. He is not only the instigator of them, but their victim as well.

Pierre et Jean, perhaps the most successful of Maupassant's novels, furnishes a fine example of the picture image which is thoroughly integrated into the pattern of the novel. Robert Niess's article on this work establishes, with its study of light and shadow, a vital fact in the development of the work, namely that it is a visual novel, constructed around the sense of sight to a degree that renders all other sensory perceptions within it of strictly secondary significance. We have already dealt extensively with the imagery which it contains, but the one image which is absolutely central to the psychological conflict which it sets out to portray must be the miniature of Maréchal which Madame Roland so carefully conceals until the last possible moment. This small item is truly the keystone of the work, for it is the portrait which gives to Pierre conclusive evidence of his mother's guilt. Immediately following its reappearance we read:

On eût dit qu'ils [Pierre et sa mère] s'épiaient, qu'une lutte venait de se déclarer entre eux; et un malaise douloureux, un malaise insoutenable crispait le coeur de Pierre. Il se disait, torturé et satisfait, pourtant: "Doit-elle souffrir en ce moment, si elle sait que je l'ai devinée!" Et à chaque retour vers le foyer, il s'arrêtait quelques secondes à contempler le visage blond de Maréchal, pour bien montrer qu'une idée fixe le hantait. Et ce petit portrait, moins grand qu'une main ouverte, semblait une personne vivante, méchante, redoutable, entrée soudain dans cette maison et dans cette famille.[22]

There can be no doubt of the fact that Pierre has made up his mind at this point about the essentials of the problem. What remains to be done will stem directly from this revelation.

It is significant that unlike previous portraits and paintings, this miniature is not directly revealed to the reader. For in this novel, Maupassant's major concern is not to portray the exterior, that is to say the physical world; he concentrates on a much more interiorized problem. Thus a detailed description of the object in question would constitute nothing more than a digression and would distract the reader's attention from what matters. The objective approach denies the concept of the omniscient author, but by drawing our attention so graphically to the significant objects, gives to the reader an omniscience which we had in *Bel-Ami* thanks to the images, but which is possible to acquire during the reading of *Pierre et Jean*. Observed reality is not a key to the inner world, but a genuine part of it.

[22] Maupassant, *Pierre et Jean*, pp. 135–36.

In this passage, two aspects of the picture are important – first of all its diminutive size, out of all proportion to its significance, and a clear, albeit somewhat brief suggestion of form. The new rôle of external objects is nowhere more vividly portrayed. The miniature is, like other objects intensely alive. What is important is not what it looks like, but the message it conveys to those perceptive enough within the fictional circumstances to comprehend. Monsieur Roland is entirely oblivious to its impact, insensitive as he is to all he beholds. Jean too dismisses it with little more than a brief mention. Only Pierre and his mother are aware of the drama contained in its frame, and it is the conflict between these two around which the novel is really constructed. The problem of identity is put in concrete terms in this fashion, and in a way in which the reader is compelled to take far greater interest in that problem than in its exterior manifestations or resolutions. The shift of emphasis with regard to the objective world is for the first time lucidly illustrated.

The central problem of *Fort comme la mort* is so strikingly similar to that of *Pierre et Jean* that it would be impossible to dismiss it as coincidental. It is again a problem of identity, centring around the youthful Annette and the slowly fading beauty of her mother, Anne de Guilleroy.

We find again an external focal point for the mental anguish of Olivier Bertin in the portrait of Anne now hanging in her home and painted by him when she was in the full bloom of beauty. The similarity between mother and daughter is so remarkable that they are the centre of a lengthy discussion during the dinner party of the second chapter. The novel is constructed around Olivier Bertin's gradual awakening to the fact that he is not in love with Anne, but with his picture of her as it now finds three-dimensional embodiment in the person of her daughter. This impasse leads him to self-destruction.

Here again the portrait in question, like the miniature of Maréchal, is never really visible to the reader, although both mother and daughter are. When Bertin finishes the work, we read:

Il avait fini le portrait de la comtesse, le meilleur, certes, qu'il eût peint, car il avait su voir et fixer ce je ne sais quoi d'inexprimable que presque jamais un peintre ne dévoile, ce reflet, ce mystère, cette physionomie de l'âme qui passe, insaisissable, sur les visages.[23]

The impact of the piece is thus distinctly visual in nature, and the work represents the high point of Bertin's career, just as his relationship with Anne de Guilleroy represents the climax of his emotional existence.

[23]   Maupassant, *Fort comme la mort*, p. 55.

Being both a product of his talent and an external object, the portrait is given a double depth for Bertin. And by hiding its physical contours from the reader's eye, Maupassant preserves its mysterious power, which, as he says, is "inexprimable". It is again a question not of appearance, but of essential nature, its importance, its impact on the fictional situation.

Nor can there be any doubt about the power of this painting. Like its immediate predecessor, it too has a strength, a vitality:

Au milieu du mur principal, le portrait de la comtesse par Olivier Bertin semblait habiter, animer l'appartement. Il y était chez lui, mêlait à l'air même du salon son sourire de jeune femme, la grâce de son regard, le charme léger de ses cheveux blonds.[24]

Initially, Bertin's confusion is linked with the two women. But as the novel progresses this distortion of his vision becomes less severe. Little by little he begins to differentiate more clearly between them. A double movement is involved. First Anne is genuinely aging as the book progresses, and second, Bertin is increasingly aware of the nature of his confusion as he becomes, little by little, more involved:

Le grand soleil les éclairant, il confondait moins à présent la comtesse avec Annette, mais il confondait de plus en plus la fille avec le souvenir renaissant de ce qu'avait été la mère.[25]

As in the case of *Pierre et Jean*, so here, events of the past begin to take precedence over the present. The reduction of objectively perceived externals is increasing as Maupassant perfects his technique. And Bertin is finally aware that the portrait has spoken to Anne when her daughter is compared to it. It takes only a re-creation of the circumstances which produced the original for the problem to come out into the open.

Essentially, Bertin is caught between two irreconcilable worlds. Emotionally he is involved with Anne, and will remain so forever. But the external world is constantly trying to destroy his love. He himself observes: "Non, je n'aime pas la petite, je suis la victime de sa ressemblance." The tragedy of the novel lies in the fact that, although Bertin becomes aware of the treachery of reality's illusion of truth he is unable to reconcile this fact with his own inner being. Bertin is incapable of taking that one step. Just as Pierre Roland extricated himself physically from an intensely difficult position, Bertin, by another and much more drastic means, repeats the process. The mirror deception of *Bel-Ami* is the portrait deception of *Fort comme la mort*.

[24] *Fort comme la mort*, p. 82.
[25] *Fort comme la mort*, pp. 217–18.

But the technique has made some progress, since the visual image so necessary to both *Pierre et Jean* and *Fort comme la mort* becomes more interiorized here. An image of an image, it is also a creation of a creation. *Notre coeur* will be the next stage in the progression. Mariolle is the victim of an inner image, that of Michèle de Burne, the only reality which he has left to cling to.

These three types of interior images which run throughout Maupassant's fiction, that is to say the window, the mirror and the painting, are thus really three manifestations of the same basic principle. Their common characteristics shed much light on the problem of Maupassant's art. They are of course all visual, and the stress on vision in this author's view of the world cannot be overstated. As well as these illustrations, both internal and external, we find Maupassant's characters constantly looking in each other's eyes to try to communicate. The shape of Paul Brétigny's eyes strikes Christiane Andermatt immediately. Madeleine Forestier is shrouded in smoke when we first meet her, and her character and activities remain enigmatic for as long as she participates in the novel. Mademoiselle Fifi enjoys nothing more than to shoot the eyes out of the portraits on the walls. Pierre and his mother cast furtive glances at each other in an attempt to make contact. For as we saw in Olivier Bertin's portrait, it is the visual, the expression on a face, which contains within it the inexplicable, the essence of life. However, the other senses, and particularly the ear, must not be disregarded. *Fort comme la mort* and "L'inutile beauté" offer us moving examples of the power of music. But in the larger scheme of things these are little more than isolated examples. Powerful as they are, there is not really sufficient auditory material within Maupassant's works to justify any suggestion that this might rival the sense of sight in significance. The author himself reveals the primacy of the eye in his approach to his material:

Mes yeux ouverts, à la façon d'une bouche affamée, dévorent le terre et le ciel. Oui, j'ai la sensation nette et profonde de manger le monde avec mon regard, et de digérer les couleurs comme on digère les viandes et les fruits.[26]

. . .

L'Oeil, le plus admirable des organes humains, est indéfiniment perfectionnable; et il arrive, quand on pousse avec intelligence son éducation, à une admirable acuité.[27]

---

[26] Maupassant, "La vie d'un paysagiste", *Oeuvres postumes* II, *Oeuvres complètes*, p. 84. First published in *Le Gil Blas* (September 28, 1886).
[27] "Vie d'un paysagiste", p. 88.

The exterior and interior images to which we have attached so much importance in these last two chapters should be more than adequate proof of the conscious application of his opinions.

Another characteristic of the three internal images is the fact that they all constitute framed objects, that is, images with clearly defined limitations. They are constantly imposing bounds on the reality they reflect or reveal, and thus impede the search for an infinity which they offer a glimpse of, and which is the constant aim of Maupassant's art. To break the barrier is precisely the goal of the Maupassant hero, to transcend the limits of the real, to effect a breach in the fortifications. And again we have only to listen to Maupassant himself to realize the degree to which he was concerned with this problem:

Ah! si les poètes pouvaient traverser l'espace, explorer les astres, découvrir d'autres êtres, varier sans cesse pour mon esprit la nature et la forme des choses, me promener sans cesse dans un inconnu changeant et surprenant, ouvrir des portes mystérieuses sur des horizons inattendus et merveilleux, je les lirais jour et nuit. Mais ils ne peuvent, ces impuissants, que changer la place d'un mot, et me montrer mon image, comme les peintres. A quoi bon?[28]

Art then becomes a narcissistic vicious circle without an exit, incapable of varying the nature and the form of things. Maupassant would appear to be caught in a trap just as strong as Flaubert's.

Again we find both interior and exterior imagery converging on the same point. Just as the constant intrusion of the vertical on the horizontal shatters the illusion of perfection and infinity at the same time as it suggests it, so the nature of the framed interior image offers an illusion of depth which is barred to the viewer. The achieving of an ultimate answer thus constitutes a seeming impossibility, and the microcosmic, as well as the macrocosmic infinity is always perceptible but just beyond reach. Identity with the universe cannot be attained. To break out of this perfect circle of perpetual motion is at the root of Maupassant's search.

This whole element of form in Maupassant – verticals, horizontals, frames – is so essential to the understanding of his art that is deserves careful analysis in its own right. It is hoped that the following chapter will reach some conclusions on a problem that has arisen with surprising regularity up to this point.

[28]   Maupassant, *Sur l'eau*, p. 44.

VII

FORM AND STRUCTURE

It has been said, and it would seem to be the generally held opinion that Maupassant represents in the development of French fiction what one might call a kind of terminal position within the framework of nineteenth century realism.[1] One cannot deny that he is to a very large extent a faithful adherent to Gustave Flaubert's beliefs in objectivity and aesthetic perfection. It is precisely this degree of objectivity in Maupassant which has unfortunately led to such oversimplification with regard to his contribution.

There is all through his work a precision and accuracy through which he is connected both with Flaubert and Zola – the little significant detail so dear to his mentor is undoubtedly the reason behind Jeanne de Lamare's calendar or Leda and the swan on the wall of the salon Jupiter. His concern with exactitude makes Boule de Suif's journey or the view of the Norman coast at Le Havre or of the Seine valley at Rouen just as accurate, just as precise as Flaubert's Yonville–l'Abbaye or Zola's Plassans. On this most superficial level the physical world has as much importance for Maupassant's concept of art as it had for his seniors'. His works are with very few exceptions placed squarely in his own times and in geographic locations with which he had first-hand experience.

And Maupassant makes great use of what has come to be called the objective method, although certain of his short stories, in particular "Miss Harriet" or "La Reine Hortense" among those we have mentioned, suggest a sympathetic approach which denies once and for all the accusation of heartlessness which has so frequently been levelled at him. Through the physical world communication takes place, and stories usually centre around that physical world. Food is endowed with great intensity of meaning in "Boule de Suif" for example, as it is again in "L'aventure de Walter Schnaffs" (1883). And physical descriptions are

---

[1] For more specific details on this subject see Chapter I, p. 4, note 11.

keys to character development in very many instances. For this reason they are located in positions of prominence in the stories, usually forming a kind of list which we have already observed in "La maison Tellier" and "Mademoiselle Fifi", to mention only two of the best known instances.

In the earlier works, passages of these types can often show some concern with form. Nevertheless it would be dangerous to assert that these factors frankly dominate all others in the presentation of the "real" world. The description which accompanies the preparations for the departure in "Boule de Suif" makes use of this objective approach, and is the result of many different observations of the scene itself. The darkness punctuated only by a lantern, the incessant falling of snow like a curtain of flakes which soak up the shadowy forms are the visual essentials of the scene. Combined with this we have the sounds of the horses' hoofs and of men's voices, the bells of the harness being made ready. At the slam of a door this activity is silenced, leaving only the sound of the falling snow. Maupassant is attempting to capture the effect of the moment, to set down in words the sights and sounds, colours, forms and shadows of a real scene carefully observed, so that the reader might have a clear impression of the activity to which he is witness. One must conclude that Maupassant is already aware of the ephemeral quality of what he is attempting to transfer on paper when one is confronted by this most effective passage dealing with the snow:

Un rideau de flocons blancs ininterrompu miroitait sans cesse en descendant vers la terre; il effaçait les formes, poudrait les choses d'une mousse de glace, et l'on n'entendait plus, dans le grand silence de la ville calme et ensevelie sous l'hiver, que ce froissement vague, innommable et flottant de la neige qui tombe, plutôt sensation que bruit, entremêlement d'atomes légers qui semblaient emplir l'espace, couvrir le monde.[2]

It would seem that he is trying to come to grips with something which evades his grasp – such terms as "vague", "innommable", "flottant", "plutôt sensation que bruit", "semblaient" – indicate his struggle with the elusive.

This problem, latent in the material considered here, will increase for Maupassant as his career progresses. Terms such as "inexprimable", "innommable", "inconnaissable" recur with surprising frequency. It would be an interesting, and indeed profitable study to trace the development of this theme of the unknowable through his work if really accurate chronology could be established. Within the framework of the present

---

[2] Maupassant, "Boule de Suif", *Bole de Suif, Oeuvres complètes*, p. 12.

analysis however, it would lead us too far afield and I must therefore limit my remarks in this regard to certain rather general observations about a limited number of stories.

The significance of the painting in the development of human relationships in "Miss Harriet" has already been clarified, but the nature of the tidescripve material within that story bears closer scrutiny. It opens with the autumn countryside just at the moment at which the sun awakens it from slumber. A composition of colour and vaguely outlined, misty forms produces a feeling of mystery in its "vapeurs blanches". This setting inspires the narrator to relate his past experiences.

The painting which captures the imagination of Miss Harriet herself is a composition dominated by colour as the sun clothes the rocks in brilliant light and illuminates the jade green sea. What the painter is seeking in his canvas, as he tells us, is instant communication, since he wishes everyone to see it immediately. Miss Harriet understands, realizes that he comprehends nature, a realization that will lead inevitably to her death. For this communication through art has revealed to the narrator that the poor old maid contains within her something deeply meaningful but impossible.

Il y avait dans son oeil une espèce de folie, une folie mystique et violente; et autre chose encore, une fièvre, un désir exaspéré, impatient et impuissant de l'irréalisé et de l'irréalisable! Et il me semblait qu'il y avait aussi en elle un combat où son coeur luttait contre une force inconnue qu'elle voulait dompter et peut-être encore autre chose ... Que sais-je? que sais-je?[3]

To me this story, dating as it does from an early part of Maupassant's productive period (1883), occupies a primary position in the development of his art in the light of his later years. First of all, it clearly states the problem of reality, since it is the setting itself which inspires the tale, and that same setting to which the central figure so noticeably reacts. Descriptive material – the painting, the coast, a ravine filled with mist – is vital to the construction of the story, and is always present before the reader's eye. And yet in the final analysis communication proves to be an impossibility. Death results. Miss Harriet's longing for love is as impossible as the constant grasping for the meaning of the world, deformed as it always is by brilliant light, mist, and other mirage-producing phenomena.

Maupassant's task is to try to grasp the essentials of this ethereal illusion, and such attempts regularly end in failure. Jeanne's portrait,

[3] Maupassant, "Miss Harriet", *Miss Harriet, Oeuvres complètes*, p. 24.

Duroy's reflection, Christiane Andermatt's interpretation of Paul Bré-tigny's physiognomy are all manifestations of this struggle. The second chapter of "Yvette", in which Yvette's inner yearnings are stirred, points up very clearly the fleeting nature of the world in which she finds herself. A series of paragraphs dealing with the Seine and its surroundings clothes the declarations of Servigny to the young girl. First the evening and its sunset:

Le soleil s'était enfoncé derrière l'île, mais tout le ciel demeurait flamboyant comme un brasier, et l'eau calme du fleuve semblait changée en sang. Les reflets de l'horizon rendaient rouges les maisons, les objets, les gens...[4]

and subsequently the brilliant morning sunlight on the water:

Ils arrivaient devant la grille, en face de la Seine. Un flot de soleil tombait sur la rivière endormie et luisante. Une légère brume de chaleur s'en élevait, une fumée d'eau évaporées qui mettait sur la surface du fleuve une petite vapeur miroitante.

De temps en temps un canot passait, yole rapide ou lourd bachot, et on entendait au loin des sifflets courts ou prolongés, ceux des trains qui versent, chaque dimanche, le peuple de Paris dans la campagne des environs, et ceux des bateaux à vapeur qui préviennent de leur approche pour passer l'écluse de Marly.

Mais une petite cloche sonna ...[5]

In the first passage, that brief moment of sunset is caught in the act of modifying through its unusual light the accepted interpretation of the "real" scene. Objects become splashes of red colour, in which outlines vanish. An illusion is effected in the second passage by the slight mist rising from the river's surface under the warmth of the morning sun. Only after this picture is painted are the visual effects combined with auditory ones to complete the impression.

For impression is the operative word here. Maupassant attempts in his descriptions with no small degree of success to capture that brief moment at which a given scene may be viewed in a given way.

We are witnessing here a thorough application of the objective method. By careful observation of the external world, always in harmony with the narrative, the dramatic situation, or the characters of those implicat-ed, impressions are conveyed to the reader without the author's personal intervention. The essence of these descriptions, as we might logically expect, is their visual aspect.

[4]   Maupassant, "Yvette", *Yvette, Oeuvres complètes*, p. 41.
[5]   "Yvette", pp. 56–57.

The impressionistic character of these passages must be stressed. Brilliant in colour, full of movement, they are not surprisingly very similar in their effect to the products of impressionist painters. The views of the Seine here, or of the seacoast in "Miss Harriet" tend to reduce form to a minimum, indeed almost to disregard it in preference to the interplay of colour, light and shadow. In all of them the source of light is clearly defined, and often its coloration, particularly in the sunset descriptions here as elsewhere (the Arc de Triomphe for example) is of great importance. Reality becomes a shimmering interaction of visual effects observed carefully under clearly defined light conditions at precise moments of the day or night. One tends to think immediately of Monet's studies of Rouen cathedral or of his series of haystacks. And Maupassant shares something else with impressionism in his interest in water. The passages mentioned are reminiscent of Renoir's boating scenes, set as they are in the identical geographical context. And water, like no other element, is a kind of visual will-o'-the-wisp.

Maupassant shares the essentials of his painter contemporaries – an overall effect in which form as such becomes nothing more than a juxtaposition of contrasting or blending colours in which even the outlines they produce are blurred.

Flaubert's teachings have undoubtedly contributed to no small extent to Maupassantian impressionism. For it is precision, accuracy, fidelity to the object under scrutiny which will lead, when pushed beyond Flaubert's own models, to description of this type. The substance which the master confers on his objects because of the extreme care of composition, that is to say essentially because of his style, will in the hands of the disciple produce quite the opposite effect. For Maupassant makes no attempt to imitate his master's work slavishly. He is not satisfied to remain in the shadow of greatness. The aesthetic goal which Flaubert spent his whole life seeking remains Maupassant's goal as well. But by the very difference in their natures the younger author must strike out on his own, and find his own route towards "le Beau". Nowhere is this belief more in evidence than in the preface which he wrote for *Bouvard et Pécuchet*.[6]

His temperament cannot lead him along the same paths as his master. One cannot find in him the overpowering pessimism as the arbiter of form, the tragic cycle so evident in Flaubert's last work, and so symbolic of his entire career. Maupassant sees the problem, as we have demonstrat-

[6]   See Chapter I, p. 1.

ed, but unlike Flaubert does not adapt his approach to fit it. The cycle, as Maupassant interprets it, becomes the product of his fictional situation rather than the governor of its every movement. He was by no means the aesthetician that Flaubert was, and his interpretation of his world must of necessity deviate greatly in practice even though or perhaps because he remains by and large faithful to the spirit of his master's teachings.

Descriptions, as Maupassant sets them before our eyes in the earlier works, are clearly illusions, deformed by light, in which nothing is really clear except the light itself. Nature has a fleeting, unreal, ethereal quality which is quite at odds with the Flaubertian aesthetic goal of permanence. To capture the fleeting, to set down the evanescent has become a goal of Maupassant's art. It is precisely this fleeting quality of reality, and indeed of life itself, which will cause him to voice his frustration to Pol Arnault in the dedication of *Au soleil:*

La vie si courte, si longue devient parfois insupportable. Elle se déroule, toujours pareille, avec la mort au bout.' On ne peut ni l'arrêter, ni la changer, ni la comprendre. Et souvent une révolte] indignée vous saisit devant l'impuissance de notre effort. Quoi que nous fassions, nous mourrons! Quoi que nous croyions, quoi que nous pensions, quoi que nous tentions, nous mourrons! Et il semble qu'on va mourrir demain sans rien connaître encore, bien que dégoûté de tout ce qu'on connaît. Alors on se sent écrasé sous le sentiment de "l'éternelle misère de tout," de l'impuissance humaine et de la monotonie des actions.[7]

Maupassant's pessimism is well known, and his travel books, particularly *Sur l'eau*, present conclusive evidence of it. The relentlessness of the life-death cycle, and the limitations on man's capacity are factors in his thought which he shares with Flaubert, although with deep regret. He could never bring himself to create anything remotely similar to Flaubert's greatest withdrawal from life itself – *Bouvard et Pécuchet*. His art remains constantly rooted in, constantly struggling with the nature of life. He is not the ivory tower artist that some would make of him. And I would seriously question the accuracy of the conclusion that his view of life terminates in the blackest of despair, with absolutely no hope for any possible outlet for man's frustrations. We have in his work what is to me conclusive evidence of a kind of "révolte indignée", which, in spite of the awareness, or more precisely the fear of futility, leads man on to continue the struggle. This revolt is by no means a kind of "existentia-

---

[7]   Maupassant, *Au soleil*, p. 3.

lisme avant la lettre" and it would be utter nonsense to propound such an argument. But he does seem to suggest, however timidly, a new direction.

Impressionism, as everyone became aware, led eventually up a blind alley. The moment, once captured, had a terrifying propensity for slipping away between one's fingers. As it was noted down, whether on paper or on canvas, the reality which artists chose to reflect moved on to assume new contrasts, new sights, new sounds. Its constant state of flux opened an unbridgeable chasm between the work of art and the world which it purported to represent. In itself, the impressionistic description lacks those qualities essential to the production of a valid and lasting work of art. It might be called the *cul-de-sac* of realism, for the capturing of the fleeting moment by observation and careful notation can only go so far along the road to the permanent. What really matters in life cannot be so immediately grasped and communicated.

Maupassant was well aware of the impasse into which this dangerous approach would lead him. The external visual approach, that is, total objectivization could not achieve the ultimate goal. As he says to Maurice Vaucaire, in a letter dated 1885:

... établir les règles d'un art n'est pas chose aisée, d'autant plus que chaque tempérament d'écrivain a besoin de règles indifférentes. Je crois que pour *produire* il ne faut pas trop raisonner. Mais il faut regarder beaucoup et songer à ce qu'on a vu. *Voir:* tout est là, et voir juste. J'entends par voir juste voir avec ses propres yeux et pas ceux des maîtres. L'originalité d'un artiste s'indique d'abord dans les petites choses et non dans les grandes. Des chefs-d'oeuvre ont été faits sur d'insignifiants détails, sur des objets vulgaires. Il faut trouver aux choses une signification qui n'a pas encore été découverte et tâcher de l'exprimer d'une façon personnelle.[8]

The emulation of Flaubert is self-evident. Such phraseology as "voir avec ses propres yeux et pas ceux des maîtres", or "d'insignifiants détails", the stress on accuracy and originality speak eloquently of his overpowering influence on Maupassant. But there is a basic difference which Maupassant expresses here, which bears witness unequivocably to the fact that he is paying more than lip service to Flaubert's teachings: "pour produire, il ne faut pas trop raisonner". Surely this represents a kind of thumbnail summary of the major tragedy of the senior author to which the incomplete *Bouvard et Pécuchet* so pathetically testifies. Flaubert's tragedy is the tragedy of the mind. Maupassant's will be that of the feelings.

[8] Maupassant, "Correspondance", *Boule de Suif, Oeuvres complètes*, pp. CLIV–V.

If the solution to the aesthetic question is for Maupassant essentially visual, then he must attach to that all important verb *voir* something beyond its dictionary meaning. For the mere sense in itself is incapable of anything beyond the superficial. And it is here that his own temperament takes over in this eternal quest for the beautiful, and objectivity harmonizes with originality. He puts it himself this way:

L'oeil, aussi impressionnable, aussi raffiné que l'oreille d'un musicien subtil, ressent au seul aspect des nuances, des nuances voisines, combinées, compliquées, un plaisir profond et délicieux. Un regard fin et exercé les distingue, ces nuances, les savoure avec une joie infinie, en saisit les accords invisibles pour la foule, en note les innombrables et discrètes modulations.[9]

Maupassant's sight is a very special gift indeed, which by its very nature has the capacity to see beyond, that is, to transcend the bounds. There must be for him a visual reorganization of material along aesthetically dictated lines in order to achieve a goal of any lasting value. Faithful to Flaubert, he agrees that reality must be interpreted in order to produce a work of art. Indeed he recognizes in the talent of Zola considerable artistic value and considers this factor essential to his success. If Zola is a Romantic with a marked propensity fo exaggeration and magnification against which he incessantly struggles, the resultant product is certainly art. Almost in spite of himself, Zola's temperament imposes a subjectivity on his material, stylizes it and renders it greater than the so-called real.

For Maupassant then, as for Flaubert, talent is an essential factor in the artist's make-up, although hard work is constantly required of that talent. In his way he represents a return from Zola's concept and restores to the novel a much greater degree of aesthetic concern than Zola's "experimental" concept would have ever allowed. But to return to Flaubert is much too simple. Maupassant is more accurately an extension of the master's views into an unexplored domain.

If Maupassant has literary talent, if he has that visual ability of which he spoke, than the nuances perceived by his "regard fin et exercé" must be summed up by one word – *form*. For it is in this direction that his production tends to move.

No novelist is static, and consequently, if one can reach some conclusions as to the modifications the author's concepts undergo, such conclusions should prove invaluable in the understanding of his goals. In

[9]   Maupassant, "Au salon", *Chroniques* ..., Dumesnil, p. 162. First published in *Le XIXe Siècle* (April 30, 1886).

dealing with Maupassant of course this is especially difficult since his productive period is so brief and dates of composition are in many instances impossible to establish. But the descriptive element in Maupassant has furnished us with material nicely suited to such an approach. For we have already established the fact that, while the impressionistic type of description is a constant in his production, there is in his later material an increased concern with and emphasis on form.

To trace this development in Maupassant, it is pertinent to return once again to "Miss Harriet". The whole elaboration of this piece depends in the final analysis on one significant visual experience. For without the painting, no communication would have taken place between the narrator and the English spinster. In other words the keystone of the study is not the visual identity with raw nature, beautiful as it may well be, but with an individual's reorganization of nature in art. The aesthetic is awarded a position of primacy from which all further development springs. It is therefore a very special way of viewing things which has established the rapport. Artistic reorganization is what gives the piece cohesion and coherence. The artist is creating order out of chaos.

It follows then that what he has succeeded in doing really is to give form to the formless. For any work of art, by its very nature has some kind of form as distinct from that of the reality it portrays. That it can vary infinitely both quantitively and qualitively no one would deny. The basic impressionism of the work in question, that is to say the lack of stress on form *per se* has already been noted, but this style does seek to give some permanency to a fleeting scene. The significant aspect of observed phenomena in the tale is thus set down on a rectangular piece of canvas before its meaning is communicable between individuals. Form is not stressed in this story, but is nevertheless a necessary factor in its comprehension.

In "Yvette", the other example of impressionism which we mentioned at some length, form again is vital to comprehension. The main body of this rather lengthy "nouvelle" contains a great deal of description and the interior crisis of Yvette herself is precipitated by the presence of Servigny in this setting. We have the same kind of relationship as that which existed between Miss Harriet and the painter before the appearance of that all-important canvas. Servigny in unable to communicate on any but the most superficial of levels with Yvette, and she is not fully aware of her own position, nor of her course of action in the future. Before she can communicate with others, she must first find her own identity. The final chapter is carefully constructed in order to resolve this dual problem.

Yvette must come to grips with life itself, and when she does, she finds suicide the only possible answer. And it is again the sense of sight by means of which she is able, however fleetingly, to comprehend her situation. Closed in her room she is confronted with two visual experiences – the mirror and the window.

Although these two images are not artistic recreations of reality, both of them have the dual effect we have already observed, in that they permit the viewer to peer deeply into the interior and the exterior aspects of her situation. Both of them clearly establish limits, that is form, in its broadest sense, on reality itself. Comprehending both her own nature and the position of Servigny leads her inevitably to her crucial decision. That she fails where Miss Harriet succeeds only heightens her tragedy, for if she has been able, by limiting her view formally, to catch some glimpse of Truth, she has been as unable as her English-speaking counterpart to hold it and retain it. Fear of Truth leads the old maid to destroy herself and the young girl to withdraw from the brink and fall into the rôle which has been laid out for her. The painting, the mirror, the window, all suggest to the viewers a potential whose realization is a frustrating impossibility.

Form is without question the essential factor in this never-ending search. The early novels, like these two relatively early short stories, demonstrate with clarity its validity. Jeanne de Lamare's entire life is punctuated by forms, portraits, tapestries, faces, landscapes and particularly windows. Indeed at one point she attempts literally to seize the beckoning possibilities of the window by running out of the house barefoot in the snow. She ends her days again at a window, her potential sadly wasted, and her life a complete void.

The "bovarysme" of this kind of imagery should of course be noted, for Jeanne is as we have said a derivative of the great Flaubertian heroine. Like Emma she has intense romantic longings, like her she is a product of the high-walled convent, for her as well marriage is a mismatch leading only to frustration and despair. But her flights of fancy are always visually inspired by these same recurring images which all suggest the ideal which she tragically cannot achieve. They run like links in a chain throughout the course of the novel, and give to the work the only real unity it possesses. There can be no doubt of the fact that *Une vie*, however successful it may be considered, is the least original of Maupassant's six completed novels. The theme it presents, and its method of presentation have little to set them apart from other and more successful treatments of the same basic idea. And the objectivity which Maupassant preserves throughout, for the most part due to the kind of visual imagery we have noted, displays minimal originality. About all one can really say about *Une vie* is that it is a curious and more or less successful application of the lessons Maupassant learned. It is interesting to the student of Maupassant for the use it makes of the visual in establishing a setting and for the suggestions of form already discernable in its visual imagery. The pattern which eventually evolves is already discernable.

Bel-Ami is a much more important and vastly more original piece of work. This can be justified to no small extent by a consideration of this same type of imagery. The mirror, window and painting, very much to the fore, function not so much as links in a chain, but rather as the blocks by means of which the personality of Georges Duroy is constructed. They build one upon the other, revealing to the protagonist the potential within him, driving him onward and upward in his unscrupulous bid for power and wealth. They are as well the channel markers on his course, guiding him accurately to his chosen goal. Like Jeanne, he too has an unrealized potential, but in the reverse of "bovarysme" he sets out consciously to realize it. His views of reality too are governed by the same forms, but his relentless search for what they reveal is as much a deception as was the earlier case. The realities that these forms reveal to him have in his mind the ring of truth, but the concluding image of the painting demonstrates to the reader the deception of it all. Powerful and successful, Duroy is as much a fake as he was initially. The imposition of form would appear to be in the final analysis as much a deception as anything else.

But the main point would be lost if we left the conclusion here. For form has meaning, and through it truth can be seen. If the mirrors and the painting delude Duroy and others in the novel, they serve as well to inform the reader of that delusion. It is through these images that Maupassant exposes his anti-hero to his public. The same observation can of course be made with regard to *Une vie* since poor Jeanne herself is never confronted directly with a revelation of the truth of her condition. But the success of *Bel-Ami* is in no small part dependent on the skill with which this imagery has been integrated into the fabric of the text. By tracing their successive appearances, we trace the rise of Duroy's star to its apogee in the closing paragraphs.

The images of identity in both novels serves thus a dual purpose. Besides communicating with the reader, they are an externalization, that is, an objectivization of the inner world of the character. By their use, Maupassant circumvents the necessity for personal inner probings. But where it was multiple, interrupted, and distinctly uneven in his first novel, the development becomes a consistent progression, as regular as the rungs of a ladder in the second. The movement of the novel as a whole, and of the protagonist in particular, is mapped out by their appearance.

By enclosing the "real" within the frame of a mirror, a window or a painting, what is formless, and therefore incomprehensible, suddenly, and perhaps only briefly acquires both form and limitations. Maupassant's characters must have an outward focus in order to understand, in order to look inward. The tragedy of the Maupassantian approach is that while these moments of truth appear, and open the window, so to speak, on infinity, on self-comprehension, they at the same time distort that essential truth so that it too becomes a deception, a barrier to the achievement of the very thing it momentarily reveals. If Duroy could pin down his own image, then he might not be the unscrupulous coward he would appear to be. For he is not entirely heartless, demonstrating as he does a concern with his parents and a love of children which incidentally provides the rather ironic title of the novel. Duroy is really to be pitied, not despised, as he somewhat in the fashion of Macbeth, seeks to achieve in life what he glimpses in the mirror. That Maupassant leaves him at the pinnacle is eloquent testimony of the frustration which deceptive reality produces in him. Whether he falls or not does not interest the author and there is indeed absolutely no evidence in the work that he will be brought down. The ever changing world is always a step ahead of man's attempts to pin it down. This is Maupassant at his blackest.

Mont-Oriol adds very little to what we have already observed, save in the final scene. It is relevant that Christiane Andermatt refuses to let Paul set his eyes on their child, who is really an externalization both of the love which once existed between them and the destruction of that love. In her deep regret there is undoubtedly a feeling of revenge, and the denial of this visual experience to the man she still loves is an attempt on her part to destroy him. The novel ends in a gaping void between them. That which the child reflects is lost, and reality and its reflection are again at odds.

It would be fair to say that the visual images in all these novels, while form is latent in their presentation, do not emphasize this aspect of their presence. The images remain by and large impressionistic, but with a marked concern for limits, frames, outlines in this constant quest for identity. And the exterior descriptions reveal this same tendency which is particularly visible in the last mentioned work. The descriptions of the Auvergne countryside which it contains resolve themselves into a surprisingly regular almost abstract pattern of verticality and horizontality.

Limits to infinity are everywhere – valleys framed by mountains, scenes framed by trees, vistas brought up short by buildings, towns and villages, extinct volcanoes surrounded by rocks. Maupassant is attempting here too to come to grips with infinity by imposing a clear-cut limitation on it, by organizing it and giving it form. For if the character in Maupassant must exteriorize in order to understand his inner self, he must also exteriorize to understand his world.

The novels and short stories up to this point offer a great deal of evidence of a growing concern with the inadequacies of the strictly visual and external method. Whether the movement be slowly downward as in *Une vie*, meteorically upward as in *Bel-Ami*, or combination of the two as in *Mont-Oriol*, the end result is a nothingness, a total blank of intense tragedy. The forms are not sufficiently clearly defined to produce something which will endure. The last page of each one produces a "table rase" to which nothing can be added.

It is with *Pierre et Jean* that a real change becomes noticeable. Maupassant is constantly searching for a solution to the Flaubertian circle and this novel is a step in that direction. I cannot see in it however the complete reversal that some critics so often attribute to it.[10] There is no break with what has come before, but simply a more thorough application and development of certain tendencies already quite discernable.

Both interior and exterior imagery are present in this work as indeed they were in previous novels. But the interior imagery is reduced from the multiplicity of its manifestations in the earlier pieces to one single overpowering object – the portrait of Maréchal which Pierre insists on seeing and which his mother is finally forced into revealing. It is this isolated object, this one form, which will lead the elder son to an irreversible decision.

The same observation can undoubtedly be made about external nature, for it is the sea in its various manifestations – under sunshine, in fog or in darkness to which Pierre constantly returns to try to resolve his problem. The novel is thus a study in contrasts between the permanent and the changing, the interior and the exterior. All movement fluctuates between these two poles, between the infinitely vast and the minute. Imagery of form becomes here for the first time a solid framework on which the narrative in all its many aspects is constructed. That this is possible is substantiated by our analysis of *Bel-Ami*, but in *Pierre et Jean* what was

---

[10]   See especially Sullivan's *Maupassant the Novelist*, in which this work is called a "novel by extension".

hesitant and multiple although systematic, becomes tightly unified. The novel builds to the revelation of the portrait through a series of quests for identity in the sea and the fog and ends with Pierre's being swallowed up by the infinity of the water. The trace of smoke left in the last paragraph is significantly not part of Pierre's perception, but of Madame Roland's. The portrait has left no doubt in his mind, but his confrontation has left an indelible mark on hers.

Thus a tightly knit unity of the imagery sets this work apart quite distinctly from its predecessors. On top of this there is a decided shift in emphasis as to the relationship of that unity to the action of the novel which is without doubt a movement away from the objective concept. By removing the portrait from the eyes of the reader, a fact already observed in the present study, Maupassant forces us to concentrate solely on its form, on its diminutive size, as a contrast with its ever increasing psychological impact. While thus retaining the techniques of the objective approach he renders essential reality a much more subjective thing than it has heretofore been. We must provide what he only suggests, we must fill in the outlined form, and we must delve into Pierre's mind in order to understand its significance. A gradual process of interiorization is under way.

But here again formlessness wins out over form. If the portrait gives Pierre an insight into his mother's past and the truth of Jean's identity, it is a truth which he cannot bear. He opts for the formless, that is to say for the sea which Maupassant goes to such great lengths to describe. Chaos conquers order. He too withdraws in terror. Again we have the same basic pattern of horizontals broken by vertical strokes – masts and ships, the steep cliffs of the Norman coast – attempts to give it perspective, to close it in, to frame it and give it form. But it escapes his grasp as Pierre escapes into it and the novel ends on the same note of oblivion as we have witnessed in the others. Reality if perceived still cannot be retained.

Like *Pierre et Jean, Fort comme la mort* is governed by a dominant image. The portrait, painted but invisible in the first chapter, rises in significance as the novel progresses. The outdoor world has only an incidental function in this novel at two important points – the walk in the Parc Monceau and the sojourn of the trio in the country during which Anne comprehends fully the trap into which her lover is falling. The outward movement brings to light the realization of a problem as it did for Pierre, but no answer can be found in the expansive. Crucial as these incidents may be, they do not occupy the central position in the work that the aesthetically controlled, reflective interiorizing visual image maintains in the development of the tension. The comparison to be made wtih "Miss Harriet" is quite obvious.

The governing image is again one in which form, this time a permanent form, is given to a reality which, while renewing itself, cannot remain constant. Olivier Bertin cannot tolerate the truth of its message, and like Pierre Roland chooses the formlessness of oblivion.

The nature of form in *Notre coeur* is much more complex than in either of the other two late novels, and offers still further proof of the double development of Maupassantian imagery – the increased concern with form and the heightened emphasis on the interior. As with both *Pierre et Jean* and *Fort comme la mort*, *Notre coeur* is controlled by an interiorized image. And as with the story of Olivier Bertin, that of André Mariolle makes vital but only incidental use of its external counterpart. The two poles of *Pierre et Jean* have been further reduced in the quest for unity. But it is the very nature of the interiorizing image in *Notre coeur* which increases its complexity. Whereas in the preceding two novels the all-powerful image was a portrait, a kind of reflection with a considerable degree of independence, in this last complete novel, the visual is suggested by the contents of that most complex of Maupassant's mirrors in which Michèle de Burne is enclosed. It is this image, as cold as a marble statue, which captivates and then tortures Mariolle. In his farewell letter to her he makes it clear. His heart is as empty as a beggar's stomach, since "vous . . . avez jeté de belles choses, mais pas de pain. C'est du pain, c'est de l'amour qu'il me fallait."

Mariolle's problem is thus essentially the same as Miss Harriet's. External visual perceptions, tempting as they are, cannot in themselves resolve man's quest for identity and communication, that is to say, love. Like the portraits of the preceding works, Michèle de Burne offers only glimpses of what she cannot fulfill.

She is an aesthetically created individual, a product of art, and thus a re-creation of reality. The artificiality of her world, its controlled environment of *objets d'art* and high society bears witness to this. Her apartment, as we have seen, is formally arranged. And the discussions between Mariolle the intelligent dilettante and Gaston de Lamarthe the celebrated novelist offer conclusive evidence of this very formal, controlled, reflective function of the beautiful Madame de Burne. For she is clearly the reflection, the fictional expression of the kind of woman Maupassant finds all too frequently in Parisian society. In an attack on realism, Mariolle explains it this way:

Au temps où les romanciers et les poètes exaltaient [les femmes] et les faisaient rêver, disait-il, elles cherchaient et croyaient trouver dans la vie l'équivalent de ce que leur coeur avait pressenti dans leurs lectures. Aujourd'hui vous vous obstinez à supprimer toutes les apparences poétiques et séduisantes pour ne montrer que les réalités désillusionnantes. Or mon cher, plus d'amour dans les livres, plus d'amour dans la vie. Vous étiez des inventeurs d'idéal, elles croyaient à vos inventions. Vous n'êtes maintenant que des évocateurs de réalités précises et derrière vous elles se sont mises à croire à la vulgarité de tout.[11]

Realism destroys true reality, the reality of the mind. This is Jeanne de Lamare's tragedy in reverse, but still the means of reconciling the seemingly irreconcilable must be discovered.

The visual image controlling *Notre coeur*'s development is immediately identifiable with Michèle de Burne. Mariolle is at first not capable of understanding the distinction which must be made between her external aspects and her true nature. In other words he is deceived by his sense of sight, just as all of Maupassant's heroes have been by an image which offers a glimpse of truth but places barriers on the road to it.

The very immediacy of the identification of exterior image and the individual which it reflects produces automatically a situation in which physical, formalized objects can no longer be clearly differentiated from internal subjective reality. Mariolle's inability to make this distinction tortures him incessantly. The shift in significance of the external world, the physical world which we have observed in progress all through Maupassant's writings moves then another step down the scale in favour of something else. The process of interiorization which all readers have observed in his later works is in no way an arbitrary break in Maupassant designed only to satisfy a changing and increasingly demanding public. Its roots can be traced into the earliest of his writings, and his entire output is without doubt a cohesive unit.

It is the created, or reflected image, the exteriorization of the self which reveals in all its clarity this progression. Maupassant is giving new dimensions to the technique of objectivity. By attempting to grasp reality by means of its essential forms, he is moving away from realism.

The short stories as well substantiate this argument. Renardet destroys his "futaie" because of its associations with the murder, and what we are witnessing is a destruction of form. It is as if the immense height of the trees under which the body was found, contained within them, whispering in the wind, and offering glimpses of the infinity of the sky beyond, the secret of the murderer's identity. By destroying their form, or in other

[11]   Maupassant, *Notre coeur*, pp. 145–46.

words by reducing verticality to horizontality, Renardet hopes to destroy the truth. But it returns to him in the window as we have seen, and his eventual death occurs from the height of a tower of his house whose flagpole he attempts to break down. Renardet reacts throughout the story to the evocative power of forms. Driven to murder by the contours of la petite Roque's naked body, he is drawn to write his letter of confession by the vision in the window, and ultimately to suicide from the height of his tower because of the existence of that same letter.

"Le Horla" also demonstrates a concern with visible form. The fact that the being which haunts the narrator is invisible is what makes the whole situation so terrifying, and when his own reflection disappears from the mirror, the destruction is complete. The awesome aspect of that most curious tale "Qui sait?" stems from essentially the same problem. The strange individual in whose Rouen establishment the narrator rediscovers his lost furniture is described to us first in terms of his shape, his form:

Au milieu d'une grande pièce était un tout petit homme, tout petit et très gros, gros comme un phénomène, un hideux phénomène.

Il avait une barbe rare, aux poils inégaux, clairsemés et jaunâtres, et pas un cheveu sur la tête. Pas un cheveu? Comme il tenait sa bougie élevée à bout de bras pour m'apercevoir, son crâne m'apparut comme une petite lune dans cette vaste chambre encombrée de vieux meubles. La figure était ridée et bouffie, les yeux imperceptibles.[12]

It is precisely this "monstre à crâne de lune" who haunts him incessantly, and drives him finally into the asylum. Here again form, for the description is essentially of that nature, is interwoven with the formless, the imperceptible eyes, and occupies the same position as we have already witnessed so many times. This little man contains within him the truth concerning the unusual disappearance of the furniture, but will not divulge it. Form is both gateway and barrier here too.

However, it would not be accurate to suggest that Maupassant abandons totally the impressionistic approach so apparent in his earlier works. The later works too are full of light, colour and movement in the descriptive passages. Renardet first sees the postman in the final scene as a patch of blue in the distance; Mariolle enjoys watching the sunlight play on the verdant green of the forest of Fontainebleau. This is the constant we spoke of earlier in this chapter, and no one can seriously deny its presence throughout his works.

[12] Maupassant, "Qui sait?", *L'inutile beauté, Oeuvres complètes*, p. 251. [First published in *L'Écho de Paris* (April 6, 1890).

But there is a clear suggestion, judging from close study of descriptive passages, that impressionism by itself is inadequate, and something more lasting is being sought. We are witnessing the application of impressionistic techniques of colour and light in combination with a factor which will restore some solidity to the exterior world, namely, form. Colours are combined and juxtaposed in order to evoke some essential, underlying, one might even say skeletal permanence. Maupassant is imposing an order on his world in the Flaubertian sense, but an order which is essentially his own. The sense of sight so important to him becomes more and more dominant in his aesthetic concept, in an increasingly controlled fashion.

The realization that realism carried to its extremes leads absolutely nowhere is by no means unique to Maupassant. The enthusiasm for impressionism, at its height in the 1870's is also by this same period being seriously questioned by some painters and modified according to new approaches to reality. Of the three contemporary painters who contributed so greatly to the evolution of painting, Van Gogh, Gauguin and Cézanne, it is the last-named who offers a very curious and interesting parallel with the work of Guy de Maupassant. Any claim of linking these two names in terms of influence would no doubt be exceedingly difficult, if not impossible to prove. All we can safely assume is that Maupassant must have been aware of the painter. Cézanne was at one time a very close associate of Emile Zola, a childhood friend, as is well known. This relationship lasted more or less until the break precipitated by the publication of *L'oeuvre* in 1886, to which it would appear Cézanne took serious exception. Maupassant's interest in painting was somewhat limited, no doubt, but knowing Zola as he did, he must have had at least some knowledge of the painter's work.

The interesting aspect here is not that of influence but rather a kind of harmony in the two men's approaches to their world. For Cézanne never denied the essentials of impressionism. His canvases glow with light and colour. But colour alone would not provide that solid grasp of reality which he sought. As one critic of him has phrased it:

He sought for essential structural ideas that had existed in eternity long before the artists had come to earth. All artists, he thought, made the mistake of painting what they saw and calling it reality. He wanted to catch the true reality beneath the appearance, the true order of form, that only the intellect and not the eye can comprehend.[13]

[13]   Henry Thomas and Diana Lee Thomas, *Living Biographies of Great Painters* (New York: Blue Ribbon Books, 1940), p. 297.

Form for Cézanne is thus the key to reality. But this is not the outline, the drawing of shapes, but rather the construction of form through the use of colour. Forms are created on the canvas by the contrasts of blended and juxtaposed colours. Impressionism is thus not abandoned, but controlled in order to probe more surely into the subject under scrutiny. In other words an order is imposed which is aesthetically determined in order to make the work of art meaningful. This is exactly what Maupassant would appear to be doing with words.

And for Cézanne this concern with form is not simply the consideration of isolated objects, isolated shapes, but also with the essential structure of reality, that is to say, with the overall pattern of his world and his interpretation of it. The structure, or organization of his canvases is a logical extension of the interest in shapes and forms. His biographer, John Rewald, discusses this aspect of his art in terms that are in my estimation almost equally applicable to Maupassant:

For a better grasp of his model, Cézanne advised Bernard to 'see in nature the cylinder, the sphere, the cone, putting everthing into proper perspective, so that each side of an object or a plane is directed toward a central point. Lines parallel to the horizon give breadth, that is, a section of nature . . . Lines perpendicular to this horizon give depth. But nature, for us men is more depth than surface, whence the necessity of introducing in our vibrations of light – represented by reds and yellows – a sufficient quantity of blue to give the feeling of air.[14]

How curiously these remarks of the painter himself coincide with much of what we have already observed of Maupassant's descriptions – forms, verticals and horizontals, and even the predilection for reds and yellows which we have so frequently seen in the writer's sunsets. And Rewald continues with the following remarks about Cézanne's art:

This theory which preoccupied Cézanne during his last years, is the outcome of his study of planes and volume. In Cézanne's work, however, one finds neither cylinders or cones, nor parallel and perpendicular lines, the line never having existed for Cézanne except as a meeting place for two planes of different colour. One might thus be permitted to see in this theory an attempt to express his consciousness of structure beneath the coloured surface presented by nature. It was this awareness of form that detached Cézanne from his impressionist friends. But nowhere in his canvases did Cézanne pursue this abstract concept at the expense of his direct sensations. He always found his forms in nature and never in geometry.[15]

[14]   John Rewald, *Paul Cézanne*, trans. by M. H. Liebman (London: Spring Books), p. 172.
[15]   Rewald, *Paul Cézanne*, pp. 172–73.

Like Cézanne, Maupassant remains firmly rooted in nature. And like him, the structural basis of that reality is what seems to matter for him more and more as his work progresses.

This artistic control of material in neither artist stops at the fragmentary. They share a concern for the totality of the concept, the interest in the work as a unified whole in which every part is coherent and significant. And again the increased control of structure is an aspect of Maupassant's rising concern with form in the novel and in the short story. We have already observed how successfully he can exploit a single image in a short story in such a way that it becomes the controlling factor in the lives of the persons involved. Among the most successful of his short works it is the object itself which would seem to take on characteristics of a living being. Whether it be jewels, an umbrella, or even a lowly piece of string, the reality each contains goes beyond its passive physical presence or absence. And in every case the vitality of the object has a visual importance: – the inability to see whether jewels are false or real; the visual mistaking of a piece of string for a wallet; the appearance of an umbrella; – these are the controlling factors in their strength. Each of them is a reflection of an incident or a relationship important in the character's life, the incident from which all consequences stem. In other words it is an image which determines the form of these particular pieces. Nothing extraneous, that is, nothing unrelated to the dominant image of the story is allowed to intrude. And indeed, in two of the stories in particular, "Le Horla" and "Qui sait?", it is the very absence of a concrete image which destroys the narrator.

André Vial makes a very good case for the concern for form in Maupassant's short stories. He notes that in about half of them the tales are told by a designated individual, clearly distinct from the author himself. He goes on to enumerate the various means by which Maupassant introduces this narrator. But it is the conclusion he reaches here that is so much in harmony with our argument. By shifting the focus away from the author, not only does he maintain his precious objectivity, but he also shifts the reader's interest away from the facts of the narrative to its method of presentation. It is in other words the form of the story that is important, not its events. For the reader hears it told, he does not witness it directly. It is in itself an organization, a selection of circumstances, details and events, a fact of which the reader is conscious. Structure thus becomes an essential of narrative, and form is so closely interwoven with fact that the two cannot be disunited.

But we must return to the novel again to find conclusive evidence of our theories. We have already seen that the imagery of *Une vie*, effective as it may so frequently be, remains in the main, fragmentary. Maupassant makes little if any concentrated attempt to link the images into a neat overall pattern. As a result the novel is strictly linear in construction, tracing the events of Jeanne's life in historical sequence, as the title would suggest. It is largely because of the unrelated nature of the imagery in successive chapters that there is still such dispute over the novel's composition. Is it a series of short stories strung together, or are the related shorter pieces parts of the novel which were subsequently extracted? According to Vial, who presents a most convincing argument in this regard, the latter is the truth of the case.[16] However, the fact remains that Maupassant had great difficulty with the transitions, as he quite openly admits. Here already his concern with form is visible although he is very far indeed from the mastery he will later achieve.

The progressive imagery of *Bel-Ami* is without doubt a step forward in the structural quest. The upward mobility of Georges Duroy is marked off in its progression by the series of related reflective images which we have examined. The novel is divided almost exactly in half, with eight chapters in the first part, ten in Part Two. The symmetry of this type of construction is obvious and demonstrates the author's careful manipulation of form. And significantly enough, the last chapter of Part One and the first of Part Two contain the only two major incidents of the novel which take place outside Paris. Both the Côte d'Azur and the Seine valley interludes are connected with Madeleine Forestier. The descriptions contained in these passages are thus a transitional device in the structure of the novel, connecting as they do Duroy the aspirant with Duroy the bridegroom. The Midi interlude is a preparation for, and a pre-echo of the wedding trip. The essential fact in the structure of *Bel-Ami* is that Maupassant seems to be trying to work out his narrative difficulties in terms of images.

Like *Bel-Ami*, *Mont-Oriol* is divided into two roughly symmetrical halves. But here the transition is far easier between the two. For it is the relationship between Paul and Christiane on the one hand and the speculations of Andermatt and company on the other, joined together by the setting itself, which unite the two parts. Like its two predecessors

---

[16] André Vial, *Guy de Maupassant* ..., pp. 486–506. Vial's arguments are much too detailed to sum up accurately. However he does offer a very interesting theory on the relationship between such stories as "Par un soir de printemps" (1881) and "Le saut du berger" (1882) to the novel *Une vie*, and maintains a similar relationship exists with regard to other short stories and novels.

this book, covering two summers in Auvergne, with the Paris winter left in the interlude between them, is basically linear in construction although the historical time involved has been much reduced in length. Imagery of a visual nature marks the stages of the relationship between the lovers in a way not unlike the technique employed with such success in *Bel-Ami*. But this novel is very much less successful than the latter, largely because it fails to integrate successfully the two major lines of interest, the love plot and the financial plot, with the result that the latter appears as nothing more than a weak excuse for an attack on certain members of society whom Maupassant loathes. Joints are not smooth, and the novel is extremely uneven. The visual link is not sustained in relation to both sub-plots and the action sways wildly and unreasonably from one to the other, with little or no artistic justification. Formal symmetry is quite insufficient for the success of the work, and the visual imagery which is so well developed in it leaves one half of the narrative almost a complete blank except for brief descriptions of the characters, and the initial scene already referred to.

These first three novels explore the possibilities of what is really one basic structural approach. They are each a series of chains, or in the latter case a double chain. Event succeeds event in regular sequence, and in the cases in which the links in the chain are too visible or too weak, it would appear that Maupassant has not integrated his visual imagery sufficiently well into the totality of the work.

It is in *Pierre et Jean* that the evolution of structure becomes for the first time truly successful, but the techniques it uses so happily are not truly innovations. Everything found in this short novel can be seen somewhere in the three which precede it. If *Une vie* demonstrates the importance of the formal visual image, *Bel-Ami* attempts to systematize that discovery, and *Mont-Oriol* tries in turn to give it new dimensions by applying it more broadly. The reflective imagery in *Bel-Ami* takes on importance as a manifestation of the character of one person. In *Mont-Oriol* this same technique is employed to give meaning not to a personality but to a relationship between characters and situations. Christiane and Paul find in the various views of Auvergne, and indeed in their own physical appearances a bond between them, whereas the mirrors and the painting in *Bel-Ami* served principally to set him apart from those around him. Images gradually become more than a means to transmit information to the reader.

This progression towards greater structural unity is nowhere more clearly evident however than in *Pierre et Jean*. The imagery here is related not simply to Pierre, but to the problem with which he is confronted, a problem which affects in varying degrees every character in the narrative. The struggle between form and formlessness dictates the structure of the book as a whole. Although we are dealing with events in sequence, the past rises out of the present situation and reduces the linear to relative inconsequence. *Pierre et Jean* is not a chain of events, but a single event viewed in evolution. It is a single unified vision given form by the author's pen. Imagery has given unity to the novel.

Fort comme la mort is another demonstration of this same essential approach to narrative fiction, governed as it is by the image of the portrait. Longer than *Pierre et Jean*, it is divided into two symmetrical parts, carefully constructed according to the visual images necessary for its evolution. The first part clearly establishes the relationship between Bertin and Anne de Guilleroy and the significance of the painting for them. By the end of it the internal struggle within the painter has begun, thanks to Annette. This is a struggle in which he is initially unaware of the implications. The second half gives us the only non-Parisian interlude of the novel in which the real deterioration of the relationship begins. Anne's beauty has been destroyed by grief, and it is now Annette who clearly takes visual precedence. When Bertin arrives at their estate he remarks to the mother:

– Est-ce étrange, hein, de voir votre fille en deuil?
– Pourquoi? demanda la comtesse.
  Il s'écria avec une animation extraordinaire:
  – Comment, pourquoi? Mais c'est votre portrait peint par moi, c'est mon portrait! C'est vous, telle que je vous ai rencontrée autrefois en entrant chez la duchesse![17]

What follows is the gradual revelation of the truth of this vision first to Madame de Guilleroy and then to Olivier Bertin. Structure is very carefully worked out in terms of a single visual image and its significance to the parties involved. The two parts are clearly the rise and fall, *crescendo* and *diminuendo* of a single movement. Here again the sequence of events is displaced by an immediacy, a unity, in which each element functions only in terms of the novel as a whole.

The last novel of the series, *Notre coeur*, having as a dominant image Michèle de Burne, produces a common motivation governing the conduct of every man in the novel, and most significantly of course, André Mariolle. But here the image does not even exist objectively in the literal sense,

---

[17]   Maupassant, *Fort comme la mort*, p. 197.

but is found rather in Madame de Burne's projection of herself in the mind of Mariolle. This novel, divided into three parts, again can be traced in its structural development along the lines of visual images.

In Part One, the vision of Madame de Burne is shown captivating the minds of all who surround her. As the narrative progresses, Mariolle too is taken into the trap. At the beginning of Part Two comes the excursion to Avranches and Mont Saint-Michel. It is at this point that Mariolle's vision of Michèle corresponds exactly with her vision of herself, and the view of the famous monument – that pronounced vertical and its surrounding horizontality – captivates most fully but only momentarily the meaning of the situation. In succeeding chapters of the central part the euphoria has vanished as Michèle de Burne can no longer live up to Mariolle's view of her. Part Three again returns to a non-Parisian location, and the struggle in Mariolle's mind to come to grips with the essentials of the situation. It is the forest of Fontainebleau, again an interplay of vertical and horizontal forms, which leads to the final solution.

Forms again are a function of structure, but this novel represents still a further progression in Maupassant's search for the real. We have already seen that the reflective images tend to become less and less visible *per se* in the novels, with the result that in spite of their externality, or their so-called objectivity, they function more and more exclusively within the framework of the fictitious world of the work itself. We as outsiders are no longer kept informed by them. While they remain physically outside the personalities involved, their significance becomes progressively more internal. This process goes as far as possible in Maupassant's last novel, since the image itself consists only of a reflection in a mirror for Michèle de Burne, and in the mind's eye of her lover. It is this image that he prolongs and protects by closing his eyes at the end of the book as he had attempted to do with the artificial garden of his "garçonnière". The formal image in other words becomes meaningful only to those who are directly involved, and the reader is forced more and more to delve to another level to grasp its message.

This progression in the novels is an unequivocable revelation of the depth of meaning which Maupassant attaches to form. Beginning with a basic approach which lacks originality, he moves progressively closer to a solution which is his own. Fragmented forms first of all become linked in a progression, and then little by little become more and more integrated into a greater whole, a greater form which is the structure of the novel. From historical progression they become unified vision, in which each element is only a function, not a semi-independent unit. The quest for the essentials of reality is in the end a quest for oneness. The reflective image becomes a more reflective art of fiction. Plot and character are increasingly controlled by image, and this combination in turn determines the form of the whole. It is increased concern with form which provides us with the key to the Maupassantian aesthetic.

The quest for unity discernable in Maupassant is without doubt an aspect of his concept which he relates very carefully to the doctrines of classicism. This association is made clear in his discussion of the novel which has come to be called the preface to *Pierre et Jean*. His first reference to Boileau here makes the point that what the realist is doing in essence is seeking verisimilitude, for truth is often very deceptive. That Maupassant is doing this is quite beyond question. His earliest attempt at realism, if not at naturalism in the novel, revealed the weakness of that approach to truth. Controlled as it has been shown to be, *Une vie* lacks the cohesion necessary for a great work of art. Reality has been shown by Maupassant to be as incoherent, as infinitely fragmented as Flaubert so tragically saw it to be. The setting down of a whole life in terms of a novel is not only overambitious, but more seriously an impossibility without an immense amount of selection and control. The end result can risk two very great dangers – an endlessly repetitive chain of empty detail, or a disjointed group of interrelated incidents. The weaknesses of *Une vie* are definitely of the latter type.

What we observe him doing is gradually limiting his vision of reality to more controllable dimensions in order to create an impression of truth in artistic terms. He describes this process best himself:

Le réaliste, s'il est artiste, cherchera, non pas à nous montrer la photographie banale de la vie, mais à nous en donner la vision plus complète, plus saisissante, plus probante que la réalité même.[18]

The artistic quest for reality is just that – a visual quest in depth. And this quest requires not only the special gift of sight which he seems to possess, but an immense amount of discipline in the choice of materials. If rules can be evolved to suit the aesthetic goal, they should be rigorously applied. The artist must limit himself to the "détails caractéristiques utiles à son sujet". Maupassant was well suited to classicism and makes great use of its teachings both in his stories and his novels. Let us consider very briefly some of the other essentials of seventeenth and eighteenth century literary criteria in the light of Maupassant's production.

If verisimilitude consists of seeking reality in its most credible manifes-

[18]   Maupassant, "Le roman", *Pierre et Jean*, p. XIV.

tation and avoiding what is improbable, it logically follows the path towards a kind of universality. Maupassant reveals in the progression of his novels the truth of this doctrine and the application he gives to it. Gradually descriptive detail disappears until the imagery achieves the broadest application possible. The novels become in themselves sustained and unified images. This is also true in a more restricted sense of some of the later short stories as we the readers are given wider latitude in interpretation. Less and less tied to one character, imagery becomes increasingly identified with situation. As a result relationships acquire a much broader, more general basis in terms of human behaviour. Characters become to a greater extent representative, and no longer so particularized by their surroundings.

But with respect to form, the most obvious parallel with classicism in Maupassant is of course the concern with unity. Incident in the novel centres more and more around one single event to which all preceding details build, and from which all following ones stem. The progression from multiplicity of incident to unity is obvious and the later novels show to what pains Maupassant went to achieve this. Imagery, structure, characterization, theme, all are so tightly interwoven that each element is a vital and necessary function of the total work of art. As he progresses, Maupassant becomes increasingly skillful in the handling of his material with a single goal in mind.

The short stories, from the very beginning, show that Maupassant was capable of and concerned with unity of effect. But in working with the novel he obviously had problems adapting to the greater and more complex genre. The unity of the short stories is in the early stages of the novel a unity of chapter which results in a disjointed kind of overall composition. Only gradually is he able to adapt himself to the larger work until he succeeds, first of all in a very short novel, *Pierre et Jean*, and then in more extensive pieces, in controlling the many threads of composition in a more complete and satisfying whole.

The greater interest in the higher levels of society and more precisely of Parisian society which is evident in his later works can also be explained in classical terms as well, since study in depth, more and more his preoccupation, should according to the doctrine of "bienséances" deal with individuals whose complexity is worthy of such examination. There is no need to accuse Maupassant of pandering to the upper classes, and indeed it does him an unmerited disservice.

Classicism had much to teach Maupassant about form, and he seems to have learned his lesson thoroughly. And yet his can hardly be called a slavish imitation. He uses what he finds valuable in the classical theory in the development of his own personal form. As a disciple of Flaubert he cannot be expected to do otherwise. And although Vial offers a very interesting breakdown of the structure of *Fort comme la mort* into the five act sequence of classical tragedy, I feel that such analysis is interesting for its cleverness rather than for its validity. Maupassant evolves a concept of structure with a basic consistency, but varies it as he varies his imagery within these confines with a considerable degree of flexibility. The form is not a mould into which the work is arbitrarily fitted. It is rather a product of the total concept of the work, one of its necessary functions, and will vary according to the nature of the subject itself.

Form in the broadest sense becomes synonymous with genre, and here again a general pattern emerges from Maupassant's work. For he worked principally with two forms of prose literature – the short story, including both "conte" and "nouvelle" (the distinction between these two being very difficult to make), and the novel. Vial here again has devoted a great deal of study to this problem and shows very convincingly that there is in Maupassant's productive period a movement away from the shorter form and an increased concern with the longer and more complex genre.[19] Apart from the fact that his early years of publication, successful as they were, were essentially years of trial and experimentation spurred on by unusual success with the reading public, this marked shift only adds to our general interpretation of the significance of form in Maupassant. For it is a move away from the fragmentary isolated incident towards something much broader in scope, much more deeply involved with the totality of existence. In his quest for the truth of life, Maupassant can become much more directly involved through the novel than through the short story. On this level as well it is form which becomes more and more a determining factor in his artistic interest.

Although I have tried to show how Maupassant differs from Flaubert on numerous occasions, it is this never-ending concern with form which gives conclusive evidence to the fact that the younger author remains faithful to the spirit of his great predecessor. Flaubert's ideal novel, in which the material content would function only as a pretext, a vehicle, would be a novel of pure style, a "livre sur rien" in which the entire interest would lie in the form and structure.

In Maupassant too, as we have seen, the artist takes precedence over the realist, or more exactly, comes to grips with the problems raised by

---

[19] Vial, *Guy de Maupassant*, pp. 434–506.

the realist. His works are in the very broadest of senses an extension of
Flaubert – the harmony of all effects, the reduction in significance of
reality as an end unto itself, the pattern of form – all these he shares
with him. André Vial claims that Maupassant is not the stylist his teacher
was. His concern with composition is much less controlled and indeed in
the later works becomes very different from the earlier pieces. In Vial's
view he degenerates, his style becomes a series of platitudes, needless
repetitions lacking in form. This is particularly visible, he says, in *Notre
coeur*. His comment on this is I think well worth quoting:

Avaient d'abord préexisté une vision, et un sentiment de ce que doit être la
phrase, comme un moule vide que le romancier emplissait au plus juste. Il
arrive à la fin, qu'aucune forme préméditée n'existe plus: un vide de souffrance
où vagabonde une onde sonore, une interminable plainte.[20]

No one can seriously suggest that Maupassant was the painstaking artisan
of language that was Flaubert. If Flaubert's dominant stylistic concern
was the sonority and flow of language, and pure form was a question
of pure style, then Maupassant is moving in quite another direction. For
his concern is not, ultimately with the achieving of an aesthetic abstraction, but rather with the discovery of an essential truth rooted in life.
The dominant element within him is vision, yes, and it is through the
control of vision or form that the goal is sought. If there is such a marked
change in the author's style, is this not in keeping with the changes already witnessed, and can it not be explained, not in terms of the mental
degeneration of the artist, but rather in terms of the goal he has in mind?
And if that goal is a vision of reality, it becomes necessary to attempt an
explanation of the nature of that essential truth which he so ardently
seeks.

[20]   Vial, *Guy de Maupassant*, p. 609.

VIII

TIME

The imagery of form as the key to Maupassant's vision of reality has within it the fourth dimension so inescapable in the presentation of the physical world – time. And it is especially here that the distinction between interior and exterior imagery becomes so important. As the descriptions of the exterior world become more concerned with form, so too they become more deeply rooted in the present time. From Jeanne's wedding trip to Corsica through Georges Duroy's trip to Rouen, Pierre's excursions to the sea and Mariolle's to Mont Saint-Michel, the great descriptive passages always are occasioned by a sensory event. They are clear-cut attempts to arrest time in the present, to capture the fleeting moment and transfix it forever. And it is the increased concern with form in these passages which gives to their impressionistic coloration the same lasting quality that one finds, as we have noted, in Cézanne. One can understand why the Auvergne landscape is so evocative for Christiane Andermatt, for example, and why the same situation takes on quite different dimensions the second summer when the moment has been forever lost:

Christiane songeait à Tazenat. C'était la même voiture! c'étaient les mêmes êtres, mais ce n'étaient plus les mêmes coeurs! Tout semblait pareil! ...et pourtant! ...pourtant! ...Qu'était-il donc arrivé? Presque rien! ...Un peu d'amour de plus chez elle! ...un peu d'amour de moins chez lui! ...presque rien! ...[1]

The fact is that externals are quite incapable of evoking this ultimate goal. But Maupassant continues the search relentlessly. His three travel books are perhaps his most concentrated effort to stop the ravages of time by this method. Forms in nature cannot be maintained. They can only try to grasp the moment as it passes. A successful demonstration of this is to be found in *Notre coeur*. The two individuals find a common bond in

---

[1] Maupassant, *Mont-Oriol, Oeuvres complètes*, p. 316.

their setting, and the peak of their communion occurs at that moment at which they walk the parapet of the church, high above the moving sand and water. For a brief moment time is standing still, interrupted by the bold vertical thrust into the relentless horizontal flow of life, and they escape together into the void:

Il la portait presque, et elle se laissait aller, jouissant de cette protection robuste qui lui faisait traverser le ciel, et elle lui savait gré, un gré romanesque de femme, de ne pas gâter de baisers cette promenade de goëlands.[2]

But nature, for all its potential, is firmly rooted in the present. Man can momentarily soar to the heights of infinity, but time carries on and the present soon becomes the past. Time the destroyer cannot be overcome by external reality. Mariolle's walk in the Forest of Fontainebleau only serves to remind him of that lost moment on the Norman coast. It cannot return him to it. This time nature is melancholy solitude. And it even goes so far as to reflect the new present in the forms of the two twisted trees, the beech and the oak, so intimately entwined and still reaching for the sky.[3]

While the interior increasingly tends to dominate the Maupassantian universe, there is this outward progression in Maupassant towards the expansive. Interior experience opens him to reality and the essential fact which stems out of this is the identification which takes place. There is a union at the point in time, that is to say the present, which is total and absolute, between the perceiving individual and the perceived object. Maupassant is at this point faithful both to Flaubert and to Schopenhauer. His originality in this regard lies with his method of dealing with his material. Gradually vision becomes equated with form and the point of identity is *immediately* perceived. It is not the gradual building up, the linear method of which we spoke, but a kind of totality with regard to the work itself.

But if as with Flaubert, the experience is only momentary it is hardly the eternal moment. It vanishes as quickly as it appears without the slow disintegration so typical of Flaubert. Mariolle is so confused the morning following the experience at Mont Saint-Michel that he is not certain how to confront Michèle de Burne. It was truly a "rêve réalisé",[4] as he says to himself on returning to Paris, something which came and went like the flash of Duroy's mirrors.

---

[2]   Maupassant, *Notre coeur, Oeuvres complètes*, p 104.
[3]   *Notre coeur*, p. 278.
[4]   *Notre coeur*, p. 111.

Time is portrayed in Maupassant not as a rhythmic series of *crescendos* and *diminuendos* but in a more abrupt stop-and-go pattern. The peaks at which things arrive at a union appear unexpectedly, with little or no preparation, and vanish with similar suddenness. Immediately after the night at Mont Saint-Michel, Mariolle knows full well that it has gone:

Il restait à André Mariolle de cette rapide, de cette bizarre entrevue (le lendemain matin), l'imperceptible déception de l'homme qui n'a pu cueillir toute la moisson d'amour qu'il croyait mûre, et, en même temps, l'enivrement du triomphe, donc l'espérance assurée de conquérir bientôt ses derniers abandons.[5]

This dream, this hallucination, leaves him with only an illusion with which to carry on. The reality he has glimpsed has left only its reflection, which obliterates all else. He is incapable of seeing, hearing, or doing anything unrelated to Michèle de Burne on his return to Paris. Olivier Bertin before him had undergone the same process. Walking with Annette in the Parc Monceau, suddenly, inexplicably, the memories of his past well up within him. It is the sight of the young girl seated by the pond which, he eventually realizes, lies at the root of his experience. It is not the regular building of one event on another, but the whole of his life which flashes suddenly before him:

Bertin sentait en lui s'éveiller des souvenirs, ces souvenirs disparus, noyés dans l'oubli et qui soudain reviennent, on ne sait pourquoi. Ils surgissaient rapides, de toutes sortes, si nombreux en même tèmps, qu'il éprouvait la sensation d'une main remuant la vase de sa mémoire.[6]

He too is confused following the vital moment. Inspired to paint on returning to his studio he is incapable of anything but dreaming. The moment of perception is past. Time present is gone.

If the present offers us these tempting illusions which cannot be captured in themselves, then the past must therefore assume greater significance. The moments lost in the present might be regained here. And it is in dealing with the past that the second series of images becomes meaningful. The reflective interior image is never related to the present, but always to a time which is important within the psychology of the fictional characters, that is, either past or future.

Both the portraits of Maréchal and Anne de Guilleroy are like a constant background to the action of their respective novels. Hidden away by Madame Roland, the image of her lover becomes in Pierre's mind the

5 *Notre coeur*, p. 109.
6 Maupassant, *Fort comme la mort, Oeuvres complètes*, p. 121.

conclusive piece of evidence. By finally revealing it, his mother unearths her past visually before the eyes of her son. It is a kind of sudden, un-expected appearance, a mirage which has broken into the family to do irreparable harm. In it the past has risen to meet the present, and the resultant explosion will destroy Pierre's image of his mother. Here too time in Maupassant is not a series of developments, but rather a series of unexpected, immediate shifts which the rational mind seems quite in-capable of really controlling.

The portrait of Anne de Guilleroy as she appeared some fifteen to twenty years earlier is another instance of the visual presence of the past. Its danger lies of course in the fact that it now corresponds to a new order of things, it is a reflection of a quite distinct reality. Time has destroyed its harmony in a slow but relentless process of decay. But the realization of this comes to Bertin with such tragic suddenness that the rational mind can in no way come to terms with it.

The mirrors of *Bel-Ami* move in the opposite direction. They are literally projections, and the basic problem of the novel is thus the attempt to force the present into a correspondence with a glimpsed future. These incidents too break unexpectedly into the action, interrupting its course and plotting its direction, that is to say Georges Duroy's direction. They explode into his mind and only then does reason take over to guide what has already been intuitively perceived.

The painting of Christ too is a part of that pattern of time in the novel, illustrating as it does the underlying falsity of Duroy's actions. It is a vision into the truth which those who view it do not have the perceptive-ness to evaluate. The essential artificiality of Georges Duroy's world, substantiated by a series of illusions, has yet to find a synthesis. The only point of union of past, present and future has been based on a lie. This is without doubt the novel of blackest pessimism, for we are left not with destruction, but with the complete degradation of human values. It is as if Maupassant were terrified to carry his point of view any farther along the road to oblivion.

If the establishment of time in Maupassant is in the final analysis a visual problem, then one can readily identify still another point of weak-ness in *Mont-Oriol* which is created by the lack of coherent imagery. The past is an essential of the narrative, but it lacks that focal point required to establish it. There is no systematic pattern to the past, only the sugges-tion of form of Brétigny's physiognomy which, while serving to explain much of the relationship between himself and Christiane, fails to draw the divergent parts of the novel together.

It is his last attempt to traverse the abyss of time which is again the most significant. *Notre coeur* follows the same basic pattern of time – the past, represented by Mariolle's mental reflection of Michèle de Burne and her own mirror-image, and the point of union in the present already examined. The abyss between these two poles opens wide, and Mariolle is about to go the way of other Maupassantian heroes, when a new element is unexpectedly introduced – Elizabeth. By a combination of the two women, some thread of possibility remains open. Past and present do not necessarily destroy each other in this novel, but attempt to fuse, timidly one must admit, to at least the potential of a new order.

Perception through vision has been the guiding principle of all of Maupassant's central figures, a principle which gradually asserts itself more dominantly as he develops his technique. Through it, repeated attempts to arrest time, to bring all to union and harmony have been made, but they end inevitably in either sham and deceit far removed from the essentials of the real and totally within the world of illusion as in *Bel-Ami*, or in the complete void of *Pierre et Jean* and *Fort comme la mort*. For vision is illusion. Objectivity in this sense is a *cul-de-sac* from which there is no possible escape. The psychological nature of Maupassant's later works demonstrates unequivocably that he was aware of the futility of the position. But unlike Flaubert, he refuses to withdraw into style. He must continue his search for something solid.

And it is through vision that he sees the possibility of destroying time. One must bear in mind the dual nature of the reflective image. It is first of all the means by which Maupassant objectifies the problem confronting his characters, and in this sense it cannot satisfy the need for reality. For objective reality has that tragic characteristic of being constantly destroyed. Whether it be internal or external in focus, the image of the physical world is constantly vulnerable to time. The present, by its very nature, vanishes immediately, the past is a mere mirage, and the future is only a deception whose truth is objectively unknowable. But by the same token these reflective images are products of the human mind. The painting, the portrait, the mirror reflection are internal as well as external. It is thus that they are able both to suggest a reality and bar the route to it. Exteriorization leads to the Flaubertian dilemma. Objectivity slips through one's fingers.

Maupassant's goal then would appear to be a kind of artistic reconstitution of phenomena by means of which the moment, intuitively perceived can be captured and arrested. The internalization of artistic focus is an aspect of his creative talent which is not to be underestimated. The timeless moment wells forth in the travel books as suddenly as in the novels:

La petite pendule suspendue contre la cloison de bois fait un bruit qui semble formidable dans ce silence du ciel et de la mer.

Et ce minuscule battement troublant seul l'immense repos des éléments, me donne soudain la surprenante sensation des solitudes illimitées, où les murmures des mondes, étouffés à quelques mètres de leurs surfaces, demeurent imperceptibles dans le silence universel.

Il semble que quelque chose de ce calme éternel de l'espace descend et se répand sur la mer immobile, par ce jour étouffant d'été. C'est quelque chose d'accablant, d'irrésistible, d'endormeur, d'anéantissant, comme le contact du vide infini. Toute la volonté défaille, toute pensée s'arrête, le sommeil s'empare du corps et de l'âme.[7]

One can notice the significance of form in this preoccupation with time. The seascape, such as this passage evokes, and the panoramic landscapes that we have already viewed are an interplay between form and formlessness. It is at that moment at which the analytical human mind loses that perception of form that sight takes on this vital temporal suggestion and is able momentarily to transcend. Such evocations of infinity and the void are thus of capital importance in Maupassant's quest for life. The vocabulary of the last sentence is deeply meaningful – *volonté, pensée, sommeil* are words charged with meaning for the author.

But the moment for Maupassant is not always that point at which forms disintegrate. Precise light conditions are very much a part of his descriptive – sunsets over the Arc de Triomphe, sunrises and fog on the coasts of Normandy or Provence, the mid-day heat of the Sahara Desert. These particular lighting effects are important in the context of time for two reasons. First, they silhouette objects, etch them against the sky, and thus stress their form in a very dramatic fashion. From a visual point of view this is a means by which objects are reduced, not to formlessness as we found in the last passage or in the fog of *Pierre et Jean*, but rather to essential, structural elements, in which all else tends to be disregarded. And secondly such special lighting conditions are but brief moments in the continuum of time. They therefore do not permit long complex analyses but must be perceived at the moment. Intuition takes priority over reason in their observation. The infinity of the firmament can fleetingly reduce observable reality to its essence, and thus deepen its significance to the observer, offer him some brief insight into the meaning of existence. This is precisely the message of the couple and the seascape

[7]   Maupassant, *La vie errante, Oeuvres complètes*, p. 13.

transposed into a painting by the artist in "Miss Harriet", a message which Miss Harriet herself receives. It is a sudden intuitive flash, an insight which drives her ultimately to suicide. She cannot retain this experience. Time destroys all, and the artistic interpretation in the form of the canvas becomes yet another external object whose deeper meaning cannot be retained. Suicide becomes then the only exit possible.

Miss Harriet also demonstrates the importance of the male-female relationship in Maupassant's fictional situations. The theme of love occupies the author's attention in his writings with perhaps as much frequency as his social escapades did in his life. From "Boule de Suif" and "La maison Tellier" to "L'inutile beauté" sexual relationships are fleeting things. The perfect union is an occurrence which is rare indeed, and like the sunsets, is ephemeral. Francesca Rondoli appears and disappears with equal suddenness. Mariolle and Mme de Burne find only a brief moment of harmony. Communication between individuals is not impossible, but this timeless state of union and bliss cannot be preserved. Time destroys the love between Olivier Bertin and Anne de Guilleroy not by the slow Flaubertian erosive process, but rather by means of a series of sudden intuitive perceptions. The slow fading of the garden in Mariolle's "garçonnière" does not parallel a slow decrease in intensity of the relationship between Mariolle and Mme de Burne, but bears tragic witness to an artificial attempt to recapture something briefly found and lost. *Fort comme la mort* is not a novel of a gradual disintegration of a relationship to which the aging of the two lovers bears tragic witness, but rather of a sudden realization of the *fait accompli* which explodes in Bertin's face. The preservation of the moment is an internal, subjective problem, important only on the psychological level. Time in these later novels is not a slow progression of measures. It is essentially stopped in the minds of the central characters, for several years in *Pierre et Jean* and *Fort comme la mort*, for one brief instant in *Notre coeur*. The internalization of reality is a development in Maupassant which cannot be overlooked, and which sets him apart from his three major literary ancestors – Balzac, Zola and Flaubert.

Time is not an analytic process in Maupassant, but rather an organic one. The *moment* preserved is the goal of his writings. Although he was not the deepest of thinkers, there is undoubtedly a metaphysical level to his writings.

All this discussion of the moment, so central to his view of life, leads inevitably to the short story. It is a fact that Maupassant is better known at least in the English-speaking world, as a writer of short stories than as a novelist. As a literary form the short story is indeed well suited to the capturing of the moment. It is by its very nature a brief and fleeting experience. The moment of time as a central problem of the Maupassantian short story takes several forms and can offer some insight into the great variety to be found in these short pieces.

The "cadre" or framework structure for example, can be viewed in this light to some advantage. The narrator of the story travels through a certain area such as is the case in "Miss Harriet", visits a friend (as in "Mademoiselle Perle"), or as a lawyer pleads a case in court (as in "Un cas de divorce"). He is reminded, either by the scene he observes or by the social context in which he finds himself, or indeed by the problem at issue, of a series of events which he witnessed or heard of previously. Time is momentarily disjointed, thrown in reverse, or even arrested, while the narrator relates these events. The "cadre" form then is a means by which time can be suddenly stopped and the moment captured. Here again we have a link between the "cadre" and the story, that is to say between time and timelessness, which is abrupt and essentially intuitive in nature.

But of course many of Maupassant's short stories do not employ the "cadre" technique. Many of his readers remember him for his celebrated "trick" endings such as we find in "La parure" or perhaps in "Boule de Suif". Here too time performs an interesting and similar function. That moment of nothingness which the Loisels experience upon the discovery of the truth about the necklace serves to reduce to futile meaninglessness the long tragic passing of years between the loss of the jewels and the revelation of their worthlessness. And one must bear in mind that this important appearance of truth is an accidental occurrence, unexpected, and unprepared. The non-rational nature of the time lapse is central to the ironic effect of the ending. By the same token the rejection of Boule de Suif is equally irrational, and reduces her great moment of patriotic self-sacrifice to total futility. The delay at the inn which her principles caused, that is to say the lapse of time so critical to her fellow travellers has therefore no value at all. Time is subjectivized and the story is geared to that moment in the *dénouement* at which time comes to a full stop. Nothing further can be added, no progression from this point is possible. The only factor which can possibly be preserved lies within Boule de Suif herself, a fact which Maupassant does not point out. Even in this very early work, despite its all-pervasive pessimism, the potential interiorization which Maupassant will come to explore is already visible.

Still another aspect of Maupassant's short stories which is well-known is of course hallucination. And here we are confronted by a multitude of conflicting literary and medical possibilities. Let me simply suggest that this too can be viewed as still another manifestation of the Maupassantian interpretation of the problem of time. By its very nature the hallucination is a non-rational experience. The mad husband of "Un cas de divorce" is haunted by the destructive power of time and withdraws from human contact in an attempt to savour perfection, that is to say, the moment, for as long a time as possible:

J'ai parfois pour une d'elles une passion qui dure autant que son existence, quelques jours, quelques soirs. On l'enlève alors de la galerie commune et on l'enferme dans un mignon cabinet de verre où murmure un fil d'eau contre un lit de gazon tropical venu des îles du grand Pacifique. Et je reste près d'elle, ardent, fiévreux et tourmenté, sachant la mort si proche, et, la regardant se faner, tandis que je la possède, que j'aspire, que je bois, que je cueille sa courte vie d'une inexprimable caresse.[8]

Time is at the very centre of this typical dilemma of the heart versus the head. Intellectually Maupassant cannot escape the destructive force of time, but intuitively glimpses of paradise reveal themselves, tempting and torturing the eye, and revealing the impossibility of the human condition. In the same diary we find the following passage:

L'oeil! Songez à lui! L'oeil! Il boit la vie apparente pour en nourrir la pensée. Il boit le monde, la couleur, le mouvement, les livres, les tableaux, tout ce qui est beau et tout ce qui est laid, et il en fait des idées. Et quand il nous regarde, il nous donne la sensation d'un bonheur qui n'est point de cette terre. Il nous fait pressentir ce que nous ignorerons toujours; il nous fait comprendre que les réalités de nos songes sont de méprisables ordures.[9]

This non-rational flight into timelessness has in an almost Baudelairian way a dual nature. The hallucinatory temptation is at once the temptation of paradise and the tortured anguish of a living hell. The Horla would appear to have the ability to transcend man's bounds, and its super-human power can drive the narrator, intuitively conscious of its presence, at least in the initial stages, to suicide. But even this creature will fall victim to time:

S'il n'était pas mort? ...seul peut-être le temps a prise sur l'Être Invisible et Redoutable. Pourquoi ce corps transparent, ce corps inconnaissable, ce corps d'Esprit, s'il devait craindre, lui aussi, les maux, les blessures, les infirmités, la destruction prématurée?[10]

[8] Maupassant, "Un cas de divorce", *L'inutile beauté*, *Oeuvres complètes*, pp. 228–29.
[9] "Un cas de divorce", p. 222.
[10] Maupassant, "Le Horla", *Le Horla*, *Oeuvres complètes*, p. 47.

But the "unknowable" perhaps dies at his appointed hour. Time is thus a known quantity and not an abstract, unpredictable force here as it is for mankind. The mastery of time pushes to the limit of existence. Its perception is intuitive and lets man glimpse both heaven and hell, permanence and annihilation. Time is at the core of human existence.

From the philosophical point of view then, time represents an impossible dilemma for Maupassant. And from the strictly practical point of view as well, it created certain serious literary difficulties for him.

If the short stories are composed of a single, or a series of moments of perception, then the novel is more a problem of duration than of moment. Maupassant's perception of his world had in this respect much difficulty in adapting to the longer literary form. The early novels have already been described as chain-like in their structure. Each incident or chapter represents one perceived moment, and Maupassant has technical problems in connecting those moments. The transitions in *Une vie* are very weak, those of *Bel-Ami* succeed because of a conscious parallelism or even duplication of the successive moments. *Mont-Oriol* tries to unify two distinct types of temporal progressions.

With *Pierre et Jean* Maupassant arrives through a reductive process already discussed at his own form for the novel. This is essentially a novel of one moment – that of the discovery of identity. That moment is given density and duration by the narrative in a way which parallels the author's approach to the short story. Time is embodied in the miniature of Maréchal here as it will be in the portrait of Mme de Guilleroy in *Fort comme la mort* and in the impassive beauty of Michèle de Burne in *Notre coeur*. These are novels of vision, vision in its deepest sense in which all factors culminate in the moment of identity.

The mystical quality, that desire to achieve a state of omniscience and omnipotence, with all its tortures and all its dreams, finds its aesthetic counterpart in a unified structure which Maupassant does not share with Balzac, Zola or Flaubert. And the intuitive transcendence of time is the key to the Maupassantian universe, a key which the author is extremely hesitant to use, and which all too frequently leads to disaster. Only Mariolle makes any attempt to reconcile the human dilemma:

Cette enfant séduite ne serait-elle pas, pour son amour aride et desséchant, la petite source trouvée à l'étape du soir, l'espoir d'eau fraîche qui soutient l'énergie quand on traverse le désert?[11]

[11] Maupassant, *Notre coeur, Oeuvres complètes*, p. 293.

IX

THE ILLUSION OF REALITY

Care and precision of observation are such an essential to Flaubert's art that his interpretation of external reality is central to the understanding of his artistic purpose. The constant search for the significant detail, the revealing gesture, the ability to see in man's world that which the ordinary man is incapable of perceiving, establish the claim to originality in art. One can see then that observation and objectivity are closely interrelated with aesthetic concerns for Flaubert and it is for this reason that he is so frequently and so inaccurately labelled a realist.

For Flaubert's principal goal is without question artistic. "Realism" is only a means, a device by means of which art can be created. The "livre sur rien" which consists of pure style and which for Flaubert would constitute the ultimate achievement would not be limited by the exigencies of the real world, since the "real" world in that sense would be valueless. Maupassant's "preface" to *Pierre et Jean*, stressing as it does observation, precision of detail and originality show how deeply the pupil is indebted to the master.

Nor will anyone deny that Flaubert is by nature a Romantic in the sense that he is intensely aware of the value and significance of personal inner experience. But the narcissism so frequently found in Romanticism is absent from his work. His approach to reality is, unlike theirs, basically expansive. His quest is a quest not for the self, but for the world. It is by identifying his world that he will identify himself.[1]

In other words, Flaubert's approach to the physical world is objective, that is, rational. It is a search for comprehension which will lead ultimately to identification.

But external reality is diffused in an infinity of space and time. Fragmentation and multiplicity are the great barriers to identification, the hurdles which art alone can attempt to overcome. The artistic process becomes

---

[1] Georges Poulet, *Études sur le temps humain* (Edinburgh: Edinburgh University Press, 1949).

thus a kind of synthesization of this diversity into an aesthetically determined unit by means of style. The artist's main objective becomes the
struggle to give a kind of homogeneity, a kind of form, to what exists in
a seemingly senseless or formless state.

The Flaubertian approach to this problem might be termed a linear
one, in which images proceed one from the other, and build one on the
other until the total perception is achieved. The process is a kind of
ascension until the whole is blended at that point at which a totality is
reached. This is a reasoned progression towards a unified view of man's
universe. But such moments cannot be sustained, and fissures appear
rapidly, eventually destroying the entire edifice. The abyss which was
momentarily bridged opens again to reveal an essential nothingness.

Flaubert's struggle with reality is thus a kind of cyclical process which
attempts to explain the universe by linking it together in a series of causes
and effects. And he finds no escape from this chain which inevitably will
lead him back to his point of departure. One can see how important his
final novel, *Bouvard et Pécuchet* becomes. Each chapter represents a full
revolution of the machine, from inspiration through the logical piecing
together of the concept to the ultimate disintegration of the whole. It
seems so fitting and almost intentional that he left the novel incomplete,
as if the process were to repeat itself to infinity.

This is the nature of Maupassant's inheritance, and it is from this
point that he will proceed. What we must decide is whether he accepts
totally this hopelessly pessimistic view of life from which the only escape
is into the ivory tower of style, or attempts to break the equilibrium and
move out of the circle.

It is again to the novels that we must turn in order to deal with this
problem, and through them try to shed some light on all of Maupassant's
production. We have already seen that structurally *Une vie* is linear,
proceeding in historical time from incident to incident. The reasons for
this are obviously not difficult to determine. The work is an application
of Flaubert's teachings with little or no deviation. We see in it the same
type of cyclical progression from early enthusiasm, through the ascension
to the synthesis which occurs on Jeanne's marriage to Julien. The wedding
trip of the fifth chapter is the turning point in the development. As they
cross the sea to Corsica the identification is at its height:

Le soir venait, un soir calme, radieux, plein de clarté, de paix heureuse. Pas un
frisson dans l'air ou sur l'eau; et ce repos illimité de la mer et du ciel s'étendait
aux âmes engourdies où pas un frisson non plus se passait.[2]

[2] Maupassant, *Une vie*, p. 95.

But already the structure is beginning to show signs of weakness. Julien's miserliness, Jeanne's first experience of physical love contain the seeds of destruction. There is an obstacle between Jeanne and her husband which she perceives for the first time as a result of this experience.[3] The rest of the novel consists of the slow but relentless breaking down of Jeanne's illusions until she is left entirely alone at the end with only fragments of her former life, on which she constantly dwells. The movement has run full circle and only a void of endless repetition remains. Maupassant has added nothing to Flaubert's concepts. Indeed he is unable to provide even an artistic unity to the work and it remains uneven and fragmentary on this level as well. Not only does *Une vie* demonstrate only very slight originality, but it also lacks the artist's control of his material which was Flaubert's greatest success.

This same approach manifests itself with only a limited deviation from the Flaubertian norm in *Bel-Ami*, but with a much greater degree of aesthetic success. The emphasis is placed with striking irony on the rising half of the movement, unlike its predecessor. The cumulative moment occurs here in the closing paragraphs of the last chapter in which all Paris is at Georges Du Roy de Cantal's feet:

Lorsqu'il parvint sur le seuil, il aperçut la foule amassée, une foule noire, bruissante, venue là pour lui, pour lui Georges Du Roy. Le peuple de Paris le contemplait et l'enviait.[4]

The protagonist's ascent has been cold and calculating from beginning to end, as he climbed from deception to deception. If the attaining of this goal is a possibility, Maupassant seems to be telling us, it can be reached only by an overpowering dishonesty which includes the perpetrator himself in its scheming web. For the most convinced victim of deceit is Duroy himself. True to Flaubert's impassivity Maupassant leaves his hero at the peak of wealth, power and influence with no comment whatsoever. The attempt to break the omnipresent vicious circle is only a delusion. Whether Duroy ever awakens from his dream is not significant. Maupassant leaves the reader with an image of it whose message is inescapable.

Mais [Duroy] ne les voyait point; sa pensée maintenant revenait en arrière, et devant ses yeux éblouis par l'éclatant soleil flottait l'image de Madame de Marelle rajustant en face de la glace les petits cheveux frisés de ses tempes, toujours défaits au sortir du lit.[5]

---

[3] *Une vie*, p. 100.
[4] Maupassant, *Bel-Ami*, p. 573.
[5] *Bel-Ami*, p. 573.

In spite of his calculations he remains attached to an image for which he has already risked the loss of his ambitious attainments. Madame de Marelle fitted into his calculations only in the initial stages of his career, and because of her social position could no longer represent an asset to him. But he cannot dispense with her as he could with Madeleine Forestier or Madame Walter. If his careful construction should crumble one can only assume that Madame de Marelle reveals the first crack in the façade. In the light of what we have said about the image in his work, her reflection which we see here will by its very nature lead to his downfall.

By the attention given in the novel to illusion and deception, one must conclude that Maupassant's view of life is at least as pessimistic here as was Flaubert's. Succcess is only self-delusion and the natural state of man would appear to be failure. He is as caught in the trap of reality as was Flaubert.

Mont-Oriol, the least successful, if not the least original of Maupassant's novels, combines, or more accurately juxtaposes the methods of presentation of its predecessors. Christiane Andermatt is to Jeanne de Lamare as her husband is to Georges Duroy. Both are caught in the *cul-de-sac* of the "real" world, the former's dreams shattered by Paul Brétigny, the latter a material success whose private life has become a series of false illusions. For all its complexity, this novel lacks the cohesiveness that only a more careful construction of images could provide. The synthesis that such imagery achieved in *Bel-Ami* exists nowhere in *Mont-Oriol* and its fragmentation is more obvious than that of *Une vie* since he fails to correlate meaningfully and consistently the two parallel plots.

The fragmentation, the multiplicity of reality which was for Flaubert the challenge to the intellect is for Maupassant too the challenge to his art. If there is an underlying unity to the universe, no matter how fleetingly it may be glimpsed, it is the artist's task to achieve an aesthetic homogeneity in his product in order to approach the problem. By proceeding in the Flaubertian tradition of cause and effect, the younger artist has had only a very partial success. Maupassant must find something more suited to his temperament, more original and less derivative.

The fact that there is some essential unifying element underlying reality is something neither Flaubert nor Maupassant would have denied. The older artist devoted his life to the search for it and found a kind of solution for his problem in what one might call an artistic withdrawal. On the illusory quality of the external world, Maupassant, in his preface to *Bouvard et Pécuchet* quotes from Flaubert's correspondence:

Vous vous plaignez que les événements ne sont pas variés – cela est une plainte réaliste, et d'ailleurs, qu'en savez-vous? Il s'agit de les regarder de plus près. Avez-vous jamais cru à l'existence des choses? Est-ce que tout n'est pas une illusion? Il n'y a de vrais que les rapports, c'est-à-dire la façon dont nous percevons les objets.[6]

The nature of reality thus depends on our method of viewing it. For Maupassant the linear approach proved inadequate and in his later novels he develops a new route, more in harmony with his personal views of life. We have already seen that the visual formal image has a large rôle to perform even in the first three novels. It is this aspect which he will explore in greater depth in order to attempt to come to grips with the evanescent truth.

Flaubert is however not the only thinker whose ideas are important in Maupassant's approach to life. As is well known he was very much attracted to certain arguments of the German philosopher Schopenhauer, and put to good use a number of his concepts.

It is particularly to that section of *Die Welt als Wille und Vorstellung* which deals directly with the artist and aesthetics that we must turn in order to appreciate much of Maupassant's effort and contribution to the advance of the art of prose fiction.

One will immediately see that Schopenhauer's view of the artist and his function is in very close harmony with Flaubert's. But where it was Flaubert's personal approach to depend very heavily on the chain of cause and effect in order to glimpse that point of essential harmony, Schopenhauer endorses a somewhat different course towards the identical goal:

If, raised by the power of the mind, a man relinquishes the common way of looking at things, gives up tracing, under the guidance of the forms of the principle of sufficient reason, their relations to each other, the final goal of which is always a relation to his own will; if he thus ceases to consider the where, the when, the why and the whither of things, and looks simply and solely at the *what*; if further he does not allow abstract thought, the concepts of the reason, to take possession of his consciousness, but, instead of all this, gives the whole power of his mind to perception, sinks himself entirely in this, and lets his whole consciousness be filled with the quiet contemplation of the natural object actually present, whether a landscape, a tree, a mountain, a building or whatever it may be; inasmuch as he *loses* himself in this object, ... i.e., forgets even his individuality, his will, and continues to exist only as the pure subject, the clear mirror of the object, so that it is as if the object

---

[6] Maupassant, "Étude sur Gustave Flaubert", *Oeuvres postumes* II, p. 98, quoting from Flaubert's correspondence.

alone were there, without anyone to perceive it, and he can no longer separate the perceiver from the perception, but both have become one, because the whole consciousness is filled and occupied with one single sensuous picture; if thus the object has to such an extent passed out of all relation to the will, then that which is so known is no longer the particular thing as such; but it is the Idea, the eternal form, the immediate objectivity of the will at this grade; and therefore, he who is sunk in this perception is no longer individual; for in such perception the individual has lost himself; but he is *pure*, will-less, painless, timeless *subject of knowledge*.[7]

The process Schopenhauer describes here at such length begins in essence where Flaubert concludes. The rational tracing of the chain of cause and effect, on which Flaubert depends so heavily to fill in all the gaps, must be relinquished, says Schopenhauer. The true, unchanging constant of reality must be attained by perception freed from the limits imposed by reason, and not created by it. Only thus can true objectivity be reached, an objectivity which is free from any modification by individuality. How similar this appears to Poulet's interpretation of the Flaubertian goal:

Celui-ci n'éprouve dans sa plénitude, conscience de lui-même que dans le moment où il sort de lui-même pour s'identifier, par le plus simple mais le plus intense des actes de la vie mentale, la perception, avec l'objet, quel qu'il soit, de cette perception.[8]

[7] Arthur Schopenhauer, *The World as Will and Idea*, trans. by W. Durant, *The Works of Schopenhauer* (New York: Simon and Schuster, 1931). The original German reads as follows: "Wenn man, durch die Kraft des Geistes gehoben, die gewöhnliche Betrachtungsart der Dinge fahren lässt, aufhört, nur ihren Relation zu einander, deren letztes Ziel immer die Relation zum eigenen Willen ist, am Leitfaden der Gestaltungen des Satzes vom Grunde nachzugehen, also nicht mehr das Wo, das Wann, das Warum und das Wozu an den Dingen betrachtet; sondern einzig und allein das *Was*; auch nicht das abstrakte Denken, die Begriffe der Vernunft, das Bewusstsein einnehmen lässt; sondern statt alles diesen die Ganze Macht seines Geistes der Anschauung hingibt, sich ganz in diese versenkt und das ganze Bewusstsein ausfüllen lässt durch die ruhige Kontemplation des gerade gegenwärtigen natürlichen Gegenstandes, sei es eine Landschaft, ein Baum, ein Fels, ein Gebäude oder was auch immer; ... d. h. eben sein Individuum, seinen Willen vergisst und nur noch als reines Subjekt, als klarer Spiegel des Objekts bestehend bleibt; so dass es ist, als ob der Gegenstand allein da wäre, ohne jemanden, der ihn wahrnimmt, und man also nicht mehr den Anschauenden von der Anschauung trennen kann, sondern beide eines geworden sind, indem das ganze Bewusstsein von einem einzigen anschaulichen Bilde gänzlich gefüllt und eingenommen ist; wenn also solchermassen das Objekt aus aller Relation zu etwas ausser ihm, das Subjekt aus aller Relation zum Willen getreten ist: dann ist, was also erkannt wird, nicht mehr das einzelne Ding als solches; sondern es ist die *Idee*, die ewige Form, die unmittelbare Objektivität des Willens auf dieser Stufe; und eben dadurch ist zugleich der in dieser Anschauung Begriffene nicht mehr Individuum; denn das Individuum hat sich eben in solche Anschauung verloren; sondern er ist *reines*, willenloses, schmerzloses, zeitloses *Subjekt der Erkenntnis*" (Arthur Schopenhauer, *Die Welt als Wille und Vorstellung* I [Stuttgart und Frankfurt-am-Main: Cotta-Insel-Verlag, 1960], p. 257).

[8] Poulet, *Temps humain*, p. 249.

But what is with Flaubert a goal to be sought and momentarily glimpsed constitutes method with Schopenhauer. In the German's view it would be the very method of the Frenchman which denies him his goal. He defines art as the "way of viewing things independent of the principle of sufficient reason". Thus and only thus, can objectivity be attained, and for him genius is the most complete objectivity. The artistic method is intuitive, not rational.

What we see in Maupassant's novels is in my view a gradual shift away from the Flaubertian method in favour of that advocated by Schopenhauer. Maupassant begins by almost slavishly imitating his teacher, and proceeds from there to develop a more suitable approach in the hope that it might lead him out of the impasse. And it is clearly by means of the imagery we have dealt with that he advances. Although *Bel-Ami* is essentially a linear novel in which events stem one from the other in a logical sequence of cause and effect, this progression is periodically interrupted at those moments at which the images of identity intervene. These brief moments are not the culminations of long slow processes. They come upon Georges Duroy totally by surprise, and he is able, by means of them, to see, or more accurately to perceive his own image. Although the working out of his ambition remains in the domain of the reason, the original impetus at each step of the way is intuitive in nature. The progression takes on a dimension which sets it apart from *Madame Bovary* or *L'éducation sentimentale*. Intuition is no longer operative only at culminating points. It constitutes a series of unexpected signposts along the way. That such a combination of processes is so successful is no small evidence of Maupassant's creative ability, and *Bel-Ami* must be regarded as one of his finest accomplishments. We are not dealing in this novel with vague romantic longings. Bovarysme gives way here to something much more precise, much more impersonal.

It would be meaningless to consider Maupassant's career as a kind of methodical, mathematical progression away from Flaubert and towards Schopenhauer. For *Mont-Oriol*, here as in so many other instances, contributes very little to what has already been worked out. If *Bel-Ami* illustrates a somewhat timid introduction of a new element into his method, this next novel is then a retrogression to the earlier techniques in its essentials. Filled as it is with Christiane Andermatt's ill-defined amorous longings and her husband's shady business dealings, it lacks the focal point necessary to render it a success. The attempts to give form to reality which we have witnessed can in themselves be successful, but their application to the whole novel is so erratic as to make the work almost totally devoid of greater meaning. It remains in other words in the realm of the particular and fails to elevate itself into the world of Ideas. It is not in the Flaubertian or in the Schopenhauerian sense, a work of genius.

It is again with *Pierre et Jean*, without doubt Maupassant's most significant novel, that we are able to discern his approach in its most original form, although not all of the problems are solved in it. Its duration is shortened to a matter of weeks, and the novel becomes a concentrated study in depth rather than in length. We do not witness here the long slow but relentless erosion of an edifice, nor do we see its painstaking construction. It is a sudden obliteration, brought on by a single event, and facilitated by a dominant image. It is a novel of vision, not of reason. It is development and expansion of one of the stages of Georges Duroy's career. Pierre's crisis begins with the vague sensing of something amiss in the circumstances surrounding his brother's inheritance, a suspicion that is substantiated by the portrait of Maréchal. It is only after his intuition has been justified by that cold harsh reflection of reality that the rational process becomes truly operative and he openly confronts his mother.

Il avait l'esprit excitable, et réfléchi en même temps, il s'emballait, puis raisonnait, approuvait ou blâmait ses élans; mais chez lui la nature première demeurait en dernier lieu la plus forte, et l'homme sensitif dominait toujours l'homme intelligent.[9]

But the rational process eventually does reveal itself, and it is herein that the tragedy lies. Essential truth, even when immediately perceived and not constructed, cannot be maintained in the presence of logic. Fog gives way to light, and all tumbles into the yawning chasm of nothingness. Pierre did not consider in detail the chain of cause and effect which would stem from his discovery until after its revelation. The human failing here is not the inability to unearth truth, but the inability to adapt to it. Pierre is driven to destroy the image that has been with him all his life, the image of his mother's perfection, by a suspicion that is brought into focus not by logical deduction, but by the suggestions of two incidental characters, Marowsko, the Polish druggist, and the café waitress. Intuition, as Maupassant states himself about Pierre, takes precedence over reason. But the cycle has yet to be broken, for Pierre, the only character in the book with the capacity to seek an ideal, has failed to attain it. The intuitive approach has served only to accelerate the process

---

[9]   Maupassant, *Pierre et Jean*, p. 40.

of disillusionment, and the pessimistic view of life would seem thus only to be intensified. Man has still less control over his environment.

But like Flaubert Maupassant carries on his search, and in *Fort comme la mort* he comes to grips again with the problem. Olivier Bertin is another hero captivated by an ideal, the beauty of his mistress, which he has exteriorized in the form of the painting. This is again a novel of vision. His attraction for Annette, bitterly witnessed by her mother, is a development of which he is not intellectually aware until it is too late. It explodes into his conscious mind and drives him to self-destruction. Bertin can distinguish between reality and its illusion, between Annette and her mother, but he cannot prevent the attraction of the beautiful daughter from destroying him. Studying a copy of the portrait in his studio, he reveals fully to the reader the nature of his torture:

Il essayait de la revoir, de la retrouver vivante, telle qu'il l'avait aimée jadis. Mais c'était toujours Annette qui surgissait sur la toile. La mère avait disparu, s'était évanouie, laissant à sa place cette autre figure qui lui ressemblait étrangement. C'était la petite avec ses cheveux un peu plus clairs, son sourire un peu plus gamin, son air un peu plus moqueur, et il sentait bien qu'il appartenait corps et âme à ce jeune être-là, comme il n'avait jamais appartenu à l'autre, comme une barque qui coule appartient aux vagues.[10]

The key to Bertin here is of course the verb. "Il sentait" lies clearly in the domain of perception, and there can be no question of sufficient reason or cause and effect.

The conflict in the mind of André Mariolle is identical to Bertin's. Like his predecessor he is aware that on a purely rational level his present experience is a total impossibility, but intuitively he cannot prevent his attraction to Michèle de Burne. The struggle between reason and intuition which destroyed Pierre Roland and Olivier Bertin risks doing the same to him. He too runs away from his problem:

Mais pourquoi lutter? Il ne le pouvait plus. Elle lui plaisait par un charme qu'il ne comprenait pas, plus fort que tout. La fuir ne le délivrait pas, ne le séparait pas d'elle, mais l'en privait intolérablement, tandis que, s'il parvenait à se résigner un peu, il aurait d'elle au moins tout ce qu'elle lui avait promis, car elle ne mentait pas.[11]

Like his predecessors he abandons the field, yields to intuition, to the "idée fixe" that dominates the character of the Maupassantian hero. But it is vital that one recognize in this last novel an important difference,

---

[10]   Maupassant, *Fort comme la mort*, p. 294.
[11]   Maupassant, *Notre coeur*, p. 292.

for here the abdication is for the first time not absolute. Weak and timid as Mariolle's final decision may seem, it is not a complete withdrawal from an impossible conflict of heart and head. By closing his eyes to the vision of the real which no longer corresponds to his interior ideal, he is able to combine the attractions of Michèle and Elizabeth, that is to say, to synthesize them by means of an internal process into a permanent, if extremely limited vision which will stay within his grasp. True identification, if not fully achieved in *Notre coeur*, is at least brought within the realm of the possible. Mariolle's decision in the closing pages of the novel should not be regarded as a total annihilation, but as a hesitant attempt to conquer and come to terms with the human condition. If it seems to the reader a rather weak compromise, it nevertheless indicates that a new order should be explored. There is a ray of optimism, admittedly very slight, which is visible in no other novel of Guy de Maupassant.

We have seen in these novels an increasing emphasis on the perceptive, non-rational element in the human make-up, particularly as illustrated by the protagonists themselves. But if the goal of art is the discovery of the true nature of reality, then a consideration of Maupassant's methods of presentation in these works is at least of equal importance to the outlook of his characters and their reactions.

In our consideration of form in Maupassant we saw him move progressively towards greater and greater unity both in the concept and the execution of his art. We have also seen that this increased mastery over form depends very heavily for its success on highly developed imagery of a reflective nature, and certainly not on style. It would I think be naïve to consider the presence of the mirror in both Maupassant and Schopenhauer as sheer coïncidence. The philosopher conceives of the artist as the "clear mirror of the object",[12] so clear in fact that all barriers between the two disappear and the end product is "one single sensuous picture". By submerging himself totally in this perception, the artist transcends the bounds of the particular and in Schopenhauer's platonic terminology enters the world of the "Idea".

The parallels with Maupassant's writings, particularly his last three novels, are indeed striking. The dominant image in each of them is distinctly reflective in nature, and the essential power of each lies not in its surface contours, but in the hidden truth contained within it, perceptible only to the specially endowed individual. Maupassant preserves in this

[12] Schopenhauer, see quotation, pp. 278–79.

way the much praised objectivity so prized by both Flaubert and Schopenhauer. He is not compelled to delve personally beneath the surface, for his images provide this necessary deeper layer of meaning. In other words the author becomes identified not with his characters, but with his reflective imagery. Maupassant himself becomes the painting or the mirror, and thus can convey to his reader the truth about the actual situation.

The image becomes the unifying factor in each situation. The resolution of conflict depends on the perception of the image it contains, and in this way the artist Maupassant becomes literally the mirror of reality in which it becomes impossible to distinguish the creator from the created.

It is precisely for this reason that the second progression we have noted in our study of the image is of such great importance – the gradual reduction of descriptive detail until only the bare essentials, the forms, remain. For if there is an underlying unity to the universe, it cannot be perceived if it is surrounded by the multiple distortions of its superficial appearance. The significant thing about Maréchal's portrait is neither its contours nor its resemblance to Jean, but the revelation of the relationship between the deceased and Madame Roland. This is its message. And the portrait does not simply tell Bertin that Anne de Guilleroy and her daughter look strikingly alike. Of this he is already aware. It does inform him that he is caught in an impossible mesh of human relationships from which the only exit he can discover is death. André Mariolle realizes that, at the end of *Notre coeur*, he is in love not with Michèle de Burne herself, but with his image of her. And he requires her physical presence, as well as Elizabeth's in order to survive. They have become in this sense the reflections, and the image is now the reality, the unity of what is fragmented in the transcendental physical world. True reality is one. The illusions of this world are disjointed and partial evidence of a superior world perceptible through form.

It is logical then that his novels become to a greater and greater extent studies in depth, in which the physical world as such has a much reduced rôle. Maupassant masters his material not by perceiving unity in multiplicity in a cumulative progression as does Flaubert, but by constantly reducing his field of vision. Whereas Flaubert's movement is basically macrocosmic, Maupassant, while not denying the expansive, becomes increasingly microcosmic.

This tendency is very much in evidence in his last novel, for here the physical object conveying the image is quite literally a mirror, the most retractive of all reflective images. Michèle de Burne finds herself quite surrounded in mirror, literally isolated from her physical world, in the same way that André Mariolle attempts to surround her, isolate her, and keep her for himself. She escapes physically, but her image remains. External reality is relegated to two isolated but important sequences in which form is the essential characteristic. The physical world has little to contribute except in those instances in which its forms are evocative of a greater reality, a deeper meaning. For it is the world of illusion and deception. The truth lies in quite another direction, and it is towards it that Maupassant is moving in his later productions.

If the quest is to be continued, and Maupassant never shows signs of abandoning it although failure seems to be inevitable, a new route must be found. By moving increasingly towards the interior, the psychological, he is thus not relinquishing his artistic concerns, nor is he simply catering to a more sophisticated audience at the price of his integrity. Greater interiorization of conflict is simply the next logical step in the progression.

Physical reality remains always a basic in Maupassant's fiction. He is rooted in his own world and there is in him no more tendency towards abstraction than in Cézanne. But the important factor in reality becomes less and less its presence and its appearance, and more and more its underlying values. It is more and more perceived rather than viewed objectively. If interior reality is the answer, and Maupassant undoubtedly has some reservations about this, then Mariolle must be regarded as the closest he ever came to a frank expression of this view. Mariolle's vision is internal, and indeed he cuts off the exterior world in the vision that will keep him alive. And Maupassant significantly stops his novel at a point at which the complete resolution of the problem remains very much in question. External reality remains as strong a force as ever – the two interlocking trees in the closing pages substantiate this – but can Mariolle overcome external vision with internal vision, or is it really another illustration of self-delusion? The closing line should dispel any doubt. Mariolle answers Elizabeth's hesitant question with clarity and conviction: "Je t'aimerai comme ici."[13] If others are deceived, he certainly is not. He is no Georges Duroy.

A comment in "L'angélus", one of two incompleted novels, indicates that Maupassant is at least on the path towards a solution. The deformed child is told in one of the fragments:

Pauvre petit, toi aussi, tu as reçu de l'impitoyable destinée un triste sort. Mais tu auras au moins, je crois, en compensation de toutes les joies physiques, les

[13] Maupassant, *Notre coeur*, p. 297.

seules belles choses qui soient permises aux hommes, le rêve, l'intelligence et la pensée.[14]

The nostalgia for an unattainable reality is intense, but there is another reality which can compensate – an interior reality – it is explored.

What Maupassant has been doing is to place the responsibility for the whole problem squarely on the shoulders of man himself. If man cannot discover reality, he must then create it. And this is certainly not the Flaubertian aesthetic despair. Its characteristics – dream, intelligence and thought – are much too positive for that. These "belles choses" must be used to continue the search; they are not an end in themselves, but tools to be applied to life. It is in that application that the difficulties emerge. Art never becomes for Maupassant an end in itself.

The way out of the impasse is of course illusion and illusion runs great risk of becoming deception. It is precisely the fact that there is a risk, or in other words, some infinitesimal chance of success that makes it so valuable. He puts it this way in a variant of *Notre coeur:*

Un affamé qui trouve par hasard du pain blanc ne peut-il pas s'imaginer qu'il savoure la plus délicate nourriture; quand on est repu, qu'importe ce qu'on a mangé puisqu'on a rêvé.[15]

The answer to the enigma of reality must come from illusion. It is for this reason that the dream ranks so high in the list of human endowments. The whole discussion of the rôle of hallucination in Maupassant as proof of mental disturbance and even degeneration thus becomes meaningless. If it is true, and it seems very unlikely, that he was little by little losing control, then the dream as it appears is an obvious attempt in his lucid moments, to come to terms with himself. If on the other hand he was lucid until the end, and what medical evidence there is seems to point in this direction, the hallucination, a visual experience in essence, is then a useful device in the pursuit of his artistic goals. It represents not a flight from reality, but a genuine struggle to come closer to it. Does the narrator of "Le Horla" really go mad? By losing his identity in a mirror he certainly came closer to the "being" than one might think. And did he destroy it by burning down his house? Perhaps the truth of the matter is that some degree of madness, of hallucination, of irrationality is essential in the perception of Truth. And it is perhaps fear of this that prevents Maupassant, the objective artist, from really exploring his discovery. If he has

[14] Maupassant, "L'angélus", *Oeuvres postumes* II, *Oeuvres complètes*, p. 230.
[15] Maupassant, *Notre coeur*, p. 297.

found a road to Truth, he cannot bring himself, as Proust could, to make
the final leap of faith. Rational man destroys intuitive man. The second
and third of man's gifts, intelligence and thought, overcome the first.
What must be achieved a reversal of this order of precedence. Of all
Maupassant's characters, only André Mariolle makes any attempt whatsoever. And important as is the development of Maupassant's thought,
the final act of *Notre coeur* is far from daring.

Time in Maupassant is a series of disjointed moments at which one
becomes aware of its passing. How curiously the following passage, used
by Georges Poulet to illustrate his argument on Proust corresponds with
Maupassant's treatment of the same theme:

Et en m'apercevant que je n'avais pas de joie qu'elle fût vivante, que je ne
l'aimais plus, j'aurais dû être plus bouleversé que quelqu'un qui se regardant
dans une glace, après des mois de voyage, ou de maladie, s'aperçoit qu'il a les
cheveux blancs et une figure nouvelle d'homme mûr ou de vieillard. Cela bouleverse parce que cela veut dire: l'homme que j'étais, le jeune homme blond
n'existe plus, je suis un autre. Or l'impression que j'éprouvais ne prouvait-elle
pas un changement aussi profond, une mort aussi totale du moi ancien et la
substitution aussi complète d'un moi nouveau à ce moi ancien, que la vue d'un
visage ridé surmonté d'une perruque blanche remplaçant le visage de jadis?[16]

One has only to read the closing paragraphs of "Fini"[17] or "Adieu"[18] to
see time spring suddenly to the mind of a man caught in the same trap.

If the only means of discovering meaning in this morass of isolated
moments lies in the domain of intuitive perception, it follows that there
must be some point of contact between Maupassant and the Symbolists.
For they too are in search of something beyond, an unexplainable *au-delà*
that cannot be rationally approached. Like them, Maupasant is very much
aware of the power of the word. How could he have been otherwise, given
his early literary training. Notice the depth of value a single one syllable
word is given in a most striking passage drawn from *Au soleil*:

Le Sud! quel mot rapide, brûlant! Le Sud! Le feu! Là-bas, au Nord, on dit en
parlant des pays tièdes "le Midi". Ici c'est "le Sud".
    Je regardais cette syllabe si courte qui me paraissait surprenante comme si
je ne l'avais jamais lue. J'en découvrais, me semblait-il, le sens mystérieux. Car
les mots les plus connus comme les visages souvent regardés ont des signifi-
cations secrètes, dont on s'aperçoit tout d'un coup, un jour, on ne sait pourquoi!

---

[16] Poulet, *Temps humain*, p. 295, quoting Marcel Proust, *Albertine disparue*, ii, p. 137.
[17] See note 5, Chapter VI, p. 105.
[18] Maupassant, "Adieu", *Contes du jour et de la nuit, Oeuvres complètes*, pp. 256–57.

Le Sud! Le désert, les nomades, les terres inexplorées et puis les nègres, tout
un monde nouveau, quelque chose comme le commencement d'un univers!
Le Sud! comme cela devient énergique sur la frontière du Sahara.[19]

And this from the pen of the man who is supposedly so lacking in feeling
for poetry! How unjust does the judgement of Henri Peyre concerning
Maupassant appear:

Le Symbolisme a vieilli pour nous Maupassant, à qui manquait le sens de la
poésie. Lorsqu'avec Gide, Proust, Giraudoux, Larbaud, l'influence du Symbolisme a contribué a poétiser notre roman, Maupassant s'est mis à dater. Proust
nous a ensuite, et Freud avec lui, fait découvrir de nouvelles dimensions dans
la psychologie; Maupassant, en regard, a vite paru mince.[20]

There can on the contrary be no doubt that Maupassant understands the
artistic effect of suggestion. During the composition of *Fort comme la mort*
he writes the following lines to his mother:

Je prépare tout doucement mon nouveau roman, et je le trouve très difficile,
tant il doit avoir de nuances, de choses suggérées et non dites. Il ne sera pas
long, d'ailleurs, il faut qu'il passe devant les yeux comme une vision de la vie
terrible, tendre et désespérée.[21]

We have seen that detail in description becomes progressively less essential
to Maupassant as he develops his method. This whole novel is designed
to be a kind of hallucination, and as a consequence the active participation
of the reader must be sought. There must be *vision* of the truth, for to
state it is to lose it.

Maupassant makes not infrequent use of poetry in his writings. Paul
Brétigny quotes Baudelaire to Christiane Andermatt in a discussion of
beauty,[22] and Maupassant himself does the same in "Sur les chats",[23]
to mention only two instances. But the clearest statement of his views on
Symbolism are found in *La vie errante*, in which he deals with these poets
very curiously and at some length. Contemplating the night and the stars,
he quotes in full Baudelaire's *Correspondances*, concluding with the
comment:

Est-ce que je ne venais pas de sentir jusqu'aux moelles ce vers mystérieux:
"Les parfums, les couleurs et les sons se répondent."

[19] Maupassant, *Au soleil*, p. 63.
[20] Henri Peyre in *Pour et contre Maupassant*, ed. by Artine Artinian (Paris: Nizet,
1955), p. 115.
[21] Maupassant, "Correspondance", *Boule de Suif, Oeuvres complètes*, pp. CLXVI–
CLXVII.
[22] Maupassant, *Mont-Oriol*, p. 114.
[23] Maupassant, "Sur les chats", *La petite Roque, Oeuvres complètes*, p. 160. First
published in *Le Gil Blas* (February 9, 1886).

Et non seulement ils se répondent dans la nature, mais ils se répondent en
nous et se confondent quelquefois "dans une ténébreuse et profonde unité,"
ainsi que le dit le poète, par des répercussions d'un organe sur l'autre.[24]

In his admiration for Baudelaire and his successors, he seems to suggest
that they have been succeeding in one genre in doing what he aspires to in
another. For they express the multiform sensibility of the artist with their
"vers euphoniques, pleins de sonorités intentionnelles, incompréhensibles
et perceptibles".[25]

But he goes on to state that the phenomenon of "correspondances" has
been medically documented as the product of "... les natures très ner-
veuses et très surexitées", and the effect on the reader is thus a kind of
transferal of the contagion. His attitude towards this literature is both
admiration and fear. Attracted by its results, he has a great deal of
difficulty accepting its methods. The "dérèglement de tous les sens" enters
the Maupassantian view of things only with a struggle. Moving on to
Rimbaud's "Voyelles" he balks at the basic irrationality of the concept,
but grasps an essential point, one which has been seen to be central to his
own artistic explorations – the search for the inexpressible through unity,
or as he says himself, the poet "essaye de chanter en effet la gamme entière
des sensations et de noter par les voisinages des mots bien plus que par
leur accord rationnel et leur signification comme d'intraduisibles sons
...".[26]

The difficulty would seem to be that the resources of the artist have run
out. Man's intelligence has five barriers "entr'ouvertes et cadenassées"
and he is at present trying his utmost to bring them down. He is seeking a
new means of perception in art. There seems to him to be no realreason
why the senses should be limited to five. People can do without one and
still easily survive, so why is it not possible to have more? Art is constantly
seeking a new sense by means of which man can break out in a new
direction and explore the unknown. If the sense which is of special value
to the novelist is sight, then some means must be found to increase its
sensitivity, increase its depth of perception. This is clearly the task of
Maupassant as he has set it out for himself.

But we see in this discussion of Symbolism the same timidity we have
already witnessed. If the procedure involves giving preference to the
intuitive over the rational, Maupassant can sympathize but he cannot
bring himself to act in accordance with his own concept. The need to

[24] Maupassant, *La vie errante*, pp. 19–20.
[25] *La vie errante*, p. 18.
[26] *La vie errante*, p. 22.

understand is so basic that he is frightened of placing it in second position, although he accepts the fact that this must inevitably come about. Like Maupassant, Mariolle too is aware of his own weakness:

Je ne suis au fond qu'un jouisseur délicat, intelligent et difficile. J'ai aimé les choses de la vie sans m'y attacher jamais beaucoup, avec des sens d'expert qui savoure et ne se grise point, qui comprend trop pour perdre la tête. Je raisonne tout, et j'analyse d'ordinaire trop bien mes goûts pour les subir aveuglément. C'est même là mon grand défaut, la cause unique de ma faiblesse.[27]

Mariolle's weakness is undoubtedly Maupassant's. No more than his creation can he let himself go. He plots the new course but has great difficulty taking the initial step. Mariolle is caught for the first time in his life in a situation in which he has become inextricably involved. He withdraws only as far as Fontainebleau before turning back. His hesitant step at the end of the novel is indeed similar to Maupassant's in writing it. Whether either was ultimately successful no one will ever know.

One must bear in mind that Maupassant's aims lie entirely within the domain of art. He makes no claim to originality as a thinker, and it would be foolish for the critic to try to substantiate any such claim. But any attempt to see in him a precursor of "l'écriture automatique" would be equally fallacious. He is from beginning to end the conscious artist in control of his material. If the nature of his product changes radically one cannot with any justice put it down to simple loss of control. It is his ceaseless quest for something lasting and durable which can account for modifications in his production. As he clarifies his thought, he corrects his method accordingly. For in his search for the unknowable, all the elements vital to a work of art must serve that end. Never does he allow himself the Flaubertian liberty of setting up one aspect of the art of prose as a goal unto itself. This is nowhere more obvious than in his style. For as his point of view shifts, so does his method of expressing it. The whole must always remain greater than the sum of its parts, and it requires *all* of the parts.

André Vial devotes an entire chapter of his most extensive study of Maupassant's novels to the problem of style.[28] It would be pretentious of me to try to improve on the essentials of his argument. The care and control of language he demonstrates can only be the product of calculation. But I certainly do question the interpretation he gives to the marked change of style which is discernable most particularly in his last writings, especially since Vial shows that such changes are not without precedent

[27] Maupassant, *Notre coeur*, p. 236.
[28] Vial, *Guy de Maupassant*, pp. 569–611.

in earlier works. If there are weaknesses, one must remember that, conscious artist or not, Maupassant was not a painstaking worker. Great care must be exercised in evaluating to what extent discipline or haste can account for stylistic lapses. There is little evidence of drastic revision of manuscript by Maupassant, but in spite of his deteriorating eyesight there are apparently more drastic editings of his last novel than of any other. I can only conclude therefore that its so-called stylistic weakness was quite intentional.

Vial thoroughly documents a ternary rhythm in Maupassant which gradually multiplies into what he calls "explosions en chaînes". He finds quite startling examples of this even in *Une vie*. But according to Vial these early examples are fully under his control, and what was originally artistic intention later descends into empty romantic oratory and stylistic monstrosity. He nevertheless admits that Maupassant's vocabulary has always been relatively limited, and that all of these weaknesses, in spite of intention, have precedent in what are generally considered to be his best works.

If such is the case, can it not therefore be suggested that the change of style so noticeable in *Notre coeur* can be accounted for without resorting to the excuse of mental or physical deterioration? If Maupassant is driven by a thirst for the real, cannot the increased complexity be still another means by which he is attempting to pin it down? Reality is such a fleeting illusory thing that it becomes progressively more difficult for language to approach it. Increases of syntactical complexity in which sentences become paragraphs and even pages are thus accountable as calculated attempts to make language conform, not to a preconceived world, but to the true nature of the problem at hand. Language is, as Flaubert realized only too well, the most difficult, the least pliable of artistic media. Surely Maupassant may be given some credit for his attempt to give it greater elasticity. If illusion is the road to reality, then language too must contribute to the hallucinatory effect. Approximation must replace precision. The apparent looseness of composition becomes then a desire to follow the convolutions of the human mind gripped with what Mariolle realizes is a basically non-rational situation. Style is only one aspect of the literary art, and all aspects must combine in harmony in order to produce a coherent, unified effect. We return thus to the same basic principle. The Maupassantian aesthetic is concerned with the totality, in which no single element will dominate.

We must of course make the same kind of reservations about his style as a manifestation of the problem of reality that we have about the other aspects of his art. Many of the weaknesses that Vial points out are undoubtedly there. The hesitation we have noticed elsewhere is present here too. It is essentially a building up of binary and ternary rhythms which is only in part effective. Here again Maupassant only lets go with regret, and enters his new reality with nostalgia for what he is compelled to leave behind.

During the course of this study a great deal of our attention has been devoted to *Notre coeur*, and it has been utilized extensively to illustrate the argument we endorse. It is of course because it is the final completed novel that it does occupy such a position. I have tried to refrain from value judgements in dealing with this most curious piece, since its importance lies not necessarily in the quality of its success or failure, but in the changing approach to reality which it so manifestly documents.

We must not neglect to mention that most of the tendencies it reveals are also visible in the last short stories. The increased concern with hallucination is well illustrated by such stories as "Le Horla" (1886), "La morte" (1887), "L'endormeuse" (1889), "Sur l'eau" (1888) or "Qui sait?" (1890). All of these depend on a visual event, unexpected and unprepared, to set the conflict in motion. And in each case a whole new world of experience is perceived, leading out of the limitations of reality as we know it. And in each one it leads to some form of disaster, as does the vision of the past in conflict with the present that is the essence of "Le champ d'oliviers". Everywhere Maupassant is dealing with the meaning of life. Everywhere he finds illusion. It is for this reason that the final scene of *Notre coeur* assumes such dimensions in assessing his accomplisments. He has consistently refused to abdicate. That he himself is unwilling to disengage himself from the struggle of life is nowhere more obvious than in "L'endormeuse". The beautification of suicide only serves to increase his horror at the thought of death. To make it the ideal solution is in itself a dream, a dream which would appear to be the road to the real. Tempting and idyllic as it may sound, it constitutes only a self-deception. For all its blackness, Maupassant opts in favour of life, but again, not without hesitation, not without nostalgia. Just as the illusion of reality will lead to ultimate reality, so the illusion of suicide will lead to ultimate finality. The stopping of time in "La nuit" (1887) brings the sudden realization that death is imminent. But it is all, as we are told in the subtitle, a "cauchemar", a dream, an illusion.

The fundamental conflict in Maupassant is of course between the reason and the intuition, in which the former intrudes to destroy the pre-determined order of the latter. It is as we have demonstrated the human mind, its logic and its reason which is, in the typically nineteenth century view of things, at the root of conflict. Only the gifted few can have for Maupassant those flashes of insight into the depth of existence, those of genius, or in Schopenhauer's view, the artists.

Art is thus the salvation for Maupassant. For if reality is in the final analysis only subjective illusion, entirely dependent on one's inner make-up and therefore not directly communicable, then art becomes the only answer, the only means of expression. The more direct a reflection of that inner reality it can be, the greater will be the communication – a communication which is admittedly indirect, but essential. The illusion that art sets up must tread the thin line between this inner world and man's physical world. It must find a balance between the dream which springs directly from the subconscious and occupies first position, and intelligence and thought, those two other vital characteristics of the human animal. For if it moves too far over the brink it brings only deception and leads ultimately to death. What is sought is a redefinition of the nature of the aesthetic experience.

It follows then that the greater the degree of realism or more accurately of verisimilitude, the greater that communication will be. And that realism, by its very nature must be an internal rather than an external phenomenon. It is for this reason that Maupassant, while remaining constantly true to the spirit if not to the letter of Gustave Flaubert, is far more than a terminal point of a novelistic tradition.

X

CONCLUSION

A traditional interpretation of Guy de Maupassant has fixed him in the most pessimistic of positions as the extreme case of the nineteenth century progression of realism – naturalism, all the while overshadowed by Flaubertian concerns with art and aesthetics. René Dumesnil expresses this view in the clearest of terms:

Il [Maupassant] n'a même plus cette foi que gardait Flaubert qui, lui, croyait au moins à l'Art. Écrire, ce qui était, au temps de ses débuts à la fois une consolation et un espoir, n'est plus que l'accomplissement des gestes habituels à l'ouvrier qui remplit sa tâche. Au moins garde-t-il jusqu'à la dernière heure de cette vie pitoyable le respect de son métier, et c'est un bien faible soutien, une superstition, vaine comme tout au monde, une illusion... .[1]

Thus, it is generally speaking his earlier works which are of greatest significance, since as we have seen they do contain the best illustrations of Maupassant's objective techniques. The final stages of his career are seen as a kind of aberration due perhaps to loss of mental control,[2] or what is even more damning, the pandering to a particular segment of the reading public under the pernicious influence of Paul Bourget.[3] At any rate the last two novels are generally considered to be little more than historical curiosities, and a number of his later short stories would appear to be products of a somewhat disturbed mind.

These views are quite at variance with the facts of the case which have been substantiated by these works. The control exercised over form proves

---

[1] René Dumesnil, *Le réalisme et le naturalisme* (Paris: Del Duca, 1962), p. 350.

[2] Sullivan comments, in dealing with *Fort comme la mort* that "the decline in his [Maupassant's] creative powers is evident not only in the quantity of works produced but in their quality as well. What is more interesting, however, is that his last novels do more than reflect the growing impotence; in essence their subject is really the theme of the sterility of the artist, the blunting of the creative force by old age and by the diversions of society" (Sullivan, *Maupassant the Novelist*, p. 121).

[3] See F. Steegmuller, *A Lion in the Path*, Part III, Chapter I, for a detailed account of this period of Maupassant's life.

conclusively that Maupassant was at all times fully aware of what he was trying to do, and true to the independent spirit of Flaubert, was pursuing at all times an artistic, if not stylistic end. He was undoubtedly concerned with his public, and particularly with the sale of his books, as his correspondence documents perhaps only too well, but he never became their puppet. It is particularly evident in his "preface" to *Pierre et Jean*, written in 1885, that independence and originality are essential to his concept of the artist. A letter of advice to Maurice Vaucaire makes his point perfectly clear:

... surtout, n'imitez pas, ne vous rappelez rien de ce que vous avez lu; oubliez tout, et (je vais vous dire une monstruosité que je crois absolument vraie) pour devenir bien personnel, n'admirez personne.[4]

It is precisely this struggle to assert his own personal view which is the unifying link to all of Maupassant's serious work. Tutored in the art of literature by Flaubert, he demonstrates an influence which is perhaps unequalled in intensity in the history of the novel. Maupassant's struggle is the struggle to uphold the basic tenets of the author of *Madame Bovary* while at the same time striking out on his own. That this new direction asserts itself so late in his career is convincing evidence of the impact of the senior writer.

Flaubert's Romanticism, and his struggle to control it, has been the subject of a great deal of study. Maupassant's concern with form is no doubt a development out of this artistic concern. But its whole emphasis is shifted. Maupassant belonged to another generation, a generation not reared on the excesses of the early part of the century. Whereas Flaubert is endeavouring to subdue and control certain natural tendencies, Maupassant is searching for a means to give form and substance to what he considers valid. If Flaubert is by nature a Romantic, Maupassant has by nature a more strictly classical bent. From *Pierre et Jean* on, his novels demonstrate the possibilities of a renovation of these teachings.

But it is precisely this concern with form which leads him into difficulty. As the form becomes more clearly defined, reality becomes progressively less vivid, and assumes the dimensions of a mirage, an illusion. Images of form conjure up an unbridgeable gap between past and present. The void that is thus visible is the source of Maupassant's intense pessimism. Already in 1881, in a letter to his mother, it is clearly defined:

Je sens cet immense égarement de tous les êtres, le poids du vide. Et au milieu de cette débandade de tout, mon cerveau fonctionne lucide, exact, m'éblouissant

---

[4] Maupassant, "Correspondance", *Chroniques...*, Dumesnil, pp. 334–35.

avec le Rien éternel. Cela a l'air d'une phrase du père Hugo: mais il me faudrait beaucoup de temps pour rendre mon idée clair dans un langage précis. Ce qui me prouve une fois de plus que l'emphase romantique tient à l'absence de travail.[5]

Combined with the Flaubert-inspired reference to hard work is there not detectable here a kind of nostalgia? Maupassant's reason, like his characters', is a force for destruction. It is its overpowering influence which leads him to a despair for which there is no real salvation. His remarks on the achievement of Balzac, significantly from a much later date than the reference in the first chapter of this study, reveal considerable admiration for certain aspects of that great novelist's art:

On ne peut dire de lui qu'il fut un observateur, ni qu'il évoqua exactement le spectable de la vie, comme le firent après lui certains romanciers, mais il fut doué d'une si géniale intuition, et il créa une humanité tout entière si vraisemblable que tout le monde y crut et qu'elle devint vraie. Son admirable fiction modifia le monde, envahit la société, s'imposa et passa du rêve dans la réalité. Alors les personnages de Balzac, qui n'existaient pas avant lui, parurent sortir de ses livres pour entrer dans la vie, tant il avait donné complète l'illusion des êtres, des passions et des événements.[6]

What Maupassant is attempting is to return to something more in keeping with Balzacian vision and perception, the movement from dream to reality, all the while not abandoning the precision of observation which Balzac's successors had taught him. Whereas Flaubert laboured to assert the power of the human reason over its imagination, and thereby brought himself into a position in which the only value remaining was an aesthetic one, Maupassant would like to attempt to restore to art that immediacy which the rational mind had destroyed. In the opposite movement to Flaubert, he might be called a frustrated classicist. "Gustave Flaubert, dans ses lettres", he says, "pousse le grand cri continu, le grand cri lamentable de l'illusion détruite."[7]

Maupassant's last novels must be considered as conscious attempts on his part to reconcile the reason with the imagination. We have seen how he achieves a greater immediacy through form and while preserving a kind of objectivity through his use of imagery, does in fact move out towards a more subjective art. In each one in succession the fusion beco-

---

[5] Maupassant, "Correspondance", *Boule de Suif, Oeuvres complètes*, p. CXXX.
[6] Maupassant, "Le roman au XIX siècle", *Maupassant journaliste*, ed. by G. Delaisement, p. 231. First published in the *Revue de l'Exposition Universelle de 1889*, 2.
[7] Maupassant, "Le roman au XIX siècle", p. 87.

mes greater. One would have to agree with at least the first part of Schmidt's remarks about the last novel:

Notre Coeur devrait être considéré comme le testament littéraire de Maupassant, dont c'est l'oeuvre la plus accomplie.[8]

The psychology of the novel may be weak, as Henri Peyre observes, but we are dealing here, as he reminds us, with a pre-Freudian period.[9] Failure it may be, but a very important and largely unrecognized contribution to the history of letters. Maupassant himself describes his conflict in what might be considered the summing up of his artistic position:

Comme j'avais raison de me murer dans l'indifférence. Si on pouvait ne pas sentir et seulement comprendre sans laisser des lambeaux de soi-même à d'autres êtres! ... Il est singulier de souffrir du vide, du néant de cette vie, étant résigné comme je suis à ce néant. Mais voilà, je ne peux vivre sans souvenirs, et les souvenirs me grignotent. Je ne peux avoir aucune espérance, je le sais, mais je sens obscurément et sans cesse le mal de cette constatation et le regret de cet avortement. Et les attaches que j'ai dans la vie travaillent ma sensibilité qui est trop humaine, pas assez littéraire.[10]

It is impossible for him to neglect the destructive power of reason, and the futility of his position is not without deep regret. The problem lies in finding an acceptable alternative. One wonders what Maupassant might have become had Flaubert's teachings not been so persuasive, or if he had lived long enough to fully reconcile these with his own changing views. It is as if he held all the keys to the unanswered questions, but was over-hesitant to make full use of them. And precisely because of the close connection with Flaubert, and to a lesser extent with Zola, critics and artists alike have consistently refused to give him credit for pointing the way towards new dimensions in the novel. He is an artist caught between two poles. To the one he clings with nostalgia and to the other he reaches out only fearfully. But of this there can be no doubt. In both his practice and his theory the route prose fiction is going to take is mapped out in some detail. His compromise solution will lead inevitably towards the swinging of the balance in the other direction.

Pour les débutants qui apparaissent aujourd'hui, au lieu de se tourner vers la vie avec une curiosité vorace, de la regarder partout autour d'eux avec avidité, d'en jouir ou d'en souffrir avec force suivant leur tempérament, ils ne regardent

[8]   Albert-Marie Schmidt, *Maupassant par lui-même* (Paris: Éditions du Seuil, 1962), p. 150.
[9]   See p. 175.
[10]   Maupassant, "Correspondance", *Boule de Suif*, p. LXXVI.

plus qu'en eux-mêmes, observent uniquement leur âme, leur coeur, leurs in-
stincts, leur qualités ou leurs défauts, et proclament que le roman définitif ne
doit être qu'une autobiographie.[11]

It is Maupassant's tragedy that he could not break the equilibrium.
The disdain for the rising generation is not without its tinge of regret.
His own introspection is achieved only by reflecting external reality from
which he could never escape.

The key to Maupassant lies therefore in his descriptive ability. René
Dumesnil sees in it an unsuspected depth.

L'art descriptif de Maupassant est beaucoup plus profond qu'il ne paraît à
première vue. Il pousse jusqu'au vif et fixe, en même temps que l'aspect transi-
toire et particulier des hommes, les caractères spécifiques et inaltérables de la
race, de la classe sociale à laquelle appartient chacun d'eux, son relief et sa
valeur générale, sa portée humaine.[12]

But Maupassant was not able, as was his master, to develop the potential
of his youth and evolve a fully mature personal mode of expression which
was his and his alone. We can only conclude that he was moving slowly,
hesitantly and unnoticed in what appears to have been the right direction.

[11]   Delaisement, *Maupassant journaliste*, p. 233.
[12]   Dumesnil, *Réalisme et naturalisme*, p. 347.

APPENDIX A

The Tables of Contents of the seventeen volumes of short stories contained in the Conard edition of Maupassant's complete works.

Mademoiselle Fifi

Contes de la bécasse

Clair de lune

Les soeurs Rondoli

Le rosier de Madame Husson

La main gauche

APPENDIX B

The following is an attempt to categorize the short stories according to background. I have divided them into four broad groups, since further fragmentation would only serve to confuse the issue. Even so, certain stories contain more than one setting. I have in these cases made a personal decision as to which of these settings I consider to be the most significant. No story appears in this list more than once.

Within each group there are two sections – those stories in which exterior description performs a vital function, and those in which it is either totally neglected, or just briefly and passingly mentioned. Again, personal judgment was necessary in a number of cases.

Since the date of composition of the stories cannot be fixed, I have followed the date of first publication as indicated in the Schmidt edition (see Bibliography), the Conard edition otherwise referred to being somewhat inaccurate in this regard. The stories are listed only according to year of publication since the exact date would have little, if any value here. In each year, they are therefore listed only in alphabetical order, ignoring definite and indefinite articles.

PROVINCIAL TOWN

Description	*No Significant Description*
1879 Le papa de Simon	
1880	
1881 La maison Tellier	
1882 Un coup d'État	Mon oncle Sosthène
La folle	Une passion
Madame Baptiste	La rempailleuse
	Une passion

1883 Denis   Le mal d'André
     L'enfant   La mère aux monstres
     L'orphelin   Le pain maudit
     La reine Hortense   Une soirée
     La serre
1884 Berthe   La chambre 11
     Bombard   Le lit 29
     La confession   Un parricide
     L'ivrogne
1885   Toine
1886 Madame Parisse
     La question du latin
1887 L'ordonnance   Madame Hermet
     Les rois   Moiron
     Le rosier de Madame Husson
1888 Alexandre   Les 25 francs de la supérieure
     Un divorce
     Le noyé

TRAVEL AND RESORT
(including Auvergne and Provence)

Description	*No significant Description*
1880 Boule de Suif	
Correspondance	
1881	
1882 Un bandit corse	Ce cochon de Morin
En voyage *(Clair de lune)*	La relique
En voyage *(Miss Harriet)*	
Un fils	
Marroca	
1883 Auprès d'un mort	L'ami Patience
En mer	Un duel
Enragée	La main
Le modèle	
Mon oncle Jules	
Première neige	
Tombouctou	
Une vendetta	

1884 L'abandonnée   **La dot**
     Adieu   ·   Rencontre
     Le bonheur
     Le bûcher
     Châli
     Découverte
     Idylle
     Mohammed-Fripouille
     Notes d'un voyageur
     La peur
     Les soeurs Rondoli
     Rose
     Le tic
1885 A vendre   Ça ira
     En wagon   Nos Anglais
     L'épingle
     Imprudence
     Joseph
     Mes 25 jours
     La roche aux guillemots
1886 L'auberge
     L'épave
     L'ermite
     Julie Romain
     Sur les chats
1887 Duchoux
     Un échec
1888   L'infirme
1889 Allouma
     Un soir
1890 Le champ d'oliviers

PARIS AND THE SEINE

Description   *No Significant Description*
1875 La main d'écorché
1877 Le donneur d'eau bénite
1878 "Coco, coco, coco frais!"

1881 Au printemps
     Une aventure parisienne
     En famille
     La femme de Paul
     Une partie de campagne
     Sur l'eau
     Les tombales

1882 Menuet   Le baiser
     Nuit de Noël   La bûche
     Le verrou   Clair de lune *(Oeuvres post.)*
     Le voleur   Le gâteau
                               Le lit
                               Magnétisme
                               Un million
                               Mots d'amour
                               Le pardon
                               Rêves
                               Rouerie
                               Yveline Samoris

1883 A cheval   L'ami Joseph
     Les bijoux   L'attente
     Décoré!   Au bord du lit
     Deux amis   Les caresses
     Lui?   La confession
     Mademoiselle Cocotte   L'enfant
     L'Odyssée d'une fille   La fenêtre
     Un sage   Fini
     Suicides   L'homme-fille
                               Monsieur Jocaste
                               Le petit
                               Le remplaçant
                               Le vengeur

1884 L'armoire   La chevelure
     L'héritage   La confession
     Lettre trouvée sur un noyé La confidance
     Misti   Un fou
     Promenade   "Garçon, un bock!"
     Le protecteur   Un lâche
     Solitude   Le parapluie

Souvenir	La parure
Yvette	La patronne
	Rencontre
	La revanche
1885 L'inconnue	Le moyen de Roger
	Le Père Mongilet
	Sauvée
1886 Au bois	Un cas de divorce
Le trou	Cri d'alarme
	Mademoiselle Perle
	Le Marquis de Fumerol
	Monsieur Parent
	Le signe
1887 La morte	L'assassin
La nuit	La baronne
	Étrennes
1888	Les épingles
	Le portrait
1889 Le rendez-vous	L'endormeuse
	L'épreuve
	Le masque
1890 L'inutile beauté	Mouche

RURAL SETTINGS

(Those stories with asterisk are essentially peasant tales)

	Description	No Significant Description
1878	Le mariage du Lieutenant Laré	
1880		Mademoiselle Fifi
1881	*Histoire d'une fille de ferme	
	Par un soir de printemps	
1882	*L'aveugle	*Aux champs
	Clair de lune (Clair de lune)	Un coq chanta
	*Conte de Noël	Ma femme
	*Farce normande	*Pierrot
	Fou?	La rouille
	*Histoire vraie	Le testament

*La légende du Mont Saint-
　　Michel
　Le loup
*Un Normand
*La peur
*Un réveillon
　Le saut du berger
　La veillée
　Une veuve
　Vieux objets

1883 *L'âne   *Le cas de Madame Luneau
　　Apparition   *La confession de Théodule Sabot
　　L'aventure de Walter Schnaffs
　　La farce   La moustache
*La ficelle
　Humble drame
*La martine
　Miss Harriet
　Le père *(Contes du jour et de*
　　la nuit)
*Le Père Judas
*Le Père Milon
*Regret
　Réveil
*Les sabots
*Saint-Antoine

1884 *L'aveu   *Coco
*Le baptême *(Miss Harriet)*   *Le petit fût
*Le crime au Père Boniface   *Tribunaux rustiques
　Un fou?   *Une vente
　Le garde
*Le gueux
　L'horrible
　Les idées du Colonel
*La mère Sauvage
*Les prisonniers
*Le retour
　Souvenirs
*Le vieux

1885 *Le baptême *(Monsieur*   *La bête à Maît 'Belhomme
        Parent)
      *Les bécasses
      *Petit soldat

1886 Amour   *Clochette
      Une famille   *Le diable
      *Le fermier   *Rosalie Prudent
      Le Horla
      *Le Père Amable
      *La petite Roque

1887 Le père *(Clair de lune)*   *Un lapin
                                     La porte
                                     *Le vagabond

1888   Nos lettres

1889   Hautot père et fils
                                    Boitelle

SELECTED BIBLIOGRAPHY

Artinian, Artine, "Guy de Maupassant and his Brother Hervé", *The Romantic Review* (December, 1948), 301–06.

—, *Maupassant Criticism in France, 1880–1940* (New York: King's Crown, 1941).

—, *Pour et contre Maupassant* (Paris: Nizet, 1955).

Balzac, Honoré de, "Avant-propos," *La comédie humaine* 1 (Paris: Bibliothèque de la Pléiade, 1951).

Beuchat, C., *Histoire du naturalisme français*, 2 vols. (Paris: Corréa, 1949).

Borel, Pierre, *Le destin tragique de Guy de Maupassant* (Paris: Éditions de France, 1927).

—, *Le vrai Maupassant* (Geneva: Cailler, 1951).

Bourget, Paul, *Nouvelles pages de critique et de doctrine* I (Paris: Plon, 1922).

Brunetière, F., *Le roman réaliste* (Paris: Calmann-Lévy, 1889).

Butler, A. S., *Les parlers dialectaux et populaires dans l'oeuvre de Guy de Maupassant* (Geneva: Droz, 1962).

Cogny, Pierre, *Le naturalisme* (Paris: Presses Universitaires de France, 1953).

Coulter, S., *Damned shall be Desire* (London: Cape, 1958).

Cox, Alan, "Dominant Ideas in the Works of Maupassant", *University of Colorado Studies* (1932).

Croce, B., "Maupassant", *European Literature in the Nineteenth Century*, trans. by D. Ainslee (New York: Knopf, 1924), 344–58.

Delaisement, G., *Maupassant journaliste et chroniqueur* (Paris: Albin Michel, 1956).

Dumesnil, René, *Chroniques, études, correspondance de Guy de Maupassant* (Paris: Gründ, 1938).

—, "Les derniers romans de Maupassant", *Revue des Vivants* (May, 1935), 709–20.

—, *Guy de Maupassant* (Paris: Taillandier, 1947).

—, *Le réalisme et le naturalisme* (Paris: Del Duca, 1962).

Flaubert, Gustave, *Correspondance* (Paris: Conard, 1910).

France, Anatole, "M. Guy de Maupassant et les conteurs français", "La Vie littéraire" I, *Oeuvres complètes* 6 (Paris: Calmann-Lévy, 1926), 52–61.

—, "M. Guy de Maupassant critique et romancier", "La vie littéraire" II, *Oeuvres complètes* 6 (Paris: Calmann-Lévy, 1926).

—, "Notre coeur", "La vie littéraire" IV, *Oeuvres complètes* 7 (Paris: Calmann-Lévy, 1926).

Grant, R. B., "Imagery as a Means of Psychological Realism in *Une Vie*", *Studies in Philology* LX, 669–84.

Hainsworth, G., "Pattern and Symbol in the Work of Guy de Maupassant", *French Studies* V (January 1951), 1–17.

—, "Un thème des romanciers naturalistes: La Matrone d'Éphèse", *Comparative Literature* (1951), 129–51.

James, Henry, "Guy de Maupassant", *Partial Portraits* (London: Macmillan, 1888).

Lemaître, Jules, "Portrait littéraire: M. Guy de Maupassant", *Les Contemporains* V (Paris: Lecène et Oudin, 1892), 1–12.

Létourneau, R., "Maupassant et sa conception de l'oeuvre d'art", *Revue de l'Université d'Ottawa* III (1933), 364–90; IV (1934), 478–90.

Luplau-Janssen, C., *Le décor chez Guy de Maupassant* (Copenhagen: Munksgaard, 1960).

Martino, P., *Le naturalisme français* (Paris: Armand Colin, 1965).

Maupassant, Guy de, *Contes et nouvelles*, 2 vols., ed. by Albert-Marie Schmidt (Paris: Albin Michel, 1962).

–, *Oeuvres complètes*, 29 vols. (Paris: Conard, 1907–10).

–, *Oeuvres complètes*, 15 vols. (Paris: Libraire de France, 1934–38).

–, *Correspondance inédite*, ed. by A. Artinian (Paris: Dominique Wapler, 1951).

Maynial, E., "La composition dans les premiers romans de Guy de Maupassant" *Revue bleue* (October 31 and November 7, 1903).

–, *Guy de Maupassant, sa vie et son oeuvre* (Paris: Mercure de France, 1907).

Neiss, R. J., "*Pierre et Jean:* Some Symbols", *French Review* XXXII (May 1959), 511–19.

Neveux, Pol., "Guy de Maupassant", Introduction to *Boule de Suif* (Paris: Conard, 1908).

Rewald, J., *Paul Cézanne*, trans. by M. H. Liebman (London: Spring Books).

Saintsbury, G., *A History of the French Novel* II (London: Macmillan, 1919), 484–515.

Schmidt, Albert-Marie, *Maupassant par lui-même* (Paris: Éditions du Seuil, 1962).

Schopenhauer, A., *Die Welt als Wille und Vorstellung* (Stuttgart and Frankfurt-am-Main: Cotta-Insel-Verlag, 1960).

–, "The World as Will and Idea", *The Works of Schopenhauer*, trans. by W. Durant (New York: Simon and Schuster, 1931).

Steegmuller, F., *A Lion in the Path* (New York: Random House, 1949).

Sartre, Jean-Paul, *Situations* II (Paris: Gallimard, 1948).

Sullivan, E. D., *Maupassant the Novelist* (Princeton: Princeton University Press, 1954).

–, *Maupassant: The Short Stories* (= *Barron's Studies in French Literature*) (New York: Barron's Educational Series, 1962).

–, "Portrait of the Artist: Maupassant and *Notre Coeur*", *French Review* (December 1948), 136–41.

Thibaudet, A., *Réflexions sur le roman* (Paris: Gallimard, 1938).

Thomas, H., and D. L. Thomas, *Living Biographies of Great Painters* (New York: Blue Ribbon Books, 1940).

Thoraval, J., *L'art de Maupassant d'après ses variantes* (Paris: Imprimerie Nationale, 1950).

Togeby, Knud, *L'oeuvre de Maupassant* (Copenhagen: Danish Science Press, and Paris: Presses Universitaires de France, 1954).

Vial, André, *Guy de Maupassant et l'art du roman* (Paris: Nizet, 1954).

INDEX

Artinian, A., 3, 175

Balzac, Honoré de, 5–6, 9, 10, 38, 40, 113, 157, 160, 183; *César Birotteau*, 5; *Le curé de Tours*, 5; *Le père Goriot*, 5
Baudelaire, Charles, 114, 175, 176
Beuchat, C., 1, 2, 4
Bourget, Paul, 181
Brombert, Victor, 7
Brunetière, F., 4, 8

célébrités contemporaines, Les, 9
Cézanne, Paul, 140–142, 172
Cogny, Pierre, 2

Delaisement, G., 9, 35, 185
Dumesnil, René, 1, 3, 181, 185

Feuillet, Octave, 9
Flaubert, Gustave, 2, 6–8, 9, 10, 25, 30, 38, 40, 57, 103–104, 113, 121, 123, 127, 128, 149, 150, 152, 155, 157, 160, 161, 171, 180, 182, 183, 184; *Bouvard et Pécuchet*, 7, 103, 127, 128, 129, 162, 164; *Un coeur simple*, 7, 26; *L'éducation sentimentale*, 7, 40, 43, 167; *Madame Bovary*, 7, 8, 25, 29, 123, 132, 167; *Salammbô*, 3, 7, 25, 26, 85
France, Anatole, 2, 4

Gauguin, Paul, 140
Grant, R. B., 4

Hainsworth, G., 4
Hugo, Victor, *Les misérables*, 5

Lemaître, Jules, 2, 4
Loti, Pierre, 9
Luplau–Janssen, C., 20, 80

Martino, P., 2
Maupassant, Guy de, *A cheval*, 21; *Adieu*, 28, 83, 105, 174; *Allouma*, 17; *L'âme étrangère*, 50; *L'angélus*, 58, 172–173; *L'armoire*, 21; *L'auberge*, 17; *Au soleil*, 61–62, 63, 64, 65, 66, 93–94, 128, 174–175; *L'aventure de Walter Schnaffs*, 123; *L'aveu*, 75; *Balzac d'après ses lettres*, 6; *Un bandit corse*, 17; *Le baptême*, 85; *Les bécasses*, 32; *Bel-ami*, 12, 38–42, 45, 46, 52, 60, 78, 79, 80, 88–89, 95, 104, 106, 108–110, 115–117, 119, 120, 126, 133, 135, 143, 144, 151, 152, 154, 155, 160, 163–164, 167; *Berthe*, 18; *La bête à Maîtr' Belhomme*, 14; *Les bijoux*, 26, 33; *Bombard*, 16; *Le Bonheur*, 17,